DATE DUE

OCT 10 2018

Terrorism versus Democracy

This book examines the terrorist networks that operate globally and analyses the long-term future of terrorism and terrorist-backed insurgencies.

Terrorism remains a serious problem for the international community. The global picture does not indicate that the 'war on terror', which President George W. Bush declared in the wake of the 9/11 attacks, has been won. On the other hand it would be incorrect to assume that Al Qaeda, its affiliates and other jihadi groups have won their so-called 'holy war' against the Coalition against Terrorism formed after 9/11.

This new edition gives more attention to the political and strategic impact of modern transnational terrorism, the need for maximum international cooperation by law-abiding states to counter not only direct threats to the safety and security of their own citizens but also to preserve international peace and security through strengthening counter-proliferation and cooperative threat reduction (CTR).

This book is essential reading for undergraduate and postgraduate students of terrorism studies, political science and international relations, as well as for policy makers and journalists.

Paul Wilkinson is Emeritus Professor of International Relations and Chairman of the Advisory Board of the Centre for the Study of Terrorism and Political Violence (CSTPV) at the University of St Andrews. He is author of several books on terrorism issues and was co-founder of the leading international journal, *Terrorism and Political Violence*.

Series: Political Violence
Series Editors: Paul Wilkinson and David Rapoport

This book series contains sober, thoughtful and authoritative academic accounts of terrorism and political violence. Its aim is to produce a useful taxonomy of terror and violence through comparative and historical analysis in both national and international spheres. Each book discusses origins, organisational dynamics and outcomes of particular forms and expressions of political violence.

The Psychology of Terrorism
John Horgan

Research on Terrorism: Trends, Achievements and Failures
Edited by Andrew Silke

A War of Words
Political Violence and Public Debate in Israel
Gerald Cromer

Root Causes of Suicide Terrorism
Globalization of Martyrdom
Edited by Ami Pedahzur

Terrorism versus Democracy
The Liberal State Response, 3rd Edition
Paul Wilkinson

Countering Terrorism and WMD
Creating a Global Counter-Terrorism Network
Edited by Peter Katona, Michael Intriligator and John Sullivan

Mapping Terrorism Research
State of the Art, Gaps and Future Direction
Edited by Magnus Ranstorp

The Ideological War on Terror
World-Wide Strategies for Counter-Terrorism
Edited by Anne Aldis and Graeme P. Herd

The IRA and Armed Struggle
Rogelio Alonso

Homeland Security in the UK
Future Preparedness for Terrorist Attack since 9/11
Edited by Paul Wilkinson

Terrorism Today, 2nd Edition
Christopher C. Harmon

Understanding Terrorism and Political Violence
The Life Cycle of Birth, Growth, Transformation, and Demise
Dipak K. Gupta

Global Jihadism
Theory and Practice
Jarret M. Brachman

Combating Terrorism in Northern Ireland
Edited by James Dingley

Terrorism versus Democracy

The liberal state response

Third edition

Paul Wilkinson

Routledge
Taylor & Francis Group

LONDON AND NEW YORK

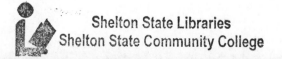

First published 2001
by Routledge
Second edition published 2006
by Routledge
Third edition published 2011
by Routledge
2 Park Square, Milton Park, Abingdon, Oxon OX14 4RN

Simultaneously published in the USA and Canada
by Routledge
270 Madison Avenue, New York, NY 10016

Routledge is an imprint of the Taylor & Francis Group, an informa business

© 2001, 2006, 2011 Paul Wilkinson
The right of Paul Wilkinson to be identified as author of this work has been
asserted by him in accordance with sections 77 and 78 of the Copyright,
Designs and Patents Act 1988.

Typeset in Baskerville by Taylor and Francis Books Ltd
Printed and bound in Great Britain by
CPI Antony Rowe, Chippenham, Wiltshire

British Library Cataloguing in Publication Data
A catalogue record for this book is available from the British Library

Library of Congress Cataloging in Publication Data
Wilkinson, Paul, 1937-
Terrorism versus democracy : the liberal state response / Paul Wilkinson. –
3rd ed.
p. cm.
Includes bibliographical references and index.
1. Terrorism–Prevention. 2. Democracy. 3. Liberalism.
4. Terrorism–Prevention–Government policy. I. Title.
HV6431.W564 2011
363.325'156–dc22
2010030733

ISBN13: 978-0-415-58800-3 (hbk)
ISBN13: 978-0-415-58799-0 (pbk)
ISBN13: 978-0-203-83231-8 (ebk)

Contents

Preface

John Adams, the second president of the United States, wrote to his wife: 'I must study politics and war that my sons may have liberty to study mathematics and philosophy'. Sadly this advice has not always been followed by his successors or by all the political leaders of other democracies. It is a sad reflection that in future our political leaders will need to study terrorism and to think deeply about how democracies should respond to both domestic and international terrorism. My hope is that my book will help to stimulate this process and encourage and assist those engaged in security studies in the universities and those serving in the security professions.

The first edition of my book was published ten months before 11 September 2001 (or 9/11). In this third edition I include a critical assessment of President George W. Bush's 'War on Terror', and conclude that fundamental mistakes in responding to terrorism can end up strengthening terrorism and create further threats to international peace and security and human rights. There is a new chapter on the problems facing President Obama in his attempts to extricate the US from his predecessor's legacy. The wider lessons for democratic and international response are surveyed. The strengths and limitations of influential 'models' of response are compared, e.g. military response, political pathways out of terrorism and the criminal justice response. I remain convinced not only that the liberal state response I advocated in the first and second editions is morally sound but also that democratic countries working closely together with the wider international community can succeed in unravelling the Al Qaeda network of cells and affiliates without sacrificing the rule of law and the protection of basic human rights in the process. On the contrary, if liberal democracies failed to act firmly and courageously against terrorists who are explicitly committed to the mass killing of civilians they would be guilty of failing to uphold the most basic human right of all, the right to life itself.

Paul Wilkinson
St Andrews
August 2010

Acknowledgements

I wish to thank the following for their encouragement and wise insights into terrorism: Professor Magnus Ranstorp, formerly of the Centre for the Study of Terrorism and Political Violence (CSTPV), University of St Andrews, now at the National Defence College, Stockholm, Dr Peter Lehr, Group Captain Affi Ashraf and Professor Max Taylor, all University of St Andrews. I also wish to thank Gillian Duncan, CSTPV for her superb work in typing the manuscript and Joseph Easson, CSTPV for his helpful assistance and Andrew Humphrys and Rebecca Brennan of Routledge for their valuable advice and encouragement. Needless to say, the author is solely responsible for any errors.

Paul Wilkinson
CSTPV
University of St Andrews
August 2010

Glossary of terrorist groups

Abu Sayyaf Group An extremist jihadi group, based in the Southern Philippines and linked to Al Qaeda.

Action Directe French extreme-left group formed in 1976: the group faded out following the arrest of its main leaders in 1987.

Al Aqsa Brigades A militant faction of Fatah, responsible for some suicide attacks on Israeli targets.

Al Jihad Zawahiri led Al Jihad and then, in 1998, it merged with Al Qaeda.

Al Qaeda Al Qaeda ('The Base') was founded in 1989 by Osama bin Laden and Abdallah Azzam. They aim to establish a pan-Islamist Caliphate (super-state) uniting all Muslims. Al Qaeda has declared a jihad or holy war against the US and its allies and has set up a World Islamic Front for Jihad declaring it is 'the duty of all Muslims to kill US citizens – civilian or military, and their allies everywhere' (bin Laden 'Fatwa', 23 February 1998). A key feature of the Al Qaeda movement is its explicit commitment to mass-killing terrorist attacks making it the most dangerous terrorist organisation in recent times.

Al Qaeda in the Arabian Peninsula (AQAP) This group has been particularly active in Yemen, where it has briefed and trained militants.

Al Qaeda in the Maghreb (AQIM) An affiliate of Al Qaeda formed out of Algerian, Moroccan and Libyan groups.

Al Qaeda Jihad Organisation Mesopotamia This is a major affiliate and support group of Al Qaeda and was previously known as Al Qaeda in Mesopotamia.

Animal Liberation Front An issue group which has committed violent attacks as protests against what they claim to be abuse or exploitation of animals.

Ansar al-Islam Al Qaeda major affiliate and support group.

Armenian Secret Army for the Liberation of Armenia The group has attacked Turkish businesses and diplomats around the world.

Army of God   An extreme anti-abortion group in the US which has used violence against clinics and medical professionals involved in abortions.

Aryan Nations   An extreme-right racist group in the US. It has used violence against minorities and programmes for minorities.

Asbat al-Ansar   Lebanon based – Al Qaeda major affiliate and support group.

ASG   Abu Sayyaf Group: this extreme Islamic separatist group operating in the southern Philippines split from the Moro National Liberation Front in 1991. Its declared aim is to create an independent Islamic state in western Mindanao and the Sulu archipelago.

Assassin Sect   A sect of Shia Islam active in Persia and Syria in the twelfth and thirteenth centuries and which used the dagger to assassinate opponents.

Aum Shinrikyo   A Japanese cult responsible for the Sarin gas attack on the Tokyo underground in March 1995.

Baader-Meinhof   See RAF (Red Army Faction).

Black Hand   A Serbian extreme nationalist group formed in 1911 and linked to the Serbian military, who assassinated Archduke Ferdinand in 1914.

Black September   Palestinian terrorist group responsible for the Munich Olympics attack in 1972.

CCC   Cellules Communistes Combattantes (Fighting Communist Cells): a Belgian extreme-left group active in the 1980s.

Contras   Nicaraguan movement opposed to the Sandinista regime and backed by the CIA in an attempt to undermine the Nicaraguan government.

DFLP   Democratic Front of the Liberation of Palestine: it split from the PFLP in 1969 under its leader Nayef Hawatmeh.

ELA   Revolutionary People's struggle: a Greek extreme left group formed in 1971.

ELN   National Liberation Army: a Colombian extreme-left group formed in 1965. Its major activity has been kidnapping for ransom.

EOKA   National Organisation of Cypriot Fighters: it waged a campaign of terrorism from 1955 to 1960 to force Britain to relinquish its colonial rule over Cyprus and to unite Cyprus with Greece (Enosis).

ETA   Euzkadi Ta Askatasuna (Basque Fatherland and Liberty): it is aimed at establishing an independent Marxist Basque state.

EYAL   Israeli extreme nationalist group bitterly opposed to the Israeli–Palestinian peace process: the assassination of Prime Minister Yitzhak Rabin was linked to this group.

rope. It lost its momentum following the suicides of its key leaders in gaol, d eventually disbanded in March 1998.

Brigades Brigate Rosse: formed in 1969, it became the major Italian left-ng group waging terrorism, aimed at overthrowing the Italian government d replacing it with a revolutionary communist system. The group was feated in the early 1980s by police and judicial measures and through its vn internal divisions and deterioration.

ng Path Sendero Luminoso: a Maoist group formed in the late 1960s, it is waged a particularly ruthless and lethal terrorist campaign aimed at erthrowing the Peruvian government, but the capture of its founder, Abimael uzman, in 1992, severely weakened the organisation.

Fein Political wing of the Provisional IRA (see above).

Symbionese Liberation Army: formed in 1973, an extreme-left group used in California. It was eradicated in 1974 when its leader Donald De eeze and five other members were shot by the police.

Sudanese People's Liberation Army: formed in 1973, it is waging an surgency against the Arab-speaking northerners who have dominated the untry since 1956.

an This extreme fundamentalist movement gained control of most of fghanistan in the 1990s. They gave safe haven to Al Qaeda's leadership and peratives and allowed them to set up training camps for terrorists. Since 001 they have been waging an insurgency in Afghanistan to topple the fghan government and regain control. The hard-line factions, including e Haqqani army, are closely allied with Al Qaeda.

l Tigers Liberation Tigers of Tamil Eelam: an extremist Tamil separatist rganisation formed in 1972. It has used terrorism and guerrilla and con-entional warfare in its conflict with the Sri Lankan security forces, which has ost thousands of lives on both sides.

Secret Organisation of Al Qaeda in Europe Al Qaeda major affiliate nd support group.

maros Uruguayan left-wing group, formed in 1963. Its name derived om Tupac Amaru, a Peruvian Indian leader killed in the eighteenth century.

Ulster Defence Association: formed in 1971, it is the largest Loyalist aramilitary organisation in Northern Ireland.

Ulster Freedom Fighters: a terrorist arm of the UDA.

Ulster Volunteer Force: formed in 1966, a Northern Ireland Loyalist group.

TA Uniao Nacional Para a Independencia Total de Angola (National Jnion for the Total Independence of Angola): established in 1966, it

FARC Revolutionary Armed Forces of Colombia: formed in 1964, a Marxist group that wages guerrilla war and terrorism, specialising in kidnapping for ransom and providing armed protection for narcotics traffickers.

FCO Fighting Communist Organisation, a term used to describe any of the 'Red Army' terrorist groups, which emerged in the late 1960s and early 1970s.

FIS Islamic Salvation Front: an Algerian Islamic fundamentalist political party that appeared set for victory in the 1992 election until the army suspended the elections and established emergency rule.

FLN Front de Liberation Nationale (National Liberation Front): formed in 1954, the FLN led the struggle for independence against the French using a combination of guerrilla warfare, urban terrorism and strikes until France conceded independence to Algeria in the 1962 Evian Agreement.

FLNC Front de Libération Nationale de la Corse (Corsican National Liberation Front): the group emerged in 1976 and has conducted a campaign of ter-rorism against French authorities with the aim of securing autonomy for Corsica.

FLQ Front de Libération du Québec (Quebec Liberation Front): the group waged a terrorist campaign in the 1960s and early 1970s against the Canadian authorities with the aim of securing the separation of Quebec from the rest of Canada.

GAL Gruppos Antiterroristas de Liberacion (Anti-terrorist Liberation Group): a Spanish death squad responsible for the murder of ETA activists in France during the 1980s. The group received covert support from high levels in the Spanish government and security forces.

GIA Armed Islamic Group: an extreme Algerian Islamist group that since the early 1990s has waged a ruthless campaign of terrorism with the aim of overthrowing the secular Algerian regime and replacing it with an Islamic state – it is now part of Al Qaeda in the Maghreb (AQIM).

GSPC Salafist Group for Call and Combat – Al Qaeda major affiliate and support group – it is now part of Al Qaeda in the Maghreb (AQIM).

Hamas Islamic Resistance Movement: a Palestinian Islamic fundamentalist group, formed in 1987, aiming to establish an Islamic Palestinian state.

Harakat-ul-Mujahedin Al Qaeda major affiliate and support group.

Herri Batasuna The political wing of ETA.

Hezbollah The Party of God: a Shia Islamic fundamentalist movement backed by Iran and established in the early 1980s. It aims to create an Islamic Lebanese republic.

Hizb-e-Islam/Gulbuddin Al Qaeda major affiliate and support group.

HUA Harakut ul-Ansar: an Islamic fundamentalist group, formed in 1993, aimed at securing the transfer of jurisdiction over the whole of Kashmir to Pakistan. It has now been renamed Harakut ul-Mujahidin.

IMRO The Internal Macedonian Revolutionary Organisation: formed in the 1890s as a nationalist underground movement against Turkish rule it later became involved in systematic terrorism and organised crime and was enmeshed in the bitter interwar rivalries of Balkan politics.

IRA See PIRA (Provisional IRA).

Irgun Irgun Zvai Leumi (National Military Organisation): a Jewish nationalist group, formed in 1931, aimed at establishing an independent Jewish state on both sides of the Jordan. Irgun used terrorism, assassination and guerrilla warfare to force the British to withdraw from the Palestine Mandate. It was disbanded in 1948.

Islamic Army of Yemen Al Qaeda major affiliate and support group.

Islamic group Egyptian Islamic group – Al Qaeda major affiliate and support group.

Islamic Jihad The name adopted by Hezbollah when claiming some of their terrorist operations in Lebanon in the 1980s.

Jaish-e-Mohammad Al Qaeda major affiliate and support group.

Jemaah Islamiyah (Islamic Group) Al Qaeda major affiliate and support group.

JRA Japanese Red Army: an extreme-left group formed in the early 1970s with the aim of overthrowing the Japanese government and monarchy and promoting world revolution.

Kach An extreme-right-wing Jewish group, founded by Rabbi Meir Kahane, aimed at restoring the biblical state of Israel.

KMT Kuomintang: Chinese Nationalist Party.

Ku Klux Klan (KKK) Founded after the American Civil War, this group was anti-black, anti-Jewish, anti-immigrant and anti-catholic. It has carried out attacks on black Americans and sometimes on members of other groups.

Lashkar-e-Jhangvi Al Qaeda major affiliate and support group.

Lashkar-e-Tayyiba Al Qaeda major affiliate and support group.

Libyan Islamic Fighting Group Al Qaeda major affiliate and support group.

LTTE See Tamil Tigers.

M19 Movimiento 19 Abril (April 19 Movement): an extreme-left Colombian Group, formed in 1974. In 1981, it split into two factions, one supporting a

non-violent political strategy, the other (CNB) com[...] 'armed struggle'.

Mafia Sicilian Secret Society, which developed into [...] crime organisation.

Mlada Bosna Young Bosnia: an extreme Bosnia Ser[...] the First World War.

Moroccan Islamic Combatant Group Al Qaeda ma[...] group.

MRTA Tupac Amaru Revolutionary Movement: a M[...] 1983 and aimed at establishing a Marxist regime in [...] from Tupac Amaru (see below).

New People's Army NPA is the armed wing of the C[...] Philippines. It was founded in 1969, led by Jose Maria [...] Liwang a.k.a. Joma. NPA is active in rural Luzon, V[...] numbering some 16,000.

November 17 Greek extreme-left group: formed in 1[...] from 17 November 1973 student uprising against the G[...]

PFLP Popular Front for the Liberation of Palestine: forme[...] George Habash, it is opposed to the Israeli–Palestinian [...]

PFLP-GC Popular Front for the Liberation of Palestine – [...] formed in 1968 and led by Ahmad Jibril, it split from P[...]

PIJ The Palestinian Islamic Jihad: formed in the 1970s by [...] it is bitterly opposed to the Israeli–Palestinian peace pro[...] up an Islamic–Palestinian state and to remove the state [...]

PKK Kurdistan Workers' Party: formed in 1974, it seeks to c[...] Kurdish homeland in South-Eastern Turkey.

PIRA Provisional Irish Republican Army: formed in 1969, th[...] dominant Republican organisation and the most lethal group [...] They declared a ceasefire in 1997 and in 1998 Sinn Fei[...] signed the Good Friday Agreement aimed at establishi[...] government in Northern Ireland.

PLO Palestinian Liberation Organisation: formed in 1964, it [...] by Arab states as 'the sole legitimate representative of the [...] In September 1993, the PLO leader Yasser Arafat, and [...] Minister Yitzhak Rabin, agreed to the Declaration of Pri[...] train the Israeli–Palestinian peace process.

RAF Rote Armée Fraktion (Red Army Faction): formed in [...] group became one of the leading Fighting Communist [...]

remained involved in political violence following UN efforts to resolve the Angolan conflict.

Weathermen US extreme-left-wing group: formed in 1969 it was an off-shoot of Students for Democratic Society (SDS).

Will of the People (Narodnaya Volya) A Russian anarchist group that believed it could provoke a people's rebellion by assassinations of the Tsar and leading officials. It succeeded in assassinating Tsar Alexander II.

Introduction to the third edition

Terrorism remains a serious problem for the international community. In the period January 2006 to December 2009, over 60 per cent of countries experienced terrorist attacks. Eleven countries (Afghanistan, Colombia, India, Iraq, Israel, Nepal, Pakistan, the Philippines, Russia, Somalia and Thailand) suffered over 1,000 attacks in this period and seven of these experienced over 2,000. The worst affected were Iraq (over 18,000 attacks), Afghanistan (over 5,400 attacks) and Pakistan (over 5,000 attacks).[1] In the same period the armed forces of the United Kingdom, the United States and other NATO allies have lost hundreds of soldiers' lives in a struggle to suppress a terrorist-backed insurgency in Afghanistan.

The global picture does not indicate that the 'war on terror', which President George W. Bush declared in the wake of the 9/11 attacks, has been won. On the other hand it would be incorrect to assume that Al Qaeda, its affiliates and other jihadi groups have won their so-called 'holy war' against the Coalition against Terrorism formed after 9/11. Al Qaeda and its allies have not succeeded in gaining full control of a single Muslim country. Moreover, despite the fact that Al Qaeda and its affiliates and supporters are still determined to mount major terrorist attacks on the United States, the United Kingdom and other Western democracies, they have not succeeded in mounting an attack on the scale of 9/11. This is not for the want of trying. The intelligence services and the police in Western democracies including the UK and the US have been able to preempt or prevent numerous conspiracies and plots through acquiring and sharing better intelligence and through improved police coordination and response. The prevention of the 2006 liquid explosives plot to blow up seven airliners en route from Heathrow to North America is a major example of this vital role of the counter-terrorism agencies. If the plotters had succeeded it has been estimated that the terrorists could have caused mass killings on the scale of 9/11.

As argued in the 2006 edition of my book, the democracies need to remain vigilant. The Al Qaeda network has suffered many setbacks and failures but it is still in the business of promoting international terrorism and recruiting and indoctrinating people to conduct their so-called 'holy war' against the democracies they are taught to hate. However, it remains a central argument of my book that the democracies should stay true to their basic values in their response to terrorism. The foundations of any operative democracy are the upholding of

the rule of law, the protection of fundamental human rights and effective representative institutions and electoral processes to ensure democratic accountability.[2]
In the first and second editions of this book, I argued that it is possible to maintain
an effective counter-terrorism policy without undermining the basic principles of
liberal democracy. I do not accept that democracies need to suspend the rule of
law and adopt draconian measures in the name of 'national security' in order to
suppress terrorism. On the contrary, as I argue in my book and elsewhere, the use
of extreme draconian measures or 'terror against terror' is counter-productive as
it serves as a recruiting sergeant and propaganda weapon for terrorists. What is
the good of governments undermining democracy by adopting measures of brutal
suppression that do the terrorists' work for them? A major factor in helping
operative democracies to fight terrorism is the support of the overwhelming
majority of their population for democratic governance. Even though their
citizens are fully aware of democracy's shortcomings, they know that it is the
least imperfect form of government. Most law-abiding citizens are also fully aware
that terrorist attacks can never be legitimate in an operative democracy because,
by definition, these political systems provide numerous channels for peaceful
campaigning for political change.

As I have argued elsewhere, operative liberal democracies have shown resilience
in the face of significant terrorist threats, despite the obvious vulnerabilities and
opportunities they provide for terrorists.[3] Sadly the front-line states experiencing
very high levels of terrorist atrocities combined with full-blown terrorist-backed
insurgencies do not share this resilience. For example in Iraq and Afghanistan,
where the efforts to establish democratic government are still at a fragile and
rudimentary stage, and in Pakistan, which is beleaguered with the challenges of
religious fundamentalism, ethnic separatism and deep political divisions and mistrust.
Nor are these the only major incubators of international terrorism; Somalia and
Yemen are other examples. In such cases, terrorist campaigns become a major
threat to national security and a huge obstacle to the development of democracy
and economic and social reform.

These trends are directly affecting the security and wellbeing of the afflicted
countries, but they also pose a major potential threat to international peace and
security. A key lesson of the early development of Al Qaeda and the 9/11 attacks
is that once a terrorist group that aims to change the international system is
allowed to establish a safe haven and base in the territory of a failed state or a
state with a weak or collaborative regime, it can more easily plan and carry
out deadly attacks on foreign targets and provoke full-scale war, possibly including war between states armed with weapons of mass destruction (WMD). This
danger has not receded since I completed the second edition of my book. I have
therefore given more attention to the political and strategic impact of modern
transnational terrorism, the need for maximum international cooperation by law-
abiding states to counter not only direct threats to the safety and security of
their own citizens but also to preserve international peace and security
especially through strengthening counter-proliferation and cooperative threat
reduction (CTR).

In my conclusions I offer some observations on the current status of the struggle against the Al Qaeda network's campaign of transnational terrorism and terrorist-backed insurgencies, including an assessment of the strengths and weaknesses of the Al Qaeda network and the international community's response. Finally, I speculate about the post-Al Qaeda scenarios and the long-term future of terrorism and terrorist-backed insurgencies.

Paul Wilkinson
St Andrews
May 2010

1 Terrorism, insurgency and asymmetrical conflict

Introduction to the concept of terrorism

A great deal of unnecessary confusion has been created as a result of the mass media, politicians and others using the term terrorism as a synonym for political violence in general. Others seek to ban the word terrorism on the spurious grounds that most of those who use terrorism as a weapon prefer to be called 'freedom fighters', 'holy warriors' or 'revolutionaries', depending on the cause they profess to be fighting for. Some so-called 'post-modernists' reject the concept of terrorism on the grounds that it is purely 'subjective', implying that there are no independent objective verifiable criteria to enable us to distinguish terrorism from other forms of activity. The public would be justifiably puzzled if lawyers and criminologists ceased to use terms such as 'murder', 'serial murder', and 'war crime' and 'genocide' simply because those who perpetrate such crimes regard these terms as pejorative.

As for identifying objective criteria for identifying terrorist activity, common sense indicates that the general public in most countries in the world can recognise terrorism when they see campaigns of bombings, suicide bombings, shooting attacks, hostage-takings, hijackings and threats of such actions, especially when so many of these actions are deliberately aimed at civilians.

Terrorism can be conceptually and empirically distinguished from other modes of violence and conflict by the following characteristics:

It is premeditated and designed to create a climate of extreme fear;
It is directed at a wider target than the immediate victims;
It inherently involves attacks on random or symbolic targets, including civilians;
It is considered by the society in which it occurs as 'extra-normal', that is in the
  literal sense that it violates the norms regulating disputes, protest and dissent; and
It is used primarily, though not exclusively, to influence the political behaviour of
  governments, communities or specific social groups.

It is true that in the burgeoning of modern international terrorism in the late 1960s and early 1970s many efforts to obtain international agreements and conventions on the prevention and suppression of terrorist crimes were stymied by governments which, for their own political and ideological reasons, wished to block such measures by claiming that there was no internationally accepted definition of terrorism. Since then almost all the major democracies have developed national anti-terrorist legislation and many individuals have been convicted of terrorist offences. We have also seen a considerable amount of international law on terrorist offences developed before and since 9/11. Moreover, in October 2004 the UN Security Council unanimously passed Resolution 1566 which defines terrorism and declares that in no circumstances can terrorist acts be condoned or excused for political or ideological reasons:

> Criminal acts, including [those] against civilians, committed with the intent to cause death or serious bodily injury, or taking of hostages, with the purpose to provoke a state of terror in the general public or in a group of persons or particular persons, intimidate a population or compel a government or an international organisation to do or to abstain from doing any act, which constitute offences within the scope of and as defined in the international conventions and protocols relating to terrorism, are under no circumstances justifiable by considerations of a political, philosophical, ideological, racial, ethnic, religious or other similar nature.
>
> (unscS/RES/1566[2004])

It is true that we may have to wait some time before we see a UN General Assembly definition. However, governmental and inter-governmental conferences on problems of terrorism no longer waste days in definitional issues: they have made genuine progress in improving cooperation against terrorism, and those who dismiss all the national and international efforts to develop a legal regime to deal with various aspects of terrorism as nugatory are simply wrong. The legal framework to deal with terrorist crimes is far from perfect and very difficult to apply effectively because the more sophisticated and dangerous groups have become more skilled at evading detection, but despite this there have been some major successes in bringing terrorists to justice (e.g. Ramzi Youssef, Shoko Asahara, Abdullah Ocalan, Abimael Guzman, Carlos the Jackal). Terrorism is not simply a label; it is a concept that has proved indispensable in legal and social sciences to deal with a complex global phenomenon.

The key statutory definition of terrorism in the UK legislation is contained in the Terrorism Act (2000):

(1) In this Act 'terrorism' means the use or threat of action where:
    (a) the action falls within subsection (2),
    (b) the use or threat is designed to influence the government or to intimidate the public or a section of the public, and
    (c) the use or threat is made for the purpose of advancing a political, religious or ideological cause.
(2) Action falls within this subsection if it:
    (a) involves serious violence against a person,
    (b) involves serious damage to property,
    (c) endangers a person's life, other than that of the person committing the action,

(d)   creates a serious risk to the health or safety of the public or a section of the public, or

(e)   is designed seriously to interfere with or seriously to disrupt an electronic system.

(3)   The use or threat of action falling within subsection (2) which involves the use of firearms or explosives is terrorism whether or not subsection (1)(b) is satisfied.

(Terrorism Act 2000, Part 1, (1) – (3))

The US Government has employed the definition contained in US Code Title 22 Section 2656f (d) since 1983 as follows:

The term 'terrorism' means premeditated politically motivated violence perpetrated against noncombatant targets by sub-national groups or clandestine agents, usually intended to influence an audience.

The term 'international terrorism' means terrorism involving citizens or the territory of more than one country.

The term 'terrorist group' means any group practicing, or that has significant sub-groups that practice, international terrorism.

(US Code Title 22 Section 2656f (d))

Typology, with historical and current examples

Terrorism is an activity or a 'weapon-system' as Brian Jenkins has termed it, which has been used by an enormous variety of non-state groups, regimes and governments. (Historically the use of terror by regimes has been infinitely more lethal than that of non-state groups, because, by definition, regimes/governments are likely to have control of far greater supplies of weapons and manpower to implement their policies of terror in the course of internal repression or foreign conquest.)

However, in an operative democracy the major threat of terror is posed by non-state movements or groups seeking to destroy or undermine democratic governments and to impose their own agenda by coercive intimidation.

Another basic division is between international terrorism, which involves the citizens of jurisdictions of more than one country, and domestic terrorism, which is confined within the borders of a single state and involves no foreign citizens or property. This distinction is useful for statistical purposes, but we should bear in mind that almost all protracted domestic terrorist campaigns targeting a specific state develop an important international dimension through their creation of an overseas support network aimed at raising finance, recruits, weapons and other resources for their colleagues leading the struggle against their chosen 'enemy', state authorities and security forces.

One useful way of categorising non-state terrorist movements or groups is by their political motivation: *ethnonationalist* groups, for example ETA (Euzkadi Ta Askatasuna or Basque Fatherland and Liberty), which continued its bombing campaign despite numerous captures of its top echelon by the Spanish and French authorities and a short-lived ceasefire declared in March 2006 that ended with ETA's attack on Madrid Airport in December 2006, killing two Ecuadorean immigrants; *ideological* groups, for example the Red Brigade which waged a campaign against the Italian Republic in the 1970s and 1980s with the aim of creating a neo-communist socio-economic system and state; *religio-political* groups, for example Hamas, which aims to create an Islamic Republic of Palestine and ultimately to dismantle the state of Israel; *single-issue* groups, such as animal rights extremists linked to ALF (Animal Liberation Front), aim to change one aspect of government policy and social behaviour rather than to remodel the political and socio-economic order as a whole. While most members of the animal welfare movement are committed to restricting themselves to non-violent protest, extreme militants are prepared to engage in arson and bomb attacks on the premises of commercial firms they wish to target and to engage in threats, and in some cases attacks, on people they describe as animal 'abusers'. It should be borne in mind that campaigns by animal rights extremists against specific firms and projects such as the Cambridge animal laboratory have caused industry research labs to lose millions of pounds.

The damage and disruption caused by violent single-issue groups should not be underestimated, but so far, at least in the UK, they have not succeeded in killing anyone.

One distinction worth adding to our typology is that between potentially *corrigible* terrorism – where there is a real possibility of finding a political/diplomatic pathway out of the conflict by addressing its underlying causes, thus very probably reducing if not ending the terrorist violence spawned by the conflict – and *incorrigible* terrorism. In the latter case the movement/group has such absolutist and maximalist aims, and poses such a major threat to the lives and wellbeing of civilian communities, that the only recourse is to use all possible measures to suppress the group before it can wreak more mayhem.

In order to begin to understand the implications of recent changes in the nature of international terrorism, it is essential to grasp the major differences between the new terrorism of the Al Qaeda network of networks and more traditional terrorist groups such as ETA and FARC. Al Qaeda is not simply another group like ETA but under a different label. ETA has certainly committed hundreds of brutal killings; however, unlike Al Qaeda, ETA did not explicitly adopt a policy of mass killing as an integral part of its strategy. As Brian Jenkins so aptly observed, terrorists in the 1970s and 1980s wanted 'a lot of people watching, not a lot of people dead' (1975: 4).

By contrast Al Qaeda's leader, Osama bin Laden, issued a 'Fatwa' on 23 February 1998, which announced the setting up of a World Islamic Front for Jihad and declared that 'it is the duty of all Muslims to kill US citizens – civilian or military, and their allies – everywhere'. The brutal language of this 'Fatwa' is one way in which the sheer ruthlessness and lethality of this movement is reflected. Their track record of brutal mass-killing in New York, Washington, Kenya, Bali, Casablanca, Saudi Arabia, Iraq and many other places is proof positive of their remorseless use of mass terror.

Moreover, whereas ETA and other more traditional groups have limited their aims to bringing about radical change in one particular state or region, Al Qaeda has an uncompromising/absolutist commitment to changing the entire international system. The Al Qaeda movement aims to expel the US and other 'infidels' from the Middle East and from Muslim lands generally. They also want to topple Muslim regimes/governments which they accuse of betraying the 'true Islam' and collaboration with the US and its allies. Ultimately their aim is to establish a pan-Islamist Caliphate uniting all Muslims. These aims may appear grandiose in the extreme, but we need to bear in mind that bin Laden and his followers fanatically believe that they will prevail in their Jihad because Allah is on their side.

A major difference between the new terrorism of the Al Qaeda network and more traditional groups is precisely its global network of networks, including affiliates, cells and support. These networks provide the movement with a presence and a capacity to act in at least 90 countries. It is the most widely dispersed non-state terrorist network ever seen and this is what gives the movement 'global reach'.

'Traditional' terrorist movements generally confine themselves to mounting attacks in one country or region, though in some cases they do develop sophisticated overseas support networks to obtain finance, weapons, recruits, safe havens and the opportunity to enlist wider support for their cause.

In a later chapter, I will assess Al Qaeda's current strategy, modus operandi, targets and tactics and ask to what extent the war on terrorism can be judged successful in its efforts to crush Al Qaeda.

Assessing the effectiveness and strategic impact of terrorism

Some terrorists appear to believe that terrorism will always 'work' for them in the end, by intimidating their opponents into submitting to the terrorists' 'demands'. In reality the history of modern terrorism campaigns shows that terrorism as a major weapon has only very rarely succeeded in achieving a terrorist group's strategic goals. The clear exception to this in recent history occurred in the period of anti-colonial struggles against the British and French after the Second World War, for example in ending British Mandate control in Palestine, ending British control of Cyprus and Aden, and in ending French rule in Algeria (Horne 1977).[1] However, there were special factors militating in favour of the rebels in all these cases; the public and the government of the colonial power had no real desire to occupy these countries or to sacrifice the lives of young soldiers and colonial police, or to expend their scarce resources, already severely denuded after six years of world war. The anti-colonial movements also had the inestimable advantage of large-scale sympathy among their own population, and the colonial authorities faced a wall of silence when they sought intelligence among the public. But, in the postcolonial period, there is not a single case of a terrorist movement seizing control in any country. Indeed the use of terrorism as a weapon by insurgents has backfired and alienated the indigenous population.

There are two other major factors to be considered here. First, historically terrorism has mainly been used as an auxiliary weapon in a conflict involving a much wider repertoire. Second, it should be remembered that the use of terror as a weapon of control by dictatorships has been generally much, much more effective than the use of terror as a weapon of insurgency, mainly because dictatorial regimes generally have more ruthless and powerful domestic agencies of repression with which to suppress any incipient opposition.

However, there is a key difference between terrorists gaining all their strategic goals and terrorists having a strategic impact on macro-political and strategic events and developments. With careful timing and skilful planning terrorists can certainly have a strategic impact on international relations and politics from time to time. There were some clear examples of strategic impact in the 1980s and 1990s:

- The 1983 truck bombing of the US marines while they were in barracks in Lebanon compelled President Reagan and his administration to pull all US troops out of the multi-national force, and thus sent the message to active or potential terrorists (e.g. bin Laden at that time) that the US could be intimidated into making changes in its foreign policy through the use of terrorism.

Other examples of terrorist attacks having a major strategic impact are:

- In the 1990s the use of suicide bombings against Israeli civilians helped to undermine the peace process between the Israelis and the Palestinians.
- Mass hostage-taking by Chechen terrorists in 1996 compelled the Russian government to make major concessions to the Chechen leadership.
- The 9/11 suicide hijacking attacks by Al Qaeda on the World Trade Center and the Pentagon had a colossal effect not only on US foreign and security policy and public opinion. They had a major influence on international relations, the US and international economy and on the patterns of conflict in the Middle East.

If terrorism rarely gains strategic goals for its perpetrators, why does it remain such a popular mode of struggle for so many groups around the world?

Even when leaders of terrorist groups recognise the fact that they are very unlikely to win their strategic goals, they may be persuaded that the potential tactical benefits to be gained by using terrorism are so attractive that terrorism is a weapon they cannot afford to discard:

- It can help weaken the enemy by a campaign of attrition.
- It is a useful way of inflicting hatred and vengeance on a hated enemy.
- It can be used as a means of provoking government security forces into over-reaction, thus driving up support for the insurgents.
- If they can mount spectacular or particularly damaging attacks they will get huge publicity.
- They may gain release of imprisoned terrorists.

- They may get huge cash ransoms.
- Another key factor is that terrorism is a low-cost, potentially high-yield and relatively low-risk method of struggle for the perpetrators.

I have argued that it is grossly misleading to treat terrorism as a synonym for insurgency, guerrilla warfare or political violence in general. It can be objectively defined as a special method of armed struggle, or in Brian Jenkins's term a 'weapons system', which can be used either on its own, or, as is more often the case historically, as part of a wider repertoire of armed struggle. Hence, just as it is possible to engage in acts of terrorism without mounting a full-scale insurgency, so it is possible to wage an effective insurgency by relying on a combination of guerrilla and conventional warfare, and eschewing the weapon of terror. Terrorist campaigns inherently involve deliberate attacks on civilian targets and are there-fore analogous to war crimes. Nor is it the case that the weapons of terror are used solely by substate perpetrators. Throughout history it has been regimes and their agents of repression which have time and time again demonstrated their capacity to employ mass terror on a truly vast scale. In the twentieth century, truly the age of terror, the obvious examples of this are the campaigns of mass terror and genocide waged by the Hitler and Stalin regimes. The tendency of modern governments to apply the terms terror and terrorism exclusively to sub-state groups is blatantly dishonest and self-serving. If the concepts of regime or reign of terror, sometimes called 'incumbent' or state terrorism, and terrorism by sub-state groups, are to have any lasting value in political science and strategic studies, they must be applied consistently in accord with clearly defined objective criteria.

Employing the criteria outlined in this chapter I conclude that a major char-acteristic of contemporary ethnic insurgencies is the widespread use of terror both by insurgents and by the counterinsurgent regimes and military and paramilitary forces ranged against them. However, I argue that there is no inevitable evolu-tionary pattern in insurgent organisations whereby they begin as exclusively terrorist groups and only later show an interest in acquiring the manpower and weaponry for a wider insurgency. Most insurgent leaders view terrorism as a useful auxiliary weapon. They are realistic enough to recognise that terrorism alone is going to be insufficient to deliver their strategic goals and that it is a faulty weapon, which often misfires and may ultimately prove counterproductive. I conclude by presenting some general conclusions on the relationships between insurgency and terrorism.

The concept of insurgency

Insurgency is a relatively value-neutral concept denoting a rebellion or rising against any government in power or the civil authorities. It should be stressed that although the idea of a rising against the government may appear to imply a large popular movement, in reality many insurgencies have involved very small numbers of rebels.

In the contemporary international system, and historically, insurgency is generally manifested as low-intensity conflict rather than as full-scale conventional warfare.

However, there are many instances where the insurgent forces eventually acquire sufficient troops and weaponry to defeat the incumbents' forces in a conventional war. This was achieved, for example, by the Taliban against their opponents in the latest civil war in Afghanistan. This assumed association of insurgency with purely low-intensity conflict is also implied in the classic distinction between insurgent and belligerent in international law, where the former is not equated with engagement in all-out war. In the reality of the post-Cold War world, where the vast majority of armed conflicts are insurgencies and internal wars of remarkable savagery, this attempt to differentiate between a state of insurgency and a state of belligerency begins to look increasingly meaningless.

The same can be said for the implied distinction between counterinsurgency and war. While it is true that counterinsurgency strategy and doctrine pays considerable attention to political, social and economic measures and inevitably involves the police and criminal justice system, it is also clear that there are numerous examples of the whole spectrum of conventional military force being deployed to suppress insurgency. This is well illustrated in the case of the deployment of US armed forces in Vietnam against the Viet Cong, the Soviet forces' efforts to suppress the Mujaheddin in Afghanistan, the recent Russian efforts to defeat insurgencies in Chechnya and Dagestan and the efforts of the US and UK troops to suppress insurgency in Iraq following the 2003 allied invasion.

A study of the chronology of armed conflicts in the period since 1945 shows that the overwhelming majority have been intrastate and by far the greater proportion of those killed in these internal wars have been civilians. One authority has estimated that as many as 84 per cent of those killed in armed conflicts since 1945 have been civilians. In fact the cumulative death toll from low-intensity conflicts is almost as high as the total number of those killed in the worst of the high-intensity conflicts. This is because there are at least four times as many low-intensity conflicts for each high-intensity conflict at any given time, worldwide.

Typical intrastate conflicts of the 1990s involved ethnonationalist or ethno-religious movements waging armed struggle to achieve ethnic separation or to topple the government. They have been fought mainly by armed militias, mercenaries and paramilitaries. Their prime targets are civilians. They typically employ mass terror and atrocities to carry out ethnic cleansing of whole areas, for example by driving people from their homes, murders, massacres, mass rape, torture and starvation. There are no clear front-lines in such wars, and there is generally not even the most minimal attempt to adhere to the Geneva Convention. It is a tragic fact that in many conflicts involving ethnic cleansing, for example in the Great Lakes of Central Africa, in Afghanistan and the Caucasus, the international community has failed to act to prevent or stop such atrocities. In Rwanda and Burundi, for example, the ethnic cleansing reached genocidal proportions, and yet UN action has been largely restricted to belated provision of some humanitarian aid and the setting up of the International Tribunal to try cases of war crimes and crimes against humanity committed in Rwanda. The former Yugoslavia international military intervention to stop further ethnic cleansing in Bosnia and Kosovo, though ultimately effective, was extremely belated, leaving tragic legacies of gross violations of human rights, huge socio-economic destruction and disruption, and simmering ethnic hatreds and thirst for vengeance, which could at any time break out into further savage warfare. In other genocidal conflict situations such as Darfur and Uganda the UN has simply not had the resources to cope.

Nor should we fall into the trap of assuming that other states have no business concerning themselves with such conflicts. Quite apart from the international community's moral obligation to try to stop the gross violations of human rights committed in these interstate wars there is a major argument for action by other states, particularly neighbouring states, on grounds of national interest. Interstate armed conflicts have led to hundreds of thousands of refugees fleeing from the afflicted states. In most cases the receiving states simply lack the resources to find food and adequate shelter and adequate health and welfare support for large numbers of refugees. In some cases, for example in the Balkans and in Africa, recipients of refugees have themselves got a fragile ethnic balance that could be fatally undermined by a huge influx. Hence there is a real danger of the political and economic stability of other states and whole regions being undermined.

In addition to classifying insurgencies on the basis of their relative intensity and lethality it is also instructive to categorise them in terms of their general political motivation.

It would be a serious error to assume that ideologically driven insurgencies are a thing of the past. In Latin America and parts of South and South East Asia, for example, there are numerous groups challenging regimes in the name of some kind of extreme-left ideology. Indeed, every significant insurgent movement in Latin America falls into this category. In addition it should be borne in mind that these categories are by no means mutually exclusive. For example, the Kurdistan Workers' Party (PKK) that, since 1974, has waged an armed conflict against the Turkish authorities, in the pursuit of independence for the Kurds, is Marxist-Leninist in ideology. A number of secular Palestinian political organisations, for example the Popular Front for the Liberation of Palestine (PFLP), also combine nationalist aims with a Marxist-Leninist ideology. One important type of conflict is the challenge to a growing number of states and regimes by religious fundamentalist groups, which see themselves as waging holy war to overthrow regimes they regard as irredeemably corrupt and evil, and to restore observance of the true religion.

This trend towards waging armed struggle in the name of religion is, however, rarely manifested in pure form. In some cases these groups' fanatical adherence to the doctrines of religious fundamentalism is wedded to a political agenda that is implicitly nationalist in character. Hence Hezbollah wants to establish an Islamic republic in Lebanon, Hamas has a similar objective for Palestine, the Armed Islamic Group (GIA) wants an Islamic republic of Algeria, al-Gama'at al Islamaiyya or Islamic Group in Egypt also wants to set up an Islamic state in their country and so on. Al Qaeda, on the other hand, aims at establishing a pan-Islamic Caliphate.

In practice, seen in the civil wars in Afghanistan and Sudan for example, the combination of religious fanaticism and a nationalist political agenda can cause particularly lethal and protracted intrastate conflict. Other evidence, for example from the Balkans and the Caucasus and from the Punjab and Kashmir, underlines the importance of taking full account of the resurgence of religious fanaticism. It has been a dangerous element in the map of conflict world-wide since the 1980s. However, the cases of the Caucasus, Punjab and Kashmir again show how religion is closely intertwined with ethnic separatism. In order to understand the key role of ethnonationalism the next section will explore the reason for the salience of this political motivation for modern insurgencies.

Why is ethnonationalism the predominant political motivation behind contemporary insurgencies?

There are two key factors which help to explain the ubiquity and strength of the ethnonationalism which underlies so many modern campaigns of insurgency. First, despite the Marxist preoccupation with socio-economic class as the prime referent for the analysis of social conflict, it is ethnic identity which has provided a far more durable and powerful influence on human behaviour. In the face of all the powerful forces of globalisation and talk of a new global 'mass culture' the reality is that ethnic distinctiveness, as manifested in a common language and culture and shaped by a shared history and values, remains as important today as it was in the heyday of the European national self-determination movement in the nineteenth and early twentieth centuries.

Second, there remains a colossal mismatch between the international state system, with its legally recognised sovereign governments and frontiers, and the demographic map of distinctive ethnic groups or national identities. This has been compounded by the fact that the borders of over two-thirds of the member states of the UN were drawn quite arbitrarily by the diplomatists of the major powers in the nineteenth and early twentieth centuries without any respect for maintaining ethnic or tribal homogeneity. Yet it was these borders, often drawn by diplomatic conferences in the capitals of the European colonial powers, which almost without exception formed the inherited boundaries of the newly independent postcolonial states as they broke free from European rule in the 1950s and 1960s. Not surprisingly multiethnic new states such as India, Nigeria and the Congo soon found themselves immersed in bitter intrastate conflicts, challenged by ethnonationalist movements demanding the self-determination they believe they were so unjustly denied in the decolonisation process. But the causes of the recent upsurge in ethnic insurgencies are to be found not only in historic hatred and rivalries, but also in the changes to the international system wrought by the ending of the Cold War. The collapse of the former communist regimes in Eastern Europe and the former Soviet Union created a fresh stimulus for a large number of ethnic groups to reassert their identities, by challenging the status quo and pursuing their various separatist and irredentism claims and rivalries through armed struggle or the threat of violence.

Although classical realists have always applied the concept of the security dilemma exclusively to states, it can be used just as legitimately to help explain conflict at substate level involving ethnonationalist movements. When one ethnic group visibly enhances its own security, for example by acquiring additional weapons or making military alliances with friendly states or groups in the belief that this is a necessary defence against other groups or states, the neighbouring ethnic groups will tend to see this as a potential threat to their own security, and in consequence take countermeasures that, paradoxically, may make a conflict between them more likely. The dynamics of escalating hostility and tension between the rival ethnic groups will also generally be fuelled by memories of outrages or injustices attributed, fairly or unfairly, to the 'enemy' ethnic group. Clear examples of this process at work can be seen in the worsening relations between the ethnic Albanian Kosovars and the Serbs in Kosovo in the 1990s, in the growing tensions between Croats, Serbs and Bosnian Muslims in the early and mid 1990s, between the Armenians and the Azeris over Nagorno-Karabakh, between the Georgians and the Abkhazians since the late 1980s, and between the Sunnis and Shiites in Iraq since 2003. It is notable that in all these cases the emergence of militant nationalist leaders capable of mobilising their own ethnic constituencies and playing on the perceived threat posed by enemy groups is a key feature.

Other important factors contributing to the ethnonationalist violence are likely to include: availability of militant leaders capable of mobilising sizeable proportions of their ethnic constituencies, by persuading them of the reality and severity of the 'threat' they face and appealing to history and historical myths; availability of weapons; and availability of political and possibly military support from friendly states, other ethnic groups or other external actors. Alternatively, in some cir- cumstances, the leaders of an ethnonationalist group may be tempted to take action because they become convinced that they have an asymmetric advantage over their opponents and that no state or other group will be willing to risk involvement in armed conflict to assist their designated 'enemy'.

Finally, it is most important to stress that there is nothing in the historical and social science research literature on insurgency to suggest that the recourse to armed rebellion is inevitable, or that the precise methods of armed struggle adopted by insurgent groups can be predicted by the use of some general formula. So much depends on the personalities, attitudes, beliefs and strategic and tactical ideas of the specific ethnonationalist groups involved and, in particular, of their leaders and mentors and those who are influential among the upper echelons of the group. Much will also depend on any experience they may have of earlier involvement in conflicts and the lessons they may have drawn from this.

We have now established that ethnonationalism is the predominant political motivation behind contemporary insurgencies, and some of the reasons for this. The following section will identify the major forms of armed struggle used by insurgents, their roles and for conflict and their wider implications.

The main forms of armed struggle used by contemporary insurgents

Conventional warfare

Most revolutionary wars in which challengers have toppled an incumbent govern- ment have moved through a guerrilla or low-intensity phase and finally developed into a decisive struggle between conventional armed forces. This is how the Bolsheviks finally defeated the White Russian forces, how Mao's Chinese communists defeated the nationalists and the Vietnamese communists defeated the South Vietnamese army. Some of today's insurgency movements undoubtedly have the manpower and range of weaponry to enable them to resort to full-scale conventional military operations if and when the opportunity arises. For example, Union for the Total Independence of Angola (UNITA), the main opposition to the Angolan government, was known to have over 50,000 fighters, tanks, anti-aircraft artillery, field guns and multiple rocket launchers as well as Stinger missiles,[2] which proved so effective for the Mujaheddin in the Afghan conflict. In Sudan the SPLA is believed to have between 60,000 and 100,000 fighters together with anti-aircraft artillery and surface-to-air missiles.[3]

However, in the vast majority of cases insurgencies are characterised by modes of low-intensity conflict as outlined below.

Guerrilla warfare

In the classic pattern the guerrilla wages a hypermobile war. It is, one could say, the natural weapon of the strategically weaker side. Rather than risking the annihilation of his own forces in a full-scale battle with his more numerous and better armed opponents the guerrilla goes over to the tactical offensive, waging what Taber has called 'the war of the flea'[4] using methods, time and places of the guerrillas' choice and constantly trying to benefit from the guerrillas' major tactical advantage – the element of surprise.

The most effective modern leaders and theorists of guerrilla warfare have stressed that it is not a self-sufficient method of achieving victory. Only when the anti-guerrilla side underestimates the guerrilla threat or simply fails to commit its full resources to the conflict does a guerrilla have a chance of achieving, unaided, long-term political aims. In most twentieth-century cases, guerrilla warfare on a major scale has been linked to revolutionary warfare, a struggle between a non-government group and a government for political and social control of a people in a given national territory. Most revolutionary wars have moved through a guerrilla phase and have finally developed into a decisive struggle between conventional armed forces. It should be noted, however, that the guerrilla warfare method has also frequently been used as an auxiliary weapon in other types of conflict (for example, partisan warfare against Nazi Germany in the Second World War and guerrilla attacks during the periods of full-scale limited war in Korea, and later in Vietnam).

Many theories of guerrilla warfare formulated by revolutionary leaders proclaim that counterinsurgency measures by incumbent regimes cannot be effective, and assume that such measures will tend only to enhance popular support for the guerrillas. Guerrilla movements often use urban guerrilla and terrorist tactics in a deliberate effort to provoke the authorities into a counterinsurgent overreaction, thereby inducing an effect on domestic and international opinion favourable to the guerrillas. Thompson is one of many writers who have argued against an over-emphasis on military aspects of counterinsurgency.

Among the twentieth-century revolutionary war theorists there have been changing emphases and doctrines of guerrilla warfare. The Leninist model for gaining political power was basically designed for urban areas and was to culminate in a form of revolutionary *coup d'état*. It was therefore found unsuitable for trans-mission to Asia. Mao Tse-tung tried the route of insurrection in the cities, but this was a complete failure. Chiang Kaishek was able to defeat the Chinese Communist Party in 1927. Mao concluded that henceforth communist revolutions could only take the form of revolutionary wars.

Mao stressed the vital importance of gaining the mass support of peasants as a basis for revolutionary struggle. He developed the strategy of protracted war as passing through three stages: the enemy's strategic offensive and the revolutionaries' strategic defensive; the enemy's strategic consolidation and the revolutionaries' preparation of the counter-offensive; and the revolutionaries' strategic victory. This emphasis on a protracted struggle was based on Mao's assumption of a lack of external assistance to the revolutionaries and the initial superiority of the enemy's military forces.

During their conflict against French colonial rule, the Viet Minh adapted the doctrine of protracted war to Vietnamese circumstances. In South Vietnam, guerrilla warfare was undertaken mainly to exploit contradictions in the American and Saigon governments, and to achieve political victory by undermining the opponent's will to fight. This aim was particularly clear after 1969, when the struggle basically became a confrontation between the conventional forces of North Vietnam and those of the United States and South Vietnam. Obviously the North Vietnamese could not have hoped to win a conventional military victory over US forces. What the guerrilla struggle helped to achieve was the American withdrawal, leaving the path clear for a conventional victory over the demoralised South Vietnamese army.

The successful guerrilla campaign of the Cuban revolutionaries led by Fidel Castro, 1956–59, saw the development of the theory of the *'foco'*, a small group of armed men who themselves created a revolutionary situation by their attacks on the government forces. The revolutionary leadership of the *'foco'* combines political and military command. The guerrilla band is seen as the party in embryo. But although these ideas did have some influence in Latin America, the Cuban model suffered a great setback when the attempt at revolution in Bolivia ended in Guevara's death. A major weakness of the *'foco'* concept was its elitism and its almost inevitable isolation from the peasant and urban masses.

In the late 1960s and early 1970s revolutionary theorists in Latin America and elsewhere tended to shift their attention from the countryside to the cities, launching a number of spectacular but relatively short-lived campaigns of urban violence. These efforts also ended in failure due to determined and ruthless efforts to suppress them, and the failure of the revolutionaries to gain substantial and lasting mass support.

It would be premature to assume that guerrilla warfare has become obsolete as a result of developments in military technology and counterinsurgency capabilities. Guerrilla warfare continues to prove effective in tying down large numbers of security forces, disrupting government and the economy, and as an auxiliary weapon in a wider revolutionary war. Guerrillas continue to be used, often highly effectively, in many parts of the world, sometimes with substantial help from friendly foreign governments. If well led and well armed, guerrillas can still present a formidable threat to weak and unstable governments in divided societies, especially where the guerrillas have ample wild and inaccessible terrain from which to operate, and a friendly state across the border.

Terrorism

Terrorism is the systematic use of coercive intimidation, usually to service political ends. It is used to create and exploit a climate of fear amongst a wider target group than the immediate victims of the violence, and to publicise a cause as well as to coerce a target to acceding to the terrorists' aims. Terrorism may be used on its own or as part of a wider unconventional war. It can be employed by desperate and weak minorities, by states as a tool of domestic and foreign policy, or by belligerents as an accompaniment in all types and stages of warfare. A common feature is that innocent civilians, sometimes foreigners who know nothing of the terrorists' political quarrel, are killed or injured. Typical methods of modern terrorism are explosive and incendiary bombings, shooting attacks and assassinations, hostage-taking, and kidnapping and hijacking. The possibility of terrorists using nuclear, chemical or bacteriological weapons cannot be discounted.

Terrorism is not a philosophy or a movement. It is a method. But even though we may be able to identify cases where terrorism has been used for causes most liberals would regard as just, this does not mean that even in such cases the use of terrorism, which by definition threatens the most fundamental rights of innocent civilians, is morally justified. Paradoxically, despite the rapid growth in the incidence of modern terrorism, this method has been remarkably unsuccessful in gaining strategic objectives. The only clear cases are the expulsion of British and French colonial rule from Palestine, Cyprus, Aden and Algeria. The continuing popularity of terrorism among nationalists and ideological and religious extremists must be explained by other factors: the craving for a physical expression of hatred and revenge, terrorism's record of success in yielding tactical gains (e.g. massive publicity, release of prisoners and large ransom payments), and the fact that the method is relatively cheap, easy to organise and carries minimal risk.

Totalitarian regimes have used huge systems of state terror to control whole populations and to persecute and silence dissidents and those designated 'enemies of the state'. Because these regimes (and other despotisms) have a monopoly of armed forces and a ruthless secret police apparatus, state terror has been a very effective method of suppressing opposition and resistance. Some states use regime terror as an international weapon to intimidate and kill exiled opposition leaders and to conduct revenge attacks on foreign countries, usually denying responsibility. However, increased international pressure and the use of sanctions against state sponsors of terrorism has led to a reduction in the number of states using state or state-sponsored terrorism in foreign countries.

In the light of recent historical experiences, what general assessment can be made of the overall effectiveness of terrorism as a weapon for non-state organisations? With the notable exception of the terrorist campaigns used against the European colonial powers in the mid twentieth century it is hard to find a single example of a terrorist group succeeding in gaining its strategic political objectives. Many groups have kept up their campaigns of terrorism to make useful *tactical* gains, such as boosting the morale of their recruits and supporters, gaining huge publicity and making large sums of money through kidnap and ransom operations. The more realistic terrorist group leaders' long-term hope is that their terrorist attacks will inspire and ignite a wider insurgency capable of seizing power.

However, it would be foolish to overlook the fact that the growing trend towards mass lethality terrorist attacks since the 1980s, and particularly since 9/11, has had significant impacts on the foreign and security policies of many states, polarising conflicts and helping to trigger interstate wars and civil wars. A striking example of strategic impact was the way Palestinian suicide bombers' attacks on Israeli targets helped to destroy the chances of further progress in the Oslo peace process. Bombings of buses full of Israeli civilians and the assassination of Israeli Prime Minister Rabin by a Jewish extremist effectively killed off the Oslo initiative.

Al Qaeda's 9/11 attacks provoked two international conflicts: the UN-endorsed invasion of Afghanistan to remove the Taliban regime that had given safe haven to Al Qaeda, and the US-led invasion of Iraq in 2003. These wars have cost the US and its allies hundreds of soldiers' lives and well over 100,000 civilian deaths. It is foolish to deny that terrorism can have major strategic impact. Terrorism, far from being *la maladie imaginaire* of international politics, is all too real and is a danger to the national security of many states, as well as a threat to international security because it is clearly capable of triggering a wider international conflict. Overreaction to terrorist attacks can prove to be just as dangerous as underreaction. Let us not forget that counter-terrorism policies can also have significant impact. Since 9/11 many governments have responded by curtailing, or indefinitely suspending, basic civil liberties and human rights. Nor should we forget the enormous economic costs of deploying the armed forces in what President Bush termed 'the war on terror'. Professor Stiglitz, a former winner of the Nobel Prize for Economics, has calculated that by 2006 the US government had spent over three trillion dollars on fighting the war in Iraq, and this estimate does not include the interest the US government has to pay on the loans it has needed to finance its military deployment.

Sabotage

Sabotage is a method used in accompaniment with all forms of low-intensity conflict, but also in conditions of full-scale war. It is the deliberate destruction, disruption or damage of equipment, power supplies, communications or other facilities. It is generally aimed at undermining the physical enemy's infrastructure rather than causing loss of life or targeting specific individuals. The term is derived from the French, *saboteur*: to spoil through clumsiness, or literally to clatter in sabots (clogs).

Sabotage is an extremely low-cost, potentially high-yielding means of inflicting damage on an enemy. It has frequently been used as a weapon of modern insurgents, for example by the Resistance during the Second World War. It is often combined with guerrilla warfare, but it is not generally used by groups exclusively engaged in terrorism because they are primarily concerned with creating fear by causing or threatening to take life or to cause serious injury. It sometimes happens that acts of sabotage do result in loss of life, but in such cases this is not terrorism as the loss of life was not *intended* by the saboteurs.

Relationship between guerrilla insurgency and terrorism

The history of modern insurgency shows that in most cases where the insurgents succeed they use a wide range of methods and tactics in the course of their struggles, ranging from occasional acts of sabotage to full-scale conventional warfare.[4] But there is no universal pattern so far as the decision to use terrorism is concerned. Some guerrilla leaders and theoreticians, such as Che Guevara and Mao Tse-tung, opposed the use of terror against the civilian population because they believed it would lose them the support and active cooperation of the peasants on which they depended so heavily, and hence be counterproductive. Others, such as Carlos Marighela in his *Minimanual of the Urban Guerrilla*, believed that terrorism was a weapon the revolutionary could never afford to relinquish. At the other extreme is the case of Pol Pot, who led the Khmer Rouge insurgency in Cambodia and conducted mass terror on the scale of genocide. When Pol Pot's movement seized power in the late 1970s it massacred well over a million Cambodians. The only contemporary intrastate conflicts of comparable mass lethality have been the genocides in Rwanda and Burundi in which, since 1993, an estimated 1 million civilians have been killed.[5] It is highly likely that the level of atrocities committed primarily by Serb forces but also by other parties in the ethnic conflict in the former Yugoslavia in the 1990s would have reached similar levels of genocidal lethality had it not been for international intervention to terminate the violence in Bosnia and Kosovo. However, it should be stressed that terror violence occupies only a relatively minor or auxiliary role in the majority of guerrilla insurgencies. If you are a guerrilla leader you do not have to read Mao Tse-tung or Guevara to realise that you are unlikely to win and retain the vital support and cooperation of the general population if you engage in terrorist attacks against civilians. It is true that many guerrilla groups do engage in kidnapping, especially of foreigners, in order to gain valuable cash ransoms, and this is clearly terroristic activity by its very nature. Some guerrilla organisations, such as the Revolutionary Armed Forces of Cambodia (FARC) and the other main Marxist-Maoist group in Colombia, the National Liberation Army (ELN), have made an industry out of kidnap and extortion, but it is clear that this has made them, both in reality and popular perception, little more than a branch of organised crime, decadent guerrillas rather than genuine revolutionaries, irredeemably corrupted by their intimate involvement with the narco-traffickers and their cynical pursuit of huge profits from kidnapping and from their 'protection' of coca and opium production, processing and shipping facilities.[6] On the other hand we should bear in mind that these guerrilla organisations now have the wealth to deploy huge well-equipped private armies, a major fact in ensuring that large tracts of Colombian territory are virtual 'no go' areas for the Colombian army and police.

If we examine the world map for organisations involved in terrorism we find that the majority are very small groups, ranging from a few dozen to a few hundred activists. Only a minority, approximately 25 per cent, number their members in the thousands. The tiny groups simply lack the critical mass necessary for launching a full-scale insurgency. Some, though by no means all, of the larger groupings, such as the Khmer Rouge, Sendero Luminoso (Shining Path), the PKK, the New People's Army (NPA), Harakut ul-Ansar (HUA) and Hezbollah (Lebanon), had the capability and resources for a wider campaign of insurgency.

Is there a discernible evolutionary pattern in these organisations whereby they begin as exclusively terrorist groups and only later acquire an interest in acquiring the manpower and weaponry for a wider campaign of insurgency? It is hard to find any evidence to support this theory. All the insurgent groups listed above began to acquire guns and ammunition and recruits on a scale far beyond what would be needed to man terrorist cells from the outset of their formation. It therefore appears more likely that serious insurgent group leaders recognise from the start that terrorist attacks alone are going to be insufficient to deliver their strategic goals. While they generally begin to use terrorist methods from the outset they implicitly, if not explicitly, acknowledge that they can play no more than an auxiliary role by immediately setting about building the critical mass of fighters and weapons needed for a wider insurgency. In their efforts to become major players in power struggles these movements frequently find it expedient to soft-pedal or suspend, in whole or in part, their terrorist activities because of their need to retain allies and supporters in the wider international system. A clear example of this was the PKK leadership's concessions to the German government in the wake of PKK's international terrorist activity, or Hezbollah's decision, taken purely on hostages in Lebanon.[7] For the serious insurgent groups, terrorism is regarded simply as a useful tool to be discarded or taken up at will, as circumstances demand.

Conclusion

The general conclusions of this chapter on the relationship between insurgency and terrorism are as follows:

- Acts of terrorism do not inevitably lead to a wider insurgency. On the contrary, the vast majority of groups using the weapon of terrorism remain locked in a cycle of individual, usually very spasmodic, acts of bombing, assassination, hostage-taking, etc. Only a small minority of terrorist campaigns succeed in expanding their struggles into wider insurgencies.
- The key factors which determine whether a terrorist campaign expands into a wider insurgency are (a) its capacity to win wider popular support among a substantial segment of the population; (b) a degree of repressive reaction by

the government and its security forces leading to an increase in popular support for an insurgency; (c) the availability of leaders capable of inspiring and sustaining a wider insurgency; and (d) access to sufficient weapons to initiate a wider insurgency.

- The predominant form of armed conflict in the contemporary world is intrastate rather than interstate, and the overwhelming majority of insurgencies are ethnic or ethnoreligious in their underlying motivation.
- A common feature of all contemporary wider insurgencies institutions of ethnic or ethnoreligious conflict is that acts of mass terror against the 'enemy' ethnic group, 'ethnic cleansing', massacres, mass rape and other atrocities against the civilian population are widely employed. Frequently the perpetrators are militias or paramilitary organisations rather than regular armies. There are no clear front lines, and there is no adherence to the Geneva Convention.
- Though they often begin on small scale, ethnonationalist insurgencies are particularly dangerous because they can quickly escalate out of control.

2 The emergence of modern terrorism

Liberal democracies and the emergence of modern terrorism

Liberal democracy is a fairly recent (nineteenth-century) development, which in theory provides ample scope for political opposition and participation within the law.[1] It is because they enjoy constitutional legitimacy in the eyes of the majority of their citizens that modern liberal democracies have proved remarkably resilient against terrorist campaigns by extremist political movements. Compared to colonial regimes and autocracies, Western liberal democracies have been remarkably free of large-scale revolutionary strife and separatist wars. However, they have not proved to be immune against terrorist attacks: on the contrary, the intrinsic freedoms of the democratic society make the tasks of terrorist propaganda, recruitment, organisation and the mounting of operations a relatively easy matter. There is ease of movement in and out of the country, and freedom of travel within it. Rights of free speech and a free media can be used as shields for terrorist defamation of democratic leaders and institutions and terrorist incitement to violence. If the government is provoked into introducing emergency powers, suspending democracy in order to defend it, there is always the risk that in using heavy repression to crush the terrorist campaign the authorities may alienate the innocent majority of citizens caught up in the procedures of house-to-house searches and interrogations.

It is clear that even long-established liberal democracies become more vulnerable when weakened by prolonged ethnic or religious conflict, by military defeat, by major economic crisis or by an erosion of popular support for democratic institutions and values. For example, Hitler was able to exploit the climate of popular resentment over the Versailles settlement, the crisis of the Depression and the erosion of popular support for democracy when he deployed a combination of political propaganda and terror to undermine the Weimar Republic and seize absolute power. Similarly Mussolini was able to destroy Italian democracy by exploiting the economic crisis and the erosion of popular support for liberal democracy, together with widespread resentment at the outcome of the peace treaties in which Italy was alleged to have been cheated in the distribution of the spoils of victory following the First World War.[2]

However, although all operative liberal democracies are intrinsically vulnerable to terrorist activities and attacks, it is those which rank among the transitional or modernising political systems, still engaged in the processes of democratisation and economic modernisation, that are the most at risk from internal violence escalating into full-scale civil wars. Hence, although terrorist attacks within Western democracies and against their citizens and facilities overseas remain a threat to innocent life, it is the newer democracies, established following decolonisation and after the ending of the Cold War, which have experienced, and are likely to continue to suffer, the severest levels of political violence and instability.

It is a tragic irony that the country which has suffered by far the greatest number of terrorist attacks in recent years is Iraq, where the neo-conservatives who advised President George W. Bush believed that following the 2003 invasion and the removal of Saddam democracy would take root and become a model for other Middle Eastern states. Putting aside the fierce controversy over the legality of the invasion it is a tribute to the courage and persistence of the majority of Iraqis and the pro-democratic leaders that free elections have been held, and the beginnings of democratic institutions and processes are painfully and slowly emerging despite continuing terrorist atrocities, many of which are an expression of bitter sectarian hatred between Sunni extremists and the Shi'ite majority and Kurds. At the time of writing (spring 2010) it is still uncertain whether President Obama will be able to withdraw US forces from Iraq by his target date, and still more uncertain whether democracy can survive in Iraq after the US forces' departure. Chapter 4, which deals with terrorist-backed insurgencies, discusses the factors which help to explain why terrorism and terrorist-backed insurgency in Iraq have proved so difficult to suppress.

The emergence of modern terrorism

It is not the aim of the present study to provide a comprehensive history of twentieth-century terrorism. The following brief survey is an attempt to identify some of the key developments that led to the emergence of terrorism as a challenge to liberal democracies in the mid and late twentieth century. (Those readers wishing to investigate the recent history of terrorism in specific countries or regions will find some useful guides to the specialist literature now available.)[3]

If the 'success' of terrorist movements is to be judged by their ability to realise their long-term political objectives, then those in the nationalist category have the best record. Wherever there is a deeply felt sense of oppression and resent-ment against alien rule on the part of large sections of the population, the nationalist rallying cry is a grave danger signal for the incumbent regime. For the terrorist movement that proclaims national independence as its major goal can bid to represent a whole ethnic constituency, however dubious the credentials of the terrorist leadership and however undemocratic their internal processes. If a nationalist terror movement is recognised as legitimate by a large proportion of its proclaimed constituency (say a quarter to a third of its members), it will have a more powerful basis on which to challenge the incumbents than any nihilist or utopian revolutionary could hope for. Moreover, if in addition the nationalist movement can use terror and agitation to neutralise a further third of the population, that is to say, to withhold positive support and cooperation from the incumbent regime, the way is open for them to exploit any military or political weakness, internal division or lack of will on the part of the authorities.

The practical advantages to the terrorist of having a large corps of activists and sympathisers, and a large passive element waiting fearfully to see who wins the struggle, are obvious. Terrorists need, in addition to plentiful recruits and supplies of cash and weapons, reliable lines of communication, safe houses and a constant flow of intelligence on what the authorities are up to. But there is a still more important advantage in having, to use the Maoist image, a favourable sea in which the terrorist fish can swim: the incumbent security forces will be denied the vital intelligence and cooperation from the public upon which they depend to catch the terrorists. This was one of the winning cards of the Ethniki Organosis Kypriakou Agoniston (EOKA) terrorists in their fight against the British Army and police in Cyprus. The British forces found themselves confronted, time and time again, by an impenetrable wall of silence that effectively cancelled out the authorities' advantage of numbers and firepower.[4]

These factors certainly help to explain the few solitary successes of movements using terrorism as a primary weapon in the struggle for power in the modern period. As a weapon against well-established liberal democracies or against indigenous autocracies, terrorism has proved an almost total failure. Only in a small number of armed colonial independence struggles in the 1940s, 1950s and early 1960s (mainly directed against British and French colonial administrations) did terrorism prove effective in persuading the metropolitan publics and their governments that the cost of maintaining their military presence outweighed the costs of withdrawal. Britain's eventual relinquishment of control in Palestine in 1948 and Cyprus in 1960 are perhaps the most clear-cut instances. Terrorist violence also played a key part in forcing British withdrawal from the Suez Canal zone base in 1954 and from Aden in 1964, and French withdrawal from Algeria in 1962.

These successes of the terrorist strategy were undoubtedly considerably facilitated by three other key factors. First, the metropolitan governments and their publics were weary of war in general and colonial wars in particular. They wanted to bring their soldiers home, for the public had no real stomach for the conflicts. Both colonialism and imperialism were no longer popular causes: jingoism had long since given way to a guilt-ridden disillusionment with any overseas military adventures. Another important factor conducive to withdrawal was the straitened economic circumstances of the mother countries, impoverished by years of world war, preoccupied with the problems of internal reconstruction and economic survival; they simply could not stand the financial cost of prolonged involvement in colonial wars. In Britain's case, there was an additional consideration: a growing popular feeling that there were no vital strategic interests at stake in such distant entanglements. Formally this new realism was reflected in the official British policy of negotiating independence for one colony after another in the 1950s and 1960s. Indeed it was a bitter irony that it was within a situation of internal communal strife, where there was no universally accepted 'bargaining agent' for the native population, that Britain found itself swept into the whirlpools of bitter internal war and terrorism (as in Palestine where Arabs fought Jews and in the Graeco-Turkish conflict in Cyprus).

Now the great era of colonial independence struggles has passed. It would be naïve to assume that this signifies the end of nationalist and irredentist movements in former colonial states. The intractable problems of struggling to sustain internal cohesion and order have simply been inherited by the successor states, many of which are pathetically ill-equipped – economically, politically and militarily – to handle them. More often than not the new states inherited frontiers that show scant regard for ethnic, linguistic and religious divisions. Hence we now have a situation in which there is hardly a single country in the third world that has not experienced serious internal conflict in the form of separatists' struggles or inter-communal strife in the past decade.[4] Movement after movement has resorted to armed struggle: the Palestinians, the Kurds, Tamils, Kashmiris and Sikhs are just a few examples of ethnic groups that have taken up arms against their new masters. As the frontiers of the third world rigidify in the postcolonial era, we may expect an increasing number of these desperate groups, trapped awkwardly astride the diplomatic frontiers, to resort to the gun and the bomb. No doubt terrorism will not invariably be the primary weapon in the struggles of these new nationalist movements, but all the signs are that this source of terrorism will increase dramatically in Asia, Africa and the Middle East.

In general terms the ideological terrorist sects and secret societies posed nothing like such a long-term threat to individual Western states or to Western strategic interests. These movements, whether of the neo-fascist far right or the new Marxist and anarchist far left, are more analogous to tiny gangs of bandits than to serious political movements.

Groups like the Red Army Faction, the Japanese Red Army, the Weathermen, the Red Brigades and the Angry Brigade typically presented a bizarre contradiction: Lilliputian membership and negligible popular support coupled with the most pretentious language of people's revolutionary war and struggles against world capitalist imperialism. A more appropriate label, perhaps, for many of these weird cults of violence and hate would be the title adopted by a small group in Heidelberg in 1970: the Socialist Patients' Collective.

Ideological terrorist sects of this kind originated exclusively within the indus-trialised liberal democracies that they professed to hate so heartily. They claimed that they were the vanguard of a people's revolution and that their actions would inspire revolutionary consciousness and solidarity with the workers. In practice their tiny memberships were drawn almost exclusively from the children of affluent and privileged homes. Most tended to be recruited from extremist political groups in the universities. Far from speaking the language of working classes, they lived in a kind of fantasy world concocted from neo-Marxist slogans and the ideals of Sartre and Marcuse.[5]

These groups were especially baffling to the outside world because they did not share the same canons of rationality: rather they created their own 'transcendental' rationality, which transvalues everything in terms of the revolutionary ideology. The chiliastic utopianism of groups like the Baader-Meinhof gang, the Weathermen and the Japanese Red Army totally rejected the existing order as being vile and beyond redemption. There was no ground for negotiating any compromise between their ends and those of the rest of society. Ideological terrorists dwelt in a Manichean mental world divided into the oppressor–exploiters and their colla-borators on the one hand, and themselves as soldiers of revolutionary justice on the other. Instead of viewing the use of terrorism in instrumental–rational terms, involving a realistic calculation of its political effectiveness and the possibilities of success, acts of violence became ends in themselves. In short, for these revolutionary secret societies, terrorism became an integral part of their ideology and lifestyle.

In contrast, then, to the movement that has a genuine nationalist legitimacy and popular constituency of support, the ideological sects are outlaws, *francs-tireurs* even in their country of origin. For the nationalist movement, the realities of political power bring their own responsibilities. Nationalists must concern themselves to a considerable extent with building up their own bases of domestic support and with winning over foreign governments and international opinion to their cause. This inevitably imposes certain restraints on the use of terrorism. They must learn when to play politics, when to exert diplomatic pressure and how to avoid alienating public opinion. The ideological votaries on the other hand are isolated and des-perate from start to finish, often hated even more among their fellow citizens than they are abroad.

Yet although the root causes of many of the terrorist campaigns that developed in the late 1960s and early 1970s were quite independent from the Cold War, there is no doubt that the ideological conflict between Western capitalism and com-munist revolutionism had a profound impact on the new pattern of low-intensity conflict that emerged in the later 1960s and 1970s. Almost without exception the leaders of the insurgent groups espoused ideologies of Marxist revolutionism. Even groups with a nationalist aim, such as the IRA, ETA, PFLP,[6] DFLP[7] and FLNC,[8] saw themselves as part of a wider 'anti-imperialist' movement challenging the alleged 'oppression' and 'exploitation' by this climate of anti-imperialist anti-Western revolutionism for their own propaganda purposes, and in order to provide useful assistance and support, on an opportunistic basis, for selected client groups.

The archetypal terrorism campaign to emerge in the late 1960s and 1970s was pursued by factions of the PLO,[9] such as Al Fatah and the PFLP. After the cataclysm of the Six Day War in June 1967 it became clear to the Palestinian leadership that their position had become desperate. The long-promised assault by combined Arab armies to recover their homeland had failed. Israel was firmly entrenched in occupation of extensive and strategically valuable territory in Sinai, West Bank, Jerusalem and the Golan Heights. The Arab states' armies were licking their wounds, and Arab leaders had been neither able nor willing to use their power over oil supplies to realise their political objectives. Hence the Palestinian radicals began a series of international terrorist attacks, such as hijackings, bombings and shootings of civilians to augment their traditional methods of guerrilla border raids.[10] This shift to terrorism was intensified after the further disastrous defeat of the Fedayeen at the hands of King Hussein's forces in Jordan in autumn 1970. The international consequences of this shift were highly significant. Other militant groups elsewhere in the world were influenced by what they perceived as the success of the Palestinians in attracting widespread publicity and international attention for their cause. Moreover, many groups began to send their activists for training in Jordan and later in Lebanon and Yemen. Al Fatah, for example, trained personnel from many other groups. Key operatives in the Baader-Meinhof gang, it is worth remembering, were trained at an Al Fatah camp in Jordan. Six weeks later they were busy establishing the Red Army Faction in Germany.[11] By the later 1970s the PLO had become a major conduit for spreading techniques of terrorism world-wide and a client of the Soviet bloc sponsorship, receiving substantial assistance from the Soviet Union and other Warsaw Pact states.[12]

Another major factor in this move towards terrorism was the shift in revolutionary theory away from an interest in the strategies of rural guerrilla warfare and towards urban guerrilla war as a major or auxiliary form of armed struggle. In part this new emphasis was provoked by the dramatic failures of attempted follow-ups of the Cuban guerrilla victory. Rural insurgencies in Venezuela, Argentina and Bolivia suffered severe defeats at the hands of increasingly better-equipped and trained government security forces. Furthermore, the revolutionaries came to realise that in heavily urbanised states like Brazil and Argentina where well over half the population was in the cities, they had to win power in the cities as a condition for seizing state powers. Carlos Marighela's mini-manual of the urban guerrilla,[13] and the widely publicised urban activities of Raoul Sendic's Tupamaros[14] in Uruguay, soon had the effect of inspiring emulation abroad. For example, Ulrike Meinhof's *Concept of the Urban Guerrilla*, which helped inspire the Baader-Meinhof's campaign, borrowed heavily from the ideas of Marighela.

The world-wide dissemination of new technology has also greatly facilitated the growth of terrorism. For example, the development of international civil aviation has created new vulnerabilities and lucrative targets for the terrorist to exploit. TV satellites have brought about a media revolution: the terrorists can exploit this by gaining almost instantaneous world-wide publicity for an outrage, thus enabling them to magnify the element of fear to disseminate awareness of their cause or demands on a scale that would have been unthinkable for the anarchist bomb-thrower or assassin of the nineteenth century. Modern weapons technology has also proved a great boon to terrorists, providing them, for example, with modern plastic explosives such as Semtex and highly accurate lightweight portable firearms. Perhaps most important of all the factor encouraging the spread of terrorism has been the sheer success of this method in achieving short-term tactical objectives of great value to the terrorist. For although it is clear that terrorism rarely, if ever, wins strategic political goals, it has an impressive record in gaining such things as massive world-wide publicity, extortion of large ransom payments, and the release of a considerable number of imprisoned terrorists.

To sum up on the underlying cause of the resurgence of international terrorism in the 1960s and 1970s, the historical evidence suggests that the major factors were:

The development of social movements dedicated to achieving national self-determination or the revolutionary transformation of the socio-economic order, or both.

The belief of many of these groups that terrorism was an effective and legitimate weapon to help attain their goals.

The acquisition of the necessary techniques and resources to mount terrorist attacks or campaigns.

The precise timing of the beginning of the upsurge in international terrorism, as the mid-point of the Cold War, was due to a combination of historical developments: the impact of the June 1967 war on the thinking of radical Palestinians, the shift in revolutionary theory from the rural-based guerrilla to the use of urban terrorism (as exemplified in the ideas of Carlos Marighela and other Latin American revolutionary strategists), and the development of small groups on the revolutionary left in the industrialised countries who were impatient with what they perceived as the weakness and failure of the new left and who believed in confronting the capitalist system they so despised with uncompromising violence.

Terrorism in Northern Ireland[15]

The political culture and traditions in Northern Ireland, on both Republican and Loyalist extremes of the political spectrum, are so steeped in violence that the Province became a virtual laboratory for deploying protracted terrorism as a weapon within a liberal democratic state. By 1998 over 3,300 had died in 29 years of conflict. From the 'Peep O'Day Boys', the Ulster Volunteer Force (UVF), the Fenians and the IRA, fresh generations of gunmen have emerged in the North and South. As Conor Cruise O'Brien has remarked:

> Young people in both parts of Ireland have been brought up to think of democracy as part of everyday humdrum existence, but of recourse to violence as something existing on a superior plane, not merely glorious but even sacred. Resort to violence, that is, in conditions resembling those that spurred the Founders into action.[16]

Insofar as IRA violence was directed against the British government since 1970 in order to force a British withdrawal from Ulster and the destruction of the Unionist regime it must be described as a campaign against liberal democracy. But it must be admitted that, from the establishment of the Unionist regime in Stormont in 1922 to the 1980s, the Northern Catholic minority suffered from political, social and economic discrimination. Moreover the Special Powers Act introduced in Ulster in 1922 gave the government sweeping powers to suppress any unwelcome forms of political opposition. The outlawed IRA did attempt a campaign of bombings and attacks on policemen and soldiers in the North from 1956 to 1962, but it was an ignominious failure. The political initiative amongst the Catholics in the North was taken by the Civil Rights Association in the late 1960s, using non-violent demonstration, petition and political pressure. The IRA was compelled to involve itself in this political work to avoid complete isolation. Apparently blind to the real grievances of the civil rights movement, the hardline

Unionists interpreted the movement as a front for the IRA conspiracy and revolution. Self-styled 'loyalists' and the Royal Ulster Constabulary (RUC) overreacted against civil rights marches and demonstrations, while the Revd Ian Paisley whipped up a campaign of anti-Catholic hatred comparable to that of Titus Oates. There is little room for doubt that the hardline Unionists mistook the angry rioting in Londonderry's Bogside in 1969 for a Fenian rising. The Scarman Tribunal produced abundant evidence of the panicked overreaction by the Royal Ulster Constabulary. As the civilian death-toll in the street-fighting rose, the Londonderry and Belfast Catholics began to arm themselves and to look to the IRA as the only available armed Catholic defence organisation. The IRA leadership in Dublin were caught off-guard by this escalation into armed conflict. They had, after all, recently swung over to a *political* strategy in the North. It was the 'Provisional' IRA who then formed and moved rapidly in 1970 to fill this vacuum.[17] Led by hardline 'physical force' men like Sean MacStiofain, the Northern Republicans began to rally to the Provisional organisation because they were ready for military action, and the Provisionals became bitter rivals of the so-called 'official' Marxist-dominated IRA for the support of the Northern Irish Catholics.

It is worth keeping in mind that Belfast was the most ideal terrain for urban terrorism. It is a city of over 400,000 people, most of whom lived in small homes in narrow streets. There were few natural boundaries within the city, and because of its featureless anonymity it was relatively simple for a terrorist to evade patrols and merge into its surroundings. Much of the property is Victorian or Edwardian, and yards are divided by high walls. There were ideal fields of fire in every street, and countless hiding places for sniping and ambush. Nor was there any shortage of privately held guns, many of them officially registered on the pretext of 'rifle-club' membership. Both the Provisionals and the Ulster Defence Association (UDA)[18] and the UVF[19] obtained up-to-date arms from abroad. The Provisionals benefited from considerable financial aid from Republican sympathisers in the US, and from expropriations and 'donations' within Ulster. They were able to obtain the highly accurate gas-operated American armalite rifle, made in Japan under licence for the Japanese Self-Defence Force! But the major source of IRA weapons, including Semtex, AK-47s, and machine guns, were huge shipments of arms from Libya in the mid 1980s. Certainly the border with the Republic was in constant use by the Provisionals both as a source of arms and ammunition and as an escape route for terrorists. In sum, all these conditions were conducive to an extraordinarily protracted and bitter ethnic sectarian feud between the extreme Republicans and the extreme Loyalists, and a war of attrition waged by the Provisionals with the aim of compelling the British army to withdraw.

Ideologically the Provisionals' campaign was callow in the extreme. It is true that they could depend on widespread sympathy among the Catholic population. The widespread Catholic hatred and resentment of the internment measure introduced by Faulkner's government in the summer of 1971 and the Bloody Sunday shootings[20] helped to fuel support for the Provisionals. By late 1972 the sympathy had been largely eroded by the revulsion against the particularly indiscriminate and bloody campaign of bombings in Belfast and Derry, which hurt the innocent population (Catholic and Protestant alike), ruined livelihoods and seemed to prove to the majority of the population the absolute necessity of a continuing British military presence. By continuing a stubborn policy of death and destruction the Provisionals forfeited all possibility of participation in, or real influence upon, the planning of a new constitutional structure for Northern Ireland to replace the now discredited Stormont system. Cathal Goulding's assessment of MacStiofain could really be applied to the Provisional movement as a whole:

> The whole thing I have against him is that he is a very narrow man, he is a man who won't accept or examine new ideas and in his rigidity he is sure that there is only one solution to this problem and that is by physical force. He has no time for politics of any kind – and a revolutionary who has no time for politics is in my mind a madman.[21]

There is no doubt that the Provisionals deployed an impressive range of terrorist techniques including car bombs, mortar attacks, assassinations, gaol-breaking, letter bombing and kidnapping. They repeatedly demonstrated capability in carrying terror bombings in London and other English cities. But terrorism can sink to the level of a corrupted and professionalised form of crime that is finally self-destroying. Nor did the Ulster Freedom Fighters (UFF) and UVF or the other Protestant extremist organisations in the Province have any better record.[22] Several recent studies have carefully documented the scale of their record of murder and destruction and show how they also actively incited violence and promoted sectarian hatred and bigotry.

The case of terrorism in Northern Ireland further supports my argument that liberal democracy is only seriously threatened by revolutionary terrorism when there is a general withdrawal of popular support from government, or when government appears entirely unable to deal with the problems that face it. This reassuring conclusion should not lead us to neglect the tragic costs of prolonged terror in a democracy: community values are destroyed; families are divided and bereaved; children are brought up in an atmosphere of suspicion and hatred and, in their teens, are socialised into terrible violence. Normal business and industry becomes impossible and new investment ceases. Whole sectors of cities are so damaged by terrorism that they take on the appearance of a land subjected to air attack. Political relations between parties and groups become poisoned, so that bargaining and compromise are instantly identified as 'betrayal'. Both extremes take on organisational forms and attitudes of paramilitary movements. It becomes increasingly difficult for the ordinary citizen to escape the terror of one or other of the armed camps. 'If you are not with us you are against us' becomes the rallying cry. Terrorism can corrupt and corrode democracy by establishing a kind of tyranny over men's souls and no democracy worth the name can afford to tolerate it.

Just as there were those in the Irish Republican movement who misread the history of Northern Ireland, and believed it was a case of British colonialism comparable to Cyprus, so there were some in the security forces who believed that they could simply apply the lessons of counterinsurgency acquired by the army in colonial situations and this would suffice to defeat the Provisional IRA. Both sides had to adapt to a much more complex reality. Eventually the more pragmatic and politically astute political leaders in Sinn Fein/IRA had to recognise that they had to enter the political arena if they were to have any chance of securing the changes they desired. Following the 1998 Good Friday Agreement and its endorsement in the 22 May Referendum, it remained to be seen whether the hardcore Sinn Fein/IRA would be willing to give up the bomb and gun for good, although the IRA's announcement in May 2000 that it was prepared to put its weapons 'beyond use' and to allow independent observers to inspect its arms dumps was a major breakthrough. Eventually in 2005, the IRA announced the decommissioning of its weapons and only the use of peaceful means to pursue its goals. On 26 September 2005 the head of the international decommissioning body, General de Chastelain, issued a statement confirming that the decommissioning had taken place.

Meanwhile the security forces and successive British governments have had to learn that combating protracted terrorism in a modern democratic society under the spotlight of the media and international opinion must be carried out in ways fully compatible with the maintenance of democracy, respect for human rights and the upholding of the rule of law. Even in this severe test, the criminal justice model of response and police primacy worked best, with the army providing invaluable support to the police.

By 2010 the Northern Ireland public was beginning to get used to the sight of Sinn Fein politicians sitting with DUP politicians in a power-sharing devolved government. It took a long time for the peace process to achieve this and there is no doubt that the overwhelming majority of both Catholic and Protestant communities would be deeply opposed to any return to the violence of the 'Troubles'. However, there remains an unreconstructed minority of hard-line Republican dissidents who remain bitterly opposed to the peace and who have been carrying out terrorist attacks in Northern Ireland; the security service still have a vital task in their efforts to prevent an escalation in this bombing campaign and to preserve public safety. In spite of this residual problem, however, the Northern Ireland case remains a rare but encouraging example of finding a political pathway out of terrorism.

The impact of the rise of radical Islamist movements

Terrorism motivated by religious fanaticism has been perpetrated throughout history. Arguably it is as ancient in origin as the use of terror regimes. However, if the late 1960s and 1970s were characterised by the rise of secular nationalist and neo-Marxist terrorist groups, such as the PFLP and the Red Brigades, the early 1980s saw a dramatic emergence of terrorism motivated by extreme Islamist movements. These organisations have developed in almost every Muslim country, but the most significant in terms of capacity to mount campaigns of terrorism have been Hezbollah in South Lebanon, Hamas based in Gaza and the West Bank and al-Gama'al al-Islamiyya[23] in Egypt and the transnational Al Qaeda network.

A common inspiration in the rise of these movements was the Iranian Islamic revolution, led by Ayatollah Khomeini, which overthrew the Shah in 1979 and attempted to construct a new Islamic republic based on fundamentalist principles. The Iranian revolution attracted growing admiration not only among Shi'ite Islamic communities but also among the Sunnis, who form the overwhelming majority of Muslims. The leaders of the Iranian revolution were seen as having struck a humiliating blow against the United States and those secular Arab leaders and regimes they perceived as 'collaborators' with the US and other Western states. The dramatic fall of the Shah, America's key ally in the Gulf region, led radical Islamists in other Muslim states to the belief that they too could overthrow their pro-Western regimes and establish Islamic republics based on a return to the *sharia*, Islamic law, as interpreted by the fundamentalists. In the case of Hezbollah in Lebanon there is clear evidence that senior representatives of the Iranian regime played a direct role in the formation of the movement and have exerted much influence upon it ever since; it has become a virtual additional arm of Iranian policy. This direct link is not so surprising when one considers the fact that Hezbollah is a Shi'ite movement and that leading members of the Lebanese Shi'ite clergy were trained in the same religious academies in Najaf as the leaders of the Iranian revolution.[24]

However, even in Lebanon the development of a more militant radical Islamist movement was able to draw on a substantial pre-existing Islamic Amal structure and could exploit the growing mood of alienation and anger felt by Lebanese Shi'ites against what they saw as the betrayal and weakness shown by Lebanese and other Arab regimes, which they saw as pro-Western, secular and corrupt, failing to protect their people adequately during the Israeli invasion of 1982.[25]

It is clear that there were strong indigenous roots in all the Muslim communities where militant Islamist movements developed in the later 1970s and 1980s. There was a deep disillusionment with the secular ideologies and movements of nationalism, Nasserism and pan-Arabism. Widespread poverty and the failure of Arab governments to meet the basic needs of their peoples provided an opportunity for Islamist radicals to develop a stronger popular base for support. They attempted this not only by forming political parties and contesting elections (where allowed to do so) but also by establishing their own structures of social, education and welfare provision better than the governmental structures have been able to deliver. If one adds to these important factors the strong resentment of US policy in the Middle East, and particularly their anger against America's support for their hated enemy Israel, and for those Arab regimes seen to be collaborating with American policies in the region, it is clear that conditions were propitious for the rise of radical Islamist movements.

It soon became apparent that movements such as Hezbollah and Hamas posed a major terrorist challenge to the United States, Israel and Western countries generally. Hezbollah used suicide truck-bombings against the US Embassy and US Marine barracks with devastating effect: in the barracks bombing they killed 241 US Marines. Under various *noms de guerre* Hezbollah conducted a series of kidnappings of US, British and French citizens. The kidnappings of US citizens brought such pressure on the US government that certain elements in the National Security Council embarked upon the Iranian-Contra arms for hostages conspiracy, which in turn led to a grave US political crisis endangering not only the credibility of US counter-terrorism policy but also the position of the president himself.[26]

The militant Islamist movements, such as Hezbollah, Hamas and Al Qaeda, have demonstrated their capacity for lethal terrorist attacks against targets of their chosen enemies. Their challenge is all the more difficult to combat because fanatical members of these organisations have been ready to martyr themselves in waging a jihad or holy war in which they believe they are carrying out God's will.[27] It is extremely difficult to prevent suicide bombings of this kind. As we shall see in later chapters, terrorism of this kind, motivated by religious fanaticism, is not the only form of terrorism that causes large-scale civilian casualties. Nevertheless this religiously motivated fanaticism now constitutes the most dangerous form of non-state terrorism.

As in earlier periods of history, religious fanaticism and terror are not an exclusive preserve of any single major religion. Christian Identity cults and sects in the United States, preaching the hate propaganda of white supremacism and anti-Semitism and armed opposition to the federal government, are linked with the shadowy groups believed to have been involved in the Oklahoma bombing, nor should we forget the strand of religiously motivated terrorism in modern Jewish fundamentalism. In 1984 the Israeli security forces managed to thwart a plot of Jewish extremists to bomb the Dome of the Rock, one of the holiest places in Islam. In February 1994, a Jewish extremist, Baruch Goldstein, a follower of Rabbi Kahane, massacred 29 worshippers in a crowded mosque at Hebron. In November 1995 Prime Minister Yitzhak Rabin was assassinated by a Jewish extremist who claimed that he was carrying out God's orders.

It is extremely important to understand that terrorism is abhorred and condemned by the leaders of all the world's major religions. It is as absurd to equate mainstream Islamic religion with the terrorism committed by extremist groups acting in the name of Islamic beliefs as it would be to blame the Christian religion for the actions of Torquemada or of the self-styled Phineas Priesthood in America. We must be vigilant in guarding against the prejudice, stereotyping and intolerance that lead, for example, to incidents of Islamophobia. As a matter of historical record, the overwhelming majority of the victims of the terrorism committed by Islamist fanatics in the late twentieth century, for example in Algeria and Afghanistan, have been fellow Muslims.

The above caveats are vitally important if we are to place the trends in terrorism in the 1990s and in the new century in proper perspective. However, it is also extremely important not to underestimate the significance of the rise of groups of extreme Islamic fundamentalists, inspired and in many cases actively encouraged by the Islamic revolutionary regime in Iran, and ready to wage jihad (holy war) against pro-Western Arab regimes with the aim of setting up Islamic republics in their place. As the examples of the GIA in Algeria and the Islamic group in Egypt demonstrate, these groups are not confined to Shia populations. The primary targets of the groups' campaigns are the incumbent regimes and their military, police and government officials, as well as the intellectuals who are identified with the regime.

As in the case of the ethnic conflicts described earlier in this chapter, terrorism is generally only one weapon in a wider struggle: others include propaganda, fighting elections (where this is permitted by the regime), and the development of a mass base of support by means of a wider range of welfare, medical, educational and cultural activities under the fundamentalist movements' control. A key feature of all these groups is that they are bitterly opposed not only to the United States and Israel but to all Western countries. Frequently they have widened their range of targets to attack Westerners within their countries, as with Hezbollah's seizure of Western hostages in Lebanon in the 1980s, GIA murders of French and other foreign citizens in Algeria since 1993 and the 1997 Luxor massacre in which the Islamic Group terrorists murdered 58 foreign tourists.

There is a growing implication in the trend in Islamic fundamentalist terrorism towards freelance attacks that has been stressed by my colleague Bruce Hoffman[28] and which concerns the *modus operandi* of fundamentalist groups' involvement in international terrorism. It appears highly likely that the group of Islamic fundamentalists responsible for blowing up the World Trade Center building in New York in February 1993 was operating as a type of independent or freelance group, inspired and encouraged by their spiritual mentor, Sheikh Omar Abd-al-Rahman, and not controlled by a state sponsor or a known major terrorist player. Such groups pose a particular problem for the counter-terrorism agencies of Western governments as they have no identifiable structure or previous track record. They would also be able to recruit fanatical members from the expatriate community in the host state with the great advantage of considerable local knowledge. However, we should not exaggerate the likelihood of such 'freelance' groups emerging. There are also huge distinctives to take into account. Most expatriates and their families wish to stay in the host country and to better themselves economically: they are unlikely to want to put their future security at risk by becoming involved in violent conspiracies against the government of their adopted home.

On balance, therefore, the more serious dangers posed by these Islamic fundamentalist groups are their violent campaigns against their prime targets: the existing governments of the Muslim countries of the Middle East and South and Central Asia and against the Middle East Peace Process to which they are so bitterly opposed. For example, Hamas has played a major part in undermining repeated US and other international efforts to restore an Israeli–Palestinian peace process to bring about a two-state solution.

Hamas is bitterly opposed to Fatah and has seized control over Gaza. Israel's fierce bombardment of Gaza in December 2008 in retaliation against Hamas rocket attacks on Israel appears to have strengthened support for Hamas and created new generations of terrorists eager to avenge Palestinian deaths.

I believe at the time of writing (spring 2010) it is far too early to predict the decline of the Islamic fundamentalist challenge in the Middle East. On the other hand, it is foolish to exaggerate its novelty or its religious significance. There is a long tradition of just rebellion and tyrannicide in the Islamic world, and concepts of jihad and martyrdom for a righteous cause are also part of the Islamic tradition. But when one examines the activities of groups such as Hezbollah, Hamas, the Algerian GIA and the Al Qaeda Network, one is struck by the predominantly *political* nature of their agendas. They may clothe their demands and justifications in Islamic language but they are all essentially engaged in power struggles with their incumbent regimes to replace them with their own preferred form of government: an Islamic Republic of Algeria, Egypt, Lebanon, or, in the case of Al Qaeda, to create a Pan-Islamist New Caliphate. Hence we see what appears to be at first sight a purely religious phenomenon is in fact in large part about political control and socio-economic demands.

Religiously motivated groups, like ethnic separatist groups, are extremely varied in their belief systems, attitudes towards violence and the capacity for adapting to changes in their strategic, political and socio-economic environments. Some groups, such as Hezbollah and Hamas, have shown an ability to engage in electoral politics and build constituencies of mass support. Other groups such as Al Qaeda, Aum Shinrikyo and the bizarre violent cults in America seem to be entirely imprisoned by their own dogma. At least some of the more extreme apocalyptic cults may well believe they have a mission to commit acts of violence. Such groups are unlikely to be constrained by the political factors which have tended to limit the violence of the more politicised and pragmatic groups. If the ultra-fanatics believe they have a monopoly of revealed truth, that their acts of violence are a sacramental duty and that those who are not converted to their beliefs are unbelievers who do not deserve to live, they are unlikely to care two hoots about causing mass casualties in public places. Hence extreme fanaticism is a dangerous feature of the terrorist trends as we enter the twenty-first century. However, the danger should not be exaggerated, and we should bear in mind that purely secular terrorist groups have been willing to engage in indiscriminate acts of terrorism on a huge scale, as for example in the 1980 Bologna railway station bombings by Italian neo-fascists that killed 84 people and injured 180, the 1974 Birmingham pub bombings by the IRA that killed 20 civilians and injured 180 and the 1987 bombing of Korean Air Liner Flight 858 by North Korean agents, killing all 115 on board. It would be a serious error to assume that fanatical religious groups are uniquely capable of the fanatical belief in their cause and hatred of their enemies that enable them to carry out acts of great carnage and destruction.

Terrorism and organised crime

Terrorist activities, such as murder, conspiracy to murder, kidnapping and extortion, are themselves obviously a form of serious organised crime, however much the perpetrators wish to see themselves as freedom fighters. Hence the various acts of terrorism almost invariably transgress the criminal law code of all civilised states. But most terrorist groups also get involved in organised crime for more mundane reasons: unless they are lucky enough to be funded by a generous state sponsor regime they will resort to crimes of armed robbery, fraud, racketeering and extortion in order to raise money to buy weapons, vehicles and other resources necessary for their campaign and generally to sustain their organisation.[29]

A common method of fundraising by terrorist organisations is the levying of the revolutionary 'taxes' among the businesses and families in their ethnic constituency of the terrorist group. For example ETA has long depended on a 'revolutionary tax' among the Basque population. Nor should we be under any illusions about what happens to those who refuse to pay. There have been numerous cases of ETA 'punishment' attacks on those who refuse to pay. A widely reported case of ETA's ruthless method of dealing with those who defy its writ was their murder of businessman Isdiro Usabiaga in July 1996.[30] Señor Usabiaga had refused to pay the 'revolutionary tax' despite having received death threats. ETA shot him in the back as he was returning home. When the armed organisations have become so habituated to committing these savage crimes it is hard to imagine them ever transforming themselves into peaceable democratic organisations.

Just as there is nothing new about the depraved criminality of the terrorist organisations so there is nothing remarkable about the continuing use of terror by traditional organised crime organisations such as the Mafia and the Triads. These gangs have routinely used lethal violence to instil fear in members of their own gangs and the communities in which they operate in order to suppress rivals and to deter anyone from informing on them to the authorities. What is remarkable is the scale of the defiance of the authorities where criminal gangs and cartels have become deeply entrenched.

However, in the early 1990s organised crime gangs in Italy and India dramatically increased the scale of the threat posed to their respective societies and legal systems by adopting the tactic of large-scale urban bombing long favoured by the politically motivated terrorists.[31] On 23 May 1992, the Italian Mafia blew up the motor convoy of Judge Giovanni Falcone, the leading judge in the fight against the Mafia. The huge bomb killed the judge, his wife and three bodyguards.[32] There had been many previous Mafia assassinations, most notably the 1982 murder of General Dalla Chiesa, the civil governor of Palermo. As in the case of Dalla Chiesa the Mafia murdered Judge Falcone because they saw him as a threat to their whole criminal syndicate. It is known that he was on the brink of examining a list of secret Swiss bank accounts, some of which were believed to contain illegally held funds and which would have established the links between Italian politicians and businessmen to the Cosa Nostra. What was remarkable about the murder of Judge Falcone, however, was that the method used was almost a carbon copy of the kind of bomb attack carried out in the past by Red Army terrorists: the typical method of assassination used by the Mafia in the past was shooting. The Mafia used the terrorist tactic again in July 1992 when they used a huge car bomb to blow up Judge Paolo Borsellino, the chief public prosecutor in Palermo who was in charge of coordinating anti-Mafia activity.[33] The judge's wife and three bodyguards were also killed in the explosion. The Italian prime minister at that time, Guiliano Amato, described the bombings as an 'act of war against a state'. In my view these murders, like the Mafia's assassination of General Dalla Chiesa, were acts of pure terrorism. Their aim was not to promote any particular political ideology but to terrorise the state and its judicial and police institutions into abandoning their investigations and prosecutions of the Mafia. It is a sad fact that despite the courage and sacrifice of leading judges and police officials the authorities' campaign against the terrorism of the Mafia has not met with the same success as the campaign against the Red Brigades in the late 1970s and early 1980s, and is still hampered by corruption at many levels. The gravity of the continuing Mafia threat was underlined in July 1997 when Sicilian police seized a cache of Soviet-made heat-seeking rocket-launchers, anti-tank grenades, detonators and AK-47 assault rifles, which the police believe were to be used in an assassination attempt on a key figure.[34] According to Guide le Forte, deputy prosecutor in Palermo, there has been a major revival of the activities of the Italian Mafia, now heavily involved in international drug-dealing, arms-smuggling and money-laundering. The Mafia is also believed to have subverted the *pentito* programme (the use of reductions in sentences to reward Mafia criminals who collaborate with the authorities), and, according to *La Republica*, 'many have used the *pentiti* for its own ends from the very beginning'.[35]

The Italian Mafia are but one illustration of the way in which terrorist methods have become the stock-in-trade of international organised crime. According to US experts global organised crime is now a £800 billion-a-year business involving Colombian and Mexican drug cartels, the Russian 'Mafiya' gangs and heroin produced on a massive scale in Afghanistan, Pakistan and the Golden Triangle (Burma, Laos and Thailand).

Leading experts on trends in global crime such as the late Dr Richard Clutterbuck and Professor Roy Godson have long been warning that the battle against the alliance of powerful drug cartels and degenerate guerrilla organisations (FARC and ELN) would be lost unless drastic action was taken. Tragically their advice was not heeded. In Professor Godson's view Colombia is now 'lost': it is being torn apart by the faction wars between the drug barons, the paramilitaries and the well-armed guerrilla forces of the 'Revolutionary Armed Forces of Colombia' (FARC), which is itself creaming huge profits from drug-trafficking, extortion and kidnapping, and gaining an annual income estimated at a billion US dollars. The Colombian army is totally inadequate to the task of suppressing this lawlessness. Huge rural areas of the country are now totally ungovernable. As a leading article poignantly observed in *The Economist*:

> ... caught terrorised in the middle are Colombia's rural people, extorted from, frightened or driven from their homes, kidnapped for ransom, 'disappeared', murdered, at times massacred wholesale. And not all the victims are even adult. Which armed men do just what is, of course, disputed conveniently but maybe rightly, the shadowy paramilitaries get much of the blame. But the results are plain, and horrible.[36]

Terrorist weaponry and tactics

The emergence of modern terrorism has been greatly facilitated by the development of a range of explosives that can be relatively easily obtained, which can be used to construct home-made IEDs (improvised explosive devices), and by the availability of accurate man-portable firearms.

Bombs are the predominant weapons of choice for terrorists because they can be made and deployed by small cells or even by an individual and they enable the bombers to kill many of their targets while escaping unharmed. In the case of suicide bombing the terrorist group is sacrificing the life of only one of its members in order to kill large numbers of its designated 'enemies'. In short, bombs are economical, readily accessible and highly effective weapons for terrorists. Moreover, bombs attract enormous publicity and hence have a psychological impact in creating fear among a wider audience.

When Alfred Nobel invented dynamite in 1867 he can hardly have foreseen that it would provide an ideal weapon for terrorists at the end of the nineteenth century. By the mid-1870s, Nobel had succeeded in producing gelatinous dynamite of higher density and greater plasticity with greater blasting action power. It was designed for commercial blasting purposes, but it had obvious attractions to groups such as the Irish Fenians and the French Anarchists in their terrorist campaigns. The bomb attacks by the Anarchists led commentators to dub the last years of the nineteenth century the Dynamite Decade.

During the upsurge in terrorism in the late twentieth century, terrorists were able to exploit the development of Semtex, a very pliable, odourless and colourless plastic explosive produced in Czechoslovakia. It is particularly attractive to terrorists because it has a very high velocity of detonation, it is very easy to disguise from normal security checks and it produces high-speed fragments, thus increasing its lethality. The Gaddafi regime in Libya sent the IRA a supply of Semtex to use in their campaign against the United Kingdom and in 1988 Pan Am 103 was blown up with a Semtex bomb over Lockerbie with the loss of all 259 passengers and crew and 11 people on the ground: by using a plastic explosive concealed in a radio-cassette player, the bombers were able to defeat seriously outdated aviation security measures. Clever improvisation rather than invention has been the hallmark of terrorists' use of weaponry. They did not invent liquid explosives but in 2006 an Al Qaeda cell devised a plot to take liquid explosives on board at least seven airliners due to fly from Heathrow to North American destinations and detonate them in mid-air. Once again the aviation security system was unprepared for this tactic and the attack was only prevented by the swift action of police in an intelligence-led operation.

Another example of improvisation was the case of a man who succeeded in boarding an airliner bound for Detroit with plastic explosives hidden in his underpants. Luckily the device failed to detonate properly as the plane approached Detroit and the man was arrested. It is believed that he was briefed and sent on his mission by Al Qaeda with the clear aim of exploiting another serious gap in airport security, the fact that the magnetometer archways used to screen passengers were not capable of identifying explosives hidden in bodily orifices or attached to body parts.

Similar trends can be seen in the field of small arms and man-portable weapons of all kinds. For instance, terrorists quickly saw advantages of small, lightweight sub-machine guns that combine ease of concealment, accuracy and a high rate of fire. They have also recognised the potential of new generations of man-portable precision-guided munitions (PGMs) and the wide range of guidance systems, ranging from radio and radar control to lasers and infra-red heat-seeking wire control. Some of them have a hit probability approaching one, over a range of two or three kilometres.

It is true that only well-resourced and sophisticated groups have been able to acquire more advanced weapons and that counter-terrorist agencies have also constantly exploited new technologies. However, the huge problem for those dealing with major international terrorist threats today is how to counter co-ordinated suicide bombings in crowded urban centres and in open societies. High-quality intelligence and swift preventive action by police is the only sure way to stop these attacks. The practical problems involved will be addressed in later chapters.

Conclusion

A close examination of trends in terrorism world-wide does not lead one to conclude that we now confront an entirely new phenomenon of 'post-modern' terrorism in the place of 'old' terrorist regimes and movements of the 1970s and 1980s. The regimes using terror against their own populations have been doing so for decades. The ending of the Cold War removed many state sponsors of terrorism from the scene at a stroke, but the major state sponsors currently active have been part of the international scene for between two and three decades. The majority of the secular international terrorist movements active in the late 1990s were established in the 1970s and most of those motivated by religion emerged in the 1980s. It is significant that only ten of the 41 active major terrorist groups listed in the US State Department's *Patterns of Global Terrorism, 1998* were founded in the 1990s; most of these groups have known aims, organisational structures and leading activists and various links with like-minded organisations and/or states.

It has been claimed that 'post-modern' terrorist groups do not claim responsibility for their attacks, but as Bruce Hoffman has argued, this is by no means a new development. It is also claimed that the 'new' terrorism is more amorphous, more diffuse, and often planned and committed by 'freelance' or 'walk-on' terrorists. Here we must be very careful not to generalise about the terrorist scene on the basis of particular terrorist attacks such as the World Trade Center bombing, which displayed some radical departures from the *modus operandi* more generally employed by terrorist organisations. If one looks at the world of domestic terrorist organisations, which still constitute the overwhelming majority of the world's terrorist groups, one is struck by their innate 'conservatism' in terms of choice of tactics, weaponry, targeting and their ability to evolve and to adapt to changes in their environment and intensified efforts by governments to suppress them.

In 2000 there was a depressing demonstration of the way the weapon of terror can be used to determine the fragile and vulnerable democracies in the global 'South'. In an effort to stave off the prospect of defeat in a general election, Zimbabwe's leader, Robert Mugabe, unleashed his ZANU-PF 'war veterans' to conduct a campaign of terror against the opposition and against white farmers, including killings and savage beatings.

The brutal violence undoubtedly affected the vote, particularly in rural areas where the opposition supports were highly vulnerable. The pre-election terror campaign was the means by which Mugabe managed to avoid total defeat in the polls. In the period May to July 2000 Fiji's democratic government was literally held hostage for two months while George Speight and his fellow hostage-takers mounted a coup. Both cases, though very different in political context and tactics used, provide clear evidence that it is a serious error to underestimate the potential of the weapon of terrorism on affecting major political changes in a democracy or even for destroying democracy itself.

By far the most worrying and significant trend in terrorism world-wide is its growing lethality and tendency towards indiscriminate attacks in public places. Yet even when it comes to the terrorist group's choice of weaponry it is by no means obvious or inevitable that they will decide to deploy weapons of mass destruction. The discussion for the future of terrorism in Chapter 12 will seek to examine both the factors that might impel terrorists towards the use of weapons of mass destruction *and* the very real constraints, disadvantages and dangers involved. In the real world of terrorism, democratic governments and societies are going to have to deal with both 'old' and 'new' terrorist organisations, tactics and weapons simultaneously, and we need to be aware of the continuities in terrorist developments as well as possible lessons from past experiences that may help us to deal more effectively with such threats in the future.

3 Origins and key characteristics of Al Qaeda

Al Qaeda ('The Base') was founded in 1989 by Osama bin Laden and Abdallah Azzam. Bin Laden is the seventeenth son of a wealthy building contractor who made a fortune carrying out major construction contracts in Saudi Arabia. Azzam[1] was a teacher of Islamic Law at King Abdul-Aziz University, Jeddah, who exerted considerable influence on Osama bin Laden while he was a student at the same university. Azzam followed in the footsteps of Sayyid Qutb, an influential Egyptian Islamist, and he taught that the world is divided between those who live according to the shari'a (Islamic religious law) and those who do not submit to Islamic law.

Qutb believed that all Muslims have a duty to wage holy war (*jihad*) in order to establish shari'a rule not only in Egypt but globally. In order to obtain this ultimate objective he was quite prepared to threaten secular Arab regimes, and those he accused of collaborating with the 'infidel' governments of the West, as legitimate targets of *jihad*.

The second most important factor in the shaping of Al Qaeda was the experience of the Muslim resistance to the Soviet occupation of Afghanistan following the Soviet invasion of 1979.[2] Bin Laden visited Afghanistan in 1980 and then began to use part of his father's construction company to build fortifications and tunnels for the Afghan resistance. Bin Laden soon became a key figure in the Makhtab al-Khidmat (Services Office) that had been founded by Abdallah Azzam and which was recruiting volunteers and raising funds for the Afghan resistance all over the world. This role provided bin Laden with a global network of contacts of radical Islamists that was to prove invaluable in the development of Al Qaeda, and provided bin Laden with the opportunity to spread the ideas he had acquired from Qutb and Azzam to other radical Islamist groups, many of whom were later to become affiliates and networks in Al Qaeda's global *jihad*.

The third key factor in the early development of Al Qaeda was the influence of the Egyptian radical Islamists, particularly Ayman Zawahiri who became the leading theoretician and strategist of Al Qaeda.[3] He had cut his teeth in revolutionary terrorist activity as leader of al-Jihad, the Egyptian extreme Islamist group that carried out the assassination of President Anwar Sadat in 1981. Although he was arrested by the Egyptians after the assassination he was released three years later due to the lack of specific evidence on his involvement in the crime. He travelled to Afghanistan in 1980 when he met bin Laden. He arranged the merger of the Egyptian al-Jihad group with Al Qaeda. Abdallah Azzam, who had major differences with bin Laden over strategy, was assassinated in 1989 while in Pakistan. It was Zawahiri, a fanatical believer in the use of terrorism as the key weapon in the global jihad, who became deputy leader of Al Qaeda.

It is a sad irony that bin Laden and his followers, elated by their success in forcing the Soviet Union to withdraw its forces from Afghanistan, an achievement partly made possible by substantial financial assistance (estimated at three billion dollars), modern weaponry (including 'Stinger' missiles) and technical assistance from the United States, then decided that it would attack the US superpower and force it to withdraw its forces from proximity to the Holy Places of Islam in Saudi Arabia. In reality Al Qaeda had much wider ambitions.[4]

What are their major beliefs and aims?

- They believe in establishing strict *shari'a* religious law rule.
- They aim to expel the US and other 'infidels' from the Middle East and from Muslim lands everywhere.
- They want to topple Muslim regimes which they claim are betraying 'true' Islam and collaborating with the US and its allies.
- Ultimately they aim to establish a pan-Islamist Caliphate (super-state) uniting all Muslims.
- Al Qaeda has declared a *jihad* or holy war against the US and its allies and has set up a World Islamic Front for Jihad declaring it is 'the duty of all Muslims to kill US citizens – civilian or military, and their allies everywhere' (bin Laden 'Fatwa', 23 February 1998).

These aims may seem utterly grandiose and unrealistic to rational students of international relations, but Al Qaeda firmly believe they will ultimately succeed because they are certain Allah is on their side, and they believe America and its allies are irredeemably corrupt and too cowardly and weak to withstand their jihad. A key part of their strategy is their commitment to using terror as their key weapon as they really believe that they can terrorise their designated enemies into submission. They aim to do this by waging holy war to win control of a base area within the Muslim world as a platform for expansion and to attack the homelands of the US and its allies by using terrorist attacks against Western targets.[5]

What are the key features of Al Qaeda's modus operandi?

Al Qaeda, unlike most traditional terrorist movements, explicitly aims at killing large numbers of people and causing maximum economic damage and disruption to create a climate of fear.

Typical methods are no-warning co-ordinated suicide attacks hitting several targets simultaneously. Its most commonly used weapon has been the large suicide vehicle bomb.

The Al Qaeda network has shown a keen interest in obtaining CBRN weapons, and its record shows it would have no compunction about using them to cause large numbers of civilian deaths. They believe their ends justify any means.

What is its area of operations, leadership and structure?

Bin Laden's Al Qaeda is more of a global transnational movement than an organisation in the traditional sense. It has a presence in at least 90 countries making it the most widely dispersed terrorist movement in history. The records show that it has 'global reach'.[6]

Bin Laden and his deputy Zawahiri provide ideological and strategic leadership and direction, and they are assisted by a Shura and specialist committees dealing with such matters as 'military' planning, Islamist doctrine and indoctrination, the media, etc. In addition they have a wide and complex network of cells and affiliated organisations (e.g. Jemaah Islamiyya, Al Qaeda in Iraq; Pakistan Taliban; Al Qaeda in the Arabian Peninsula, Lashkar-e-Tayyiba, Jaish-e-Mohammad, etc.) which they use as vehicles for waging terrorism around the world.

Why is the Al Qaeda network far more dangerous than traditional groups?

Many Europeans are still under the illusion that Al Qaeda is just the same as any other terrorist group. This assumption is not only misinformed, it is positively dangerous because it grossly underestimates the nature of the threat the Al Qaeda movement poses to international peace and security.

From an early stage in its development it was clear that Al Qaeda was not going to resemble the traditional terrorist groups with their monolithic structures and centralised control: instead it was developed into a worldwide network of networks.

This 'horizontal' network structure means that although bin Laden and Zawahiri provide ideological leadership and inspiration it is left to the affiliated networks and cells to carry out attacks against the types of targets designated in Al Qaeda ideology and combat doctrine. The Al Qaeda movement is able to maintain its 'global reach' through its widely dispersed network of cells and affiliates in over 90 countries, making it the most widely dispersed non-state terrorist network in history. Thousands of militants from many countries have been through the Al Qaeda training camps in Afghanistan prior to the overthrow of the Taliban regime that gave Al Qaeda safe haven up to the autumn of 2001.

Another key feature of Al Qaeda is that although it uses the language of extreme fundamentalist Islam its core ideology is a grandiose plan to wage a global jihad against America and its allies and against all existing Muslim governments in order to bring about nothing less than a revolutionary transformation of international politics. Al Qaeda aims to expel the US presence and influence from every part of the Muslim world, to topple all existing Muslim governments on the grounds that they are all 'apostate' regimes because they maintain friendly relations and cooperation with what Al Qaeda terms the 'crusaders and Zionists', i.e. America and its allies including, of course, Israel. Ultimately Al Qaeda wants to create a pan-Islamist Caliphate to rule all Muslims along lines dictated by bin Laden and Zawahiri. Their ideology is absolutist and hence 'incorrigible', i.e. there is no basis for diplomatic or political compromise.

However impracticable this ideological project may seem to most in the West, Al Qaeda certainly believes that their revolutionary global transformation will happen because they believe that Allah is on their side and that they will ultimately be victorious, however long it takes.

A key feature of the Al Qaeda movement is its explicit commitment to mass-killing terrorist attacks. In a notorious 'Fatwa' announced to the world in February 1998, bin Laden and a group of leading fellow extremists declared that it was the duty of all Muslims to kill Americans, including civilians and their allies, whenever the opportunity arises.[7] The 9/11 attacks which killed almost 3,000 and a whole series of other Al Qaeda attacks, including those in Nairobi, Bali, Iraq, Madrid and London, demonstrate that the movement has no hesitation or compunction about killing hundreds of innocent civilians including fellow Muslims.

Closely connected with Al Qaeda's congenital tendency to engage in mass killing is their modus operandi in tactics, targets and areas of operations. Their typical tactic is to mount coordinated no-warning suicide attacks using car or truck bombs designed to maximise carnage and economic destruction. Their choice of targets shows that they have no compunction about attacking soft targets where crowds of civilians are likely to be gathered, such as public transport systems, tourist hotels and restaurants, etc. These suicide no-warning coordinated attacks on the general public are particularly difficult for the police to prevent in open, democratic societies.

Bearing these key features of the Al Qaeda network of networks in mind, we can clearly differentiate their form of terrorist threat from the typical patterns of terrorism committed by more traditional groups. A leading example of a traditional group was the Irish Republican Army (IRA). The IRA was, prior to the Good Friday Agreement, the best armed, richest and most experienced terrorist group active in Western Europe. It was responsible for killing more civilians than any other terrorist group in Europe, but it did not aim at committing mass lethality attacks against civilians.

However, it is clear that there are many striking differences between the terrorism posed by the IRA prior to the Good Friday Agreement of 1998 and the threat posed by Al Qaeda. In contrast to Al Qaeda the IRA's aims are focused specifically on their ethno-separatist objectives in Ireland. They aim to rid Ireland of the British presence in the North and to unite the whole of Ireland under a single Republican government. Their leaders and their political wing, Sinn Fein, have shown a degree of realism and pragmatism in recognising that they were not going to achieve their aims by terrorism, but that they have a better chance of pursuing their political agenda by political means. They signed up to the Good Friday Agreement, and have maintained their ceasefire; although the peace process is still fragile it is still holding and has saved hundreds of lives that would have undoubtedly been lost if the Northern Ireland conflict had continued. Contrast Al Qaeda's stance.

Another key difference between traditional terrorist groups and the Al Qaeda movement is that the former have not been conducting a global war, they have concentrated most of their violence on the country or region where they claim to have the right to a separate state.

It is true that the IRA and other traditional groups went to great trouble to establish diaspora support networks to raise money and weapons and political support for their campaigns but they did not aim to alter the whole international system.

Another crucial difference is that traditional groups used terror, as Brian Jenkins once expressed it, to have 'a lot of people watching, not a lot of people dead'. Al Qaeda, on the other hand, specifically aims to have a lot of people watching as well as a lot of people dead.

How serious is the current threat from the Al Qaeda network? Is the war against terrorism inflicting major damage on Al Qaeda?

Was the 9/11 Commission Report justified in warning that there could be another major terrorist attack by Al Qaeda, perhaps even more lethal and destructive? (9/11 Commission 2004).

Was the Bush administration justified in claiming that the war against terrorism is being won, or does the evidence in the 9/11 report and arising from other investigations around the world support the opposite conclusion?

Looking at the positive items in the balance sheet, one could be forgiven for assuming that President Bush's optimistic assessment was fully justified. The Coalition Against Terrorism is the largest alliance in the history of international relations and despite the deep disagreements between members of the Coalition over the justifiability and desirability of the invasion of Iraq, it is clear that most members, including the Muslim Coalition states, are continuing to share intelligence and cooperate in the wider aspects of counter-terrorism. The divisions over the invasion and occupation of Iraq did not result, as some commentators had feared, in weakening the UN Security Council's stance on combating terrorism or undermining its key Resolution (1373) (2001) requiring that 'all states ... c) Deny safe haven to those who finance, plan, support or commit terrorist acts, or provide save havens; d) Prevent those who finance, plan, facilitate or commit terrorist acts from using their respective territories for these purposes against other states or their citizens' (UNSC, S/RES/1373, 20 September 2001). Nor has the UN abandoned its innovative Counter Terrorism Committee with the proactive role of monitoring member states' compliance with UN resolutions and conventions against terrorism. In an unprecedented step, NATO invoked its collective defence article, Article 5 of the North Atlantic Treaty. Other regional organisations including ANZUS and OSCE have continued to attach high priority to the War Against Terrorism.

The unexpectedly swift toppling of the Taliban regime in Afghanistan by a combination of Northern Alliance and Coalition forces removed Al Qaeda's ability to use Afghanistan as a major base for planning, training, indoctrination and propaganda and caused huge (though by no means fatal) disruption of the Al Qaeda leadership and its communications with its global network of cells, affiliated organisations and support groups.

Hundreds of suspected Al Qaeda militants and members of their support network have been arrested around the globe. Many of those listed by the US as the most wanted terrorists have been captured or killed including Mustafa Abu al-Yazid, regarded as the senior Al Qaeda leader in Afghanistan, experienced in financing and planning operations, who is believed to have been killed with members of his family in an American drone attack in the tribal areas of Pakistan in May 2010. Even so, the policy of 'decapitation' of the leadership of Al Qaeda has not put the network out of business. It is still recruiting and training fresh militants and when it suffers severe setbacks in one area, as it did after the US troop surge and the backlash by the 'Awakening' movement in Iraq in 2007–08, it is able to point to successes in other theatres in its global jihad, e.g. in its backing for the Taliban insurgencies in Afghanistan and Pakistan.

Another significant gain by the Coalition has been the blocking of millions of dollars of terrorist funds in the banking system. This has not resulted in denying Al Qaeda all sources of funds, but it has reduced their ability to finance their global 'holy war' against the US and its allies.

Despite the intensification of Al Qaeda's efforts to destabilise the regimes of the front-line Muslim states, Pakistan, Afghanistan, Saudi Arabia and Iraq, they have not so far succeeded in toppling a single government and replacing it with an Al Qaeda or pro-Al Qaeda regime.

Last but by no means least, Al Qaeda has so far failed, despite repeated efforts since 9/11, in its efforts to carry out a successful attack on the homeland of the US.

On the other side of the balance sheet, it is obvious that there have been some serious failures and mistakes, which help to explain why Al Qaeda remains very much in business and why the Coalition has a long way to go before success in quashing the Al Qaeda threat can be achieved.

First, Al Qaeda's key leaders (Osama bin Laden, Ayman al-Zawahiri) are still at large. This is a highly significant factor. Bin Laden and his deputy are particularly important as symbols, propagandists and ideologists, and provide both general strategic direction and inspirational propaganda. Moreover it is clear that far from being sidelined or rendered powerless by the Coalition's actions, as some commentators have claimed, Al Qaeda's core leadership and its key role as the central hub in the global network has adapted in the face of its setbacks and survived.

One of the key factors enabling them to survive their major setbacks is their fanatical belief in the ultimate invincibility of their 'holy war'. They believe their setbacks are but temporary reversals in specific countries. In the long term (and they have a totally different perception of the historical calendar from the secular West), they are convinced that Allah is on their side and will bring them victory. Another major factor helps explain the ability of Al Qaeda to adapt and survive in spite of the severe countermeasures taken by the US and the wider international community: bin Laden's network has been able to sustain its campaign by enlisting affiliated groups it has penetrated or hijacked to carry out attacks in the name of Al Qaeda and in pursuit of its wider aims. For example, the major attacks in Bali, Riyadh, Casablanca, Istanbul and Iraq have all been carried out by regional affiliates of the Al Qaeda network, while bin Laden has immediately claimed them as his own.

Whatever the rights and wrongs of the invasion of Iraq it could hardly be claimed as a major victory against Al Qaeda – on the contrary, it provided a gratuitous propaganda gift to bin Laden, who could portray the invasion as an act of Western imperialism against the Muslim world. More recruits could be mobilised for Al Qaeda's 'holy war', and more donations could be obtained from Al Qaeda's wealthy backers. The author warned the House of Commons Foreign Affairs Select Committee of this danger in 2003. In a document leaked to the *New York Times* in July 2005, the UK's Joint Terrorism Analysis Centre (JTAC) warned that: 'Events in Iraq continue to act as motivation and as a focus for a wide range of terrorist related activities in the UK' (*New York Times*, 2005).

In addition, the post-war insurgency, terrorism and general lawlessness, which have resulted from the war, provided a strategic opportunity for Al Qaeda. Thousands of Coalition targets (troops and civilians) were suddenly made available in a country without effective border controls, surrounded by Muslim countries with Al Qaeda militants within their populations.

One of the most damaging consequences of the conflict in Iraq has been the deflection of funding and military resources away from Afghanistan. The Afghan people are desperately in need of security and economic development after decades of civil war. Al Qaeda, in alliance with Taliban and local warlords, are creeping back in alliance, especially in the areas bordering Pakistan and in the southeast of Afghanistan. The attempt to bring stability and democracy to Iraq is likely to cost billions more US dollars and many more US, British and Iraqi lives. Yet it is vital that Coalition troops stay until Iraq's security forces can maintain basic security.

Despite the failures of policy and intelligence by the US and its NATO allies and the very real continuing threat of another major attack on the homeland of a Western state, the greater long-term danger to international security and stability is the intensification of efforts by Al Qaeda and its affiliates to destabilise and undermine the governments of some of the front-line Muslim states and to create new lawless zones, which they could use as platforms to attack neighbouring states. The fragile interim government of President Karzai is particularly at risk. Pakistan's leader has been the target of repeated assassination attempts and Al Qaeda is undoubtedly trying to exploit what it sees as the golden opportunity to destabilise the new interim government of oil-rich Iraq.

In spite of the setback experienced by the Al Qaeda network (or networks) as a result of the 'War on Terror', the network remained active and dangerous both in the 'front-line' states in the Muslim world where it continues to try to find more secure bases from which it can launch more effective attacks in neighbouring countries, and in Western countries where they have established fresh networks, mainly comprising diaspora Muslims, in order to plan terrorist actions within the homelands of the designated enemy. In other words, in the period 2002–10 the Al Qaeda movement has again morphed, adapting to a situation in which it is forced by circumstances to leave the planning and implementation of terrorist conspiracies to the network affiliates and cell leaders in the relevant region or country. Bin Laden and Zawahiri still provide the ideological leadership and inspiration, but the 'core' leadership is unable to coordinate and centrally control actions undertaken in the movement's name. In one sense this is an advantage: it enables them to maintain global reach and exploit vulnerabilities in a wide range of countries simultaneously (Gunaratna 1999). However, this policy also entails considerable risks of fragmentation and ideological, strategic and tactical divisions between the affiliates and the Al Qaeda leadership. These cracks in the Al Qaeda movement structure have been widened by the fierce criticisms of the policy of mass killing of fellow Muslims by radical Islamists such as Dr Fadl, which have certainly damaged Al Qaeda's propaganda efforts. For example, the US government claims that it intercepted a letter sent by Ayman al-Zawahiri, bin Laden's deputy, to Abu Musab Al-Zarqawi, in summer 2005, warning him to change his tactics and in particular his practice of slaughtering hostages and then posting the images on the internet. An interesting example of the movement's network-building in a European country can be found in the Netherlands. In November 2004 Theo Van Gogh, a Dutch film director and critic of Islam, was assassinated in the Netherlands. The Dutch police investigation discovered that the alleged killer was linked to a larger cell of 15 extremists with links to the Al Qaeda movement. This network, labelled the Hofstad Group by the police, planned further assassinations. The murder of Van Gogh led to the tit-for-tat burning of places of worship and schools. The Dutch intelligence service, AIVD, estimate that there are around 200 extremists liable to commit violence and roughly 1,200 who support them. This is a tiny minority of the one million strong Muslim communities in the Netherlands, but small numbers of fanatics are fully capable of carrying out deadly and determined terrorist attacks.

The March 2004 Madrid train bombings, which killed nearly 200 people, and the July 2005 bombings of the London Underground transport system, which caused the deaths of 52 innocent civilians, and the ensuing police investigations provided conclusive evidence of the presence of fanatical Al Qaeda networks within major EU countries, comprising extremists recruited within the diaspora Muslim communities, yet linked to international terrorism.

However, despite the obvious potential for using extremist networks within the Muslim diaspora to carry out major terrorist attacks in Western countries Al Qaeda has found its efforts to mount successful conspiracies thwarted by increasingly effective intelligence and police work and national and international coordination of counter-terrorism efforts. This helps to explain why it is no longer the case that the Al Qaeda network is winning its global jihad. However, at the time of writing (spring 2010), it is also clear that the Coalition against Terrorism is not yet winning the overall struggle against the Al Qaeda network. Future chapters will examine the reasons for this.

4 Terrorist-backed insurgencies

As explained in Chapter 1, it is possible to distinguish the concept of terrorism from the concept of insurgency. It is clear that the majority of terrorist groups never succeed in recruiting enough militants and accumulating enough cash and weapons to conduct an all-out struggle with government security forces. Insurgencies inevitably involve battles to seize and occupy territory, and aim to ultimately defeat the government's security forces; terrorists operating without any accompanying insurgency operate clandestinely seeking to emerge from the shadows to inflict deadly, destructive and (they hope) terror-inducing hit-and-run attacks. It is also important to note that although there are numerous examples of a combination of terrorism and insurgency campaigns, many insurgent leaders have been opposed to the use of terrorism on the grounds that it is likely to alienate many of the population whose support they need for the insurgent campaign to overthrow the government.

The Western mass media are so preoccupied with coverage of terrorist incidents around the world that they only rarely provide reports and analysis on wider insurgencies. For example, few Western journalists have investigated the major Maoist insurgency by the Naxalist movement (the term derives from Naxalbari, the village in West Bengal where there was a peasant rebellion in 1967). The insurgents are believed to have amassed an army of 14,000, and they control large, mainly jungle, areas in eastern and central India. Prime Minister Manmohan Singh has stated that the Naxalite insurgency is India's biggest internal security problem. In 2010 the problem was clearly getting worse: in April, a convoy in Chhattisgarh carrying armed policemen was attacked by around 200 Maoist guerrilla fighters and 76 policemen were killed. In May 2010 insurgents detonated a landmine under a bus killing 11 police and 24 civilians, again in Chhattisgarh. It is reported that in 2009 the Maoist insurgents killed almost 1,000 people. No less than six Indian states are affected by the insurgency. An estimated 75,000 Indian troops have been deployed for counterinsurgency duties in the area, a small number when one is aware that the total population of the affected region is nearly 500 million.

Insurgency and the origins of Al Qaeda

It is sometimes forgotten that Osama bin Laden's first contact with armed conflict was during the insurgency against Soviet occupation forces in Afghanistan in the

1980s. During this campaign by the Mujahedeen, his main contribution was in logistic support and recruitment of Mujahedeen fighters from the Arab world to support the insurgency in Afghanistan. So far as is known, he was involved in the battle of Jaji in 1986, though he was not known for his expertise in combat, but because his family was well connected to the Saudi royal family and elite he was very successful at getting donations to support the campaign in Afghanistan. His family links with the wealthy Bin Laden Corporation were invaluable in helping Osama to arrange for the construction of bunkers and tunnels needed by the Mujahedeen to protect them against air attacks.

In the mid 1980s bin Laden began his work for the Maktab al-Khadamat (Service Bureau), which he ran with Abdallah Azzam. Its job was to handle the recruitment and induction of volunteers for the Mujahedeen and involved contacts in the Arab world, Pakistan and other Muslim countries. This enabled bin Laden to develop an extensive network of contacts with militant Islamists who, like himself, had been influenced by the Jihadi ideology of Abdallah Azzam – a network that was to prove invaluable when Al Qaeda was formed in 1988.

Bin Laden boasted of his involvement with the Mujahedeen's insurgency in Afghanistan in his lengthy message to the American people:[1]

> ... we have experience in using guerrilla warfare and attrition to fight tyrannical superpowers, as we, alongside the Mujahedeen, bled Russia for ten years, until it went bankrupt and was forced to withdraw in defeat, thanks be to God. So we are continuing this policy in bleeding America to the point of bankruptcy. God willing ... and nothing is too great for God.

Many observers have commented on the extreme irony that bin Laden and his followers, exhilarated by their victory over Soviet forces in an insurgency which depended heavily on US financial support and weaponry (including US stinger missiles) channelled via Saudi Arabia and Pakistan, should then have decided to inflict humiliation and defeat on the US. What has not been sufficiently understood is that Al Qaeda was from the outset committed to using both forms of asymmetric conflict, insurgency and terrorism, in its conduct of a global jihad. However, the main expertise on terrorism came from Ayman al-Zawahiri and the experience of Egyptian radical Islamists. Zawahiri had been leader of the Egyptian group, Islamic Jihad, which had been seeking to overthrow the Egyptian government. In June 2001 this group merged with Al Qaeda and Zawahiri became deputy leader under bin Laden. Zawahiri is the main theoretician and strategist of Al Qaeda. It is worth noting that when the British police discovered a copy of an Al Qaeda manual it contained detailed guidance on terrorist methods and tactics and had been compiled by Egyptian radical extremists. Hence, Al Qaeda has been able to exploit the insurgency in Iraq that followed the invasion by US and UK forces in 2003, using coordinated mass-casualty suicide bombing attacks in urban areas, while at the same time it has been able to back the Taliban insurgencies in both Afghanistan and Pakistan that have been waged primarily in rural areas; its affiliates in these conflicts are also increasingly combining these largely rural insurgencies with urban terrorist attacks. Let us now look more closely at the case of Iraq.

Combating terrorism and insurgency in Iraq

The first point that needs to be made about the military intervention in 2003 by the US and the UK in Iraq is that it was not a necessary part of the campaign to suppress Al Qaeda. There is no evidence that Saddam Hussein was in alliance with Osama bin Laden or that he played any part in the planning or implementation of the 9/11 attacks on the United States. It is true that Saddam had given safe haven to secular groups such as the Abu Nidal Organisation and that his regime provided money for the families of Palestinian suicide bombers attacking Israeli targets, but this had nothing to do with Al Qaeda.

The earlier military intervention to topple the Taliban regime in Afghanistan could be argued to be a vital part of the effort to suppress Al Qaeda because the Taliban regime had given safe haven to bin Laden's organisation. Hence, although the international community generally saw the intervention in Afghanistan as legitimate and indeed the UN brokered the appointment of a new democratic government under President Karzai, the invasion and occupation of Iraq caused deep divisions in the international community as a whole and in the Coalition against Terrorism. The UN Security Council did not approve it, where it was strongly opposed by permanent members France, Russia and China. Moreover, unlike the military intervention in Kosovo, there was not seen to be an overriding case for intervention because of an imminent threat to the human security of the Iraqi people, or an imminent threat by Saddam to the security of neighbouring states: on the contrary, Saddam's regime was the subject of the most comprehensive policy of containment and deterrence including 'no-fly zones' and swingeing economic sanctions. The real motivations behind the Bush administration's invasion of Iraq had more to do with the neo-conservatives' aim to democratise Iraq and to use this as a catalyst for the wider democratisation of the Middle East. The UK government's case for invading Iraq was built largely on the claim that Saddam's regime was a threat to international peace and security because of Saddam's alleged possession of weapons of mass destruction. The US and the UK insisted on going ahead with their invasion before the chief UN weapons inspector, Dr Hans Blix, and his inspection team could complete their work and report back to the UN. It later emerged that the Saddam regime did not possess weapons of mass destruction, and therefore this justification for the war turned out to be bogus.

Although the war in Iraq started with a devastating allied air bombardment, aptly called 'Shock and Awe', as the Inquiry into the Iraq War chaired by Sir John Chilcot heard from key witnesses there had been no plan for the occupation of Iraq or for dealing with an insurgency. The invasion force did not have enough troops or equipment for the post-invasion tasks. The allied forces on the ground soon found themselves in a protracted and bloody campaign to suppress a campaign of insurgency and terrorism, mainly by Iraqis opposed to the occupation, and a campaign of terrorist attacks in many cases carried out or led by so-called 'foreign fighters' including Al Qaeda. Indeed Al Qaeda in Mesopotamia (Iraq), led by Zarqawi, committed some of the most terrible atrocities using suicide bombing attacks, for example against Shi'ites' gathering places, indeed some of the worst attacks against civilians in recent terrorism. This campaign of violence continued after January 2006, despite the successful holding of a general election and a constitutional referendum.

The willingness of Iraqis to turn out for elections, despite threats of retaliation by the extremists, and the emergence of a fragile Iraqi government with a democratic mandate are the most hopeful developments to emerge from this tragic venture in Iraq, in which over 151,000 Iraqi civilians are estimated to have been killed, together with well over 4,400 US troops and over 179 UK troops, and billions of dollars have been expended.[2]

For all the above reasons, the first lesson of the military intervention in Iraq has been that it is a major strategic blunder to commit military forces to invade and occupy a foreign country without the explicit permission of the UN and widespread international support. It is a classic error of foreign policy to use military force as a first resort to achieve political goals rather than as a last resort, when military force is justifiable as an act of collective or national self-defence. The new US strategic doctrine of 'pre-emptive attack' used by the Bush administration is in fact *extremely* dangerous. What is sauce for the goose is sauce for the gander. Using the precedent of US action, it is possible that the North Korean regime would use a similar excuse for an attack on South Korea. China might use it to justify an attack on Taiwan, etc.

No doubt readers will have their own views about the case for and against the Iraq war, and may well come to a different view on the legality of invading Iraq in 2003. However, whatever their views on the justifications given for the invasion, students of terrorism and counter-terrorism can learn lessons from the ways in which the allied forces attempted to combat terrorists and insurgents in Iraq.

The first point to be made about the performance of the allied forces involved in the challenging and dangerous environment of the occupation of Iraq is that the overwhelming majority have carried out their tasks with enormous courage and discipline and have made a huge effort to assist in the reconstruction of Iraq's infrastructure and the recovery of at least a minimal level of security and stability needed to make reconstruction and recovery and indeed the holding of free elections possible. Secondly we should note that for the most part the British troops had a less challenging task in the Southern (Shi'a) area of Iraq. US troops have inevitably had a more continuous and far more lethal problem in attempting to suppress insurgency in the Sunni Triangle where support for the insurgency and terrorist groups is much stronger.

However, many knowledgeable observers have been highly critical of the tactics and methods used by the American troops. Brigadier Nigel Aylwin-Foster, a Senior British officer, wrote an extremely critical article in the influential US journal, *Military Review*,[3] in which he claimed that US tactics early on in the occupation alienated the civilian population and greatly aggravated the difficulties already inherent in acting as an occupation force. His article accused the US military forces of being ignorant and insensitive about the local culture and even went so far as to accuse American officers of 'institutional racism', which may have been a contributory factor in boosting the insurgency. Brigadier Aylwin-Foster also claimed that US efforts to secure peace were vitiated by a hierarchical outlook and a 'predisposition to offensive operations and a sense that duty required all issues to be confronted head on'.

There is no doubt that many US officers will feel that these criticisms are unfair and claim that they have gone to considerable trouble to brief their soldiers on local culture and sensitivities.

However, Aylwin-Foster does have strong evidence on his side regarding the US propensity to resort immediately to offensive operations, with all issues 'confronted head on'. A tragic example of this, in the view of many observers, was the November 2004 Operation Phantom Fury, an air and land offensive to eradicate insurgents who had based themselves in Fallujah.

An experienced journalist specialising in the Middle East and who had been one of the last to leave Fallujah before the US assault described her impression of the city when she returned in 2005: 'Huge areas of what were once homes have been flattened ... Fields of rubble stretch as far as the eye can see.' Her account of the effect of the offensive on the civilian population is even more depressing. She observes: 'It is not only that promises to reconstruct the city have been broken. The bitter truth is that the actions of the US and Iraqi forces have reignited the insurgency. Anger, hate and mistrust of America are deeper than ever.'[4]

Such tactics fly in the teeth of all the knowledge about counterinsurgency and counter-terrorism operations acquired, for example, by the British Army in campaigns at the end of the colonial era and in Northern Ireland from 1970 to 1998. Any successful counterinsurgency campaign must succeed in winning the support and trust of the majority of the civilian population, and must exercise restraint and sophistication in using major military force against insurgents/terrorists and not against the general population. Using overwhelming military firepower as a kind of bludgeon in counterinsurgency tends to play into the hands of insurgents and terrorist groups such as Al Qaeda who are clever at exploiting the propaganda and mobilisation opportunities presented in their situations. It is clear, at the time of writing (June 2010), that Al Qaeda's leaders still hope to derail the coalition project to help establish a viable democracy in Iraq, to force the US and UK to withdraw their troops, and thereafter to try to establish a platform for their wider operations in Muslim countries. Despite the elections the insurgency and terrorism have not yet been finally defeated. Thus, paradoxically, although the author was one of those who argues that the invasion of Iraq was a major strategic blunder, I am now one of the observers who believes that premature withdrawal from Iraq, before the Iraqi forces are fully capable to take over the security task, would be an even more disastrous blunder that could lead to another major boost for the Al Qaeda network's global jihad.

I hope that these observations on the way in which military operations have been conducted in Iraq will underline for the reader the importance of avoiding precipitate and unnecessary use of massive military force for counter-terrorism.

The major dangers of such operations are that you cause a protracted terror war worse than the terrorism you are aiming to combat, and you will very probably end up by giving a gratuitous boost to the terrorists' campaign.

The terrorist-backed insurgency in Afghanistan

The origins of the conflict between NATO forces and the Afghan Army versus the Taliban in Afghanistan are different from the circumstances that led to the Iraq insurgency in some key respects. In contrast to the invasion and occupation of Iraq, the military intervention by US forces in Afghanistan in combination with the Northern Alliance had the full backing of the United Nations Security Council because the Taliban had been giving safe haven to Al Qaeda, the terrorist group responsible for the 9/11 attacks, and allowing them to operate training camps for terrorists. There is no doubt that the swift overthrow of the Taliban regime was a major blow to Al Qaeda, disrupting their communications and operational capability. Building on this success the UN brokered the replacement of the pro-terrorist dictatorship by a new government under President Karzai, endorsed by democratic elections and committed to the reconstruction and development of a country shattered by decades of civil war.

Despite this promising start things began to go badly wrong for the Karzai government when the Taliban, still under the 'spiritual' leadership of Mullah Omar, began to wage a full-scale insurgency, with Al Qaeda under its wing, to regain control over Afghanistan. It was one of the unfortunate consequences of the Bush administration's unnecessary but increasingly expensive invasion and occupation of Iraq that the resources available to help the Karzai government were pathetically inadequate. Many of the initial pledges of financial aid made by foreign governments failed to materialise. The troops sent to help provide security and stability were too few in number and some NATO governments placed restrictions on the deployment of troops in the country, so that they were unable to help fend off the incursions of the Taliban already controlling large parts of the huge inhospitable Afghan terrain.

There are many key differences between the Iraqi insurgency and the insurgency in Afghanistan. Although both Iraq and Afghanistan suffered from deep ethnic divisions, Al Qaeda found it much easier to exploit the Afghan conflict. Mullah Omar and the hard-line factions of the Taliban are close allies of Al Qaeda and share much of its ideology. In Iraq the Sunni majority became alienated from bin Laden's movement's terrorist atrocities. The Shi'ite majority was bitterly opposed to Al Qaeda from the outset. In Afghanistan where there is no tradition of a strong central government, the Taliban and its Al Qaeda allies have been able to make alliances with some of the local warlords and tribal leaders. Compared to Afghanistan, Iraq has a developed infrastructure (despite the damage inflicted on it in the 2003 invasion), a sizeable well-educated professional class, and a better level of education among the general population. The Taliban insurgency however has considerable advantages, which the Iraqi insurgents did not enjoy. They can move easily across borders to Pakistan where they can find safe haven and considerable support from extreme fundamentalist Islamists, and where it is easy for them to obtain funds and weaponry and places where they can train their recruits. Indeed in 2010 serious allegations resurfaced claiming that the Pakistan ISI (Inter-Services Intelligence), which channelled assistance to the Taliban in the 1990s, continues to give secret assistance in direct contradiction of the declaratory policy of the Pakistan government. The source of the latest allegations is a Harvard Researcher, Matt Waldman.[5] In his report, published by the London School of Economics in June 2010, he writes: 'Insurgent commanders confirmed that the ISI are even represented, as participants or observers on the Taliban supreme leadership council.' If this proves to be true, in sprite of official denials in Islamabad, it would indicate a huge asset for the Taliban. An additional asset we know is enjoyed by the insurgents is the fissiparous nature of ISAF. The multiplicity of contributing NATO forces and the difficulty of establishing and enforcing a unified strategy make it easier for the Taliban to strike damaging blows against NATO and the Afghan Army.

However, by far the biggest obstacle to progress in combating the insurgency in Afghanistan is the absence of effective governance at a national level. In 2010 it became clear that relations between President Karzai and the US government had become extremely difficult: Karzai was becoming increasingly and openly critical of the conduct of the counterinsurgency operations by the US and other NATO forces. The US government and other NATO countries contributing to ISAF were angered by the evidence of widespread vote rigging in the Afghan elections and the high level of corruption. There was also evidence of bad relations between General McChrystal (the US commander in Afghanistan), Richard Holbrooke, the US envoy, and Karl Eikenberry, the US Ambassador in Kabul. General McChrystal was relieved of his command in June 2010 when a journalist published statements by the General and his aides, which were strongly critical of President Obama and his senior officials. It is true that the US government immediately announced that the strategy being followed by General McChrystal would not change but this political embroilment did not indicate a well-coordinated strategic direction of the campaign. Yet, as argued earlier in this chapter, a fully coordinated political and military strategy is prerequisite for success in any counterinsurgency campaign.

The UN Secretary General's report on violence in Afghanistan, issued in June 2010,[6] underlines the seriousness of the security situation. It stated that roadside bomb attacks increased by 94 per cent in the first four months of 2010 compared with the same period in 2009. Another worrying finding was that on average there were three suicide bombings per week. The report also noted: 'the shift to more complex suicide attacks demonstrates a growing capability of the local terrorist networks linked to Al Qaeda.' The only hopeful finding in the report to the UN Security Council was that, in spite of the rise in the level of violence, the electoral commission had successfully registered over 2,500 political candidates for polls to be held in September 2010, and they included 400 women. However, a press briefing by NATO spokesman Brigadier General Josef Blotz also in June 2010 stated that 'the situation is tending in our favour as more forces flow into the area'. General Blotz also reported that due to more stringent rules of engagement there had been 44.4 per cent less Coalition-caused civilian casualties in the previous three months compared to the same period in 2009. The level of military casualties, however, was the highest recorded in the nine-year war. Total numbers of British soldiers killed in Afghanistan since 2001 totalled over 300 by the end of June 2010, and the total number of US troops killed in the same period totalled over 1,100.[7] It is understandable that public admiration for the courage and dedication of the troops serving in Afghanistan, and sympathy for the families whose loved ones have been killed or seriously injured in action, is mixed with even more insistent questioning both of the justification for the mission in Afghanistan and about why military commanders, particularly in the British case, do not appear to have been given the number of troops and sufficient suitable equipment and weaponry to do the job in such a vast country. Third, if the mission is essential and the US and UK governments and other NATO allies are prepared to see it through, what lessons can be drawn from recent experience to help design a winning long-term strategy for defeating the terrorist-backed insurgency in Afghanistan?

The author will proceed to tackle these questions, but first he should make clear that he is not a pacifist. I firmly believe that some wars have been just and that there are times when it is a duty to defend our values and life against incorrigible enemies who seek to destroy them by the use of war or terrorism.

The Second World War was a classic case of a just war. The consequences for Europe and the rest of the world if Hitler's Nazi regime had won are too awful to contemplate. The insurgencies backed and exploited by the Al Qaeda network are very different types of conflict, but it is vital for the public to understand that this network of ruthless jihadis is a transnational phenomenon and a threat to international peace and security. Those who are well informed about world affairs are fully aware that conspiracies led and inspired by Al Qaeda, at that time based in Afghanistan, were responsible for the 9/11 atrocities in New York and Washington, which killed nearly 3,000 people, and hundreds of other attacks around the world causing the deaths of thousands of innocent people. It is not only in the interests of the Afghan people that action is needed to prevent the Taliban and its close Al Qaeda allies from regaining control of their shattered country: it is in the interest of the peace, security and wellbeing of the entire international community. Mullah Omar is recognised by Al Qaeda as the 'spiritual' head of both the Afghan and Pakistan Taliban, and the latter is recognised as being used as the strike arm of Al Qaeda in Pakistan. There probably are some more pragmatic factions among the Afghan Taliban and the warlords who have sided with them who might be willing to negotiate a ceasefire with the Afghan government, but in 2010 it was very clear that the hard-line incorrigibles, the jihadis who will never agree to depart from the ideology promoted by Al Qaeda, have no wish to enter into any formal peace talks with the US and other NATO governments. Indeed, when President Karzai rather optimistically summoned a peace conference in 2010 the Taliban refused to take part: they signalled their attitude by firing rockets at the location of the conference and sending a suicide bombing squad to attack the meeting. Fortunately it failed to complete its mission, but the message is clear enough. The hardliners believe they can defeat the NATO forces and the Afghan Army and regain control of the country. NATO's mission and civilian development efforts under the auspices of the UN are vital. The young men and women serving in NATO forces in Afghanistan are not risking their lives in vain: they are playing a key role in the international struggle against the worst kind of terrorist threat the modern world has experienced. They are preventing the territory of Afghanistan once again becoming a major base and launching pad for the Al Qaeda network's terrorist and insurgency campaign in South West Asia, the Middle East and worldwide. Why is this not understood by large segments of the American and British publics? First, because it is hard for the public to get their heads round the idea of a network of transnational terrorists waging a global jihad that will very often involve links between Western countries and Afghanistan, Pakistan, Yemen or other faraway countries. Second, the politicians and the Western media have not been very good at explaining the reasons for the mission in Afghanistan. Third and often overlooked, many of the public on both sides of the Atlantic became very cynical about their governments' stated reasons for waging war when they found out that they had sold the War on Iraq on a false prospectus. But if NATO governments broadly agree on the importance of the mission, why has it taken so long to obtain a generally agreed strategy and the necessary troop levels, weaponry and equipment to put a winning strategy into effect? One obvious reason is that the US and the UK switched their attention to Iraq in 2003 and spent huge amounts on sustaining the occupation forces. Professor Stiglitz, a Nobel Prize winner in economics, has estimated that by 2006 the US government had spent three trillion dollars on the war in Iraq. The economic recession and the huge public expenditure deficits that have accumulated on both sides of the Atlantic have made it more difficult for the Allies to find the necessary resources to sustain a winning strategy in Afghanistan. Another reason for the abysmal weakness in the way the Western democracies have responded to threats is the lack of knowledge of strategic and security problems and issues among prime ministers and cabinets of democratic countries. It is also getting harder to find former military officers of junior and middle ranks among the government and legislatures of NATO states. This was true of the Clinton and George W. Bush administrations in the US, and the government of Blair and Brown in the UK. This helps to explain not only poor strategic decision-making by political leaders but also the lack of mutual understanding and effective cooperation between generals and their political masters in the democracies. In the UK prime responsibility for the inadequacy of the defence budget and the failure to recognise the vital needs of the campaign in Afghanistan lies with the Blair government. As one highly respected military analyst has put it: ' … the MOD is buying a great deal of what is not needed and has failed to buy enough of what it demonstrably does need for current operations.'[8]

In the British case the gap between the urgent needs for current operations in Afghanistan and what was actually provided was totally unacceptable. Most of the public have heard about the acute shortage of helicopters. Many may not be aware of the inadequate and poorly protected armoured vehicles and the lack of bomb-disposal capability the UK troops have been expected to manage with. How many of the general public are aware that British troops have been expected to manage with a 40-year-old tank, the Scimitar, which troops report 'is worn out, its gun is often jammed and it frequently broke down'.[9] It was reported that the Ministry of Defence stated 'replacement of Scimitar will not be in service until 2015'.[10]

What are the prospects of success for the current counterinsurgency strategy in Afghanistan? Has it taken into account the lessons of previous COIN operations? It is hardly surprising that the overall strategy of Afghanistan is determined by the US, by far the largest contributor of troops and air power. Hence, although the mission is endorsed by the UN and by the NATO allies, and many NATO countries contribute to the task, it is the US President and his senior advisers who make all the key strategic decisions. President Obama and his team took many months to review the strategic options. In December 2009 the President ordered 30,000 additional US troops to be deployed to Afghanistan. When General McChrystal was relieved of his command in June 2010 and General Petraeus, the author of the 'surge' policy in Iraq, was appointed to succeed him it was announced that there would be no change in the strategic plan for Afghanistan. This consists of three key elements: (1) increasing troop numbers; (2) giving greater protection to the civilian population; and (3) giving greater responsibility to the Afghans to look after their own security. It should be clearly understood that the US government is aiming at a swift exit from Afghanistan, with withdrawals of US forces beginning in 2011 if conditions are right. NATO's rules of engagement have become more stringent and considerable progress towards meeting objective (2) is already being made. Objective (3) makes very good sense: it is a cardinal principle of effective counterinsurgency that as far as possible the major role should be performed by local forces who are familiar with the terrain and who will be more likely to get the cooperation of local people because they are not seen as foreign occupiers and invaders of their territory. This is particularly important in a Muslim country where the insurgents can use the claim that they are expelling the 'infidel' as a useful way of rallying support.

It is understandable that both the US and UK governments are anxious to try and arrange an honourable exit from Afghanistan as soon as possible. The war is increasingly unpopular with voters and is costing the Allies billions of dollars at a time when the governments of the US and Western Europe are desperately trying to reduce their deficits. However, it is important to have a realistic strategy, and the position taken at the G8 meeting in Toronto in June 2010 when they gave Karzai five years to get his country stable and secure enough to be able to stave off further insurgencies seems more credible. Experience shows that announcing a date for withdrawal is unwise. If, in the event, it cannot be met it damages credibility. Above all it gives hope to the insurgents that if they can just keep battering away until exit day they will be in a position to seize control much more rapidly than they had hoped. A number of NATO countries had already decided unilaterally to withdraw their forces from Afghanistan before the G8 meeting, so it was important for the US and the UK to strongly reiterate their commitments to stay in Afghanistan until the mission is completed, what Liam Fox, the British Defence Secretary, described as a conditions-based withdrawal plan rather than a calendar-based plan.

There are three other key requirements if the strategy outlined above is to have any chance of succeeding: (1) President Karzai must make a big improvement in the quality of governance, especially cracking down firmly on the widespread corruption and the vote rigging so damaging to the standing of his government; (2) more effective steps need to be taken to ensure that Pakistan is not turning a blind eye to the ISI giving secret help to the Taliban; and (3) a major effort to staunch the flow of financial aid and weapons across the frontier from Pakistan. Last but not least, the Allies need to conduct a far more intensive and effective 'hearts and minds' campaign, combining public information efforts aimed at the general population of Afghanistan, explaining the reasons for the presence of the international security force and the important fact that their mission is not to colonise or exploit the country but to provide Afghans with the level of stability and security needed to enable reconstruction and economic development of the country to take place. The information should also give a factually accurate account of the cruel and tyrannical actions of the Taliban and the crimes committed by its Al Qaeda allies. To be effective, such information efforts need to be backed up by the actions of ISAF. This is why greater protection of civilians is such an important part of a winning strategy. Coalition forces are already following more stringent rules of engagement and are absolutely right to do so. People who have seen family members and neighbours blown to pieces in a coalition-caused incident are hardly likely to rally to the support of the government and its security forces. However difficult it is, especially in a complex counterinsurgency situation, the armed forces of fully operative democracies should always seek to abide by international humanitarian law (IHL) as set out in the Geneva Conventions and protocols.

As argued earlier in this chapter, it is important to have a realistic strategy. Hoping that Afghanistan will quickly turn into a fully fledged Western-style democracy is pie-in-the-sky. It will probably take years to eradicate the endemic corruption and to establish a genuine rule of law system with full respect for human rights. Nor is it very realistic to expect the Taliban leadership to agree to a ceasefire and a peace process. There may be some more pragmatic individuals and warlords who are willing to find a political pathway to influence in Afghanistan. The hardliners who dominate the leadership and groups such as the faction headed by Jalaluddin Haqqani,[11] and based alongside the Al Qaeda in North Waziristan, are incorrigible and confident that they will ultimately defeat the Western armed forces however long it takes.

Other insurgencies linked to Al Qaeda

Pakistan has recently been suffering from a serious insurgency challenge in the North West of the country at the hands of the Pakistan Taliban, which is extremely violent and ruthless and operates as a virtual strike arm of Al Qaeda. At one point it did supposedly make a deal with the very fragile democratic government of Pakistan whereby if they abided by a ceasefire no military action would be taken against them. The Pakistan Taliban treated this agreement with contempt, retained its weapons and proceeded to occupy other areas adjoining Swat.

At one point they had extended their zone of control to just over 30 miles from Islamabad. In response to this threat the Pakistan army was for the first time deployed in strength to regain control of the areas seized by the Taliban. Traditionally the army had always been deployed to confront what the Pakistan government considered was the threat from India, the long-standing dispute with India over the status of Jammu and Kashmir. It was a major shift in Pakistan's security policy, and the first clear signal that Islamabad now saw that the Al Qaeda network, with its significant presence in South and South West Asia, was a potential threat to Pakistan's own security. However, the Pakistan government's major concern does not appear to be a threat from Al Qaeda or from the constant cross-border linkages between the Afghan Taliban and extremist Islamist movements in Pakistan. The military leaders and the ISI still perceive India as the greatest threat to their security, despite all the evidence of the bitter hostility of the Al Qaeda network and its resentment at Islamabad's closer cooperation with the United States. We must remember that Pakistan's hostility towards India was deepened not only by the bitter dispute over the status of Kashmir but also by India's military intervention to assist the separatist rebellion in East Pakistan in 1970–71, which led to the formation of the independent state of Bangladesh. Many in India's political and military elites reciprocate this hostility and mistrust and blame Pakistan for hosting and assisting a number of terrorist groups responsible for deadly attacks on Indian targets. It is well known that the Lashkar-e-Tayyiba, a major Al Qaeda affiliate and support group, responsible for the multi-site assault on Mumbai in 2008, travelled from Pakistan, where many suspect that the terrorists obtained training and weapons. As both India and Pakistan are armed with nuclear weapons the danger of future insurgencies and terrorist attacks triggering a wider conventional war, possibly leading to the use of nuclear weapons, should be borne in mind. The US government and other countries in the UN Security Council are right to worry about the dangers and also about the risk of Pakistan's growing stock of highly enriched uranium and knowledge of nuclear technology getting into the hands of terrorists.

For all the above reasons, I believe President Obama's administration and European NATO states are correct in recognising that the Afghan/Pakistan frontier area is still the epicentre of the most serious terrorist threats to the international community.

However, one should not neglect other areas in the Middle East and Africa where Al Qaeda is busy exploiting the opportunities afforded by a failing or failed state to recruit and train more suicide terrorists. Yemen provides a clear example. It has become a useful base for Al Qaeda in the Arabian Peninsula (AQAP).

There is a separatist insurgency in the remote interior, and AQAP has been taking full advantage of the confused internal security situation to use Yemen as a base for training and briefing militants for terrorist missions. It is believed that

Farouk Abdulmutallab, the man charged with trying to blow up the airliner he was travelling in as it approached Detroit by using explosives smuggled through airport security in his underpants, was trained and briefed for his mission in Yemen, and that other recruits are being trained for similar missions in the same training camps in south east Yemen. Serious concerns about Yemen being used as an AQAP base have led the US government to authorise an increase in the number of US troops in the area to work in partnership with local forces to collect intelligence on AQAP's activities there. Similar assistance is being given to local forces in Somalia and elsewhere to monitor Al Qaeda-linked activity.[12]

Some lessons from recent counterinsurgencies

Counterinsurgency is one of the most challenging and complex tasks that the armed forces of a democratic state can be ordered to undertake, especially when it is undertaken overseas in an entirely unfamiliar environment. The secret of successful counterinsurgency operations is to win enough confidence and support of the local population to be able to gather vital intelligence on the identities and location of insurgents. This is very hard to achieve in situations where the counterinsurgency troops have little or no knowledge of the local language and only a sketchy knowledge of local culture, history and traditions, and where the civilian population is in constant fear of retribution by the insurgents.

The author does not profess to be a military expert in the practicalities of counterinsurgency, but as a political analyst he believes that it is possible to draw some useful general lessons from the recent experience of the armed forces of democracies in combating terrorist-backed insurgencies in foreign countries. First, and most obviously, the wisest course is to take all possible measures to avoid the necessity of such involvements. The insurgents and their terrorist backers, and a high proportion of the indigenous population, are bound to view such foreign interventions as 'colonial' or 'imperialist' whatever the justifications of the intervening states, and this provides useful propaganda and a rallying call for recruits to the insurgency and the terrorist groups that back them.

The second reason why involvement in countering insurgencies in foreign countries should be avoided if at all possible is even more fundamental: recent history shows that in order for a counterinsurgency campaign to succeed it is essential to have unified and fully coordinated political and military strategy, fully integrating social, economic and external relations policy, within the overall political-military framework. It is all too obvious from both official and independent sources that the integration of overall political and military aspects was never fully achieved in Iraq and at time of writing (spring 2010) it had not been achieved in Afghanistan. On the contrary, there is abundant evidence that in both cases the national governments and the Western forces that have been trying to assist them have been working at cross purposes.

In the case of Pakistan, the problem is somewhat different. Government rhetoric suggests that there is a unified overall strategy against the insurgents in the north-west, FATA and Waziristan but in practice it appears that some officials and some of the ISI may be pursuing their own priorities, seeking to secretly allow help to be channelled across the border to the Taliban in Afghanistan as a means of ensuring that India does not develop greater influence in Afghanistan.

Yemen and Somalia are countries where the Al Qaeda network is clearly exploiting the current insurgencies in order to gain additional bases and safe havens from which to extend their influence. In both these cases the lack of a strong national government is a huge help to insurgents and terrorists, but it makes any large-scale involvement of American and other Western armed forces all the more high-risk with no suitable exit in sight.

Experience in India and Latin America suggests that local forces, well trained and familiar with the cultural environment, local language and terrain, are the most suited to counterinsurgency tasks. Hence, in both Iraq and Afghanistan, the efforts to train local armed forces for these tasks deserve every encouragement.

However, what about conflict situations which develop into massive humanitarian emergencies where militias unleashed by, or encouraged by, a regime mount terror attacks, massacres against an ethnic group they designate as enemies? In cases such as these the international community has resorted to using the UN or regional organisations such as the African Union to try to prevent the violence from escalating and to improve human security. The international interventions in East Timor, Sierra Leone, Sudan and the former Yugoslavia are examples of international intervention of this kind. They have had varying degrees of success, largely depending on the numbers of troops contributed to the operations, their effectiveness and the level of humanitarian aid provided by the international organisations and NGOs. As the tragic case of Darfur shows, the resources available to help in these humanitarian crises are often extremely limited. There is an overwhelming case for increasing the UN's budget for emergency peacekeeping and humanitarian interventions.[13]

Three other important lessons can be derived from the recent history of military deployments to counter insurgencies in foreign countries. The first is one that should be part and parcel of the basic training of all the armed forces of a law-abiding democratic state. They should at all times abide by the International Humanitarian Law (IHL) as codified in the Geneva Conventions and Protocols. These concern the protection of civilians and non-combatants, the treatment of the wounded and prisoners of war, the responsibility of the occupying power in occupied territories and many other aspects of human rights in time of conflict. Cynics will point out that some states and most insurgents ignore IHL, but those who disclaim any interest in the laws of war should be reminded that even in the darkest days of the Second World War millions of military personnel, particularly those wounded and those taken prisoner, benefited from the observance of at least some of IHL's provisions. It is therefore in the mutual interest of all states to ensure that their armed forces are trained to abide by the Geneva Conventions and Protocols and to strengthen them when the opportunity arises. The fundamental reason why we should support the full implementation of IHL even in the most difficult counterinsurgency situations is that it is morally right to try to uphold respect for the most fundamental human rights even in times of war.

There cannot be a decent-minded citizen in any rule of law state who does not feel shocked and saddened when incidents that reveal serious cases of mistreatment of prisoners, such as Abu Ghraib prison events, show a tiny minority of a democracy's armed forces falling below the standards of conduct we rightly expect of them.

Second, and extremely important, every effort should be made to reduce civilian casualties caused by 'collateral damage'. The new strategy in Afghanistan adopted by President Obama in 2010 rightly makes this a cardinal principle of the campaign against the Taliban.

Last but not least is another key lesson (again one reiterated in discussions about the Afghan strategy): it is crucial to take all reasonable measures to reduce the number of casualties inflicted on the soldiers of a democratic society. In a world in which we pay greater attention to human rights, I do not believe that governments are justified in treating our solders as expendable cannon-fodder. Soldiers risk their lives by the nature of the job but they have a right to expect that they will not be put in the line of fire without the best available equipment and weaponry and sensible, properly planned strategy. The Blair government sent British troops into both Iraq and Afghanistan without any clear military strategy and with hopelessly inadequate equipment and weaponry. They were allocated a tank, the Scimitar, brought into service decades ago: it often breaks down and its gun often jams and it is not due to be replaced until 2015. They did not have adequate supply of up-to-date bomb-disposal equipment and they had an absurdly limited number of helicopters, vital in Afghanistan's terrain for medical evacuation and for rapid movement of personnel from A to B. All this has leaked out from press reports, the Chilcot Inquiry and from personal testimony of soldiers. It can only be guessed how many of the over 300 soldiers killed in Afghanistan by June 2010 could have returned home safe and sound if they had been properly equipped for the job.[14]

5 Politics, diplomacy and peace processes

Pathways out of terrorism?

One of the major reasons why terrorism has become so ubiquitous in the contemporary international system is that it has proven a low-cost, low-risk, potentially high-yield method of struggle for all kinds of groups and regimes. And there is no sign that the ending of the Cold War has eradicated the underlying ethnic, religio-political, ideological and strategic causes of conflicts which spawn terrorism.[1]

On the other hand, twentieth-century history shows 'terrorism is a faulty weapon that often misfires'.[2] It very rarely succeeds in delivering strategic goals, such as the overthrow of governments and their replacement by the terrorists. Wanton murder and destruction – for that is how indiscriminate bombings in city streets will be *perceived* by the general population – may have the effects of uniting and hardening a community against the terrorists, of triggering a violent backlash by rival groups or of stinging the authorities into more effective security measures in the ensuing period of public revulsion.

It is also clear that liberal democracies have been extraordinarily resilient in withstanding terrorist attempts to coerce them into major changes of policy or surrender in the face of the terrorists' demands.[3] In contrast to dictatorships and colonialist regimes, liberal democracies have the key advantage that they enjoy legitimacy in the eyes of the overwhelming majority of the population and can mobilise them and depend on their sustained support in their efforts to suppress terrorism.[4] They are in serious trouble if they begin to lose their popular legitimacy and their terrorist opponents begin to acquire it.

Political and socio-economic reform

However, this is extremely rare. All the cards are stacking in favour of liberal democratic governments, or mainstream mass parties engaged in constitutional opposition which can offer voters the prospect of alternative policies. Major political parties that can share in the government of the country have both the opportunity and the resources to at least respond sensitively and rapidly to deeply felt discontents and feelings of injustice voiced by citizens. Moreover, it is a mistake to assume that political violence and terrorism will inevitably arise in conditions where there are high levels of perceived socio-economic deprivation. Research shows that it is very often the grievances of minorities concerning perceived lack of political and civil rights which trigger violence.[5] However, if one examines the history of the political struggles of ethnic and religious minorities in the United States and Britain since the late nineteenth century, or in continental European democracies since 1945, it is clear that an overwhelming majority have found effective channels of protest, lobbying and influence through the medium of constitutional politics or through the channels of both parliamentary pressure and extra-parliamentary protest, demonstrations, marches and rallies. This phenomenon is well illustrated by the struggle for blacks' civil rights in America both past and present.[6] In retrospect it is astonishing that the black civil rights movement was so peaceful, especially when one considers the severity of discrimination and oppression of the black population in the segregationist areas of the South. This is not to deny that some militant activists opted for a strategy of violence, but they were very few in numbers and had only the most marginal influence on mainstream politics.

Yet if one reflects on the reasons for this there is no cause for complacency about the positive appeal of the liberal democratic principles and practice. One obvious reason for the predominantly peaceful nature of the majority of civil rights movements in democracies has been that the penalties for violence, or any involvement in any activities deemed to be aimed at subverting or overthrowing the government, have been very severe. Prudence rather than idealist views of civic duty may have been the predominant constraint against more violent dissent.

Nevertheless, it is also clear from the history of political violence in the major democracies that much of the success of liberal and social democratic governments in avoiding violent conflict has been due to the introduction of enlightened political and socio-economic reforms and ameliorative measures by successive governments.[7] Attention to much needed reforms to adapt to changing popular needs should be a central concern in the daily business of governments, not simply in order to head off potential civil conflict and violence but because it is the central duty of democratic governments and political parties to serve the needs of the people. There is overwhelming historical evidence that effective and preferably timely programmes of political and socio-economic reform are the best antidote against the rise of anti-democratic mass movements of the extreme left or the extreme right. The tragedy of the Weimar Republic of Germany between the wars was that it conspicuously failed to meet the basic needs of the people and was unable to mitigate the effects of the economic blizzard of the great depression which struck Germany. Thus the ground was prepared for Hitler's Nazi movement to hijack control of the German political system to establish a totalitarian dictatorship.[8]

One very positive demonstration of the power of democratic processes and values to win mass support, even in countries that have major problems of terrorism and instability and socio-economic deprivation, was the astonishing degree of popular support among Iraqis for free elections and the constitutional referendum in the face of dire threats by terrorist groups and extremist movements engaged in insurgency. Sadly, the election of governments with a genuine and broad-based mandate does not of itself solve the grave problems of insecurity and instability. Indeed, at the time of writing, atrocities such as the terrorist bombings of the Shia community and their holy shrines are continuing. Nevertheless, the courage of Iraqi voters was once again demonstrated in the March 2010 elections when they defied death threats from terrorist groups in order to cast their ballots. Sunni militants bitterly opposed to the election tried to deter people from voting, but they failed. The Iraqiya bloc led by former Prime Minister Iyad Allawi narrowly defeated the State of Law alliance led by Prime Minister Nouri Maliki, but no single party obtained enough seats to form a government on its own. However, the election showed that there is a genuine hunger for democratic government and the freedoms and rights that only democratic forms of government can bring, even in a country where there has been little or no experience of democracy. The promotion of genuine democracy may well become the best *long-term* antidote to terrorism in such societies, but the struggle to achieve it in the teeth of bitter hatred and violence from terrorist and insurgent groups has to be won if this is to happen, and it is for this reason that it would be tragic for Iraq and the future of democracy in the wider Middle East if the Coalition countries and the wider international community failed to give the fragile Iraqi government the security assistance needed to enable the Iraqis themselves to take over the security role successfully. If democracy succeeds in consolidating itself in Iraq it will be a case of some real progress coming out of tragedy.

It would be foolish to pretend that democratic governments can in some way immunise themselves against the contagion of terrorism simply by pursuing enlightened policies of socio-economic amelioration and reform. Many of the groups involved in terrorism are very small and may be totally divorced from the wider social movements. In some cases they may be offshoots of an international terrorist organisation directed and funded from abroad. In other cases the group may be part of a fanatical religious cult or an extreme neo-Nazi organisation. No democratic government worthy of the name could have dreamt of attempting to accommodate or compromise with the bizarre and dangerous apocalyptic ideas of the Aum Shinrikyo cult,[9] for example, or with the white supremacist ideas and conspiracy theories of, say, the neo-Nazi right in America.[10] Or take, for example, the case of the cruel murderers responsible for planning and perpetrating the massacre of 58 foreign tourists at the temple of Queen Hatshepsut in the Valley of Queens, near Luxor, on 17 November 1997.[11] The idea that such criminals should be accepted as legitimate interlocutors for their professed aims would surely cause general revulsion and in my view is totally unacceptable. There is only one appropriate response to those guilty of such a grave violation of human rights and that is to bring them to justice. Prophylaxis and socio-economic reform are simply not appropriate or relevant for combating many of the varieties of terrorism faced in modern democratic societies, especially from Al Qaeda and its affiliates, none of which has an economic programme. In any event, once a democratic government faces the onset of terrorist violence, from whatever quarter, it will need to have in plan an effective counter-terrorism policy and the expertise, specialist agencies and resources to carry it out.

Notwithstanding all these difficulties, it is the case that the possibilities and potential value of political and diplomatic approaches to reduce violence have generally been seriously underestimated.[12] Although, in a sense, the ending of the Cold War took the lid off a large number of ethnic conflicts that had been simmering beneath the surface for decades and thus brought long-suppressed conflicts to the surface again. The collapse of the former Soviet Union also cleared the way for a much more active role for the UN in mediation, peace-keeping and peacemaking in numerous regional conflicts around the world.[13] Many of these efforts have succeeded, at least to an extent, in reducing overall violence even though there are hardline factions in many cases that have continued to use violence.

There have been a number of successful UN peacekeeping operations, for example in Namibia, Angola, El Salvador, Nicaragua and Cambodia, which led to the holding of free elections and a transition to a period of relative peace and stability, though the situation in Angola and Cambodia has been particularly volatile and there is always the danger of major escalations of violence.[14] The key players in the remarkable South African peace process were President Nelson Mandela and former President F.W. de Klerk.[15] However, the Commonwealth Eminent Persons Group and UN observers also played a valuable role.

It is sad to have to report that the UN's efforts in this important field are being crippled by lack of funds and by lack of will on the part of member states to provide the necessary troops and other resources.[16] The total budget adopted for the 2004–05 peacekeeping operations was only 2.8 billion US dollars, considerably less than the budget for UN peacekeeping operations in 1995!

The United States is making a major contribution to peace efforts in Bosnia and Kosovo. However, there is deep reluctance in the US Congress and among the American public to increase US participation in UN peacekeeping especially in view of the heavy US burden in Iraq. Many other countries are also unwilling to get involved in new UN missions. This is partly because they are worried that they will be making an open-ended commitment. So many of the conflicts involved are protracted internal wars that seem to flare up repeatedly despite efforts to negotiate and implement peace accords. In many cases governments will be reluctant to commit troops because of lack of public support and because they fear that they will have grave difficulty in extricating their troops from the conflict.

In the absence of adequate UN capabilities to meet the growing demands for peacekeeping and humanitarian intervention there has been a growing tendency for regional organisations to fill the gap. For example, it was the Commonwealth of Independent States (CIS) which provided a peacekeeping force in Tajikistan, and it was NATO that provided the bulk of the implementation and stabilisation forces (IFOR and SFOR) in Bosnia and Kosovo (KFOR) and the International Security Assistance Force in Afghanistan. In the case of Bosnia this multinational effort has been highly successful. But there is always a danger that regional initiatives to set up 'peacekeeping' forces will lack the necessary impartiality and legitimacy to perform this role adequately.

There are considerable dangers involved in this 'peacekeeping exhaustion' which the international community is displaying. Civil wars in countries such as the Sudan, Afghanistan and parts of central Africa can undergo major escalations creating huge humanitarian problems both in the countries and among their neighbours, as massive numbers of refugees flee the fighting.

Peace processes

The most remarkable of all the peace initiatives launched since the end of the Cold War was the Oslo Declaration of Principles of September 1993 between the Israeli government and the PLO.[17] The Israeli–Palestinian conflict was the catalyst for the rise of modern international terrorism.[18] If a peace process between these historic enemies could be made to work surely this would bring a dramatic reduction in international terrorism?

Sadly, as many specialists in the study of terrorism could have predicted, the Israeli–PLO peace process has been under terrorist attack since its inception. Rejectionist groups and state sponsors, such as Iran, have dedicated themselves to derailing the peace process because they believe that the PLO leadership has betrayed both the causes of Islam and the Palestinians. At the other extreme are the right-wing fanatics in Israel who believe that the agreement betrays Israel by conceding what they believe to be an integral part of the biblical Greater Israel to the Palestinians and threatening Israel's long-term survival. In the year following the Oslo Accords, Hamas and the Palestinian Islamic Jihad showed their ability to mount sophisticated and deadly terrorist attacks on Israeli targets. Fifty-five Israeli soldiers and civilians were killed in terrorist attacks in 1994. The worst single incident against the Israelis was the bombing of a commuter bus in Tel Aviv, killing 22 Israelis. The worst single attack on the Palestinians in 1994 was carried out by a member of the extreme-right organisation Kach, who murdered 29 Palestinian worshippers at a mosque in Hebron.

In 1995 terrorist attacks by Islamic militants, aimed at derailing the peace process, killed 45 Israeli soldiers and civilians and two American civilians and injured over 270 Israelis. There were fewer attacks than in the previous year, but several suicide bombs caused large numbers of casualties. These attacks were claimed by Hamas and Palestinian Islamic Jihad.

The following year this tactic continued when suicide bombers struck in Tel Aviv in February and in Jerusalem in March, killing 65 people. Hamas claimed responsibility for three of these bombings. A further major blow to the peace process came in November 1995 when Prime Minister Yitzhak Rabin was assassinated by an Israeli extremist who belonged to the extreme-right group, EYAL, and who claimed that Prime Minister Rabin was betraying Israel through the peace process policy.[19] There is no doubt that the loss of Prime Minister Rabin, a man widely admired and trusted by the public to protect Israel's vital security interests, combined with the strong feelings of anger and insecurity engendered by the terrorists' suicide bombings, helped to ensure the defeat of Shimon Peres, Yitzhak Rabin's successor. The coming to power of Prime Minister Netanyahu in 1996 and a right-wing-dominated government, which for the most part was fundamentally opposed to the underlying principles of the Oslo Accords, radically altered the prospects for peace. Hence terrorism from both Palestinian and Israeli rejectionists and the outcome of the Israeli general election led to a situation where the peace process was very nearly extinguished.

In 1997, following further devastating suicide bomb attacks on Israeli civilians, the Israeli Prime Minister, Binyamin Netanyahu, threatened to suspend implementation of the peace accords until Yasser Arafat and his colleagues had proved that they were taking effective security action against the terrorists.[20] Meanwhile the Palestinians were becoming ever more disillusioned with the peace process. Far from experiencing a significant improvement in their socio-economic conditions, the majority of the inhabitants of West Bank and Gaza found themselves worse off as a result of the Israeli government's policy of closing the frontiers with Israel in the aftermath of successive Palestinian terrorist attacks. This prevented Palestinians employed in Israeli enterprises from earning the wages so vital to their economy. There was also particular resentment against the expansion of the Israeli housing projects in east Jerusalem and the expansion of Jewish settlements, and what the Palestinians perceived as Israel's failure to honour agreements on the withdrawal of Israeli forces from West Bank territory.

It is true that under considerable pressure from the Clinton administration, Prime Minister Netanyahu was persuaded to join Yasser Arafat in signing the Wye Agreement, designed to bring new life to the peace process. But Mr Netanyahu moved swiftly to suspend the agreement on the grounds that the Palestinian Authority was failing to carry out its vital obligations to crack down on terrorism.

Mr Ehud Barak's convincing victory over Binyamin Netanyahu in the May 1999 elections in Israel renewed hopes of resuscitating the peace process. However, the Israeli–PLO process remained in deep trouble. The Palestinians were still deeply suspicious of the new Israeli government and a final status agreement still seemed a distant dream. Meanwhile the peace process remains under attack from extremists on both sides. It has not been able to stop terrorist attacks. The so-called 'roadmap to peace' developed with the support of President George W. Bush, the EU and Russia rekindled hopes for a two-state solution. Prime Minister Sharon's policy of Israeli withdrawal from Gaza again provided some impetus towards a peaceful solution but extremists on both sides still threaten to derail the process. It is surely in the interests of the international community to prevent terrorism from achieving this aim of destroying the chance of a political solution.

A fundamental problem with the entire Israeli–Palestinian peace process was that the Oslo Accords themselves, and the whole process of attempting to implement them, reflected the asymmetry of the power relationship between protagonists. The Palestinians did not have any power, other than street protests, to redress those aspects of the Accords with Israel that are clearly one-sided and unfair in the eyes of the Palestinian population. When the Israeli authorities insist on so limiting the scope of the Palestinian Authority that they are unable to exercise any real autonomy, when the economic measures taken by the Israeli government following terrorist attacks – for example closure of borders – are so economically devastating, and the Palestinians are powerless to do anything about it, one can well understand their frustration. The victory of Hamas in the Palestinian elections of 2006 made the prospect of a peace process seem still more remote: Hamas does not recognise

Israel's right to exist and Israel's government is unwilling to negotiate with Hamas on the grounds that it is a terrorist organisation. After Hamas gained control of Gaza in 2007 the prospects of a revival in the Middle East peace process faded rapidly. Israel launched a fierce bombardment and invasion of Gaza in December 2008 and early January 2009 in retaliation for growing numbers of rocket attacks on Israel by Hamas. There were hundreds of Palestinian casualties and Gaza's creaking infrastructure was devastated. The severe economic blockade imposed on Gaza by Israel has caused great suffering for the people of Gaza. In May 2010 a flotilla of peace activists carrying humanitarian aid for Gaza was intercepted in international waters. Israeli commandos stormed one of the vessels, *Mavi Marmura*, a Turkish paddle steamer, killing nine peace activists in the process. This tragic incident caused grave damage to President Obama's efforts to promote a revival of the Israeli–Palestinian peace process, as well as rupturing Israeli–Turkish relations and increasing Israel's international isolation.

A very different kind of peace process has been attempted in Northern Ireland after over a quarter of a century of terrorist violence waged by the Provisional IRA, Irish National Liberation Army (INLA) and the Loyalist terrorist groups: the UVF and UFF. The peace initiative has its origins in a series of discussions between John Hume, the leader of the SDLP, the non-violent nationalist party in Northern Ireland, which once enjoyed the support of the majority of the Catholic minority population, and Gerry Adams, President of Sinn Fein, the political wing of the IRA. John Hume's hope was that he could persuade the Republicans to abandon violence and participate alongside the Social Democratic and Labour Party (SDLP) and other parties in political talks to shape the political future of Northern Ireland. In the Downing Street Declaration of 1993 the Irish and British prime ministers issued a bold challenge to the IRA, making it clear that if they renounced violence their political representatives could qualify for entry into political talks on the future of Northern Ireland. Although the IRA decisively rejected the Downing Street Declaration at its meeting in Letterkenny in 1994, it did, with strong encouragement from the US government and the Irish caucus in Congress, declare a unilateral ceasefire from 1 September 1994. The Loyalist terrorist groups reciprocated with their own ceasefire a month later.[21] However, the Unionist political parties, representing the Protestant majority population in the North, were deeply suspicious of the sincerity of the IRA's ceasefire from the outset. They had good grounds for their apprehension that the IRA would simply return to the gun and bomb if they did not get what they wanted at the conference table. The IRA's ambivalence about the ceasefire was clear from its inception: they refused to declare a permanent ceasefire; they maintained their terrorist cell structure in being and continued practising operations, selecting and reconnoitring targets, and storing weapons and explosives on both sides of the Irish border and on the mainland. They also continued their brutal punishment beatings of those who incurred their displeasure within their communities, as did the Loyalist terrorist groups.[22] Frustrated at their failure to bulldoze their way into all-party talks on their terms, the IRA returned to its terrorist campaign in the Canary Wharf bombing in London in February 1996, in which two civilians were killed and a large number injured. They followed this by a series of bomb attacks in the British mainland and Northern Ireland, though some of their most potentially devastating or disrupting attacks were thwarted by a greatly enhanced counter-terrorism response by the Security Service and the police.

In July 1997, two months after Labour's general election victory, the IRA renewed its ceasefire in order to secure Sinn Fein's entry to inter-party talks on Northern Ireland, which Prime Minister Tony Blair said would go ahead without them if they did not declare an unequivocal ceasefire and show that it was genuine in the period leading up to the start of the talks in mid September 1997.

However, although IRA/Sinn Fein signed up to the principles laid down by former US Senator George Mitchell's committee – including the commitment to using exclusively peaceful means and respecting the democratic principle of the consent of the majority – and thereby gained entry to the inter-party talks, it soon became clear that they were not at that time really prepared to transform themselves from a terrorist organisation to a normal political party.

The IRA has now, at last, in 2005, formally decommissioned its weapons. The main challenge now was to rejuvenate the suspended power-sharing institutions.

The proposals for the future government of Northern Ireland agreed on Good Friday 1998 represent a remarkable achievement of negotiation by any standards. The conflict between the Unionist and the Nationalist traditions has for decades seemed almost insoluble. Unionists' have feared enforced integration into a Catholic-dominated Ireland. For their part, the Nationalist minority in the province fears domination by an Orange hegemony. The great strength of the agreement is that it provides recognition and protection for both identities and full equality of rights and status in a genuine power-sharing system of government. It contains a unique and complex structure of checks and balances designed to overcome the deep ethnic and religious division of Northern Ireland. In political terms the Good Friday Agreement created a unique opportunity to build a lasting peace. It was a credit to the politicians and officials who laboured so hard to achieve it. But, sadly, politics is not enough to secure the end of terrorist conflicts. It is important to recognise that the new agreement is only a document. A great deal more has to be done to make it work. Comparisons are already being made with the Sunningdale Agreement of 1973,[23] which led to a Northern Ireland Assembly with a power-sharing executive and proposals to establish a Council of Ireland. The Sunningdale Agreement was wrecked by the loyalist paramilitaries who organised and enforced the Ulster Workers' Council strike in key industries. A basic requirement for success in 2010, as in 1974, is effective security policy to back up the Agreement and to create more confidence on both sides. In 2010, when at last the power-sharing government and the devolved assembly agreed to police and security powers being devolved, there was a worrying increase in terrorist activity by Republican dissidents.

Another major stumbling block is terrorist activity by extremist groups that totally reject the peace process. Continuity IRA and the Real IRA, the military wing of the 32 County Sovereignty Committee, have demonstrated they command considerable amounts of weaponry and expertise. The Real IRA, responsible for the bombing of Omagh, which killed 29 civilians, initially embraced the ceasefire but later recommenced its terrorist activities and remains a potential focus for anti-Agreement Republicans. It carried out a series of bombings in Northern Ireland in 2000 and is believed to have been responsible for a bomb which damaged Hammersmith Bridge in London.

The remarkable political agreement in Northern Ireland should have been strengthened not only politically but also by the physical measures to prevent it from being undermined by violent extremists. The political and security efforts to make the peace agreement work must go together hand in hand. There are severe limits to what a democratic government can achieve by purely political means in countering terrorism, but the Good Friday Agreement and the Northern Ireland peace process show great progress can be made and hundreds of lives have been saved as a result.

Terrorism and peace processes: the requisites for success in attaining a democratic peace

'Peace process' is a much abused term that has been used in many contexts frequently to denote a predetermined political or ideological 'solution' to a conflict designed and imposed by one party to the conflict. The term can be applied to any sustained political and diplomatic efforts to resolve either international or internal conflicts: hence it has been used in situations as varied as the Israeli–Palestinian relationship, South Africa, Bosnia, Northern Ireland, Colombia, Nicaragua, El Salvador, Mali, Angola, Mozambique and Cambodia!

Much of my academic work has focused on the relationships between terrorism and liberal democracy, and hence my concern is with the concept of peaceful methods of conflict resolution to prevent or terminate terrorist violence in democratic societies while ensuring that democracy is safeguarded in the process. The new strategic environment with the ending of the Cold War appeared propitious for such peacemaking efforts. For the first time since the establishment of the United Nations the Security Council was no longer completely paralysed by the ideological and strategic conflict between the superpowers. Not surprisingly we have seen a record number of UN peacekeeping and peacemaking efforts during the 1990s. Most of these efforts have involved the extraordinarily difficult problems of terminating and resolving protracted internal ethnic or ethnoreligious or ideological wars in which terrorism has played a relatively minor or auxiliary role, or has not been a significant feature. There are very few clear-cut cases where conflict resolution has been used as a means of ending violence by factions using terrorism as their primary weapon.

Sometimes even a carefully planned and internationally supported peace process can go badly wrong. For example, despite the patient efforts of the Norwegian government and the Peace Commission in Sri Lanka to end the conflict between the Tamil Tigers and the Sri Lankan government the peace efforts began to collapse in 2006 following attacks by Tamil extremists that killed many Sri Lankan soldiers and sailors. Eventually the government forces inflicted a devastating military defeat on the insurgents but left some major human rights and political issues unresolved.

Far more difficult is the problem of trying to persuade incorrigible groups to even consider a ceasefire and negotiation of a peace agreement. A dramatic example of this occurred in May 2010 when President Karzai was opening a Loya Jurga, or Grand Assembly, with the aim of bringing the Taliban into peace negotiations. Eyewitnesses reported that at least five rockets were fired at the event. As *The Times* correspondent in Kabul put it: 'The Taliban – conspicuous by their absence – had, nonetheless, managed to get their point across.'

The harsh reality is that although there probably are some factions in the Taliban who may be interested in negotiating peace, the hardliners are as incorrigible as ever. As Ahmad Behzad, a Herat MP, observed: 'it shows they are not ready for peace'.

As was noted in Chapter 4, the challenge of a terrorist-backed insurgency in Afghanistan is likely to confront the international community for some time ahead.

Conclusion

The recent experience of efforts to pursue peace processes in conflict situations does, however, enable us to reach some tentative conclusions concerning the prerequisites for an effective peace process compatible with democratic principles and values:

- There must be a sufficient political will among both parties in a conflict to initiate and sustain a peace process.
- The role of individual leaders in mobilising and guiding their population/ community/movement through the peace process is crucial.
- In many cases, though not invariably, external mediators or brokers for peace may be invaluable in the process, and this may mean a key role of the UN, or a regional organisation, or for a major power such as the United States, capable of bringing not only enormous influence but also the substantial economic resources that may be crucial in rehabilitation and recovery following severe conflict.
- Patience and a spirit of compromise together with the courage to take risks for peace are essential qualities for the leaders and negotiators on both sides if they are going to avoid being blown off course by inevitable crises and setbacks during what is likely to be a very protracted and highly complex process.
- A key requirement is for at least a minimal degree of bipartisan consensus in favour of the peace process among the major political parties in the legislature. This proved an essential element in the long and difficult route to Northern Ireland's Good Friday Agreement. For example: as illustrated by the 1997–98 impasse in the Israeli–Palestinian peace process, if this mainstream consensus is lacking and parties fundamentally opposed to the assumption of the peace process come to power the survival of the process itself is immediately in jeopardy.

Lastly, but every bit as important as the other prerequisites of peace, political advances must go hand in hand with adequate security safeguards to meet the security concerns and fears of both parties in the conflict. If this fails to be delivered there is a real danger of key parties pulling out of the peace process, or alternatively trying to impose a solution entirely on their own terms, if necessary by resumption of violence. To overcome these security fears and to build vital confidence some degree of properly supervised disarmament and demobilisation of armed forces/groups is normally a vital phase in a successful peace process.[24]

It is extremely important to beware of 'miracle breakthrough', a euphoria based perhaps entirely on paper agreements. Reaching an agreed formula or document of agreement is not enough in itself: much care must be taken to monitor the agreement and to ensure that it is comprehensively and fairly implemented. Without proper follow-through violence can so easily be rekindled and another peace effort may be even more difficult to achieve.

Last, but by no means least, in the process of attempting to mobilise initial support for peace initiatives and in sustaining the momentum crucial to success, a peace movement with genuine mass support, as broadly based as possible, is of inestimable value.

6 Law-enforcement, criminal justice and the liberal state

Suppose conflict prevention and deterrence fail? How should the liberal state respond to terrorism once the bombs start going off? It will not escape the readers' notice that Chapters 5, 6 and 7 examine three different dimensions or aspects of responses to terrorism: the use of politics and diplomacy, the use of the law-enforcement and the criminal justice systems, and the role of the military. Some academic commentators appear to view these as alternative models for the response of a liberal democracy. In *Terrorism and the Liberal State* (1977 and 1986), I elaborated on an approach which I have termed the 'hardline approach' of the liberal state to deal with terrorism. In developing the main elements of this approach I took the view that the three models should not be regarded as mutually exclusive, and I proceeded to combine elements of all three models into a set of policy guidelines capable of being applied to a whole variety of terrorist conflicts in widely differing political contexts. It offers a multipronged approach aimed at enabling a liberal democratic state to combat terrorism effectively without undermining or seriously damaging the democratic process and the rule of law, while providing sufficient flexibility to cope with the whole range of threats, from low-level spasmodic attacks to intensive mass-casualty bombing campaigns amounting to a state of war.

The hardline approach and the rule of law

The key elements of this approach can be summarised fairly briefly:

1. Overreaction and general repression, which could destroy democracy far more rapidly and effectively than any campaign by a terrorist group, should be avoided.
2. Underreaction – the failure to uphold the constitutional authority of the government and the law – will bring the threat of sliding into anarchy or the emergence of no-go areas dominated by terrorists, warlords, Mafia gangs and drug barons, and to do this should be avoided.
3. The government and security forces must at all times act within the law. If they fail to do this they will undermine their democratic legitimacy and public confidence in, and respect for, the police and the criminal justice system.

4. The secret of winning the battle against terrorism in an open democratic society is winning the intelligence war: this will enable the security forces, using high-quality intelligence, to be proactive, thwarting terrorist conspiracies before they happen.
5. The secret intelligence agencies and all other institutions involved in combating terrorism must be firmly under the control of the elected government and fully accountable to it.
6. If emergency laws are found to be needed in a particularly serious terrorist conflict the laws must be temporary, subject to frequent review by parliament and subject to parliament's approval before any renewal.
7. Despite or perhaps because of the dilemmas facing governments in hostage crises, governments should avoid granting major concessions to terrorists. Giving in to key terrorist demands encourages terrorists to exploit the perceived weakness of the authorities by trying to wring further concessions out of them. It also damages confidence in the rule of law and the democratic process if terrorist blackmail is seen to succeed. By releasing imprisoned terrorists or by paying large cash ransoms, the authorities will be increasing the capabilities of the terrorists to sustain their campaign. Any major concessions will be a propaganda and morale boost for the terrorists.

In reflection on this framework of general guidelines for counter-terrorism policy in a liberal state, I am struck by the fact that they have stood up pretty well over the past 30 years. It summarised the underlying assumption of the predominant counter-terrorism policy adopted by the major liberal democracies, with the exception of Japan, during this period, at least for most of the time.

Bush's war on terror: international law and criminal justice sidelined

The administration of President George W. Bush adopted a strategy of preemptive military action in response to 9/11. Many critics in America and abroad pointed out that this doctrine was incompatible with the UN Charter. However, President Bush and his advisers believed they were justified in adopting a unilateral strategy despite the fact that they had received unprecedented support from the UN, NATO, the EU and the wider coalition against terrorism. Although the decision to combine with the Northern Alliance to topple the Taliban regime in Afghanistan, which had given safe haven to Al Qaeda, was supported by the UN, the decision to invade Iraq (for reasons that had nothing to do with Al Qaeda) was a clear demonstration of the Bush administration's disdain for any possible international legal constraints, even though it caused a major split in NATO, and despite the fact that it deflected vital resources from the task of bringing the top leadership of Al Qaeda to justice.

In a radical departure from the US proud tradition of respect for the law and the constitution, the Bush administration decided to circumvent the US criminal justice system in its treatment of those who were classed as 'unlawful combatants' and were suspected of involvement in terrorism. These suspects were cast into a kind of limbo of apparently perpetual imprisonment without any chance of proving their innocence and gaining release. The prison at Guantanamo Bay, or other prisons such as Bagram, were used because the administration believed they had put them beyond the reach of the US federal criminal justice system.

Instead of indicting prisoners suspected of terrorism for trial in the federal courts, the US government devised a system of Military Tribunals, which were supposed to try the suspects on the basis of evidence of their involvement in terrorism. However, very few detainees have ever had the chance of appearing before a tribunal; the tribunals are conducted by the military, the suspect is not allowed to choose their own lawyer, and the standards of proof are much less rigorous than those used in the federal criminal courts. Friends and allies of the US have been baffled by the way in which the federal criminal justice system has been circumvented. In many famous cases, such as those involving Ramzi Youssef and the four terrorists convicted by a New York court for their involvement in the August 1998 US Embassy bombings in East Africa, the federal courts have shown that they have the capability of dealing with complex terrorism cases and delivering appropriate sentences on the basis of *overwhelming* evidence. In such cases both domestic and international opinion can be satisfied that justice has been done. Guantanamo, the degrading treatment of prisoners at Abu Ghraib prison, and the condoning of torture, all did great damage to the traditional reputation of the US as a champion of the rule of law and individual human rights.

What possible justifications can there be for this abandonment of due process? Those hawks who see themselves as fighting the 'Third World War' argue that the only way to deal with terrorists is to suppress them with crushing military force on the assumption that 'the only good terrorist is a dead terrorist'. They believe that the end, i.e. crushing the Al Qaeda network, justifies any means, and that terrorists have forfeited their human rights. They also argue that the criminal courts are too cumbersome, too slow, and too unpredictable in their results, and as they have already decided that the detained suspects are guilty, trials before courts of law would be an expensive waste of time. Those who are in favour of this position, not unexpectedly, also tend to take the view that in some circumstances inhuman and degrading treatment of suspects and even torture may be justified in the name of the 'war on terrorism'.

Those who take the opposite view including the author would object that by abandoning the due process under the rule of law and by violating the human rights of suspects, we betray the very values and principles which are the foundation of the democracies we seek to defend. We are also corrupting our democracies and those public officials, members of the military and others who are ordered to carry out such policies. We are perpetrating major injustice in the name of national security. How can the security authorities be sure that the detained suspects are actually guilty of any terrorist crime? Are we to believe that intelligence agencies are always correct in their information? Is it justice to deny captives who may have to suffer decades of imprisonment any opportunity to prove their innocence before a court of law? Surely not. And what effect is such a cruel policy likely to have on Muslim communities around the world? Al Qaeda propaganda, for example, dressing captured Western hostages in Guantanamo-style orange clothes and showing pictures of prisoner abuse at Abu Ghraib gaol in Iraq, constantly seeks to exploit these images in their efforts to recruit more alienated, angry young Muslims into their network. In other words, not only are these violations of the rule of law by a leading democracy morally and legally wrong, they are ultimately a gratuitous weapon for the terrorist movement.

The Obama doctrine

In a clear repudiation of the Bush doctrine of pre-emptive military action, President Obama's national security aims to strengthen global engagement and partnerships with leading powers, such as China and Russia, thus avoiding the need for the United States to act unilaterally. Bush's doctrine was a lurch into unilateralism whereas President Obama's approach is a return to the multilateral strategy favoured by most administrations since America's entry into the Second World War. Mr Obama does not claim to have a magic immediate solution to the major problems that confront the international community but he has a far broader concept of security than his predecessor, discarding what he regards as the over-emphasis by the Bush administration on the 'war on terror' and stressing the importance of multilateral cooperation to tackle threats from climate change, economic collapse and cyber terrorism. He clearly recognises the threat from Al Qaeda terrorism and is determined that America should take a leading role in countering it, but he does not believe that fighting all kinds of terrorism all over the world is sensible or practicable.

The Obama administration's intensive diplomatic engagement had already by 2010 begun to deliver some significant successes. In a number of speeches Mr Obama set out to improve relations with the Muslim world, which generally have greatly improved, and although he has not succeeded in persuading Iran to bring its nuclear programme into line with international safeguards, it is significant all the permanent members of the UN Security Council supported the resolution imposing tougher sanctions on Tehran for its defiance of UN demands to bring Iran's programme firmly within the non-proliferation framework. The agreement with Russia on mutual reductions in their stocks of nuclear weapons is also a success for quiet diplomacy.

On counter-terrorism policy, President Obama made a bold start by pledging to close down Guantanamo Bay detention centre a year after his inauguration.

This was welcome news for all those who value human rights law, because the treatment of detainees at Guantanamo is clearly in violation of international human rights law and Protocol I of the Geneva Convention. The Obama administration made another bold move when it announced that it would put those who allegedly planned the 9/11 attacks on trial before a Federal criminal court. The decision to shut down Guantanamo Bay detention centre and the decision to put Khalid Sheikh Mohammed and his alleged co-conspirators on trial have both run into considerable opposition. Detainees' countries of origin are reluctant to take them back because a high proportion of those already released appear to be re-involved in terrorism. Moreover, the public in the US are opposed to having people believed to have been linked to Al Qaeda relocated in their home state penitentiaries. President Obama and his cabinet and advisers are finding it extremely difficult to extricate themselves from the Bush legacy while at the same time winning the struggle against Al Qaeda and its terrorist-backed insurgencies.

Concessions to terrorists and the law

The current debate on concessions to terrorists has been somewhat further complicated by arguments concerning concessions or alleged concessions by the British government to the IRA/Sinn Fein before and after the commencement of the interparty talks on the future of Northern Ireland (15 September 1997). But the crucial difference between these alleged concessions and the demands made by, say, the MRTA at Lima, is that a peace process is being attempted in Northern Ireland. The IRA declared a renewed ceasefire in July 1997 which has, however, not been comprehensive. Following the Good Friday Agreement of 1998, the IRA refrained from attacks on the security forces, but continued to commit murders and carry out brutal punishment attacks against Roman Catholics. There is a crucial difference between concessions made to terrorists when they are conducting a bombing campaign or holding hostages at gunpoint and concessions made in the context of a peace process designed to bring a permanent end to violence. It is important to stress that the counter-terrorism guidelines summarised at the beginning of this chapter apply to the former situation and not the latter. In the first edition of this book I warned against the dangers of the British government making premature and unilateral concessions to IRA/Sinn Fein in the course of the peace efforts. At the time of writing the IRA had not parted with a single ounce of Semtex, or a single bullet. However, in May 2000 the IRA did make a very useful confidence-building gesture by allowing the international arms inspectors to visit their arms dumps and in 2005 General de Chastelaine, head of the international decommissioning body, reported that the IRA had decommissioned all its weapons.

Critics of the hardline rule of law counter-terrorism policy outlined above have argued that the main argument against it is that it does not work. If by that they mean there is a great deal of terrorism going on in many parts of the world then it is true: but the hardline approach is not being applied at international level because there is no supranational sovereign body or law-enforcement body capable of implementing such a policy on a global level, and there are many democratic governments which, for one reason or another, have not adopted the hardline policy to combat terrorism within their borders. Nor should we lose sight of the fact that there are still regimes actively sponsoring international terrorism and providing safe havens for terrorist groups. It is also clear that many countries have vacillated between a hard policy and a policy of weakness or overt appeasement.

However, if we look at the cases of the democratic states that have adopted the hardline policy to combat a specific domestic terrorist challenge we find that some have succeeded in defeating quite serious terrorist campaigns without inflicting irrevocable harm on their democratic process or legal systems.[1] Italy, Germany, France and Belgium, all of whom have deployed a hardline approach against the Red Army or fought Communist terrorism in the 1970s and early 1980s, succeeded in these efforts.

For example, the Italian authorities introduced wide-ranging additional legal powers to help combat terrorists as early as the mid 1970s. In 1975 Oronzo Reale, then Minister of Justice, introduced what became known as the 'Legge Reale' which gave the police increased powers of arrest, search merely on suspicion and a greater use of firearms. However, it was not until the later 1970s that the Italians introduced a system of more effective coordination between the various police forces and secret agencies such as the intelligence services. The key vehicle providing this urgently needed central direction, leadership and coordination for counter-terrorism was the newly established Ufficio Central per le Investigazioni e le Operazioni Speciali (UGIGOS), under the aegis of the Interior Minister and with General Dalla Chiesa as 'Supremo'. There is no doubt that the defeat of the Red Brigades was hastened by their own internal crisis of morale and solidarity, and by the fact that they became increasingly alienated and isolated from public opinion after they had kidnapped and murdered the former Italian prime minister, Aldo Moro.[2]

Nevertheless, it was the greatly strengthened central direction of the counter-terrorism effort and its enhanced proactive intelligence capability which enabled the Italian police and judicial authorities to deliver the *coup de grâce* against the Red Brigades.[3] In the early 1980s the judicial authorities were given the scope to offer real incentives to convicted terrorists to turn state's evidence. The so-called *pentiti* (repentant) law gave courts the discretion to reduce sentences very substantially where convicted terrorists provided tangible information leading to the arrest and conviction of fellow-terrorists. By 1982 no less than 389 *pentiti*, of whom 78 had actively cooperated with the police and judiciary, had come forward. This new measure was introduced at just the right moment, when the terrorist movement's morale was sagging badly. It was brilliantly successful in providing the police with detailed information which helped them to crack open the Red Brigade cells and columns. By 1985 the Government could report that no less than 1,280 terrorists were in gaol. Moreover, the success was achieved without undermining the independence of the judiciary and without abandoning the democratic process.

German, French and British experience

In the 1970s the main West German counter-terrorist laws were aimed at apprehending suspects and improving coordination of the police forces' activities in combating terrorism. However, additional laws that came into force in 1987 defined terrorist offences in some detail and broadened the concept of complicity. Minimum penalties for terrorist offences were raised.

A parallel development was the establishment of strong centralised structures of coordination and control in counter-terrorism intelligence and policing. A specialist anti-terrorism unit was set up within the BKA (Bundeskrimindant; Federal Office of Criminal Investigation in Germany). In 1972 GSG9 was established as a crack counter-terrorist paramilitary unit, and this first proved its worth with the brilliantly successful rescue of passengers and crew on board a Lufthansa airliner hijacked to Mogadishu in October 1977. But by far the most significant innovation in the FRG's response was the development of a formidable computerised bank of counter-terrorism data. It was this data which helped the West German police to capture some of the key members of the Red Army Faction who were on the run. A small residue managed to evade capture, but once the leadership and hard-core of the organisation were captured, the RAF ceased to be a significant threat and it has gradually withered away.[4] As in the Italian case, the authorities' success against the terrorists was not bought at the price of the democratic process and rule of law, though this is not to deny that there are many well-informed observers who believe that serious mistakes of overreaction were made and that these had a counterproductive impact. Even so, the police were successful overall in the quelling of the RAF.

The case of France is far more complex. French policy on terrorism has undergone major vacillations from a hard line to a soft line and then back again. When it came to power in 1981 the Mitterrand government followed a softer and more conciliatory policy towards terrorists than its predecessor. It gave an amnesty to hundreds of terrorists, and many of those freed went back into active terrorism. The death penalty was abolished and the state security court, despite its reputation for expertise and effectiveness in dealing with terrorist cases over the previous 18 years, was closed down. It soon became apparent that this policy was a dismal failure. Two terrorists released under amnesty became key figures in a wave of terrorism. The figures of deaths caused by terrorism began to rise sharply.

In 1982 the government reverted to hardline measures. It proscribed Action Directe, set up a 'council on terrorism' within the government to oversee the counter-terrorism policy, established the new position of Secretary of State for Public Security to deal with terrorism, and tightened the laws on the sale of firearms. In May 1986 the Chirac government introduced further hardline measures, following another spate of terrorist attacks in France. Gaol sentences of 20 years were instituted for the most serious offences, and the law was changed to allow incentives of remission of sentences to convicted terrorists who informed on their fellow terrorists – a French version of the Italian *pentiti* legislation. The police were given the power to stop any person and request identification. The length of time those suspected of terrorism offences could be held for questioning was increased from 48 hours to four days. These measures undoubtedly contributed to the undermining of extreme-left terrorism in France, although French police also had the good luck to be able to discover and arrest the hardcore leadership of Action Directe's international wing at a farm near Orleans!

It must be admitted that the French have not been so successful in their efforts to combat the spillover of GIA terrorism into France and other terrorist incidents related to the Middle East. But in dealing with the spillover of ETA terrorism France has, since the mid 1980s, played a major role in assisting the Spanish authorities to capture the top leadership of the movement and in helping curtail

ETA's use of the French side of the border as a base of operations and safe haven. In dealing with this particular problem they have followed a commendably consistent and highly effective hard line.

But, say the critics, what about Britain's counter-terrorism track record? Why was it that the British government and security forces were unable to defeat the IRA in 27 years leading up to the latest IRA ceasefire? Why is it that the hardline approach has apparently failed in this case? It is certainly true that the British have been unable to defeat the IRA. But they have been able to reduce considerably the number of deaths from terrorism. In 1972 there were 467 deaths as a result of terrorist violence in the Province. By the later 1980s and early 1990s the total annual figure had fallen to less than 100.[5] This represents a considerable achievement on the part of the security forces when one bears in mind the inherent intractability of the conflict and the fact that the IRA has been able to exploit the long border with the Republic to mount attacks in the Province. It has also used the Republic as a safe haven, to store its huge supply of weaponry and for planning, training, recruitment and other important aspects of its activities. Given these uniquely difficult circumstances it was a major achievement for the British security forces to prevent Northern Ireland from escalating into full-scale civil war and thus to buy time for the politicians to find a political solution to the underlying conflict which would be acceptable to the majority of the population on both sides of the sectarian divide. Hence, it can be reasonably argued that by following a consistent hardline approach on the security front, the police and the British Army (which is deployed to assist the civil power) have helped to make the current peace process possible. The British government did not enter the peace process out of weakness, or because they believed that the IRA was becoming too powerful to be defeated. The position between the IRA and the security forces at the start of the peace process was a stand off.

Furthermore I would argue that it would be reckless to assume that the hardline response to terrorism can be safely discarded. The peace process is not guaranteed to succeed. There is a possibility that the IRA will return to violence if they do not succeed in getting their demands at the conference table. We should bear in mind that there is no previous case in Western Europe of a terrorist movement succeeding in transferring into a peaceful political party. It is also wise to bear in mind the possibility of a split in the Republican movement leading to a splinter group continuing[6] with terrorism rather than accepting anything that smacks of political compromise which emerges from the conference table. In these circumstances hardline counter-terrorism will need to be pursued with even more determination and vigour than before. One of the most serious weaknesses of Britain's counter-terrorism policy in Northern Ireland over the years would need to be addressed: the criminal justice system would have to be strengthened sufficiently to be able to prosecute and convict the leaders and godfathers of terrorism for their role in organising the campaigns of murder. I know of no example in the world where the hardline counter-terrorism policy of a liberal democracy succeeded without having brought the terrorist leaders to justice.

Some critics of the hardline approach dismiss it on the grounds that it fails to resolve the underlying political causes of the conflict concerned, and that it 'criminalises' those who are waging a political struggle for their ideals. I have argued strongly in Chapter 5 that politics and diplomacy should be used to the fullest extent to try to prevent internal and international conflicts from breaking out, or try to terminate them once they have already begun. This is unlikely, however, to satisfy the irreconcilable groups who believe they must continue to wage violence until they achieve their maximum demands: all one can hope is that political and diplomatic agreements and reforms may leave those who wish to continue waging violence relatively isolated and hence less politically powerful. But I fail to see how the pursuit of political and diplomatic agreement with those prepared to dispense with the use of violence invalidates the hardline approach involving law enforcement and criminal justice. How else is the government going to contend with those extreme factions that refuse to compromise and continue to wage terrorist violence, defying the rule of law and the democratic majority and violating and threatening the most basic human right of their fellow citizens: the right to life?

It is also naïve to assume that all groups waging terrorism or planning to do so are susceptible to a conflict-resolution approach based on bargaining and political compromise. What possible basis is there, for example, for a political agreement between the Japanese government and a bizarre and dangerous religious cult such as Aum Shinrikyo,[7] the group which mounted a nerve gas attack on the Tokyo underground system? Should President Clinton have held some political negotiation with the shadowy extreme-right group responsible for the Oklahoma bombing? Should President George W. Bush have been ready to negotiate with Osama bin Laden? Obviously not. Law-enforcement and criminal justice are the only sensible ways of dealing with dangerous fanatical groups of this kind.

As for the claim that it is wrong to 'criminalise' terrorists, the short answer is that by using terrorism they criminalise themselves. It is precisely because terrorists, by definition, follow a systematic policy of terror, that their acts are analogous to crimes. The very notion of crime, even in the most primitive legal systems, implies the moral responsibility of individuals for their actions, and hence for any violation of the legal code. We cannot make a general rule that terrorists are to be exempted from criminal responsibility unless we are either prepared to plead their irresponsibility on grounds of insanity or are willing to allow the whole moral or legal order to be undermined by deferring to the terrorist. In most legal systems the typical acts of terrorist groups (such as bombings, murders, kidnappings and wounding) constitute serious offences under the prevailing codes. Murder is, without exception, punishable under the legal codes of all states.

It must be admitted that all the major democracies have from time to time failed to uphold the highest standards in their application of counter-terrorism policies and laws. It ill behoves the UK and other EU governments to criticise the grave departures from the rule of law by the administration of President George W. Bush while turning a blind eye to their own failings and grubby compromises.

A glaring example was the release of Abdelbaset al-Megrahi, the only man convicted for the bombing of Pan Am 103 over Lockerbie, Scotland in December

1988, killing 259 passengers and crew and 11 people on the ground in Lockerbie. It was the worst crime of mass murder committed in the British Isles. After a long and extremely complex international investigation, al-Megrahi, a Libyan working for the Gaddafi regime, was the only person to be convicted for the Lockerbie bombing. The UK government promised the United Nations and the US Government that al-Megrahi would serve his sentence in a British gaol. It must be remembered that although this atrocity took place in British airspace, the aircraft was an American airliner and the majority of the passengers were American. Because the bombing of Pan Am 103 was carried out over Scotland, the trial of al-Megrahi and another Libyan suspect, who was acquitted, was held under Scots law and before very senior Scottish judges in a special court held in the Netherlands.

The decision in August 2009 to release al-Megrahi on compassionate grounds was apparently made as a result of the Scottish devolved administration being presented with a medical opinion that al-Megrahi was suffering from prostate cancer and had only three months to live. However, this decision appears extraordinary when one bears in mind the seriousness of the terrorist crime involved, and the important foreign policy and national security implications of any decision to release al-Megrahi. While it is true that Scotland has its own judicial system of which it is justly proud, the UK government should of course have been able to exercise a veto over al-Megrahi's release because of the major foreign policy and UK wider security implications of releasing a prisoner who had been convicted of a crime of mass murder, when the majority of the victims were citizens of Britain's closest ally and when the bereaved relatives were bound to be shocked and angered by al-Megrahi's release. Prime Minister David Cameron (leader of the opposition at Westminster when al-Megrahi was released) condemned the decision at the time. In an article in the *Wall Street Journal* (20 July 2010) David Cameron compared the way al-Megrahi was treated with the fate of the victims of the Pan Am 103 bombing: 'They [the victims of the bombing] weren't allowed to go home and die in their own bed with their relatives around them.' A particularly damaging long-term consequence of the al-Megrahi release is that it weakens the UK's credibility as a partner in international judicial cooperation, including with our closest allies. Why should they rely on the UK government's pledge to honour agreements about the handling of cases of international terrorism and the punishment of convicted terrorists?

At the time of writing (summer 2010) there was no evidence that the Scottish Justice Secretary, Kenny MacAskill, was influenced by the UK's Labour government's desperate wish to help BP obtain lucrative Libyan oil contracts. We know that BP lobbied the British government to push through a prisoner transfer agreement with the Gaddafi regime and that Libya insisted it should cover al-Megrahi, but we also know that the SNP minority government in Scotland opposed the transfer agreement, and insisted that the decision to release al-Megrahi was made purely on medical grounds. However, it was, to say the least, mighty convenient for the Labour government in London to be able to disclaim any responsibility for al-Megrahi's release, convenient but certainly not honourable. The Scottish First Minister, Alex Salmond, insisted that the Scottish devolved administration was kept in the dark about the negotiations with the Gaddafi regime on oil contracts. As Scotland is not an independent sovereign state its devolved administration did not have the background knowledge or the authority to make a decision with such serious implications for foreign and security policy. The main lesson of this murky affair is surely that such matters must be the responsibility of central government.

The role of the military

Let us now consider the third line of attack by critics of the hardline liberal democratic counter-terrorism policy based on the primacy of the law-enforcement and criminal justice systems. The critics I refer to here are those who argue that terrorists are in reality waging war and that the most effective and appropriate way of dealing with such a threat is by a fully militarised response, that is by deploying the armed forces to fight an all-out war, with no holds barred, in order to suppress it.[8]

This concept of a fully militarised response is quite distinct from the use of the military in aid of the civil power (MACP), so clearly exemplified in Northern Ireland since 1969. Under MACP the military's role is strictly limited to support of the police and the civil authorities, and the army is responsible to the Chief Constable of the PSNI (previously the RUC) for assisting in the maintenance of law and order and the protection of the community and can be held accountable for its actions under the criminal and civil laws. As discussed in the next chapter, this peacekeeping or quasi-constabulary role is a very difficult one for the army to adapt to and sustain for a prolonged period. The armed forces are trained for the external defence role and for the use of maximum force or a peacekeeping role. In a quasi-constabulary or peacekeeping role the task of the army is to use minimum force in assisting the police to enforce the law and to protect the community. I argue in Chapter 7 that there are very strong reasons why governments of liberal states should only employ troops for internal security purposes with the very greatest reluctance, and that if they are compelled to deploy them they should seek to withdraw at the earliest opportunity. This is not meant as a criticism of the policy of using the army in aid of the civil power in Northern Ireland. In 1969 the then Labour Home Secretary James Callaghan and his colleagues had no alternative but to commit troops to Northern Ireland: it was essential because of the escalation of sectarian or inter-communal conflict and the total loss of confidence in one section of the community in the police. Moreover, as I argue in Chapter 7, despite occasional serious errors of judgement and policy, perhaps unavoidable in such a sensitive and intractable conflict situation, the British Army's overall contribution in support of the police and in reducing the lethality of the IRA's terrorist campaign has been vital: without it Northern Ireland would almost certainly have been plunged into all-out civil war.

There is all the difference in the world between the skilful utilisation of the military within a carefully controlled liberal democratic response to terrorism by the civil authorities and a fully militarised response. A fully militarised response implies the complete suspension of the civilian legal system and its replacement by martial law, summary punishments, and the imposition of curfews, military censorship and extensive infringements of normal civil liberties in the name of the exigencies of war. By adopting a totally militarised response the government inevitably finds it has removed all constraints of legal accountability and minimum force, enabling the military commanders to deploy massively lethal and destructive firepower in the name of suppressing terrorism. A tragic example of this in a supposedly democratic state was Russia's use of air power to inflict devastation on Grozny, causing between 30,000 and 40,000 deaths among the civilian population.[9] Far from crushing the separatist movement of the Chechens, the brutality of the Russian armed forces' assault on Chechnya only served to strengthen the determination of the militants who in 1996 achieved the withdrawal of Russian forces following further acts of political violence, including mass hostage-taking, against the Russians. The final irony is that unleashing a totally militarised response at huge cost in human rights may ultimately prove counter-productive. Sadly, in the summer of 1999 the Russian government repeated these tragic errors in response to a rebellion led by a Chechen, Shamil Basayev, and Moscow apartment bombings in which several hundred died, blamed on Chechen terrorists.

A switch to a full-scale militarised response has particularly dangerous implications at international level. The governments of many countries, including the United States, Israel, India, Turkey and South Korea, have frequently blamed foreign states for their role in sponsoring or masterminding acts of terrorism against them. The hawkish politicians, think-tanks and commentators who advocate 'waging war' on terrorism are to be found advocating military reprisal attacks on alleged sponsors. This view became particularly influential in the United States during the second Reagan administration. Indeed, the Reagan administration adopted this policy when it launched bombing raids on Tripoli and Benghazi in April 1986 in retaliation against Libya's role in the La Belle discotheque bombing in West Berlin in which one US serviceman was killed and 230 customers injured. The Gaddafi regime was militarily powerless to prevent US air attack or to take any direct military action in response. But Gaddafi did use terrorist methods to exact vengeance on both the United States and on Britain, which had given the US government permission to launch the bombing attack on Libya from British air bases.[10]

However, quite aside from the question of whether such actions as the US bombing of Libya actually 'work' in deterring further terrorism from the sponsor states, there are two other major problems about the idea of waging a 'war against terrorism' in the international arena. First innocent members of the civilian population in the state targeted for retaliation may be killed or injured, as indeed was the case in the US raid on Libya. Given the scale of modern military firepower this is bound to be a risk in any act of military retaliation. Morally most people would find it easier to justify military retaliation if it was aimed at those actually responsible for sponsoring and planning terrorism. Second, there is an obvious danger, especially where the state accused of sponsoring terrorism shares a common border with the state launching military retaliation, that the outcome will be full-scale war. This has already happened in the Middle East, when in 1982 a terrorist attack triggered the Israeli invasion of Lebanon,[11] and in Kashmir where allegations and counter allegations concerning terrorism helped spark conflict between India and Pakistan and could do so again.[12] Now terrorism is undoubtedly an evil, but war is a far greater evil involving infinitely greater numbers of deaths and far greater destruction, with the attendant dangers of other states being drawn into the conflict. When one poses the basic questions about international consequences of the militarised response to state-sponsored or supported terrorism, one becomes more aware of the irresponsibility of those who assume that there is a simple 'military solution' of this nature. Surely the only thing that entitles states to call themselves 'civilised' in terms of international relations is behaviour which is consistent with respect for the rights of the innocent and for the basic principles of international law. Those who do not maintain these basic standards put themselves on the same level morally as the terrorist states. These criticisms of the 'war against terrorism' approach do not imply, however, that the military should have no role in the liberal democratic response. (I seek to explore what the role might be in Chapter 7.)

Having defended the underlying principles of the hardline liberal democratic response to terrorism, with its emphasis on law-enforcement and criminal justice, I will now move the discussion forward to identify the key institutions and resources required to carry it out effectively: (1) the intelligence services; (2) the police; and (3) the legal system. For the purposes of illustration I shall look at the roles of those institutions in British counter-terrorism policy before proceeding to examine some of the key problems and obstacles in developing enhanced international counter-terrorism cooperation among the democracies.

The role of the intelligence services

The archetypal terrorist organisation is numerically small and based on a structure of cells. These generally exercise a fair degree of operational independence and are obsessed with their own need for security and secrecy. Overall control by the terrorist leadership is ensured by the insistence on internal discipline and total loyalty to the organisation: those deemed to have committed serious offences against their organisation are ruthlessly punished. In cases where a member of the organisation is suspected of acting as an informer the punishment is likely to be death. Experienced terrorists develop sophisticated cover against detection. They are adept at hiding in the anonymity of the urban landscape and at swiftly changing their bases of operation. These features of the terrorist organisation face the security authorities with special problems, making them an extraordinarily difficult quarry, while the ready availability of light portable weapons and materials required for making home-made bombs makes it difficult to track down their lines of supply.

For all these reasons, a crucial requirement for defeating the terrorist campaign must be the development of high-quality intelligence, for unless the police are lucky enough to capture a terrorist red-handed at the scene of the crime it will only be by sifting through comprehensive and accurate intelligence data that the security authorities have any hope of locating the terrorists, uncovering their conspiracies and bringing them to justice. Therefore, in order to make the hardline counter-terrorism policy effective, the security authorities need to know a great deal about the groups and individuals seeking to pursue their aims by terrorism, about the precise nature of the objectives and plans, their political motivations and alignments, leadership, membership, logistic and financial resources and their links, if any, with other terrorist groups, terrorist states and international organised crime. Human intelligence (HUMINT) is the key method of gaining this knowledge about terrorist networks, and it is the acute shortage of this form of intelligence which has hobbled democracies in the efforts to unravel the Al Qaeda network.

The primary objective of an efficient intelligence service must be to prevent any insurgency or terrorism developing beyond the incipient stage. It is obvious that it will need a national remit, to avoid rivalry and duplication between regional police forces, and that it should be firmly under the control of civil authorities, and hence democratically accountable. In most liberal democracies the tasks of gathering, collating and analysing intelligence in the counter-terrorism field are shared by the foreign and domestic intelligence services, the Special Branch of the police, or its equivalent, and the technical agencies responsible for signals intelligence and other sources. Normally input from the police is very important because the routine police tasks of law-enforcement and combating crime at every level of the community give the police service an unrivalled 'bank' of background information from which contact information can be developed.

In October 1992 the British government gave the Security Service, better known as MI5, the lead role in intelligence operations against the IRA on the British mainland. This was criticised at the time, especially by the Metropolitan Police Special Branch, which had traditionally performed this task. On practical grounds, there was much to be said in favour of giving MI5 this new role. The service already had a great deal of experience in countering terrorism, and its then new director general, Stella Rimington, had previously headed MI5's counter-terrorism department.

The ending of the Cold War meant that the service had the resources for this new role, and it was uncomfortably clear that there was a huge gap in police intelligence on IRA cells on the mainland, and this meant that the 'active service units' were able to mount spectacular and hugely destructive attacks, such as the City of London bombings, with impunity.

Evidence of intensive MI5 intelligence and surveillance, which surfaced in the trials of the key IRA terrorists captured on the mainland prior to the September 1994 IRA ceasefire, gave graphic examples of the value of MI5's contribution to the fight against the IRA. The extent of their commitment to combating the threat from the Irish terrorists was emphasised by Stella Rimington in her Dimbleby Lecture in June 1994, when she described it as the service's most important task, taking up nearly half of its resources.

But the IRA ceasefire in 1994, and the real prospect of the removal of any long-term threat from Irish terrorism, now faced MI5 with an acute dilemma.

How could they resist Treasury demands for sharp cuts in manpower and funding? Clear signs that MI5 had been seeking to expand into new missions in fighting drug-trafficking and international organised crime emerged in January 1995 when the Chief Constables' Committee on Drug Crime expressed concern at reports that MI5 was hoping to take on an expanded role in fighting serious crime, and the Chief Commissioner of the City of London Police was reported to be seeking clarification on MI5's plans.

In May 1995, in reply to questions from Michael O'Brien, MP, a parliamentary adviser to the Police Federation, Michael Howard, the then Home Secretary, stated that he was prepared to consider proposals for MI5 to mount intelligence operations to combat serious crime. Some experts, such as Rupert Allison (author Nigel West), believed that MI5's expansion into fighting serious crime would require a change in the 1989 Security Service Act, under which MI5 was only allowed to operate in areas affecting national security, such as espionage, subversion and terrorism. Mr Howard implied that the language of the Security Service Act was not in itself an obstacle to MI5 undertaking these new tasks if a way could be found for the service to play a useful role in supporting the police. This would involve defining the growth of drug crime, money laundering and other forms of serious crime as a threat to national security. However, these definitional and legal issues were ultimately resolved and parliament approved the extension of MI5's role. Sadly in the process of devoting more effort to the IRA and organised crime, MI5 neglected the emergence of Al Qaeda's network

In tandem with the debate on the future role of MI5, in the light of the IRA ceasefire, there has also been intensive discussion on the future role of Scotland Yard's anti-terrorist branch. Despite the undoubted success of MI5 in its new lead role in intelligence against the IRA, it would be a grave mistake to assume that the Security Service is in a position to devote all its major resources to counter-terrorism and to ditch its traditional responsibilities for dealing with subversion, espionage and economic warfare. These are far from being irrelevant in the post-Cold War world. On the contrary, I would argue that the present new world disorder of bitter ethnic and religious conflicts and rivalry over resources is so volatile that we need a sophisticated intelligence capability more than ever. It is a harsh fact that many political leaders in Western governments, including Britain, were caught totally unprepared for Iraq's invasion of Kuwait and the bloody conflict in former Yugoslavia. It is not clear whether this was due to failures by intelligence services or by their political masters neglecting to use intelligence more accurately. Either way, it is unarguable that we still need intelligence capability of the highest quality. Nor can we depend wholly on signals intelligence and the sophisticated technology of GCHQ. Human intelligence is still indispensable in interpreting conflict and threat assessment, particularly to counter international terrorism.

This is an argument for a more efficient deployment of the intelligence services in their traditional roles, not for allowing them to colonise traditional police work. In any case, it should be remembered that the police in Britain have their own extremely effective intelligence function and the new and highly professional

National Criminal Intelligence Service. If extra intelligence resources are needed to fight serious crimes these should be invested in the police's own intelligence operations.

But what of the future of the secret intelligence agencies? Britain is not alone in experiencing bitter behind-the-scenes in-fighting as major intelligence agencies fight against swingeing cutbacks or in some cases for their very survival. In the wake of the exposure of Aldrich Ames as a Russian mole, the CIA faced demands for the resignation of its director, for a special investigative commission to examine the whole future of the intelligence agencies and, from some members of the Congress, even a call for the abolition of the CIA. Congress contains a number of fierce opponents of the agency and even its intelligence committees – traditionally more sympathetic to the aims and activities of the CIA – have been expressing strong dissatisfaction about the way in which the agency has handled not only the Ames affair but the whole business of adjusting its role to the post-Cold War environment. A major reason for the pressures on the American intelligence agencies is their sheer cost. Christopher Andrew, in his magisterial study *For the President's Eyes Only*,[13] observes that the US was spending approximately 20 times as much on SIGINT (signals intelligence) as Britain! In the early 1990s, Andrew estimates, the financial cost to the United States of remaining the sole intelligence superpower was 28 billion dollars in budgetary terms.

However, despite much agonising about costs and evidence of the fallibility of the CIA, it is obviously absurd to believe that the United States could manage its role as a global superpower without resort to the traditional weapon of all major states: a high-quality intelligence capability to anticipate, evaluate and monitor threats to its military, political and economic security. The intelligence failures over 9/11 only underline the need to reform and strengthen US intelligence.

The idea that the 'peace dividend' should enable these tasks to be carried out at a vastly reduced cost in the post-Cold War is obviously attractive to a hard-pressed president and Congress. The Clinton administration planned to cut the intelligence budget by roughly 25 per cent in 1998, and this was very much in line with the level of cuts in US defence spending. However, 9/11 showed that these dramatic reductions were the result of an over-optimistic assessment of the post-Cold War strategic environment.

A second major task for the intelligence agencies in the new world disorder is to monitor, evaluate and attempt to prevent the threat of proliferation of nuclear weapons and other weapons of mass destruction in regions of growing tensions and conflicts. The complexity and urgency of this task can be well illustrated in the case of Iran, which is clearly far closer to obtaining nuclear weapon capability than has previously been realised. Western intelligence experts now believe that Iran has been obtaining invaluable help from the Russians and Germans in developing its secret nuclear weapons programme, and some former Soviet experts in weapons of mass destruction technology have found some lucrative employment there. A senior Israeli intelligence official has stated: 'When we ask ourselves what is the biggest problem we face in the next decade … Iran's nuclear bomb is at the top of the list.'

The urgent need for Western intelligence agencies to monitor the proliferation of biological, chemical, radiological and nuclear weapons is underlined by Al Qaeda's known interest in obtaining weapons of mass destruction. The relevance of the intelligence services' work in monitoring the proliferation of weapons of mass destruction is, alas, all too evident in the field of counter-terrorism.

The task of counter-proliferation also has a direct bearing on counter-terrorism. The intelligence services have the important additional task of seeking to prevent weapons of mass destruction getting into the hands of terrorists.

The role of the police

The main burden of containing and defeating terrorism in liberal democratic states is carried by the police services. The countermeasures appropriate for the police in fighting terrorism are closely analogous to those required for combating other serious crimes of violence. But the tasks involved, if they are to be performed effectively, require an extensive knowledge of the *modus operandi*, weaponry and tactics of the terrorist groups involved, together with a range of resources and specialised knowledge, for example in the field of bomb disposal and the techniques of crime scene investigation at the site of an explosion, which are beyond the scope and resources of criminal investigation departments lacking experience in this field. Hence all the police services of major countries, which have experienced terrorism, have developed specialist anti-terrorist units.

The fact that the Security Service (MI5) has taken over the lead intelligence-gathering role on the Irish Republican threat may have misled members of the public into thinking that the Metropolitan Police role in combating the IRA threat has been discontinued. Nothing could be further from the truth. The police have a crucial and continuing role in counter-terrorism, and have developed a closely coordinated approach which has led to extremely successful joint operations with the Security Service.

An outstanding example of the success of a joint operation of this kind was the complex and unprecedented undercover operations by MI5, Special Branch and the Anti-Terrorist Branch which led to the conviction of an IRA gang at the Old Bailey in July 1997 for conspiring to bomb six electricity sub-stations in London and the southeast. If the plot had not been uncovered by the massive surveillance operation, London would have been paralysed by the blacking out of power supplies, and vital services, including hospitals and emergency services, would have been disrupted. In sentencing the six members of the gang to 35 years each in gaol for their part in the conspiracy, Mr Justice Scott Barker said: 'You were reckless to the number of people who might have been killed and maimed as a consequence of your planned bombings.' Commander John Grieve, head of the Anti-Terrorist Branch, described the conspiracy as 'the most sophisticated … they have ever launched', and the gang as being among 'the most dangerous, long-term criminals I have ever seen in one place'.

It emerged during the trial that tens of thousands of hours of surveillance work was involved in this joint operation, and 5,000 pages of documentary evidence and hours of surveillance film were provided by the prosecution. When the police raided a house used by the IRA gang in Peckham, south London, they discovered 37 timers and power units ready to be fitted with Semtex and detonators. For the prosecution, Mr Nigel Sweeney said: 'Had the conspiracy succeeded, it would have resulted in serious and widespread loss of electricity to London and the South East. Supplies to customers would have been affected over a considerable period, with little likelihood that supplies would have returned for months or more.'

It is clear that in order to combat sophisticated terrorist conspiracies, constituting not only a threat to life but also a major potential threat to the economy, a highly coordinated and sophisticated counter-terrorism capability is absolutely essential, and the police and the intelligence services need the resources required to maintain it. In view of the obvious danger of further attacks by cells linked to Al Qaeda it would be the height of folly for the UK to dismantle or weaken its counter-terrorism agencies and resources.

Hence, Britain has a particularly strong reason for maintaining its guard. As Al Qaeda operates globally, one could sensibly argue that no country can really afford to be without a specialist counter-terrorism intelligence-gathering and police capability.

There is an additional problem created by the highly fragmented local police force structure in the United Kingdom. The lion's share of the counter-terrorism expertise and resources is held by the Metropolitan Police in London. Police forces in the other major conurbations, Manchester and Birmingham, have certainly built up some resources and expertise of their own. However, there is a need to create a more effective nation-wide capability of police response which can be called upon in the event of a terrorist attack outside these major cities.

The role and effectiveness of legislation as a weapon against terrorism

After almost 30 years of experience of international terrorism there is still great uncertainty and controversy among jurists and other specialists on the role and effectiveness of law and legal systems generally in combating terrorists. Among practitioners and leading government officials, there tends to be far more agreement about what works and what doesn't, and particularly strong agreement about the relatively small number of laws that have been of exceptional value against terrorism.

Part of the difficulty involved in assessing the efficacy of specific legislation stems from the wide range of functions and aims for which it can be employed. Some legislation is clearly aimed at *prophylaxis*, reforms designed to have a preventative effect by attempting to redress underlying grievances that might otherwise lead to extreme disaffection among sectors of the population. A clear example of this was the statute passed by the Spanish parliament in 1978 to give a large degree of autonomy to the Basque region. Other laws are aimed at *deterrence*, such as the laws produced in the United States and other countries instituting severe penalties for aircraft hijacking. Much anti-terrorism legislation is designed to increase the level of protection of life and property by *providing law-enforcement authorities with the powers needed to assist them in apprehension and conviction of those who commit crimes of terrorism.* Obvious examples of this are laws designed to enhance international cooperation, such as laws regarding extradition and prosecution under the *aut dedere aut judicare* principle, or the law passed by Congress in 1996 requiring the 'tagging' of explosives. Some legislation appears to have primarily symbolic or psychological functions of *expressing public revulsion* at particular outrages and *reassuring the public that something is being done.* One normally thinks of emergency powers legislation as being exclusively concerned with measures to *enhance public security* and to *facilitate the suppression of terrorist organisations.* However, it is clear that a primary function of the section of Britain's Prevention of Terrorism Act proscribing the Provisional IRA was to give legislative expression to public revulsion and reassurance that severe measures were being taken against the terrorists. In many ways proscription makes the task of gathering intelligence on the terrorist organisation more difficult. But in the atmosphere of public anger following the Birmingham pub bombings of 21 November 1974 it would have been totally unacceptable for the IRA to have been allowed to continue to raise funds and distribute propaganda openly. Last, but not least, we must bear in mind that many other areas of criminal law, for example those dealing with the control of firearms and explosives, extortion, racketeering and drug-trafficking, have a crucial bearing on society's ability to combat terrorism. If key sections of the criminal law become outdated, this will enormously hamper anti-terrorism efforts. For example, the British authorities were given the results of telephone intercepts by the US National Security Agency which could have been crucial in identifying and convicting the Omagh bombers, but in Britain, unlike the United States, tapped telephone conversations are not admissible as evidence in Court. It is worth noting that intercepts obtained in the United States played a vital role in the trial in the UK which convicted conspirators in the liquid bomb plot to destroy seven airliners en route from Heathrow to North America. It seems extraordinary that the US along with other democracies are able to use intercepted evidence in terrorist cases when the UK cannot. The UK authorities should take a fresh look at this issue.

It was clear by the mid 1990s that the UK's Prevention of Terrorism Act was hopelessly outdated. Anti-Terrorism Legislation needed to incorporate the safeguards of the European Convention on Human Rights (introduced into UK law by the Human Rights Act) and the Police and Criminal Evidence Act. Lord Lloyd's wide-ranging and far-sighted *Inquiry into Legislation Against Terrorism* highlighted these problems and proposed much needed measures to deal with international terrorism. The Terrorism Act 2000 was largely based on Lord Lloyd's recommendations.

However, in 2001, in the immediate aftermath of 9/11, the then UK Home Secretary, David Blunkett, brought in the Anti-Terrorism Crime and Security Act which reintroduced detention without trial in Section 4 of the Act, permitting the internment of a small number of foreigners who had arrived in the UK, were suspected of involvement in terrorism, but who the police felt unable to prosecute through lack of evidence and who could not be sent back to their countries of origin because of the real danger that they might be tortured.

We also need to bear in mind the inherent limitations of any legislation effort to curb terrorism. By definition terrorist groups are making war on legality. They claim that their ends justify their means: that they are for 'true justice' and to avenge the injustices committed by the system they so bitterly oppose, whose institutions and judicial procedures they view with such hatred and contempt. It is an illusion to believe that the fanaticism and determination of well-established terrorist organisations can be defeated by laws alone, even of the most severe and punitive kind. Among modern democratic states, Israel has had to confront the most protracted and intensive long-term struggle with organisations and state sponsors using the weapon of terrorism. Israel has responded with some of the most draconian measures ever used by a democratic state since the upsurge of modern international terrorism in the late 1960s, ranging from military courts, curfews for 'collective punishment' of whole areas, the blowing up of homes of the families of alleged terrorists and a mass expulsion of Hamas militants.

It is ironic that neither the severely repressive measures, nor the Labour Israeli government's efforts to achieve a peace process with the Palestinians following the Declaration of Principles signed in September 1993, succeeded in curbing attacks by the extremist groups, Hamas and Islamic Jihad. Between the signing of the Declaration of Principles and 4 March 1996 a total of 203 Israelis were killed in terrorist attacks inside Israel's own borders. In the two-year period from 6 April 1996 to March 1998, 136 people were killed in 13 attacks by suicide bombers, mostly on buses.

Legislation intended to help combat terrorism can thus be defeated by the fanaticism, ruthlessness and cunning tactics of terrorists. It can also be gravely weakened, if not totally undermined, by lack of political will on the part of the governments, cowardice by judiciaries and professional incompetence, negligence and, in some instances, corruption, on the part of the police and prison officers. Many experts believe that the Italian authorities showed a conspicuous lack of will in their failure to bring the perpetrators of extreme-right-wing terrorism to justice in the 1970s and early 1980s. The existence of an adequate framework of laws is not enough: a legal system is only as good as the people who operate it.

Most democratic states that have experienced prolonged and lethal terrorist campaigns of any scale within their borders have at some stage introduced special anti-terrorist measures aimed at strengthening the normal law in order to deal with a grave terrorist emergency. However, these emergency powers carry risks for the democratic system and it is important to identify them.

It must be a cardinal principle of a liberal democracy in dealing with the problems of terrorism, however serious they may be, never to be tempted to use methods which are incompatible with the liberal values of humanity, liberty and justice. It is a dangerous illusion to believe one can 'protect' liberal democracy by suspending liberal rights and forms of government. Contemporary history abounds in examples of 'emergency' or 'military' rule carrying countries from democracy to dictatorship with irrevocable ease.

Therefore, even in its most severe crises, the liberal democracy must seek to remain true to itself, avoiding on the one hand the dangers of sliding into repression, and on the other the evil consequences of inertia, inaction and weakness, in upholding its constitutional authority and preserving law and order. Another kind of betrayal is the deliberate suspension or limitation of civil liberty on grounds of expediency. However hard the going gets in coping with severe internal or international terrorism, or both, a liberal democratic government has a primary duty to preserve constitutional government. The attempt to rule by emergency decree, abandonment of democratic processes and fundamental abridgements of a democratic constitution must be resisted. The government must show its measures against terrorism are solely directed at quelling the terrorists and their collaborators and at defending society against terrorist attack.

As argued above, the fundamental objections to repressive overreaction to terrorism rest on moral and political principle. However, there is also abundant evidence to show that such responses play into the hands of terrorists and, if prolonged, become totally counterproductive. An example of an emergency measure employed by the British authorities which is now widely recognised as having been counterproductive was internment without trial in Northern Ireland, a power which has not been used since the mid 1970s and which the Labour government formally abandoned in 1998. The Northern Ireland Stormont government urged its use in 1971 on the grounds that normal judicial processes were proving incapable of providing essential protection for society. Witnesses, juries and magistrates were being intimidated and the police were frustrated in their efforts to bring known terrorists to trial to have them convicted. When the government decided to use this measure in 1971 the intelligence on which the operation was based was gravely deficient, and large numbers of the people netted by the security forces had little or nothing to do with Provisional IRA terrorism. Internment without trial involves a major abridgement of civil liberties: the removal of the right of Habeas Corpus. Its use should only be contemplated in the eventuality of an all-out civil war, when all other means of curbing the escalation of violence on a massive scale have failed. The use of internment in 1971 provided a powerful recruiting sergeant for the IRA. It convinced many Catholics that repression and discrimination against the minority community had to be resisted. Terrorist violence greatly increased following the introduction of internment, and the total number of deaths from terrorism in Northern Ireland in 1972 (467) is the highest ever. Political and funding support for the IRA in America greatly increased. Another serious consequence of internment is that the process injects a fresh cohort of extremely bitter and also better-trained and determined people into the ranks of the terrorist organisation. Internment became a kind of 'Staff College' for terrorists. The only satisfactory way for a liberal state to put terrorists safely out of action for a very long time is to convict them, and if they have committed serious offences, to insist on them serving appropriate long prison terms.

Emergency powers tend to be introduced as a package of measures. Some of these are likely to have little discernible effect on the level of violence. Others, as we have seen above, may ultimately prove counterproductive. However, it is important to remember that some of these measures have proved remarkably effective. An example of a highly effective strategy was the introduction in the early 1980s by the Italian authorities of the *pentiti* laws to help in their struggle to suppress the Red Brigades (see p. 80). This measure (as we have seen) led to the conviction and imprisonment of many terrorists, and to the virtual collapse of the Red Brigades.

It is therefore essential to assess the individual components of emergency powers adopted to combat terrorism before coming to hasty conclusions about the role and value of special anti-terrorist legislation in democratic states. Certain additional powers are almost invariably sought by police in really severe terrorist campaigns: increased penalties for terrorist offences; powers to stop and search pedestrians and vehicles and to search houses without warrant; the proscription of organisations; wider powers of arrest and extended detention without a criminal charge being brought against the suspect.

It is certainly the view of the police in the UK and other democratic countries within the European Union that in the circumstances of a terrorist campaign which threatens security of the public such powers are essential. However, if special anti-terrorist legislation does have to be used it should be subject to three crucial safeguards:

1. All aspects of the anti-terrorist policy and its implementation should be under the overall control of the civil authorities and hence democratically accountable.
2. The government and security forces must conduct all anti-terrorist operations within the law. They should do all in their power to ensure that the normal legal processes are maintained, and that those charged with terrorist offences are brought to trial before the courts of law.
3. Special powers, which may become necessary to deal with a terrorist emergency, should be approved by the legislature only for a fixed and limited period, at the very minimum on an annual basis. This should be subject to the legislature's right to rescind the special powers in whole or in part if circumstances alter. Emergency powers should be clearly and simply drafted, published as widely as possible, and administered impartially.

The influence of reform legislation

If it is difficult to assess the effectiveness of emergency anti-terrorist legislation in curbing terrorism, it is even more challenging to try to evaluate the influence of reform legislation in preventing terrorism. There are some fairly clear-cut cases. For example, the Italian Senate's far-sighted measure in 1972 to accord autonomy to the predominantly German-speaking province of South Tyrol (Alto Adige) most probably prevented a major upsurge of terrorist violence between the German-speaking and Italian-speaking communities. The measures taken by the United States to give greater autonomy to Puerto Rico had a similarly dampening effect on extremist political violence in the island. Yet there are also cases where terrorist violence appears to have actually intensified in the wake of a particularly significant political reform measure. For example, in the year following the suspension of the Stormont government (long hated by the IRA) the monthly average of Provisional IRA killings rose from 13.3 in 1972 to 17.1 in 1976.

Under the March 1973 Constitution Act in Northern Ireland Catholics achieved an end to gerrymandering (the division of electoral constituencies so as to give one party an unfair advantage), a guaranteed role in government and the principle of 'one man, one vote'. Yet despite these victories and the much needed reforms in housing allocation and employment in the 1970s (the Fair Employment Agency started its work in 1977) the monthly average of Provisional IRA killings actually rose again from 7.3 in 1975 to 15.5 in December 1980.

In the Basque region on the other hand, ETA's monthly average of killings did decline steadily from 10.5 in March 1979, the month of elections to the newly autonomous Basque regional assembly, to 5.8 in October 1979 when the Basque Autonomy Statute was finally approved, to 4.8 in December 1981. It is clear that reforms which provide significant advances in the eyes of the moderates and large sectors of the population can have the effect of further isolating extremist groups and reducing levels of terrorist violence in the longer term. However, although levels of violence were reduced in the case of the Basques, the ETA maximalists continued to carry out lethal terrorist attacks.

In summary, one can say that reform legislation that makes considerable concessions to the legitimate concerns and demands of moderates can greatly reduce levels of terrorist violence. However, there are very few cases where the violence is totally eradicated, and the more common pattern (e.g. Northern Ireland, the Basque region, Corsica) is continuing residual terrorist violence by an irreconcilable minority of a minority.

The role and effectiveness of international legal measures against terrorism

The primary legal weapons against terrorism are national laws, and the task of applying them rests with the national criminal justice systems. But a great deal of modern terrorism is inherently international and many states perceive that they have a shared interest in enhancing international cooperation in order to suppress those forms of terrorism which they believe to be a threat to their national security. Hence there has been a series of international legal measures at global, regional and bilateral levels aimed at facilitating and strengthening international cooperation against such activities as aircraft hijacking, attacks on diplomats, and hostage-taking.[14] The main value lies in setting international standards and symbolising general awareness of international problems.

However, efforts for improvements in international legal cooperation are beset with considerable difficulties. Let us briefly identify some of the key constraints that limit the effectiveness of existing international conventions and which make the whole process of developing further international law both painfully slow and marginal in its contribution.

Nation-states have traditionally clung tightly to their monopoly of internal legal sovereignty. There is no current indication that they are now more willing to even consider relaxing this hold. Despite the spasmodic expressions of willingness to make daring innovations on the part of some EU states it seems highly unlikely that they are about to pool their sovereignty in sensitive matters crucially affecting national security, the suppression of crime and the maintenance of law and order. Such developments might one day become feasible if the EU countries at some future date decide to unite under a single federal government. While they remain independent nation-states, however, countries will continue to treat terrorism primarily, if not exclusively, as an internal responsibility.

This may seem curiously illogical in a European Union which has developed a single market and which, under the Schengen Agreement, has already experimented with the virtual abandonment of internal border controls between certain member states. After all, the terrorists and other criminal groups can now take full advantage of free movement across borders. They can shift their bases and their operations swiftly from capital to capital and can criss-cross frontiers to evade detection. Why then has there been such a snail's pace in the EU's response, with responsibility for cooperation in this field being left to intergovernmental cooperation between senior officials, working through the 'K4' Committee under the Third Pillar?[15] Why has there been so little effort even to explore the possibility of more significant EU innovations on this important issue?[16]

The major difficulty is that each state is proud of its own national laws and traditions. National publics may often criticise aspects of their own systems and demand reforms in the law, but they are not sympathetic to the idea that their own system should have to change in order to accommodate some supranational or intergovernmental design.

In addition to national difference and national chauvinism, there is a considerable residue of popular mistrust and suspicion concerning the quality of their neighbour's political and legal systems. Sometimes this is rooted in an earlier history of conflict and the feeling that you can never really rely on professions of good faith and goodwill by the government of a former enemy. Often it is based on sheer xenophobia.

A more intractable problem arises when one European government comes to the conclusion that the government of a neighbour state is actually shielding terrorists they wish to have extradited, or that neighbouring states are delaying or obstructing the process of rendering *mutual assistance* as required under Article 8 of the European Convention.

In really serious cases of interstate disagreements – as, for example, in the dealings between the Northern Ireland and Irish Republic judiciaries over the questioning of suspects and witnesses – the whole process of judicial and police cooperation can become jeopardised.

It was partly due to recognition of these profound problems that the drafters of the European Convention on the Suppression of Terrorism wisely allowed enormous flexibility.[17] They were particularly concerned not to exclude from the Convention states that had a deep attachment to constitutional traditions or guarantees of political asylum. This is, of course, the rationale behind Article 13 of the Convention which permits any state:

At the time of the signature of when depositing its instrument of ratification, acceptance or approval, to declare that it reserves the right to refuse extradition in response of any offence mentioned in Article 1 which it considers to be a political offence, an offence connected with a political offence or an offence inspired by political motives.[18]

At first sight this Article of Reservation appears to negate the whole value of the Convention and its important core proposition that crimes of terrorism should be treated as serious common crimes.

There is no doubt that Article 13 does in a very fundamental sense contradict the basic philosophy of the Convention. It is a powerful testimony to the deep differences in constitutional and legal traditions to which I have already referred. However, it is also important to recognise that the Article of Reservation does not, in effect, totally undermine the Convention's efficacy. There is a crucial rider to the effect that when a state invokes Article 13 it has an obligation to take into due consideration, when evaluating the character of the offence, any particular serious aspects of the offence, including whether:

a. It created a collective danger to the life, physical integrity or liberty of persons;[19]
b. it affected persons foreign to the motives behind it;
c. cruel or vicious means were used in the commission of the offence.

On signature of the Convention, France, Italy and Norway all declared their intention to invoke the Article of Reservation (though in the case of France, the declaration is couched in such cloudy ambiguous terms that it implies that additional Reservations will be entered). Five states have invoked Article 13 when depositing ratification.

However, in June 1996 the EU member states announced an agreement on the 1957 Council of Europe Extradition Convention. Under this agreement the political motivation of an offence will no longer be used as grounds for refusing extradition. It is true that member states will still have the option to limit the application of this general rule to those offences listed in the 1977 European Convention of the Suppression of Terrorism, Article 1, but as these cover all the major types of terrorist crime, the new agreement should greatly assist in securing the extradition of terrorists. Moreover, it also allows for the extradition of persons who knowingly and intentionally contribute to the commission of terrorism by criminal association: either member states will consider such behaviours as extraditable offences *per se*, or they will renounce the dual criminality of principle. Under this new agreement, and in contrast to the 1957 Extradition Convention, the extradition of a person between EU states can no longer be refused solely on the grounds that the person sought is a national of the requested state. However, states may enter into reservations to the effect that they will not extradite their own nationals or will only do so under certain circumstances. It should be stressed that this EU agreement has been formulated on the basis that it must be fully compatible with the European Human Rights Convention. In principle there is no doubt that this agreement enhanced the EU's legal arrangements for dealing with terrorist crime. We must wait and see whether the EU member states will demonstrate their political will by translating these declaratory principles into more effective and consistent judicial cooperation against terrorism.

By late 2005 the EU states had adopted and begun to implement another valuable measure of judicial cooperation, the European Arrest Warrant, which avoids the need for lengthy court cases to establish a prima facie case for extradition.

The experience of the past 30 years shows that the most valuable international cooperation in preventing and suppressing terrorism among democracies both within and without the EU is bilateral cooperation on such matters as intelligence sharing, cross-border policing and the extradition of suspects. It should be added that much of the most efficient collaboration of this kind takes place at a highly informal level between intelligence and police services. There is a need for more general multilateral treaties to cover the terrorism issues, but more general multilateral conventions often end up representing the lowest common denominator of agreement and tend to be of about as much practical use as statements in favour of motherhood. For a closer look at the EU's response to 9/11 see Chapter 11.

7 The role of the military in combating terrorism

The basic questions this chapter seeks to examine are of potential interest to all major democratic governments and societies. What role, if any, should the military play in combating terrorism? Chapter 4 has discussed the crucial role of the military in countering terrorist-backed insurgencies. We must now turn to the part the military play in countering terrorism unaccompanied by any wider insurgency. Most of the well-established democracies have sophisticated military forces; including Special Forces units trained for tasks such as hostage rescue, bomb-disposal units, etc. Hence, although the police and intelligence services play the major role in preventing and combating terrorism, for specialist roles such as hostage rescue from an embassy or an airliner on the tarmac, or bomb disposal, for which the police may not have the appropriate training and resources, specialist military units may be essential if lives are to be saved.

However, experience shows us that we should be wary of assuming that the 'solution' to any terrorist campaign is a fully militarised campaign. Militarising the response in such cases may become a counter-productive over-reaction. The terrorists can point to soldiers on the streets as evidence that they are fighting a 'war' against a ruthless 'enemy', 'occupier' or 'invader', and we use this as a propaganda and recruitment tool. Putting uniformed personnel on the streets greatly adds to the number of targets for the terrorists, blending in with the civilian community. Moreover, when the authorities and the police become too dependent on the military it becomes even harder to withdraw the troops. Last but not least, misuse of the military in an overreaction to terrorism detracts from the military's capability for external defence tasks.

The military warfare model

War can be briefly defined as armed conflict between two or more parties, nations or states. The days when international lawyers could claim that the term war only applied to armed conflict between states have surely long gone. The twentieth century and the opening years of the new century are replete with examples of internal wars of all kinds – civil wars, ethnic and tribal wars, religious wars and insurgencies. In common usage the term war is widely used to refer to any conflict relating to war or with the characteristics of war.

Is the Coalition against Terrorism involved in a war against the Al Qaeda network? It would seem absurd to deny it. Al Qaeda's leaders declared war on the US and its allies. President George W. Bush declared a war on terrorism after the 9/11 attacks. We can hardly claim that the term war is being used purely metaphorically in this context. 9/11 killed more people than the Pearl Harbor bombing. US, British and other troops have been fighting Al Qaeda militants in Afghanistan, Iraq, Yemen and other countries. It is a different kind of war, an asymmetrical war in which one cannot judge success or failure in terms of battlefield or the numbers of tanks and aircraft destroyed or captured. The enemy is largely unseen, hiding among the civilian environment in cities around the world.

However, it is one thing to recognise that the struggle against Al Qaeda terrorism has some of the characteristics of war, albeit a new kind of warfare: it is quite another to adopt the *military warfare model* as the framework for democratic and international response. If the military are accorded the dominant role in formulating counter-terrorism strategy it is perhaps predictable that they will give the armed forces the predominant role in implementing the strategy. In some respects the military warfare model is a tempting route for democratic governments, especially in circumstances where the terrorists have access to significant conventional weaponry or even some weapons of mass destruction, and when armed forces deployed against them have superior firepower, are well trained, experienced and of proven effectiveness in counter-terrorism roles. The military warfare model appears to offer some important additional advantages:

- It answers inevitable public and media demands for tough action against sponsors/perpetrators.
- By inflicting heavy costs on the terrorists and/or their sponsors, it offers a chance of deterring further attacks and sponsorship.
- It offers a possibility of conveying the deterrence message to a wider range of potential attackers/state sponsors internationally.
- It offers a possibility of inflicting a psychologically damaging blow at the enemy leadership which might undermine them or hasten their removal from power.

On the other hand there are grave problems and policy dilemmas involved in undertaking strategic offensive operations and military reprisals against terrorist groups abroad and their sponsor states:

- In many cases of terrorist attack it is extremely difficult, if not impossible, to obtain sufficient high-quality intelligence to determine with certainty the identity of the perpetrator responsible for the attack.
- A military attack/reprisal could provoke a wider conflict in which the advantages of the originally conceived counter-terrorist blow are outweighed by much wider costs.
- A reprisal which causes the death of innocent civilians carries the risk of losing the 'moral high ground' and the sympathy of international opinion.

- A military reprisal which is undertaken unilaterally may not carry the support of important allies and may cause added stresses and strains on alliances.
- A military reprisal may arouse false expectations among the general public of success in defeating terrorism, and lead to expectations of similar or intensified military action next time.

There is, at the strategic level, the much greater danger of military overreaction undermining the values of the rule of law and protection of human rights which democracies have a duty to uphold. For example as the activities of the Russian army in Chechnya and Bosnian Serb militia in Bosnia tragically demonstrate, military forces do not automatically deal with separatism or other forms of rebellion with due regard to human rights principles, democracy and the rule of law. In these and many other cases the military have become perpetrators of mass terror against the civilian population, in total defiance of international humanitarian law. It is not my intention to examine numerous current and recent examples of military forces as agents of mass terror and their crimes against humanity: genocide, ethnic cleansing, massacre, mass rape and torture. However, I cannot move on without observing that the response of the major powers and the international community generally in the face of these campaigns of terror by armies and militia has been pathetically inadequate. Even while the Russian army was planning to intensify its savage bombardment of Grozny, the IMF was meeting to award Russia an $8 billion loan. The Russian authorities were quick to label the Chechens 'terrorists and bandits'. The world knows that the large-scale terrorism in that conflict was applied by the Russian army in yet another campaign of ethnic cleansing. The tragedy in Chechnya was a reminder of the fact that even when a state has acquired new procedures for democratic elections, a multiparty parliamentary assembly, an independent judiciary and a constitution guaranteeing basic rights, it does not guarantee that the army and other sections of the armed forces, the secret intelligence agencies and the police will conform to democratic ethos. In Chechnya the Russian army used the same crude and brutal repression which it employed to suppress the revolution in Hungary in 1956, though on a bigger scale.

The secret intelligence battle, the work of the police and criminal justice systems, the suppression of terrorist finances, measures to prevent proliferation of WMD into the hands of terrorists, sanctions against regimes that assist or sponsor terrorists, and many other methods, in addition to deployment of military forces in counter-terrorism missions, are all part of the multi-pronged struggle to suppress the Al Qaeda network. This does not alter the fact that we are witnessing a kind of warfare, a global war involving the use of terror and counter-terror.

Historically terrorism has often been an auxiliary method or weapon in a wider war. Military and paramilitary forces have frequently used systematic terrorism against civilian populations as a means of trying to break the will and morale of the enemy's population. Repressive regimes resort to the use of this weapon almost instinctively because they use it to suppress dissent within their own borders, and even among their exiles living overseas.

Dictators can become addicted to the use of terror and come to believe that it 'works' although there is considerable historical evidence that it is a faulty weapon and that it often has psychological effects the reverse of those intended by the perpetrators. Liberal democratic governments, on the other hand, should at all times be conscious of their obligations under the Geneva Convention to avoid deliberate attacks on civilians and to treat captured combatants and those injured in battle humanely. Adoption of the methods of terror to defeat terror leads democracies into a moral and legal quagmire in which they will no longer be perceived by world opinion to be acting in accord with their self-proclaimed democratic values. Their international credibility is undermined.

The key features of the terror wars which have now become the predominant manifestation of armed conflict are: there are no clear front lines; attacks on civilians become the norm; particularly savage violence is used in 'ethnic cleansing' of whole villages and communities; massacres, mass hostage-takings, mass rapes and destruction of civilian homes become the pattern. Typical examples of 'terror wars' in which terror is used by all sides are the conflicts in the former Yugoslavia, the Chechen conflict with the Russians, and the genocidal ethnic conflicts in central Africa. One key feature of such conflicts has been that non-state actors (paramilitary and terrorist groups) are often responsible for massive violations of human rights on a scale comparable to, or in excess of, the war crimes committed by the regular military forces of states.

A striking feature of these 'terror wars' is their durability. There is no easy exit from such conflicts. The sheer savagery that characterises them tends to lead to greater polarisation, making efforts at obtaining ceasefires and peace negotiations all the more difficult. Both sides come to see themselves as waging total war. The levels of brutality become particularly intense when the perpetrators of the violence are led or orchestrated by ideologists preaching ethnic or religious hatred. In many of the recent terror wars one side or both obtain assistance from supporters/sympathisers abroad and it helps them to obtain more finance, weapons and recruits to sustain the conflict. Last but not least the UN and regional IGOs are generally either reluctant or unable to attempt peacekeeping or even humanitarian efforts because they know that such commitments may involve them in long-term, costly and dangerous assignments with no prospect of exit, and no help to finance such deployments.

Above all, military forces are inherently handicapped in their efforts to suppress terrorism. Sophisticated modern terrorists of the Al Qaeda network and its affiliates know how to hide and operate covertly in cities around the world, how to melt into their surroundings and to keep communications secret.

To win the struggle against Al Qaeda you need to win the intelligence war and use law-enforcement agencies worldwide as well as cooperation in the finance sector, civil aviation industry, private sector and between the public and private sector. The military can be of enormous value when they have specially trained units, equipped and configured for the purposes of counter-terrorism for specific operations. An example of this would be the toppling of the Taliban regime, which had given safe haven to Al Qaeda. But, over-dependence on military operations and heavy-handed use of firepower in civilian areas is likely to cause heavy casualties among innocent civilians and is a huge strategic blunder.

What lessons can be drawn from recent experiences of military deployment against terrorism?

British Army experience in MACP in Northern Ireland[1]

The British Army has achieved a truly impressive record in countering revolutionary war and major terrorist outbreaks around the world since 1945. British soldiers have shown enormous skill, courage and patience in carrying out these tasks, and their loyalty in carrying out instructions from the civil government has never been put in question. The army is steeped in the democratic ethos. The British Army was deployed in the most difficult circumstances in Northern Ireland in 1969–72 and it undoubtedly made some serious mistakes.[2] But it is doubtful whether any army in the world could have performed the tough role in Northern Ireland with such humanity, restraint and effectiveness. In 1972 and 1973 the army chiefs in Northern Ireland clearly recognised that they could not defeat the Provisionals simply by acting as 'substitute policemen' giving effect to the ordinary law. The Provisional IRA in effect declared war on the government and the whole system of law, and by terrorism and intimidation they rendered normal policing in certain areas (the so-called 'no-go' areas) impossible. Moreover, by intimidating witnesses and juries and terrorising whole districts, they had succeeded in causing a breakdown of the normal procedures of law. The army was charged with restoring order, but political constraints ruled out the use of martial law, i.e. the complete takeover of the machinery of civil government for the period of an emergency. Hence the British government adopted the only sensible alternative: the use of special powers legislation for the emergency to give the army and the civil authorities the necessary measures to suppress the terrorists. The middle course involves maintaining the independence of civil power, while at the same time establishing special army–police cooperation at all levels. By means of operations such as 'Motorman' the army was swiftly able to end the no-go areas; the 1973 Northern Ireland (Emergency Provisions) Act enabled the army, by late 1974, to get on top of the security situation in Ulster.

In the period 1971–72 the army's role was vitiated by the clumsily implemented and counterproductive policy of internment without trial, and the tragic aberration of Bloody Sunday, when 13 civilians were killed when British soldiers fired on a crowd of protestors in Londonderry. In February 1972, the British government appointed Lord Chief Justice John Widgery to undertake an inquiry into the events of Bloody Sunday, but although 114 witnesses gave evidence, some key eyewitnesses were not called. A new inquiry chaired by Lord Saville was set up in January 2008 by the Blair government and finally published its findings in June 2010.

The inquiry, which heard 2,500 witness statements and cost £191 million, concluded that unjustifiable shooting by soldiers had killed the 13 protestors.

What this shows is that even a disciplined and well-trained force such as the British Army can, in certain circumstances, commit gross violations of human rights of the civilian population during internal security situations. However, it is important to bear in mind that the IRA were responsible for 1,771 deaths during the 'Troubles', from 1966 to 1999.[3] By contrast the British Army carried out its difficult security tasks with extraordinary patience and restraint, ensuring a degree of stability that enabled politicians to initiate and sustain the peace process.

But in the climate of greater optimism engendered by Sunningdale, and with the phasing-out of internment, the emphasis of British security policy underwent a significant shift. The decision was made that the RUC should be reformed, strengthened and expanded so that it could become a thoroughly professional and impartial police force accepted by the law-abiding citizens of both Protestant and Catholic communities and capable in due course of taking the major burden against terrorism. This policy of 'police primacy' was well under way in 1976 and the dynamic leadership of Sir Kenneth Newman, who later moved from Ulster to be the Commissioner of the Metropolitan Police, played a considerable part in converting the RUC into the modern professional force it is today. Few outsiders can fully appreciate the stresses and risks faced daily by this courageous and highly disciplined body of men and women. Between 1969 and the end of December 1986 the force lost 235 officers through terrorist violence. By the early 1980s they were able to patrol in all the major urban areas. The so-called 'bandit country' of the rural borders were the only districts where the British Army, with its greater firepower and mobility, of necessity, took the major role.

Yet it would be a great mistake to assume that 'police primacy' meant that the army became of only marginal value in combating terrorism. Against such a ruthless, experienced and heavily armed terrorist foe the RUC would simply have been unable to continue its patrols and investigations without army support. In addition to its greater firepower and tactical mobility the army also provided certain specialisms that are absolutely crucial in any major counter-terrorist campaigns. An outstanding example of this is the technological innovation of the Army's Explosive Ordnance Disposal (EOD) experts. As early as 1972 they introduced the remote-control tracked robot known as Wheelbarrow.[4] This device, and its later variants, proved to be one of the finest anti-bomb robot vehicles in the world. It provided a highly effective and reliable means of giving the bomb-disposal officer a close-up view of a bomb without having to approach the device, and of delivering a means of neutralising the bomb. With the aid of such skills the army has been able to prevent the death and injury of hundreds of innocent people.

There has recently been a heated debate in the British and Irish Press regarding the case of soldiers serving in Northern Ireland tried and convicted for the murder of civilians in the course of their duties. It would be improper for me to comment on the details of each case. However, I do wish to add my strong support for making a change in the law in order to enable a court to make a finding of culpable homicide, allowing for considerable flexibility in sentencing. I firmly believe in the maxim 'make the punishment fit the crime'. The death of any innocent member of the public is a profound tragedy. Yet there is a vast difference between the position of a young solder making a split-second judgement while on duty to defend the community, and a terrorist who deliberately goes out to bomb or maim his fellow citizens.

But the central point I wish to make is this: mistakes and acts of misconduct by a handful of serving soldiers should not blind us to the fact that the British Army, UDR, the RUC and the RUC reservists, at the cost of hundreds of their members' lives in the 27 years of terrorism, have made a colossal achievement in preventing the conflict from escalating to civil war level, and in buying time for the politicians to negotiate political solutions. This is a truly heroic record, and it should be fully recognised as such both by the British public and internationally.

MACP: SAS hostage rescue at the Iranian Embassy, 1980

In May 1980 a group of 'Arabistan' terrorists seized control of the Iranian Embassy at Princes Gate, taking a large number of hostages. The Metropolitan Police, drawing from its substantial experience of IRA terrorism, reacted with impressive efficiency. They first tried patient negotiation with the terrorists to persuade them to release the hostages peacefully. When the hostage-takers killed one of the hostages, the police commander rightly decided to call in the crack SAS hostage-rescue squad. The rescue operation was brilliantly planned and executed, the remaining 19 hostages were released unharmed and five terrorists were killed. This operation, unique on the British mainland, proved the value of close police–army coordination and joint planning and exercising. It was also very useful in teaching the police more about the intricacies and complexities of such sieges, especially where Middle East politics are involved, about the problems of handling the news media, and about the additional demands for police manpower and resources created by the siege itself as well as by the political demonstrations that built up as an accompaniment to the Embassy siege. In the longer term, the total defeat of the terrorists has almost certainly helped to deter other groups from similar attempts to seize embassies in London. This lesson was not lost on other Western countries, and many of them proceeded to establish or radically improve their own capabilities for hostage rescue. Similarly firm responses in other incidents helped curb the fever of embassy takeovers that had afflicted many capitals in 1980 and 1981. However, in December 1996, the MRTA seized 500 hostages at the Japanese ambassador's residence in Lima. The siege was ended after 126 days, when a brilliantly executed operation by a military commando unit rescued the remaining hostages. The decision to send in the military rescue team was taken by President Fujimori and his advisers. The Japanese government was clearly annoyed at being left out of this crucial ultimate decision to deploy force, but most counter-terrorism specialists agree that the Peruvian president was right to act decisively and that the valuable contribution of specialist counter-terrorism units was once again being clearly demonstrated.

The Mumbai multi-site assault

Ten terrorists believed to have been members of Lashkar-e-Tayyiba, a group closely linked to Al Qaeda, mounted a multi-site terrorist assault on Mumbai, the financial and commercial capital of India, on 26 November 2008. The coordinated attacks were on such a scale and showed such audacity and ruthlessness that the civil police were totally outgunned. India's specially trained commandos had to be called in to defeat the gunmen and it took the authorities three days to regain control of all locations seized by the terrorists. The young men had clearly been fully indoctrinated and trained to cause maximum carnage, and were armed with AK47s and grenades. They arrived in Mumbai by sea with their weapons and were able to move into the centre of the city without any hindrance.

The terrorists' first target was the Café Leopold restaurant where they fired indiscriminately at the customers before moving on to attack the Taj Mahal Palace Hotel, a famous landmark in the city, popular with Mumbai's businessmen as well as foreign tourists and visitors. At least four gunmen attacked the hotel, shooting at guests indiscriminately as they assembled for dinner. A huge fire was started and spread through other parts of the hotel. It took Indian commandos longer to clear the Taj hotel of gunmen than it took to regain control of the other five locations the terrorists had stormed. The Taj was not finally cleared of gunmen until the morning of Saturday 29 November.

In the multi-site coordinated assault on the city the terrorists also attacked the Oberoi-Trident Hotel, located in the main business district. Two terrorists rounded up diners, including many tourists. Indian commandos did not complete the operation to clear the hotel of gunmen until the morning of Friday 28 November.

Chhatrapati Shivaji Terminus (CST) railway station was attacked by two of the terrorists while the hotels were being seized. The station was crowded with passengers waiting for long-distance trains when the gunmen opened fire indiscriminately and threw grenades.

Also attacked on Wednesday night was Nariman House, which includes the Jewish Chabad Lubavitch outreach centre that is used as a place for prayer and study. Although police surrounded the centre they were unable to regain control of the building. Indian commandos were sent in on Friday and soldiers abseiled down ropes from a helicopter to secure the roof. By 6.00pm on Friday the commandos had secured the building, but by then six people including a rabbi and his wife had been killed.

Following their attack on CST rail station, the two gunmen who had attacked the passengers in the terminus moved to Cama Hospital where they again fired indiscriminately. They then hijacked a police van, shooting as they travelled. One of the terrorists was killed, but one survived and he became a useful source of information for the Indian authorities.

The police and the public in Mumbai have experienced previous terrorist attacks and showed resilience and courage during this unprecedented multi-site assault. However, it is clear that the deployment of specially trained Indian commandos with greater firepower played a crucial part in ending this multi-site assault and preventing more mass murder of civilians. If, as many observers believe, the Mumbai multi-site assault is the shape of terrorism to come, the role of specialist counter-terrorism units in the military is going to become even more important. It is true that there have been many allegations of intelligence failures in India leading to a failure on the part of the authorities to take preventive action. We should remember, however, that terrorism intelligence is often inadequate or mistaken. Any major city in any part of the world is potentially vulnerable to this type of attack by a suicide squad of gunmen using simple, readily accessible weapons.

Needless to say, the Mumbai terrorists took 'hostages' not for ransom but for tactical reasons, i.e. as cover and to prolong their ability to kill.

The November 2008 multi-site assault on Mumbai led to the deaths of at least 166 innocent people, 300 injured and mayhem in a major city centre for three days. Counter-terrorism units need to learn from this case. WMD attacks are a real possibility but the Mumbai experience constitutes a different but even more likely scenario.

Is there a role for the military in combating international organised crime?

It will be clear from the foregoing that I adhere firmly to the principle that the prime institutions for maintaining the rule of law should be an independent and professionally trained judiciary and a legally accountable, efficient and impartial police force. While it is true that there are many well-documented cases of abuse of power by judicial and police systems in various countries and localities, there are also many examples of the police and courts working very effectively and enjoying widespread respect and support among the population.

In attempting to combat international organised crime, national judicial and police systems clearly labour under some major disadvantages. Their jurisdiction begins and ends at their national borders. In a world of sovereign states, all of which tend to regard matters of security and law and order as internal responsibilities, it may be difficult, if not impossible, to secure concerted multilateral action. The intelligence agencies and police of one country may be unwilling to share their information with another country, for example on the grounds that the intelligence may be leaked or sources compromised. Even where a mutual desire for judicial and police cooperation exists, there may be insuperable problems caused, for example by major differences in criminal codes and procedures or the absence of an extradition agreement. A more fundamental obstacle is that a government will very often place its overriding priority on protecting its perceived strategic and economic interests. If these interests are seen to be placed at risk by a proposed judicial or police action, the latter are likely to be subordinated to the perceived requirements of national security/national interest.

The above list of obstacles to international judicial and police cooperation, though far from exhaustive, appears to present formidable problems in the context of efforts to combat international crime. This has led to the search for short cuts or for alternative remedies, such as adopting an entirely militarised response, or some form of economic sanctions or covert action. The more effective way of dealing with these problems, however, is to address the weaknesses of the criminal justice response at both national and international levels. Considerable scope can be found for enhancement of law, organisation, leadership and training and resourcing of national police and judicial organisations. National systems are the building-blocks of a more effective international response: hence such improvements have an added value. But the really urgent need is to strengthen cooperation in the criminal justice field at the international level. Historical experience suggests that this cooperation can best be achieved by more creative international institution building (for example, at EU level) and not by simply waiting for national systems to converge, which may take centuries! If the international system of states fails to develop its capacity to respond to the escalation of international organised crime, criminal activity may soon far outstrip the capability of the international system to contain it.

However, there is also abundant recent evidence that the military can play an invaluable role in *assisting* the democratic state's response to international organised crime. Outstanding examples would be the hostage-rescue operations by Israeli and British Special Forces against terrorist gangs at Entebbe and the Iranian Embassy siege, respectively. In both cases, the hostage commandos had the firepower and techniques to carry out operations that were beyond the capability of police units. The American Green Berets also have a distinguished record in this special field.

A second clear instance where military Special Forces have played a key part in fighting international organised crime is the work of the Americans and allied troops in helping to interdict drugs and suppress cocaine production in Colombia and elsewhere. To many observers this seemed, at first sight, to be a misapplication of American armed forces. It was also feared that the presence of such units might alienate the population and provoke conflict. The fact that this has not happened is largely due to the professional and scrupulous way in which these forces carried out difficult tasks. Unfortunately, in the case of Colombia and other drug-producing countries, the indigenous government and armed forces rarely enjoy a reputation for independence and honesty. They have on many occasions behaved corruptly, and are all too frequently dragged into the power struggles of the drug factions, which wield enormous financial power. In many cases the drug barons can exercise a kind of local political power. For example, in 2010 the Jamaican government's attempt to extradite Christopher Cope to the US, where he was accused of drugs and arms trafficking, was frustrated by his armed supporters who became involved in shootouts with the police and army in the heart of Kingston. It was claimed that Cope had become a local hero because he had distributed largesse to many Jamaican families.

Even in well-established democratic political systems, there are some major risks involved in deploying the military abroad or on their own territory for the purposes of combating international organised crime. The military are trained to fight external foes and to use maximum force. The police, on the other hand, are trained to use minimum force, and, if possible, to bring suspects to trial, following criminal investigation. The military have generally been trained and equipped, at considerable expense, to carry out the important and difficult duties of external defence. They get bored and demoralised by months of policing duties that take them away from the jobs for which they have been trained. Last but not least there is a great danger that, once having committed the military, the government will be unable or unwilling to withdraw them, thus making the community and the police increasingly dependent on the military presence.

In an increasingly dangerous and volatile strategic environment we expect the military to do more and more with less and less. Hence, it is in the long-term interests of the military to ensure that civil police, customs and other civilian agencies bear the main brunt of fighting international organised crime. The military should only be deployed as a last resort when the civil agencies cannot cope, or when the military are needed to perform special tasks for which they are uniquely prepared.

However, the capability to double up in a specialised role against international organised crime should certainly be one of the criteria examined when various units of the armed forces are being scrutinised with a view to cuts. When one considers the multiplicity of key roles the SAS has performed with such distinc-tion, it would be extremely unwise to proceed with axing the two territorial regiments of the Special Air Service Regiment (SAS) (21 SAS and 23 SAS). When one considers the multiplicity of key roles the SAS has performed with such distinction in the Falklands War, the Gulf War (Operation Desert Storm) and other recent conflicts, together with its expertise in intelligence gathering and in counter-terrorism and hostage-rescue roles, the case for protecting SAS from further cuts is overwhelming.

Thus it is clear that there are some very powerful arguments against using the military for internal security duties and fighting international organised crime, even where such forces are requested. Such forces may appear locally as a form of illegitimate interference, thus calling into question the credibility and legiti-macy of the host government and the foreign government sending the troops.

In conclusion, military aid to the civil powers in tackling certain forms of international organised crime (piracy, hostage-taking, arms and drug smuggling) is of proven value. In other areas of crime (fraud, racketeering, money laundering, etc.) the military is not the appropriate form of response. Even when the military are uniquely suited to performing tasks in combating international organised crime, such tasks should always be performed under the direct control and authority of the civil power and – whenever possible – within its own borders.

8 Hostage-taking, sieges and problems of response

Hostage-taking is a characteristic tactic in the repertoire of modern terrorism.[1] By exercising a terrible threat against the lives of their victims, the terrorist hostage-takers seek to exert a degree of psychological pressure to obtain changes of policy or major concessions, such as huge ransom payments, the release of fellow terrorists from gaol or the broadcasting or publication of their grievances and demands. The vast majority of kidnappings are carried out by common criminals to gain ransoms. In Latin America this has become a major industry with huge profits to be made.[2] It is estimated that in Colombia alone there are several thousand such kidnappings annually.

Since the late 1960s politically motivated terrorists in many parts of the world have taken to using kidnap and ransom as a means of financing their activities. They have also targeted the symbols of their 'enemy' national government, for example by kidnapping diplomats, seizing embassies and other diplomatic premises, and by hijacking the civilian airliners of national 'flag' airlines, a particularly dramatic form of hostage-taking which always brings wide international media coverage.

It is easy to see why hostage-taking has enjoyed a growing popularity in recent years as a terrorist tactic. It is extremely cheap and requires only small numbers of hostage-takers armed with standard widely available weaponry. Above all, it is one of the very few terrorist tactics with a track record of success in forcing governments into major concessions, such as the release of large numbers of imprisoned terrorists and even, in some instances, changes in government policy.

Roberta Wohlstetter has argued that it was Raul and Fidel Castro who pioneered the modern wave of political kidnappings that 'used foreign nationals ... as pawns in a domestic struggle for power'. She points out that '[t]hey violated not only internal rules of political order, but also the meagre international rules that lend stability to relations among states'.[3] It is clear that the sensational publicity gained from the rash of kidnaps of US citizens in the American and Canadian press considerably aided Castro in his campaign to intimidate the United States into withholding assistance to the Batista regime. (By late June 1958, the Castro guerrillas had kidnapped at least 47 US citizens, including 30 servicemen. Castro even used the US captives as a weapon to make the United States force the Cuban air force to cease the bombing of the rebel zone in Sierra Cristal.[4] Raul Castro told the United States that the guerrillas would hold the US captives in the bombing zone.) In the late 1960s and early 1970s the political kidnapping of foreigners (especially Americans) in Latin America, South East Asia and the Middle East reached epidemic proportions. Between 1968 and April 1983 diplomats from 113 countries were victims of international terrorism.[5] Among them were 23 ambassadors from 13 different countries who were assassinated, including the US ambassadors to Lebanon, Cyprus, Sudan, Guatemala and Afghanistan, and the Turkish ambassadors to Australia, France, Spain, Austria and Yugoslavia.

During 1979–80 a new scourge developed: the terrorist fashion of seizing whole embassies and their staffs and occupants. This is still a fairly easy operation for well-armed terrorists in countries where the security forces are too ill-trained, ill-equipped and ill-prepared to protect embassies adequately. In the notorious case of the seizure of the US Embassy in Tehran[6] by about 400 Iranian students, on 4 November 1979, the Iranian regime totally failed to carry out its obligation under international law. The Islamic revolutionary authorities made no attempt to assist the US mission staff. They provided no police or military protection for the US personnel or property; they made no attempt to return the embassy to US control by expelling the students. On the contrary, they compounded their offences against international law of diplomacy by 'adopting' the siege as their own, not only giving the official blessing of the Ayatollah Khomeini but also by manipulating the hostage crisis to inflict maximum international embarrassment and humiliation on the United States. This was the first time in recent history that any state has so flagrantly defied the norms and conventions of diplomatic relations.[7] To most ordinary Americans, the hatred and abuse hurled at them by the screaming mobs paraded before their embassy in Tehran seemed quite incomprehensible. The feeling of helplessness and frustration, provoked by these scenes, displayed on US television screens, week after week, undoubtedly did much to undermine the domestic support and credibility of the Carter administration, and the reaction against it inevitably helped Ronald Reagan, with his more hard-nosed and assertive stance, to win his overwhelming election victory.

However, the Americans were by no means alone among the major democracies in experiencing the feelings of frustration and helplessness in the face of terrorist hostage situations. The whole world has been stunned by the terrorist attack on the Munich Olympics in 1972.[8] The risks of terrorist attack on the Olympic Games had been underestimated. The Olympic Village was particularly vulnerable, and lacked adequate perimeter security. On 5 August, eight terrorists climbed the perimeter fence and headed for the Israeli accommodation block. Two athletes were shot dead and nine others taken hostage. The terrorists demanded the release of 200 imprisoned Palestinians.

Expert advice from Israeli officials was ignored, and the task of rescuing the hostages was placed in the hands of the Bavarian police. The response team was ill-prepared, ill-equipped and outnumbered. The Israeli hostages were killed in the tragically bungled rescue attempt. It was this disastrous hostage crisis that led to the United States and other Western governments to make an urgent review of policies and resources for combating terrorism, including hostage-taking.

The case for reviewing the response to hostage crises currently is every bit as strong as it was in the 1970s. The RAND–St Andrews international terrorism chronology data shows that in the early 1990s there was a 33.5 per cent rise in incidents of the kidnappings of foreigners world-wide. The US Department of State's *Patterns of Global Terrorism* statistics for the mid 1990s indicates that between 14 and 15 per cent of all international terrorist incidents world-wide fall into the category of kidnappings or barricade and hostage situations. We should also bear in mind that these statistics exclude politically motivated hostage-taking by fellow nationals within the same state. They also exclude the use of mass hostage-taking by regimes and factions as a weapon in the period preceding full-scale international or internal war, or during such conflicts. The growth of this phenomenon, which flagrantly breaches the humanitarian laws of war, should be a cause of major concern to all democratic governments. Mass hostage-taking was used by Saddam Hussein in his notorious 'human shield' tactic,[9] a crude attempt to coerce the coalition allies into backing off from military action to liberate Kuwait from Iraqi occupation. A similar tactic was used by Serb militants in an attempt to intimidate soldiers in the UN Protection Force (UNPROFOR) in Bosnia and to dissuade the NATO allies from taking any forceful action against further aggression by Serb forces.[10] Also, in the mid 1990s, the Chechen militants employed the weapon of mass hostage-taking against the Russians, with lethal and dramatic effect. (We will examine the key aspects of these events later in this chapter, as they have major implications not only for the fragile emerging democracies of the former Soviet bloc, but also for the governments of Western democracies as a reminder of the folly of abandoning their expertise, resources and mechanisms for hostage crisis-management, or of allowing them to fall into disrepair.)

Barricade and hostage sieges

The politically motivated barricade and siege situation presents the democratic government and its security forces with very different problems and dilemmas from those confronted when kidnap victims or hostages are held in an unknown location, perhaps in remote and inhospitable terrain or in the urban jungle of a huge city. In a barricade and hostage situation the government and security forces have a key advantage: the terrorists themselves become hostages and a part of the deal they seek will be a safe exit. This can be used as a powerful lever in police siege tactics. Also a siege provides the authorities with *time* and an opportunity for a planned security agency response which, if skilfully implemented, may have a chance of rescuing the hostages without surrendering major concessions to the hostage takers. Few other terrorist tactics offer similar opportunity to the security forces: it is true that in some incidents a bomb will be preceded by a warning, but frequently the warning time is so brief and the information on the location of the bomb is so vague, that there is no chance for the police to be able to evacuate the area.

Democratic governments are faced with the most adverse circumstances of all when the hostage incident involving their nationals is in a foreign country where the government and a high proportion of the general population are hostile. The seizure of the US diplomatic mission in Tehran was just such a case. The Iranian regime brazenly adopted hostage-taking and defied all calls from the United States and the international community for the release of the diplomats. President Carter, frustrated by the failure of diplomatic and economic pressures to bring the release of the hostages, embarked on a military rescue operation, Operation Rice Bowl, in April 1980.[11] It was a tragic failure, leading to the deaths of eight American military personnel, but even if it had been better coordinated and equipped, the odds were stacked against its success. The Reagan administration experienced similar frustration when TWA Flight 847[12] was hijacked by Hezbollah terrorists who then proceeded to turn it into a hostage situation by moving passengers to unknown locations in the sprawling suburbs of Beirut. The domestic demand for the release of the TWA Flight 847 hostages placed such pressure on the US government it led them to press their Israeli allies to release over 700 prisoners demanded by the hostage-takers, thus conceding an enormous political and psychological victory to the terrorists and demonstrating the potential of hostage-taking as a high-yield weapon against even the most militarily powerful democracy, where public opinion insists on paying almost any price for saving the lives of fellow citizens. Similarly, Western governments were forced to rule out the idea of sending elite commando forces into Lebanon to rescue Terry Waite, John McCarthy, Brian Keenan, Terry Anderson and the other Western hostages held for much longer periods, mostly by Hezbollah.[13] The terrorists, however, took no chances and constantly moved their captives from one secret hideout to another in order to confuse Western intelligence services and forestall a rescue attempt. The ultimate release of the Western hostages was due to a combination of propitious circumstances: the Israelis were interested in striking a deal with Hezbollah in order to discover the whereabouts of missing Israeli servicemen; the Iranian regime, which sponsored Hezbollah and could exert considerable influence upon its leadership, decided that the hostage crisis in Lebanon had become an obstacle to their efforts to improve their economic links and to meet the crippling costs of their war of attrition with Iraq; Syria, the dominant military power in Lebanon, wished to gain credit for being seen to help facilitate the freeing of the Western hostages in order to improve its diplomatic position in the Middle East; and, last but not least, the UN provided a patient and skilful negotiator, Mr Picco, who played a vital role in brokering the deal that led to the hostages' rescue.[14]

In dealing with barricade and hostage situations, however, the United States, Britain and other Western democracies began to develop an increasingly effective law-enforcement response. Initially police hostage tactics were developed mainly in confronting sieges where the hostage-takers were criminal gangs or mentally disturbed persons in domestic siege situations. Frank Bolz of the New York Police Department pioneered many of the police techniques of hostage negotiation that were later acquired by the Metropolitan Police in Britain and other law-enforcement agencies in the United States and elsewhere. By studying the complex psychology of the siege situation, and by thorough debriefing and reassessment after each incident, the police began to perfect tactics and techniques which would maximise their chances of success.

A famous hostage-taking incident in Stockholm in 1973, involving bank robbers who took four hostages during a bank raid, gave its name to the psychological bonding process between captor and captive: the Stockholm Syndrome.[15] During the siege, one of the female hostages formed a deep emotional bond with one of the gunmen, and she refused to cooperate with those who wanted to liberate her. Forming such a bond is believed to have saved the lives of many hostages, and it has been claimed that it explains why, during the 1977 siege at Lima, the life of one of the Peruvian hostages, the Minister of Agriculture, was saved.[16] However, it would be a great mistake to see the Stockholm Syndrome as an automatic or inevitable process. So much depends on the personalities of the individuals involved. Moreover, in many hostage-taking incidents the terrorists appear to have gone to considerable lengths to prevent any bonds of personal attachment with their captives by changing guards frequently, ensuring that hostages are regularly abused, beaten and subjected to constant humiliation.

In the 1970s and early 1980s, however, there were some dramatic successes for the security forces in siege situations which began to indicate that in 'close quarters' hostage situations, at least, the balance of advantage was swinging in the direction of the authorities. For example, in December 1975, the Metropolitan Police had to deal with a gang of four IRA terrorists who had taken refuge in a flat in Balcombe Street and had taken the occupants, Mr and Mrs Matthews, hostage.[17] The police played a softly softly waiting game. They kept talking to the terrorists, but did not give in to their demands. The Home Office called in the SAS, but kept their availability a secret. Electronic surveillance equipment was installed to enable the police to monitor conversations between hostages and terrorists. The police waited until the sixth day, when they judged that the terrorists were getting hungry and their resolve was weakening. A key factor in persuading the terrorists to surrender peacefully may well have been the deliberate leaking of the news through a broadcast bulletin that the SAS were at the scene.

The strategy of patience does not always result in a peaceful surrender by terrorists. For example, the Dutch were compelled to use a marine rescue force to rescue passengers held hostage on a hijacked train south of Groningen in May 1977, and 105 children and six teachers held hostage in a simultaneous operation by Moluccan terrorists at a primary school in Bovensmilde.[18] In the Dutch cases the value of concealed microphones in gathering precise information on the position of hostages and terrorists in the train, as well as thorough planning of the entire rescue operation, was clearly demonstrated. In the storming of the train by the marines 53 hostages were freed, two hostages died and six terrorists were killed. Considering the great difficulties involved in mounting such a rescue it was a remarkable achievement.

A dramatic illustration of Britain's growing expertise in handling siege situations came in 1980, when six anti-Khomeini terrorists seized the Iranian Embassy in London, with 26 hostages.[19] Initially the police employed the strategy of patience. There followed five days of negotiation, during which five hostages, including pregnant women, were released. The terrorists were delighted when the British authorities granted the concession of permitting their political message to be read on BBC World Service. But the terrorist leader became more aggressive on the sixth day because not all the demands had been met. The terrorists killed one hostage and threatened to kill another every 40 minutes until their demands had been granted. As soon as it became clear that the terrorists had started to murder the hostages the decision was taken by the Cabinet Crisis Committee to send in the SAS to end the siege and rescue the remaining hostages. The SAS executed the rescue with impressive speed and efficiency. All the remaining hostages were rescued, and only one of the hostage-takers survived. There is little doubt that this display of highly professional military force used against terrorists acted as a stimulus to other states to develop their own hostage-rescue capabilities, and as a considerable deterrent to similar embassy takeovers by terrorists not only in London but also in other major cities. It is true that there was a confrontation with the police involving the Libyan 'People's Bureau' (the Libyan regime's designation for an embassy) in 1984, but this was not triggered by hostage-taking but by the killing of WPC Yvonne Fletcher, on duty in St James's Square, by a gunman inside the Libyan People's Bureau.[20]

It would be a major mistake, however, to assume that the deployment of military force in a rescue operation is invariably the correct or most effective ultimate solution to a siege situation. There have been some highly successful resolutions by negotiation leading to the hostages being released unharmed. For example, this was the outcome of one of the most internationally complex sieges in the history of terrorism in Latin America: the seizure of the Dominican Embassy in Bogotá in February 1980 by 18 M-19 terrorists.[21] There was a diplomatic reception on at the time and 80 hostages were taken, including 18 ambassadors. The hostage-takers threatened to kill all their captives if the police stormed the embassy. They demanded: the release of over 300 prisoners from gaol in Colombia, including 200 suspected M-19 terrorists captured from the previous year; the payment of a ransom of $50 million; safe passage for themselves out of the country and the publication of their manifesto by all the countries represented among the hostages. The terrorists appeared prepared to hold out for as long as was necessary to get their demands, and observers were impressed by the planning and organisation that had gone into the mass hostage-taking. The siege lasted 61 days and was ended not by force but by negotiation. The basis of the deal was that the Colombian government would set up a panel of ten leading lawyers to process trials for the imprisoned M-19 members. The Inter-American Human Rights Commission of the Organisation of American States was brought in to monitor the trials. Safe exit to Cuba was arranged for the hostage-takers and the Castro regime offered them asylum. In return the hostages were released. The government refused to pay the ransom demanded, but did permit the private business community to pay a ransom of $2.5 million. Some might argue that the concessions granted to the terrorists were too large a price to pay for the lives of the hostages. Against this, one has to weigh the fact that the terrorists were known to be well armed and ruthless and that their key demands were refused. A major complication for the Colombian government was the fact that it was difficult to get agreement from all the countries involved in the incident. In view of the circumstances the compromises can be fully justified as a means of avoiding large-scale loss of life, while at the same time minimising as far as possible the gains of the hostage-takers.

Premature or clumsy use of military force to end a siege situation can be particularly dangerous where the law-enforcement agencies are dealing with religious or political fanatics with a tight control of the mindsets of their followers and with some adherents or sympathisers at large in the community. The case of the siege at the Branch Davidian cult's compound at Waco,[22] Texas, in 1993 offers a dramatic illustration of the problems involved. The 51-day siege was triggered when the Alcohol, Tobacco and Firearms Unit entered the compound. There was an effort to negotiate but it appears that serious mistakes were made; insufficient use was made of the expertise that exists on extreme religious cults, and on the Branch Davidian cult and its leader, David Koresh, in particular. There was no proper plan for ending the siege with the use of force. Eighty people, including 25 children, died when the authorities sought to end the siege, most of them from asphyxiation in the fire which, arson investigators claim, had been started by cult members. The FBI has taken rapid steps to learn from this tragic experience, and the formation of the Critical Incident Response Group is an attempt to bring the very best skills in hostage negotiation, the most sophisticated technical resources and the most highly trained rescue team to deal with future sieges. The major reason for hoping these enhancements to the FBI's capability to respond to sieges works effectively is that they should result in saving lives. But we do not overlook the unfortunate longer-term effect of an event such as Waco on the overall levels of violent extremism. For many in the militia movement and other organisations of the American extreme right Waco provides yet another yardstick with which to beat the federal government. It is worth noting that testimony given at the trial of Timothy McVeigh, convicted for his part in the Oklahoma bombing, suggested that one of his motivations for the bomb attack was his desire for revenge against the federal law-enforcement authorities for their role at Waco.[23]

Mass hostage-takings by Chechen militants

Russia, like America, has also been experiencing problems of domestic terrorism and hostage-taking in the 1990s, but the scale has been much greater; the political impact of the hostage crises in 1995 and 1996 on Russian policy has been far more dramatic than that of any hostage crisis in Western countries. Perhaps the most dramatic and effective of the mass hostage-takings by Chechen militants against Russian targets came in June 1995, when a group of Chechens under the leadership of Shamil Basayev carried out a cross-border raid into the Russian town of Budennovsk.[24] Having tried unsuccessfully to seize the police station, they seized a hospital and around 2,000 hostages, including children and pregnant women. The scale of this was unprecedented. Russian troops and police surrounded the hospital, and in their initial assault 37 army personnel and police were killed. Many civilians were caught in the crossfire and pleaded with Russian troops to stop firing. The Chechen gunmen were heavily outnumbered but fought with fanatical determination and stuck to their key demands: an end to Russian military operations in Chechnya and negotiations to discuss the withdrawal of forces. In response to this unprecedented hostage crisis the Russian prime minister, Viktor Chernomyrdin, offered huge concessions. He announced in a TV broadcast: 'I am asking you to let the hostages go. Here, before millions of people watching us on television. I am officially making an order to halt military actions in Chechnya and start negotiations.'[25] Negotiators did sign an agreement the following month, but continuing clashes led to failure of the pact.

A highly dangerous precedent had been set. Hostage-taking of civilians, explicitly prohibited under the Geneva Convention, had been carried out on a massive scale and had been rewarded by a massive policy change by the Russian government. Many observers share the view that Chechen demands for autonomy are fully justified on both political and moral grounds, especially in the light of the appalling treatment they received during the communist period. But by making dramatic changes in policy to obtain the release of hostages the Russian leaders were sending the message that mass hostage-taking works, and were storing up trouble for the future.[26]

It was therefore no great surprise when in January 1996 a group of militant Chechens, this time led by Salman Raduyev (the son-in-law of Dzokhar Dudayev, leader of the Chechen independence movement), seized over 2,000 hostages, including pregnant women, new-born infants and children,when they occupied a hospital at Kizlyar in neighbouring Dagestan.[27] Raduyev threatened to avenge every Chechen death with 15 Russian deaths. It was a carbon-copy of the mass hostage-taking at the hospital at Budennovsk six months previously. What is surprising is that the Russian authorities, their intelligence services, police, military and security advisers, appear to have been totally unprepared for this attack. The Chechen fighters were able to carry out their mission without any opposition, despite the fact that they had traversed two major emplacements of Russian soldiers to enter Kizlyar. President Yeltsin's fury at this humiliating turn of events was understandable. At a Cabinet meeting confrontation shown on television, President Yeltsin shouted at the Defence Minister, Pavel Frachev: 'What are you Generals up to? Why have you learned no lessons from previous events? We have been dealt with another blow. We had information in advance that the rebels were coming, but no action was taken. What have you Generals been doing?'[28] Despite Yeltsin's promise to take the 'most resolute action' to restore law and order, the initial reaction of officials in Dagestan who sought to save the hostages' lives was to strike a deal with the Chechens, almost identical to the bargain struck in the Budennovsk hostage crisis in June 1995. The Chechens freed over 2,000 hostages in return for a guarantee of safe exit across the Chechen border. They took over 150 hostages from Kizlyar, including children, in a convoy of buses heading for the Chechen border. But the convoy was halted when its exit was blocked by the blowing up of a bridge by the Russian Army at the village of Pervomayskaya. There was a tense stand-off between the Chechen fighters: Russian troops surrounded the convoy, the Chechens threatened to kill their hostages if the Russian troops failed to guarantee safe passage. On the night of

15 January, Russian troops stormed the village of Pervomayskaya, using artillery and helicopter gunships to end the mass hostage crisis. The village was virtually destroyed and there were heavy casualties. Inevitably a large number of hostages were killed in the ferocious Russian assault.[29] It became almost inevitable that the Russian authorities would use force to end the crisis even at heavy cost in lives, because they had been so heavily criticised for allowing a second mass hostage-taking in seven months and for their weakness and confusion in responding to the crisis. Russian television reported that the decision to attack had been taken after the Chechens shot six Siberian policemen among the hostages, but the Chechens deny that they had killed any hostages and claim they were willing to negotiate.

It is clear that the tragic mass hostage crises of June 1995 and January 1996 did serious damage to the reputation of President Yeltsin and the Russian government and security forces as a whole. However, it was the reputation of Mr Viktor Chernomyrdin which suffered most directly, because his televised order to halt Russian military action in direct response to the hostage seizure was seen as having set a dangerous precedent.

An additional and potentially dangerous consequence of major confrontations between hostage-takers and the security forces of the government they oppose is that they sometimes provoke further terrorist actions by sympathisers acting in support of their rebel colleagues. Where there is a network of sympathisers in an ethnic diaspora these sympathetic or supportive actions may well occur. The Chechens have a diaspora with small communities not only in the Middle East but as far afield as the United States. During the second major Chechen hostage-taking in January 1996, a group of sympathisers seized a Turkish ferry at the port of Trabzon[30] and threatened to blow it up with all its 118 Russian passengers aboard when it reached the Bosphorous, unless the Russian forces halted their attacks on the Chechen militants holding hostages at Pervomayskaya, near the Dagestan–Chechen border. The Chechens released the ferry passengers and the incident ended peacefully, but the Russians criticised the Turkish authorities for their leniency to the gunmen. However, it would be foolish of the Russians to alienate the Turks. The Turks feel some affinity with and sympathy for the Chechens, but they have no wish to see an escalation of terrorism in the area. In view of the volatile ethnic relations between the Russians and other ethnic groups in the Caucasus it would be sensible for the Russian authorities to seek improved cooperation with neighbouring states to help prevent any other embryonic terrorist campaigns from emerging. And, after all, the outcome of the Turkish handling of the ferry hijacking was successful in preventing bloodshed. All the hostages were freed without loss of life. This is a stark contrast to the heavy-handed Russian tactics which resulted in the virtual destruction of the village of Pervomayskaya, and the deaths of many of the hostages the troops were supposed to be rescuing. If the prime aim of the assault at Pervomayskaya had genuinely been to free the hostages, a surgical rescue operation by a special forces commando using highly accurate man-portable weapons should have been used. In reality the main aim of the Russian authorities seems to have been to win the grudging approval of the right-wing Duma by a crushing display of military force against rebels. However, this could not disguise the underlying political reality. The two tragically botched mass hostage crises had played a part in wearying the Russian public of the Chechen conflict. There was a serious upsurge of fighting between Russian troops and Chechens in Grozny in August 1996. Then, General Lebed, given responsibility for solving the Chechen crisis, managed to obtain a ceasefire agreement just in time to prevent another Russian bombardment of Grozny[31] at the end of August. On 29 December 1996 Russian combat troops withdrew from Chechnya,[32] effectively handing over control to the rebel government. However, in 1999 Russia invaded Chechnya again, following apartment bombings in Moscow for which Chechens were blamed.

The Chechen militants continued to plan further mass hostage-takings in their increasingly desperate struggle against the Russians. On 23 October 2002 one of the Chechen terrorist leaders, Barayev, led a group of 40 terrorists in a mass hostage-taking in a Moscow theatre during the performance of a musical show set in the Second World War and seized 1,000 people. The terrorists were heavily armed, the women terrorists had explosives strapped to their bodies, and they threatened to blow up the theatre unless Russia withdrew its troops from Chechnya. The Russian authorities were faced with an apparently impossible task: how could they free the hostages without the Chechens blowing up the theatre? They had at their disposal Special Forces Units with some experience of confronting Chechen terrorists, but the traditional hostage-rescue technique of launching a coordinated multiple entry point attack on the hostage-takers, using to the full advantages of surprise and speed, was unavailable. The Chechens manned every entry point and would have been able to detonate their bombs and blow up the theatre, probably killing all the hostages. It was clear to the authorities and to the hostages that Barayev's terrorist group were all prepared to die for their cause. It was the worst mass hostage situation any modern government had ever been faced with.

The Russians decided to use gas to knock out the hostage-takers and rescue the hostages. Government scientists in many countries had been searching for years to find a gas powerful enough to knock out terrorists almost instantaneously without causing death, thus enabling them to save hostages without any loss of life. The Russians clearly believed they had found this elixir and infiltrated the gas through the ventilation system.[33] It was certainly very potent: the Russian soldiers had waited an hour before entering the theatre and shot dead all the terrorists, including their leader, Barayev. At first the Russians thought they had mounted a completely successful rescue operation. They soon discovered that a large number of hostages had died in their theatre seats. Many of the 129 hostages who died choked to death when their heads lolled back and they stopped being able to breathe. The soldiers had held back over an hour before intervening, even then were not properly briefed on the kind of swift medical intervention needed to revive the hostages who had been more seriously affected by the mystery gas. Hostages were taken out onto the street and laid on their backs. When hostages were at last taken to hospitals in Moscow the medical staff had no idea how to revive them because they had not been told what kind of gas had been used to end the siege. We will never know how many of the 129 hostages who died could have been resuscitated if these elementary mistakes had not been made. However, the Russian authorities hailed the outcome as a great success for the security forces. It is true that they saved over 800 lives, but at enormous costs.

In the longer term, the Moscow Theatre Siege of October 2002 is likely to intensify research in the West to discover an effective knock-out gas to end mass hostage situations. Western scientists were puzzled at the nature of the gas used by the Russians, but the most informed guess is that it is a derivative developed from *fentanil*, an opiode well known in the medical profession. The fact that the gas caused a less than 20 per cent level of fatalities shows it was not as powerful as the well-known derivative *carfentanil*, and was designed to mitigate the chances of those exposed to the gas dying through cessation of respiration and the ensuing cardiac arrest. It is also to be hoped that scientists in Russia, America and Western Europe can combine efforts and share knowledge in order to perfect a knock-out gas capable of ending all kinds of siege situations and saving large numbers of innocent lives.

For the Chechen militants, the Moscow Theatre Siege was clearly a major defeat. Yet this did not deter them from making another major attempt to blackmail the Russian government through a spectacular mass hostage-taking. In September 2004 a Chechen terrorist gang seized an entire school of children and parents at Beslan in North Ossetia at the start of the new school term. Three hundred and thirty-one hostages, including dozens of children, died when mines planted in the school by the terrorists started to explode and the security forces stormed the school. Many of the children were killed when they tried to escape from the building. Those who watched TV pictures of the siege were struck by the apparent chaos of the security forces' response. There was no effective cordon to seal off the area around the school. Parents appeared to be rushing past the security forces and into the school grounds without any effort being made to stop them. But mistakes were not confined to the incompetent action of the security forces. According to Alexander Torshin, leader of the federal inquiry appointed by Moscow, the Russian Interior Minister had sent telegrams, based on intelligence, to the regional police in North Ossetia, ordering them to strengthen protection of all educational facilities on 1 September, but the order was ignored. Mr Torshin's report contradicts the earlier report by a prosecutor exonerating the security forces. Once again the Chechen terrorists had shown utter ruthlessness in their tactics, again seizing a soft target. The cruelty shown towards the children and parents at Beslan was fully in keeping with the previous Chechen hostage-taking when they were willing to put the lives of pregnant mothers and babies at risk when they seized control of a hospital. Sadly the Russian authorities' handling of the situation at Beslan showed no improvement over their performance in the mass-hostage situations in 1995 and 1996.

The mass hostage crisis at Lima

On 17 December 1996, 14 terrorists belonging to the Tupac Amaru Revolutionary Movement (MRTA) seized the Japanese ambassador's residence in Lima during a diplomatic reception. They took 500 hostages, including high-ranking members of the Peruvian government, diplomats and Japanese businessmen, in addition to the Japanese ambassador and members of his staff. Eight US officials were among the hostages held when the ambassador's residence was seized, but they were released after five days – an indication that, for once, the US government was not the terrorists' target.

The MRTA is a Marxist revolutionary group formed in 1983,[34] inspired by the example of Castro's Cuba, bitterly anti-American, and aiming to destabilise and topple the Peruvian government. Unlike Sendero Luminoso, it has primarily used the methods of urban guerrilla warfare and cultivated close links with other Marxist revolutionary groups in the region. It takes its name from Tupac Amaru II, executed by the Spanish after leading the 1780 Indian revolt. In the 1980s most MRTA attacks appear to have been aimed at property. But since 1992 they have killed policemen, soldiers and civilians, including a Peruvian businessman who refused to pay a large ransom after they kidnapped him in Lima.[35]

The demands of the MRTA in the Lima siege were for the release of over 300 of their gaoled comrades, an improvement in prison conditions and changes in Peru's economic policies to curtail the involvement of Japanese and other foreign business interests. Their key demand was for the release of their imprisoned comrades. The terrorist movement wanted them to be flown to a jungle hideout where they could then have used them to rebuild their movement, seriously depleted by the action of the Peruvian security forces, so they could then continue their struggle.

The Lima siege came as a major shock to President Fujimoro and his colleagues. They clearly believed that the MRTA, a smaller and weaker movement than the Sendero Luminoso, had been virtually wiped out by the security forces' capture of key leaders. (It is always dangerous to underestimate the tenacity of 'old' groups and the appeal of well-tried tactics.)

President Fujimoro was understandably adamant in his refusal to give in to the MRTA's demands. Since 1982 terrorism has cost Peru at least 27,000 lives and an estimated $23 billion. Any release of prisoners under duress would have threatened the stability and survival of the Peruvian economic and political system. After all, Fujimoro had won 64 per cent of the vote in the 1995 general election. MRTA had no democratic mandate and is a criminal organisation.

The international community as a whole had a clear interest in backing President Fujimoro in his firm stance against the blackmail of the hostage-takers. There is no shadow of doubt that taking diplomats and civilians hostage is a serious violation of international law.[36] The international community should never condone or encourage such crimes. It is therefore not surprising that the Peruvian president received backing from the G7 countries for his firm refusal to give in to the terrorists' key demands. In a significant change of policy the Japanese government gave its support, albeit reluctantly, to this firm policy. (In the 1970s and 1980s Japanese governments facing demands from Japanese Red Army hostage-takers or hijackers followed an unusually conciliatory policy, meeting ransom demands in order to secure the release of hostages.)[37] In the Lima crisis the

Japanese authorities were for the first time made forcibly aware that they had become a key target in the eyes of certain foreign terrorist groups. Moreover, despite its distaste for the use of force, Japan has increasingly come to recognise that appeasement sends dangerous signals to others who might be tempted to use terrorism to attack Japanese targets and who might damage the economic interests of both Japan and its key economic partners.

The Peruvian president wisely played for time by opting for a strategy of patience.[38] Periodic attempts were made to negotiate the safe release of the remaining hostages (reduced to 72 by the end of the siege), but the hostage-takers stuck firmly to their key demand for the release of prisoners. At one stage the Peruvian authorities hoped that they could persuade the terrorists to release their hostages in return for a safe exit to Cuba, which President Fujimoro had negotiated. The hostage-takers turned this down and reaffirmed their main demand.

After 126 days, after long and thorough planning, and frustrated by the lack of any breakthrough in the efforts to gain the release of hostages by peaceful means, President Fujimoro decided to send in a military rescue team.[39] It was a brilliant success. Tunnels were constructed beneath the ambassador's residence. Explosive charges were placed in the tunnels and detonated when some of the terrorists were playing football above, and the rescue troops stormed the building. Their careful training and planning, using a mock-up of the building, paid off handsomely. Seventy-one of the 72 hostages were freed and 14 MRTA terrorists, including their leader, were killed. The contribution of advice from elite hostage-rescue units from friendly countries is evident in the outcome. This in no way detracts from the outstanding success of the Peruvian authorities' handling of the situation.

There has been much discussion of the fact that the Japanese government was not consulted before the rescue troops were sent in. While it is true that the Japanese government technically held legal jurisdiction over the territory of the Japanese ambassador's residence one must take account of the following factors:

Under the Vienna Convention on Diplomatic Relations the host state (in this case Peru) has a clear responsibility for taking measures to protect the embassy and its staff.

The Peruvian security forces were the only available force on the ground in the correct location and were fully equipped to undertake a rescue role.

It was the Peruvian authorities who had most at stake, even more than the Japanese, in a successful outcome. The government had been engaged in a long and bitter war of attrition with terrorists on a scale scarcely imaginable in Japanese experience. From the perspective of President Fujimoro the hostage crisis was a threat to his whole policy of the eradication of terrorism and hence a threat to the stability and survival of Peru's economy and political system.

It was essential to achieve total surprise against the terrorists. Had there been wider international consultation on a rescue plan, details might have been leaked and the whole rescue plan jeopardised.

Kidnappings in Iraq and Gaza 2004–05

Between spring 2004 and spring 2005 there were over 260 kidnappings of foreigners in Iraq. Criminal gangs took advantage of the endemic instability and lack of basic law and order to kidnap for ransom. Criminal gangs which seized foreigners often sold them on to extremist groups such as Zarqawi's Al Qaeda in Iraq which wanted to use hostage-taking as a political weapon in order to terrorise foreigners into leaving the country, to show their supporters that they could inflict blows on the 'enemy', and above all to blackmail foreign governments into withdrawing their troops and civilian contractors from Iraq.

One might have thought that it would be difficult to add any cruel refinements to kidnapping tactics so fully deployed in other conflict situations (for example in Colombia, Lebanon and the Philippines), but the political terrorists in Iraq exceeded even the cruellest of those recent hostage-taking events. In order to maximise the fear and suffering of their victims' families, communities and the victims themselves they issued video images of the hostages dressed in Guantanamo-style orange jumpsuits pleading for their lives and then carried out their threats to kill them by beheading the hostages and showing pictures of the beheadings being carried out.

A terrorist murder which caused great outrage in the UK and internationally was the beheading of a British hostage named Ken Bigley, a civilian contractor, by the Tawhid and Jihad Group, led by Zarqawi, leader of Al Qaeda in Iraq.

One of the kidnappings which caused particular outrage not only internationally but in Iraq itself was the abduction of Mrs Margaret Hassan. Margaret Hassan had joint British, Irish and Iraqi citizenship, was married to an Iraqi and had a record of years of dedicated humanitarian aid to Iraqi people through Care International, a respected humanitarian NGO. In spite of numerous passionate pleas for her release from Iraqis, from Muslim organisations and from the governments of Britain, Ireland, all EU member states and from the UN, the terrorists refused to release her and then killed her. The readiness of Al Qaeda and its affiliated extremist groups to seize aid workers indicates another worrying trend and makes it difficult for humanitarian NGOs to deploy staff to the very troubled areas where their skills and commitment are so needed. Hostage-taking remains a huge problem in Iraq: there were 3,762 cases of hostage-taking in Iraq between January 2006 and December 2009; this is hardly a good omen of growing stability and security.

Another widely reported hostage-taking occurred in Gaza in December 2005 where Ms Kate Burton was employed as a human rights worker for the Al Mezan Centre for Human Rights. Ms Burton was accompanied by her parents when she was seized and all three were held hostage by a terrorist group calling itself the Mujaheddin Brigades, Jerusalem Branch, a previously unknown group. It is truly ironic that Kate Burton is a passionate supporter of the Palestinian cause.

Fortunately the combined pressure of the Palestinian Authority, the militant Palestinian groups, including Hamas and the al-Aqsa Martyrs Brigades, resulted in the release of Ms Burton and her parents. It was clear from Ms Burton's interviews with the press after her release that she wanted to continue with her humanitarian work, but felt understandably angry and betrayed by the militant group who inflicted such an ordeal, albeit brief, on her parents and herself.

Meanwhile the German authorities faced another complication from a hostage-taking of Ms Ostoff, an archaeologist working in Iraq. She was released, it is alleged, by the payment of a considerable ransom, yet she stated her intention to stay on working in Iraq, clearly placing herself in danger of a replay of the hostage-taking.

This prospect has clearly caused some alarm in Germany and more widely. It may be that this is yet another argument for resisting the payment of ransoms, a practice which we know from experience gives massive encouragement to terrorists to take further hostages.

Conclusion

Terrorist hostage-taking presents democratic governments and law-enforcement agencies with acute dilemmas. The tactic of mass hostage-taking has now been sometimes used as in Spain and Fiji to overthrow elected governments. Fragile ethnically divided democracies are particularly at risk: because of the high value we place on each individual life there is a natural urge to concede to terrorist demands in order to save the lives of hostages. But suppose that by so readily giving in to terrorist blackmail we encourage more hostage-taking, putting more lives at risk? Very often terrorists' demands include the release of large numbers of their imprisoned comrades. Would it be morally right to agree to release a large number of terrorists back into circulation when they will then be able to cause more deaths through their campaigns of violence? Sometimes terrorists demand changes in policy or in the law: is it morally right to make such changes to appease the terrorists and in so doing ignore the will of the legislature, the courts and the democratic process? Governments, unlike families and private business organisations, have responsibilities to the whole of society. In a hostage crisis involving one of their embassies abroad they have a duty not only to the unfortunate victims of this particular incident, but also to the staff in other embassies who could be the targets of such incidents, and to those who in the future might be at higher risk if potential hostage-takers could see that the government had caved in to ransom demands on previous occasions. If the US government had not upheld the 'no ransom' policy in respect of its diplomats during the 1970s it would have faced a tidal wave of hostage-taking of diplomatic and consular staff.[40]

Another problem faced by governments dealing with politically motivated hostage-takers or terrorists motivated by religious fanaticism is that they may just be using hostage-taking as a tactic, e.g. to give them cover or to give them more killing time, or they may be expressive rather than instrumental: that is to say that the hostage-taker may simply be giving vent to hate, anger or desire of vengeance rather than to achieve clearly defined tactical goals. Expressive terrorists are particularly difficult to deal with: if their hatred or desire of vengeance is strong enough there is nothing the authorities can do other than try to reach the hostages before they are murdered. In some cases the terrorists may also want to make the ultimate statement of fanatical belief by taking their own lives as well as the lives of the hostages.

A recurrent theme of the hostage crises examined in this chapter has been the importance of careful planning and coordination, high-quality intelligence, and expertise in hostage negotiation, crisis management and tactical response for a successful outcome. The expertise and training required for these tasks cannot be achieved overnight. Therefore it would be the height of folly to allow these specialisms to be abandoned in the name of economy or to become badly run down and out of date. They should be part of the law-enforcement and security resources of every democratic country. A crucial requirement is the availability of expert hostage negotiators and a specialist back-up staff of interpreters, terrorism experts and psychologists, vital in helping crisis managers facing hostage situations with terrorists, many of whom are highly trained and experienced in dealing with the authorities. It is not a job for amateurs, and it is deeply regrettable that many countries have failed to take the business of selection and training of negotiators seriously. The necessary skills take time to acquire, but states with highly experienced police–negotiator teams are generally willing to provide training facilities for friendly countries. This form of training is not vastly expensive, and it is in the international interest that it should be made available even to the poorest countries, if necessary by making the training courses part of an aid programme.

In most cases it will probably be desirable to use trained police negotiators. The authorities should always be suspicious of private individuals recommending themselves for the job, or external organisations offering their 'good offices' to negotiate. In many cases the real motives behind such offers have much to do with self-publicity or furthering a political agenda rather than a satisfactory and speedy resolution to the hostage crisis.

The negotiator should be selected with great care. He or she must be firm and tough, while also being skilled at building up some rapport with the terrorists and using all available bargaining chips to coax concessions out of them, and to play for time. A good negotiator needs considerable courage, coolness and determination to stand up to the bullying and often brutal aggression of the hostage-takers, and to cope with the considerable stress involved. The job calls for enormous patience, a high degree of intelligence to spot clues to the terrorists' intentions, motives, interpersonal relations and likely tactics and behaviour.

It is also vital for the crisis managers to understand fully the limits of the negotiator's role, and to use the negotiator skilfully. The negotiator is not a decision maker. He must refer hostage-takers' requests to a higher authority while at the same time building up a working relationship with the terrorists' negotiator and using persuasion and force of personality to get the hostage-takers to release their captives unharmed. The upsurge of hostage-taking of aid workers and other civilians in Iraq, the Gaza Strip and elsewhere in 2004–05 underlines the need for expertise in both hostage negotiation *and* hostage rescue.

As we saw in the case of the Russian hostage crises of 1995–96 the absence of appropriate expertise, training and planning was a crucial factor leading to tragic failures in response. The history of modern terrorism shows that highly trained hostage-rescue commandos and tactical response teams have just as vital a role as highly trained hostage negotiators. It is true that many dangerous hostage situations have ended without a shot being fired. But, as was clearly demonstrated in the Balcombe Street siege, often the mere knowledge that a highly trained elite armed force could be unleashed against them can have a salutary effect on persuading hostage-takers to release the hostages peacefully. For all these reasons, in my view, urgent attention should be paid to enhancing cooperation among the G8 states to improve the training, expertise and planning capabilities of those states that are lagging behind in this field.

But the central lesson for democratic governments on the problems of response to hostage-taking is that prevention is far better than cure. If they wait until a hostage-taking crisis is upon them, they are already too late to avoid a great deal of disruption, damage and the inevitable high risks of decision making in these agonising circumstances. An effective proactive counter-terrorism policy, founded upon the highest possible quality of counter-terrorism intelligence, national security coordination and international cooperation, offers the best chance of avoiding such events, or at any rate significantly reducing the chances of their occurrence.

9   Aviation security

Terrorists make it their business to threaten the most basic of human rights – the right to life. The civil aviation industry has since its inception been dedicated to protecting the safety of passengers and crews. Indeed it is the incredibly good safety record of the world's airlines that has helped to make air travel such a phenomenally successful mode of transport and one of the fastest-growing industries in the world. Therefore even if there were no legal obligations on airlines and airports to provide security there is an inescapable moral obligation resting on both governments and the civil aviation community to collaborate in taking all possible measures to protect passengers, crews, ground staff and the public in general against the scourge of aviation terrorism.[1]

Liberal democratic governments and the public now have other powerful reasons, in addition to the principle of protecting the lives of the innocent, which should spur them to help create effective aviation security. The horrific suicide hijack attacks of 9/11, the most lethal acts of aviation terrorism in history, provide the most powerful argument for establishing an effective aviation security system, and it is one which should add far greater urgency to our efforts. The most dramatic and tragic evidence of Al Qaeda's interest in civil aviation terrorism as a method and a target was the 9/11 suicide hijackings. It would be a serious mistake to assume that this exploitation of the vulnerability of aviation was a one-off, a unique departure from their normal pattern of tactics and targeting. In the eyes of Al Qaeda, 9/11 was a huge victory, a blow struck at the solar plexus of the US economy and the headquarters of the US military. They proved to themselves and to the world that they could turn airliners filled with aviation fuel into the equivalent of cruise missiles capable of killing thousands of people and causing mass destruction on the ground. For an estimated cost of around $500,000 they inflicted damage and disruption costing many trillions of dollars, not counting the billions of dollars expended by the US and the Coalition allies on the war in Iraq and the ensuing occupation, all in the name of fighting war on terrorism. The suicide-hijacking tactic enabled Al Qaeda to carry their 'jihad' into the heartland of America, to kill thousands of Americans (an explicit objective of the terrorist movement), and to gain unprecedented global publicity. Moreover, long before 9/11 the 'new terrorists' had already clearly demonstrated their fascination with civil aviation as both a method and a target. Ramzi Yousef, a terrorist master bomb-maker who was closely linked to Al Qaeda's leadership, bombed a Philippine Airlines plane in midair as a dry run for his 'Bojinka' plan to blow up a dozen US carriers in the Pacific region, a plan which would have cost thousands of innocent lives and which was only prevented by the accidental discovery of the plan on Yousef's computer in a Manila apartment. We also know that Al Qaeda was involved in a plan to cause an explosion at Los Angeles International Airport at the time of the millennium celebrations.

Nineteen Al Qaeda suicide hijackers seized control of three US airliners and attempted to hijack a fourth airliner with the aim of crashing them into key US targets. At 08.48am an American Airlines Flight 11, carrying 92 passengers and crew, was flown into the North Tower of the World Trade Center in New York. United Airlines Flight 175 with 65 passengers and crew was flown into the South Tower of the World Trade Center. Thirty-seven minutes later American Airlines Flight 77, with 64 passengers and crew, was crashed into the Pentagon in Washington DC. At 10.03am United Airlines Flight 93, with 45 passengers and crew, crashed into a field in Pennsylvania following a fight between hijackers and the passengers and crew. It is believed that the Al Qaeda terrorists intended to fly Flight 93 into the Capitol building in Washington but were prevented through the courageous efforts of the passengers and crew.

The South Tower of the World Trade Center collapsed at 10.05am and the North Tower collapsed 24 minutes later. The suicide hijack attacks killed almost 3,000 people, a greater number than those who died in the Pearl Harbor attack. In previous chapters we have considered the wider implication of the 9/11 attacks on US policy and international relations. In this chapter we will examine the implication for aviation security. We have already examined the major intelligence failures that helped to make the US so extraordinarily vulnerable to the 9/11 attacks, but it is important to remember that inadequate and incompetent aviation security at all the US airports involved also contributed to the suicide hijackers' success. Even though the intelligence-warning process failed dismally the coordinated suicide hijackings would have been prevented if the aviation security at the airport boarding gates had been efficient, thorough and comprehensive. In this chapter we will examine some of the security lessons which can be drawn from the challenges of designing an effective aviation security system, and the complex problems of combating emergencies and future threats.

Lessons from earlier aviation terrorism

Thirty-six years ago the major terrorist threat to aviation was conventional hijacking.[2] This problem has by no means disappeared; the 1988 Kuwait Airlines hijacking demonstrated extreme cunning and ruthlessness on the part of the terrorists, who proved more than a match for the aviation authorities in the countries where they landed.[3] However, the danger of conventional hijacking has been sharply reduced by three factors: (1) a combination of simple but effective technology and procedures; (2) improved international cooperation, including such measures as the US–Cuba Hijack Pact which closed down Cuba as a terrorist bolt-hole; and (3) the deterrent effect of dramatically successful commando-style rescues of airline passengers and crews at Entebbe and Mogadishu. Conventional hijackings are not necessarily low-lethality in outcome. In November 1996 an Ethiopian Airlines 767 crashed into the Indian Ocean when it was seized by three hijackers who refused to accept the pilot's word that the aircraft needed to refuel in order to get to the hijackers' desired destination in Australia. When, as a result, the plane crashed off the Comoro Islands 127 people died.[4] Over the past decade terrorists have tended to switch from hijacking to far more cowardly tactics of smuggling a bomb on board an airliner and timing it to explode in mid air, suicide hijacking and suicide sabotage bombing. As was demonstrated in the horror of the Pan Am explosion over Lockerbie in 1988 and the UTA explosion over Niger the following year, when a bomb exploded on an airliner at an altitude of over 30,000 feet, the passengers and crew have no chance whatsoever of survival. It is mass murder in the skies. Modern plastic explosives and sophisticated timing mechanisms provide an ideal weapon for terrorists and this purpose. The huge payloads of modern jumbo jets serve to maximise the carnage. In the decade 1960–69 there were nine sabotage attacks against civil aircraft resulting in 286 deaths. In the period 1980–89 there were 12 attacks causing a total of 1,144 deaths – a tripling of the number of fatalities per incident over the 20-year period.[5] By the end of the 1980s aviation terrorism rivalled technical failure and pilot error as a cause of fatalities in civil aviation. Nor should we overlook the potential for much higher levels of casualties if an airliner were to be blown up above a major centre of population.

As I argued in my 1989 report *The Lessons of Lockerbie*, the sad fact is that our aviation security systems had become hopelessly outdated by the 1980s.[6] They were geared solely to dealing with the hijacking threat. The magnetometer archways and X-ray machines introduced in the early 1970s were designed to prevent passengers from smuggling metallic objects, potential hijack weapons, on board aircraft. Although the sabotage bomb threat was clearly evident by the mid 1980s most of the world's aviation authorities had made little or no effort to put in place the explosive-detection systems, stringent baggage reconciliation procedures, effective perimeter and access controls, and other measures necessary to counter it.

The only airline that proved fully capable of coping with the new challenge was El Al. They compensated for the lack of an effective explosive-detection system (EDS) by exploiting their unique assets in counter-terrorism intelligence, their well-honed techniques of passenger profiling and interrogation and their comprehensive manual searches of luggage. In fact it was an alert El Al security officer at Heathrow who discovered the bomb Nizar Hindawi had duped his pregnant Irish girlfriend to take aboard an El Al jet. Yet although all airlines have much to learn from El Al in terms of intelligence, motivation and the importance of the human factor in aviation security, it would be totally impracticable for the major aviation states to adopt El Al's overall approach. Even El Al's tight security sometimes fails, however. In April 1996 a Hezbollah agent travelling under a stolen UK passport conspired to destroy an El Al airline in mid air. He arrived in Israel on 4 April on a Swissair flight from Zurich. He planned to blow up an El Al jet leaving Israel and succeeded in smuggling almost a kilogram of US-made RDX explosive through Zurich and Ben Gurion airports (200grams/ 7oz would have sufficed to destroy the jet). He failed because he blew himself up in a Jerusalem hotel.[7] The Israeli airline has much smaller total air traffic, and no short-haul flights, and its passengers are sufficiently motivated to accept much earlier check-in times than would be customary for American or European airlines.

The conventional hijack problem

The airliner hijacking phenomenon has been with us for over 30 years. It has become less frequent recently, but it shows no sign of disappearing. Much now depends on the ability of crisis managers and aviation specialists to handle the situation successfully. It is important to send a clear message to deter other groups from a fresh wave of hijacking.

Our policy should be to prevent the hijackers refuelling and flying off with their hostages, and to use expert negotiation to bring the release of all passengers and crew unharmed. The British track record in achieving this result is excellent. The use of an SAS hostage-rescue squad should only be considered as a last resort if negotiation fails and the hijackers start killing the hostages.

There are key lessons to be drawn from the hijackings of the Indian Airlines plane over Christmas 1999 and the Afghan plane that went to Stansted: there are still massive weaknesses in security in many of the world's airports and these must be urgently rectified. The security failures in both Kathmandu and Kabul enabled the terrorists to get hijack weapons aboard. Full investigation into security at these airports is needed to discover how this happened.

In many countries there are no trained negotiators or hostage-rescue squads available. The Indian Airlines hijack revealed the abysmal state of international cooperation among the South Asian countries. Both hijacks demonstrated how many airports receiving hijacked aircraft now ignore their responsibilities as host states under the international conventions and allow the aircraft to refuel and fly off to another destination, thus prolonging the trauma for the hostages and making their rescue all the more difficult.

The recurring threat to the lives of airline passengers reminds us of the importance of maintaining high standards of aviation security against all types of threat. It also reminds us that in some countries with lawless regions the threat of domestic hijackings is as grave as the more publicised international threat. Yet all too often standards of security for domestic flights are far lower and this provides an obvious opportunity for terrorists. Nor is this just a feature of poorer countries. The United States, the world's leading aviation state, has grave weaknesses in security for domestic flights even though measures to improve protection of international flights have been greatly strengthened since the 9/11 attacks.

But reforms purely at national and local levels will not be enough. Sadly, we are still far from achieving a really effective global aviation security regime. Terrorist organisations will seek out the weakest links. Hence security-conscious governments should exert pressure on the International Civil Aviation Organisation

(ICAO) to establish a proper international security inspectorate with powers to carry out spot checks on airports, and real sanctions to deal with defaulting airports and airlines.

A radical and proactive approach of this kind would greatly reduce the global aviation system's vulnerability to the hijack menace and to other forms of aviation terrorism. It is foolish and irresponsible to adopt the fatalist position that 'there is nothing we can do' to combat the threat. The rational and positive approach is to plan ahead and thereby ensure that civil aviation remains the safest and most popular form of transport in the world.

The first wave of hijackings after the Second World War were mostly committed by refugees escaping from communist countries. In the whole history of hijackings since 1947, 61 per cent have been refugee escapes. In 1968–69 there was a veritable explosion of hijackings. In 1969 there were 82 recorded hijack attempts worldwide – more than twice the total attempts for the period 1947–67. There were two major new kinds of hijacker active from 1968: US criminals seeking ransom or flight to Havana to escape the law, and Palestinians using hijacks for the first time as a political weapon to publicise their cause and to force Israel and Western governments into releasing Palestinian prisoners from gaol.

Boarding gate security searches and screening of passengers and luggage, introduced initially in the United States in 1973, together with the US–Cuba Hijack Pact, certainly had a significant effect in reducing the number of aircraft hijacking attempts. Airliner hijacking has undergone a welcome overall decline since the peak of 385 incidents in the decade 1967–76. In the following decade the total had dropped to 200 incidents, and in 1987–96 the figure was further reduced to 212. In the 1980s and 1990s, after the Air India bombing of 1985 and the Pan Am bombing over Lockerbie in 1988, the main focus of aviation security switched from hijacking to sabotage bombing.

It would be a great mistake, however, to assume that the hijacking threat has disappeared. The TWA hijack to Beirut in 1985 and the 16-day hijack of a Kuwait Airways plane in 1988 showed how sophisticated and ruthless hijackers could still gain publicity for their cause. Moreover, the TWA hijackers were able to use the threat against the US hostages to get 756 prisoners released from gaol in Israel and South Lebanon.

Hijacking provided terrorist groups with convenient symbols of their designated 'enemy' nations and a supply of hostages or victims, often including VIPs and influential people from several countries all in the passenger list. It would be a grave mistake to underestimate the threat to life posed by terrorist hijacking.

In December 1994, the armed Algerian Islamic group, GIA, hijacked an Air France airbus to Marseilles. They planned a novel refinement in terrorist tactics. They aimed to blow up the airliner with its 283 passengers over Paris as a kind of flying bomb in a final act of suicide terrorism. Fortunately, the expert French counter-terrorism commandos, GIGN (Group d'Intervention de la Gendarmerie Nationale), were able to storm the aircraft and rescue the passengers and crew.

The hijacking over Christmas 1999 of the Indian Airlines airliner by Kashmiri militants to Amritsar, Lahore and ultimately Kandahar attracted huge world-wide publicity because of the dramatic nature of the threat to the hostages, one of whom had already been murdered by the hijackers, and because of the extremely tense relations between two nuclear-armed neighbours: India and Pakistan.

India has traditionally followed a strict policy of no concessions to hijackers, but the BJP government was compelled to heed the powerful pressure of the hostages' relatives and the Indian media. They did not concede the hijackers' full demands, which were for the release of 36 Kashmiri militants from gaol and $200 million ransom. But they did ultimately agree to release three key militant leaders from gaol. This was regarded as a great victory by the hijackers, who were also able to escape from the scene. It has been suggested that this incident may have encouraged the hijackers of the Afghan airliner to adopt this tactic.

Designing an effective aviation security system

In designing an effective aviation security system, I suggest that we should be encouraged and inspired by the lessons of America's response to the hijacking plague of the late 1960s and early 1970s. If you examine the statistics of world-wide hijacking in the period 1968–72 you will find that in 1969, 1971 and 1972 almost half of the hijack attempts originated in the United States.[8] In the peak year, 1969, no less than 37 of the 82 hijacking attempts worldwide took place aboard flights starting from the United States. The programme of anti-hijack measures adopted by the US authorities in 1972 was an audacious one, inspired by the broad vision of the man who was appointed Director of Aviation Security, Lieutenant General Benjamin Davis.

Lieutenant General Davis immediately recognised the measures taken to combat the hijacker in the air were merely palliative: once the hijacker was airborne it was too late to do very much. He therefore adopted the policy of thorough screening and searches at the boarding gate to prevent the hijacker and his weapons getting aboard. Davis and his advisers were told that this radical scheme would not work, that the airlines and the airports would refuse to cooperate, and that the American public would not accept universal boarding gate security checks. The critics were proved wrong on all counts. The secret of making the checks acceptable to the travelling public was to ensure that adequate staff and machines were available to check passengers very rapidly, thus ensuring that any delays that occurred happened at the check-in desks or through unavoidable technical, weather or air traffic control hold-ups and not at security. The airports and airlines cooperated to make the new system work, initially because they had no other choice. In 1973 legislation made the boarding gate security measures mandatory throughout America. However, the aviation industry was fairly rapidly won over to the value of the new system. In 1973, the year after its introduction, US hijack attempts dropped from 31 to three and in the course of boarding gate searches 3,500lb of high explosives, 2,000 guns and 23,000 knives and other lethal weapons were found.[9]

The American airport security measures were so successful that other major aviation countries rapidly adopted similar measures, and eventually they spread worldwide. We can therefore learn some useful lessons from the US anti-hijacking measures which could be applied to the design of an effective system to combat the sabotage bombing threat: (1) the system was centrally designed and coordinated and was made mandatory for all airlines and airports throughout the United States; (2) the system used effective, widely available and affordable technology for boarding gate screening of all passengers and carry-on luggage; (3) the system was designed to be fully compatible with a rapid throughput of passengers without any significant loss of passenger comfort or convenience, and hence with no reduction in the commercial viability of the industry.

Let us bear these lessons in mind in defining the essential components of an aviation security system capable of dealing with today's infinitely more complex and dangerous problems of international aviation security. It would be foolish to underestimate the difficulties involved in getting our present governments and the aviation industry to act effectively at both national and international levels. Bismarck once said 'Fools say they learn from experience. I prefer to learn from others' experience'. Let us hope that other countries do not have to experience more tragic outrages on the scale of Lockerbie before they are mobilised to take the necessary action.

The most important general lesson we must learn from the recent history of aviation terrorism is never again to allow terrorists to get so far ahead of the world's airport security system. We should already be anticipating the tactics terrorists are likely to use once the methods of sabotage and suicide hijacking have been blocked. For example, we should be devising ways of preventing terrorists from obtaining and using surface-to-air missiles against civil aviation.[10] We should be planning defensive and countermeasures to deal with the possible terrorist use of chemical and biological weapons against such targets as airport terminals and airliners.

Nor is there any evidence that post-9/11 Al Qaeda has lost interest in civil aviation as a method and a target in its global terrorist campaign. On the contrary, there is abundant evidence that they continue to recognise that aviation terrorism can still provide a low-cost, potentially high-yield means of achieving their tactical objectives. We know that Al Qaeda was behind Richard Reid's attempt at the suicide bombing of an American Airlines jet using a bomb hidden in his shoe. It is also clear that the Al Qaeda network was behind the attempt to shoot down a chartered aircraft full of Israeli tourists when it was taking off from Mombasa Airport in Kenya. The missiles, of Soviet manufacture, narrowly missed the aircraft. We also know that the intelligence services in the US, the UK, other EU countries and in the Middle East continue to be concerned at the amount of intelligence they have gathered, which suggests that Al Qaeda is continuing to plan suicide bombings, suicide hijackings and the use of MANPADs as a method of attacking civil aviation. It is clear that, despite the best efforts of the US and its allies to curtail Al Qaeda funding and block their funds held in the Western banking system, the terrorist network is still capable of circumventing these controls and certainly has sufficient assets to acquire additional supplies of surface-to-air missiles.

To sum up, the threat of international terrorist attack against civil aviation, not only against UK airliners but also against other carriers using British airport facilities and carrying British passengers, remains very real. Indeed since 9/11, which Al Qaeda sees as a great victory, the threat has been considerably heightened. We know from Al Qaeda's track record that they not only favour no-warning coordinated suicide attacks: they also tend to repeat the same tactics and return to the same targets once they are convinced that this will bring them success in their 'holy war' against the US and its allies.

Statistics on the annual totals of terrorist incidents may therefore become dangerously misleading and must not be allowed to create complacency. There is no doubt that aviation security measures and standards have been greatly improved in the US, and that European Union countries' aviation security, which was already well ahead of US standards prior to 9/11, has continued to improve incrementally. However, many other countries, especially the poorest countries of the global South, have pathetically inadequate airport security measures to deal with the suicide hijacker or suicide sabotage bombers' threats. It is clear that the Al Qaeda terrorist network has the resources, sophistication and ruthlessness to find weaknesses in UK and international aviation security and to commit mass murder on the airways on a scale we have not seen before. One of the key lessons we should have learnt from the 9/11 attacks is that *qualitative* changes in terrorists' *modus operandi* can lead to a massive increase in the lethality of attacks. There is ample evidence that the UK government, the Security Service, the Metropolitan Police and TRANSEC (the Department for Transport Security Inspectorate) were fully aware of the heightened level of threat, but it is a matter of concern to find some senior staff in the aviation industry, including some members of the Airline Pilots' Association and some senior commercial managers, ill-informed about the changed nature of the threat, reluctant to adopt any additional security measures and, in some cases, anxious to discard or suspend some of the measures introduced or proposed in the wake of 9/11.

Why government should take the lead role in aviation security

There are frequent complaints from Chief Executive Officers and other figures in the commercial world of aviation that they are subject to too much oversight and 'interference' by government ministers and officials in security matters. (We recall the loud complaints over the efforts to introduce a UK 'sky marshal' programme to enhance in-flight security, for example.) We would draw the reader's attention to the latest academic research by Hainmuller and Lemnitzer – 'Why do Europeans Fly Safer? – The Politics of Airport Security in Europe and the US', *Terrorism and Political Violence*, Vol. 15, No. 4, pp. 1–36, who have concluded:

> ... we have shown that the different performance of the American and German security regimes before September 11 can be largely attributed to institutional factors. In the US, responsibility for airport security was assigned to airlines whose cost-cutting efforts resulted in low performance and lax

controls. In Germany, in contrast, responsibility was delegated to the government, which shielded the provision of airport security from market pressures and led to high performance. Drawing upon the in-depth study of both cases, experience from other European countries and the theoretical arguments developed above we claim that the delegation of responsibility for airport security to government is a necessary condition for a satisfactory security performance.

These findings are confirmed by an examination of UK experience. The policy implications are very clear. It is generally agreed that US airport security has been greatly enhanced since the Federal authorities took over responsibility for its implementation in all major airports. This adds further weight to the Hainmuller–Lemnitzer thesis and strengthens our case for recommending that governments should not relinquish or diminish their key regulatory role in aviation security matters.

Another powerful argument for ensuring that governments and their relevant security and counter-terrorism agencies maintain their lead role in preventing and combating aviation terrorism is of course the vital requirement for efficient overall strategic direction and oversight. One of the most important reasons for maintaining the government's lead role in the field of aviation security is the need to fund and conduct top-calibre scientific and technological development in fields such as the detection of IEDs, the bomb-proofing or strengthening of airliners, airport terminals and other potential terrorist targets, perimeter and access control, computerisation of passenger profiling data, enhancing cyber-security to help prevent sabotage and disruption of air traffic control systems, etc. Research and development of this kind is extremely expensive but nevertheless essential if we are to keep ahead of increasingly sophisticated ruthless and fanatically dedicated international terrorists who have already demonstrated their capacity for technical and tactical innovation.

New and emerging threats: the need to keep ahead of the terrorists' tactics and technology

Aviation authorities should have learned this lesson in the 1980s especially in the wake of the Air India Flight 122 and Pan Am 103 sabotage bombings, which together caused the death of almost 600 people: the civil aviation authorities and the industry in the 1980s were still dependent on boarding gate search technology that was capable of detecting guns and other metallic weaponry of the kind used by hijackers but was incapable of detecting explosives hidden in passenger or hold luggage. We paid a heavy price for our failure to introduce appropriate measures and technology to protect civil aviation from the sabotage bomb threat.

One important area of emerging terrorist innovation is in the choice of explosives. In recent years terrorists have favoured the use of powerful military explosives such as PETN, RDX and TNT, easily obtainable by means of theft, purchase or supply through illegal arms market or by a state sponsor. But as the explosives-detection technology currently deployed in most airports is geared to detecting these well-known military explosives, so the terrorists have a strong incentive to try switching to explosives or pyrotechnics which do not conform to the classic formulas for military explosives. For example, peroxides can be used as stand-alone explosives or as oxidisers in composite explosives, triacetone triperoxide (TATP) can be synthesised from acetone, as is believed to have been used in a number of terrorist incidents. The methods for making this and a wide range of nitrogen-free explosives are easily accessible in do-it-yourself explosives manuals and from the internet.

The fact that this threat was already being posed by terrorists linked to Al Qaeda was brought home to the public by the August 2006 pre-emptive arrest of young men who plotted a suicide mission to blow up seven airliners in mid-flight from Heathrow to North American destinations using liquid bombs which would have been assembled on board the aircraft. Approximately 2,000 passengers and crew would have been killed, and if the stricken planes had fallen onto cities the total death toll could have matched that of the 9/11 attacks. The police and the intelligence services in the UK, where the arrests were made, believe that they intervened in the nick of time to prevent these atrocities. Emergency measures to prevent passengers carrying liquids onto airliners were introduced at airports, thus creating delays and inconvenience to passengers. Once the details of the liquid bomb plot became known most passengers recognised that the aviation authorities had to take swift action in case there were members of the conspiracy still at large and able to mount liquid bomb attacks.

Emergency airport security measures were essential because existing security technology and procedures were not configured to prevent the liquid bomb tactic. Once again, a serious gap in aviation security had been revealed and it was only prompt action by the police and intelligence services that prevented mass murder in the skies.

Another major gap in aviation security was revealed on Christmas Day 2009 when a passenger on an airline approaching Detroit airport attempted to blow up the plane by detonating explosives hidden in his underpants. Existing aviation security systems were not capable of identifying explosives cleverly concealed in body orifices of passengers. It is alleged that Farouk Abdulmutallab, the young Nigerian who was arrested and charged with this attempted bombing, was recruited to carry out this suicide sabotage attack by Al Qaeda and that he was briefed on his mission by Al Qaeda in Yemen. Once again it was luck which saved the lives of the passengers and crew and potential victims on the ground. There was clearly an intelligence failure, as the father of the young Nigerian who had been arrested reported his fears about his son's involvement in Jihadi extremist violence to the US embassy in Nigeria. The worry for aviation security authorities is that others have been recruited to carry out similar missions, and that airport passenger search procedures will not be improved in time to prevent mass murder in the skies by exploiting this gap in security.

Aviation security authorities and personnel need to be fully aware of the growing interest being shown by terrorist groups in a wide range of non-detectable home explosives. What progress has been made in research and development to develop, test and deploy detection technologies capable of identifying non-nitrogenous explosives and other 'exotic' explosives? In addition to using nitrogen-free explosives, terrorists could make use of a wide variety of incendiary devices, self-igniting materials, hydrides and phosphorus. Nor should it be assumed that it is only the 'new' terrorist groups, which are aware of the possibilities of non-nitrogenous explosives. (For example, Hamas has used TATP in its bombing campaign against Israel.)

In addition to the terrorist search for 'non-detectable' and exotic explosives, there is worrying evidence that some terrorists, particularly the Al Qaeda network and its affiliated groups, are seriously interested in acquiring and using CBRN weapons. As explained in the threat assessment in Chapter 3 of this study, Al Qaeda, unlike most of the 'traditional' terrorist groups, explicitly aims at mass killing. They do not observe any humanitarian limits to their 'holy war' terror. They totally ignore the Hague and Geneva Conventions and do not recognise any distinction between combatants and non-combatants. Nor do they appear to be persuaded by any particular arguments for restraint in attacks on the civilian population. They are not constrained by any concern that the use of WMD might endanger the lives of their operatives as they believe in suicide attacks and they seem convinced that they have a limitless supply of potential volunteers for 'self-sacrifice' for the jihad. Hence, aviation security authorities need to prepare for the possibility of attacks using chemical, biological or radiological weapons. Even if the terrorists only succeed in improvising very crude devices of this kind, we should be aware that their deployment in the enclosed space of, for example, a busy airport terminal building or subway system or on board a jumbo jet could have extremely serious consequences, including the loss of large numbers of lives. In light of the above dangers and threats referred to in Chapter 3 of this study that indicated some form of CBRN attack by 'New Terrorists' is no longer simply a low-probability event, it is a major consideration for contingency planning by aviation security authorities. This must involve the closest possible coordination with the emergency services and hospitals. A key requirement is for rapid detection and identification of any CBRN agent that may have been used. Without adequate and rapid means to do this it is impossible to make appropriate decisions about how to deal with treatment of casualties, and how to mitigate the scale of lethality. The experience of Japanese authorities dealing with the 1995 Sarin gas attack on the Tokyo subway system showed the value of calling on the expertise of the defence forces. Training exercises to practise civil military coordination in such emergencies are vital and should be held in all major airports. Where there are known antidotes to specific chemical or biological weapons, it is important to ensure that hospitals in all regions can call on local stocks to deal with a mass casualty terrorist emergency. Similarly it should be an urgent priority to equip hospitals and ambulance services of all regions with supplies of decontamination units sufficient to provide rapid processing in a mass-casualty attack; that there is a proper training and exercise programme to ensure that the coordination of all services involved work effectively and smoothly; and that not only paramedics but *all* emergency personnel know how to use the equipment and the appropriate antidote, if one is available. In view of the interest shown by Al Qaeda in civil aviation targets it is important to ask whether airports and airline staff are regularly offered briefings and training on this type of threat and provided with regular opportunities to participate in appropriate exercises with the emergency services.

All experts in civil aviation agree that another rapidly emerging threat to the civil aviation industry stems from 'cyber-terrorism' or the use of information technology to cause great damage and disruption, including possibly mass-killing of passengers and crews in multiple coordinated cyber-sabotage attacks on the aviation computer systems. What progress has been made in finding possible measures to help to give some protection against this threat?

However, taking full account of these threats, it is clear that the three most serious current threats to civil aviation are the MANPAD, suicide hijackings and suicide sabotage bombing. These will be dealt with in the ensuing discussion. All major aviation countries are still searching for more effective countermeasures against these types of threat – all of which have been posed by Al Qaeda.

The UK, in common with all major aviation countries, now faces a range of new or emerging threats, all of which are extremely difficult to counter. The first and most challenging of these is the MANPAD threat, the use of man-portable air defence systems, or shoulder-launch surface-to-air missiles. This type of weapon has been used for many years against primarily military targets. Annually since 1996 there have been several attacks on civilian aircraft and 19 civilians have been killed per year. However, the Al Qaeda network, which is, as we know, waging a 'holy war' involving mass killing, has access to surface-to-air missiles[11] and has used them in attempts to down aircraft in Saudi Arabia and Kenya. It has been estimated that up to 700,000 such weapons are in circulation, in the hands of various regimes and terrorist and insurgent movements around the world, including Al Qaeda and its affiliates. What are the main options for countering this threat?

First there is the possibility of installing anti-missile defence systems on all airliners. El Al is reported, in 2004, to be fitting the Flight Guard systems to all its passenger aircraft. The system works by automatically releasing diversionary flares if an on-board sensor detects a heat-seeking missile approaching. According to most experts, to adopt this measure for all passenger aircraft in major aviation countries would be prohibitively expensive. It is estimated that it would cost billions to adopt the measure for all the passenger fleets and would take six to ten years to install.

A far cheaper though more uncertain protection is to greatly enhance the intelligence efforts to gain advance warning of a conspiracy to use MANPAD weapons and to intercept the perpetrators before they can launch their attack. The most practicable countermeasure is to combine this intelligence effort with intensive surveillance and monitoring of the vulnerable areas around major airports, which provide the most likely points for launching MANPAD weapons. It is known that the British authorities have completed MANPAD defence plans of this kind for Heathrow airport.

What of the suicide hijacking threat? It might be assumed that in the wake of the devastation and loss of life caused by the 9/11 hijackers the UK authorities would have acted swiftly and effectively to block the threat of this type of attack. It is claimed by the government that we have now set up measures to protect against this threat. The suicide hijacking threat is a product of the 'new terrorism' of Al Qaeda and its affiliates, though there had been earlier plans and threats by extreme Islamist terrorist groups to crash aircraft on to urban targets, for example the GIA group who threatened to force an Airbus they had hijacked in Algeria to fly to Paris where they would crash the plane onto the city. However, it was the 19 Al Qaeda suicide hijackers who brought this idea to reality by crashing airlines into the World Trade Center and the Pentagon. The details of these attacks, how the terrorists planned and prepared for them, why the US authorities failed to obtain advance warning and how the US responded are authoritatively covered in *The 9/11 Commission Report* (2004) and it is not our purpose to re-examine these matters here. However, it is of vital importance for the UK and the international community to learn from the tragic experience of the US attacks, in order to enhance our strategies, policies and measures to prevent or protect against this form of mass casualty terrorism. The first key area requiring examination is the intelligence failures, which in large part explain why the US authorities did not have advance warning and why they lacked any effective countermeasures. Some counter-terrorism and intelligence officials had enough indications to know that a very big Al Qaeda attack was about to happen but they did not know in what form it would take. Their political masters did not attach a high enough priority to the problem of combating the Al Qaeda threat, and were thus caught completely off guard. The US public had been generally oblivious to the threat and were therefore shocked and stunned by the magnitude and severity of the attacks.

The 9/11 Commission Report concluded that:

> During the spring and summer of 2001, US intelligence agencies received a stream of warnings that Al Qaeda planned, or as one report put it, 'something very, very, very big'. Director of Central Intelligence George Tenet told us, 'The system was blinking red'.
>
> Although Bin Laden was determined to strike in the United States as President Clinton has been told and President Bush was reminded in a Presidential Daily Brief article briefing him in August 2001, the specific threat information pointed overseas. Numerous precautions were taken overseas. Domestic agencies were not effectively mobilized. The threat did not receive national media attention comparable with the millennium alert.

Intelligence failures

The 9/11 Report, and the Senate Intelligence Committee Report on the intelligence failures agree that there were points of vulnerability in the 9/11 plot and there were opportunities to disrupt the plot, which, tragically, were missed. These missed opportunities included: failing to put two terrorist suspects on the watch-list; failing to trail them after they travelled to Bangkok; failing to inform the FBI about one suspect's US visa or his companion's journey to the US; failing to take adequate measures to track the two suspects in the US; failing to connect the arrest of Moussaoui, described as being interested in flying training simply to use the plane for an act of terrorism; failing to give adequate attention to clues of an impending major Al Qaeda attack; and failing to discover manipulation of passports and false statements on visa applications.

Moreover, in addition to the specific 'missed opportunities' listed above, there were more fundamental weaknesses in the US intelligence community, which contributed to the overall failure to anticipate the 9/11 attacks. There was an acute shortage of high-quality intelligence on Al Qaeda. HUMINT, which is the best means of learning about terrorist plans and intentions, had been neg-lected at the expense of reliance on electronic intelligence. The efforts of the plethora of intelligence organisations, including the major agencies, the CIA and the FBI, were inadequately coordinated and there was no proper inter-agency review of National Intelligence Estimate on terrorism through the whole period from 1995 and 9/11. Meanwhile the FBI, which is primarily a Federal law-enforcement agency rather than intelligence organisation, had become increas-ingly worried about the threat of terrorism from Islamic extremist groups, but its efforts were primarily case-specific and aimed at bringing prosecutions of individuals rather than aimed at preventing terrorist attacks. The FBI had very limited capabilities for intelligence collection and strategic analysis and for sharing intelligence with domestic and friendly overseas agencies. They also had to cope with a shortage of funds and inadequate training for the counter-terrorism role. Some of these endemic weaknesses have been addressed by the Bush administration. The FBI and CIA have now been directed by the President to closely coordinate their counter-terrorism efforts. The FBI has been given more resources and improved training. In response to the *9/11 Commission Report* the President has appointed a National Director and a National Counter-terrorism Center. (However, the National Director is not apparently being provided with a budget, and the first appointee was a Republican Congressman with only very limited and junior experience as a CIA employee in the 1970s who is widely regarded as a *political* appointee rather than as an intelligence professional.)

The establishment of a National Counter-terrorism Center is clearly a highly encouraging development. As the 9/11 Commission explain in their report, ' ... the problems of coordination have multiplied ... and a new National Center would help to break "the older mould of organization stovepiped purely in executive agencies"'.

It is to be hoped that an effective and well-resourced National Center will overcome the major weaknesses that the establishment of the Department of Homeland Security failed to address: i.e. the lack of coordination between the CIA and the FBI, which has been the subject of criticism both by the Senate investigation and the 9/11 Commission.

Crisis management and military options

Just as successive US administrations prior to 9/11 had always seen terrorism as a threat to American personnel and facilities overseas rather than in the American homeland, so the US crisis managers and military planners prepared a variety of strike options for attacking bin Laden and his movement overseas. Prior to 9/11 the only case where military action was taken was on 20 August 1998 when the US used missile strikes to hit Al Qaeda targets in Afghanistan and a factory in the Sudan, which US officials alleged made precursors of chemical weapons, though this was never proved. Following this action, which was the Clinton administration's response to Al Qaeda's bomb attacks on US embassies in Kenya and Tanzania, it was claimed that there was no sufficiently actionable intelligence to justify further military attacks. The use of the military to protect the US homeland against terrorist attacks was not even considered as a serious issue.

As the *9/11 Commission Report* explains, officials were completely unprepared to respond to the 9/11 attacks. As the Commission states:

> On the morning of 9/11 the existing protocol was unsuited in every respect for what was about to happen. ... What ensued was the hurried attempt to create an improvised defence by officials who had never encountered or trained against the situation they faced.

Time and again air-traffic controllers lost the hijacked planes. One airliner (the one heading for the Pentagon) was lost track of for over half an hour. Air Force jets were ultimately scrambled, but they believed that the Pentagon had been hit by Russian missiles, and were heading away from Washington. Communications among those supposedly responsible for handling the crisis were appallingly bad. By the time Vice President Cheney's order to shoot down the airliners was received by the Air Force, three of the hijacked airliners had already been crashed into their targets, and apparently for a time, Cheney was under the impression that two of the planes had been shot down by US forces. One of the major problems had been that civilian officials were far too late in alerting the military of the developing attack.

In other words, the immediate response of the US authorities shows an appalling weakness in crisis management, communications and coordination.

Suicide hijackings as acts of war: the dilemmas posed for crisis managers

September 11 inaugurated a new and infinitely more dangerous era of aviation terrorism. Traditional hijacking is naturally still of concern and has, on occasion, led to deaths and injuries among passengers and crews. However, there are tried and tested means of dealing with such events. In cases of traditional hijacking that are politically motivated the hijackers' aim is generally to obtain international publicity for their cause and to wrest concessions from the authorities they are targeting. Most hijackings of this type end peacefully with the majority of passengers and crew physically unharmed. The aim of suicide hijackers is entirely different. They want to turn the aircraft into a missile and crash it into a target on the ground, causing destruction, disruption and, in the case of Al Qaeda and its affiliates, mass killing of the target population. They know that such attacks will help to create a climate of fear in the targeted population, but, in essence, they are turning the tactic of hijacking into a weapon of asymmetrical warfare. Prior to 9/11 aviation security measures around the world were based on the assumption that the terrorists would not wish to sacrifice their own lives if they could avoid this. Al Qaeda's suicide hijackers are indoctrinated to prepare them for 'voluntary self-martyrdom' and they believe they will go to paradise for striking a blow in what they believe is a 'holy war' against the infidels. It is for obvious reasons very difficult, especially in open societies, to prevent and combat this form of terror warfare.

Obviously the best form of prevention is to intercept and pre-empt the would-be suicide hijackers' conspiracy through high-quality and timely intelligence on the terrorists' intentions and plans. Yet, as was seen on 9/11, the intelligence may be lacking. Airport boarding gate security becomes a key final opportunity to prevent the suicide hijackers from boarding the plane. CAPPS (Computer Assisted Passenger Profiling System) is one tool that may be useful here: this would be particularly useful in cases where would-be hijackers are found to be travelling with forged or stolen passports under false identities. The standard process of screening passengers, their hand luggage and hold luggage for weapons and explosives may also play a key role in such cases, provided that they conduct their duties with maximum diligence and vigilance. However, although there have been big improvements in standards of airport boarding gate security in the US and other countries since the disastrous failures of airport security on 9/11, it is clear that there are weaknesses and gaps in airport security which can still result in hijackers getting aboard with items that can be used as effective weapons to seize control of an airliner. One obvious reason for this is human fallibility. It only needs one airport/airline security screener to be distracted or lax in their task to allow the hijacker access to boarding. Moreover, there are still many airports around the world where the authorities are complacent, where they believe they are immune from attack, and may therefore allow would-be suicide hijackers on board an airliner which could then be turned into a missile for use against a target country's homeland or against a designated strategic, diplomatic, business or symbolic facility of the target country located overseas. Moreover, the level of airport security around the world is extremely variable, and terrorist movements such as Al Qaeda and its affiliates are known to undertake careful reconnaissance to find loopholes in security, including airport security, which they can exploit. In other words, it would be foolish to regard airport security as a guaranteed method of preventing hijackers from boarding airliners.

For this very reason, it is particularly foolish to dismiss or neglect measures to maximise in-flight security. In-flight security is literally the last line of defence for preventing hijackers from seizing control of an airliner. Two measures now introduced into UK airlines, despite some fierce opposition within the Airline Pilots' Association, make very good sense in the light of 9/11. The installation of intrusion-proof doors dividing the pilot's cockpit from the passengers' cabin is a sensible protective and deterrent measure. If the would-be suicide hijackers are unable to gain access to the cockpit this effectively blocks their efforts to turn the airliner into a weapon. Of course this does not prevent would-be hijackers from threatening the lives of passengers and cabin crew. For this reason, and to help forestall the would-be suicide sabotage bomber who aims to blow up the airliner in mid-air, the deployment of armed, highly trained sky marshals on board air-liners is also a sensible additional in-flight security measure. It is obviously impracticable to provide sky marshals for every flight, but the knowledge that they are being employed on a wide range of flights can act as a deterrent against suicide hijacking attempts. The reason for this is that Al Qaeda and similar organisations want their attacks to succeed. There is no point in wasting the lives of 'martyrs' for the cause if they are simply going to die in a shoot-out with sky marshals and fail in the real objective of taking control of the airliner. Provided the sky marshals are trained to a very high standard, and that the protocols on their precise role and their relationship to the captain of the aircraft are clear, the new measure is certainly a logical enhancement of in-flight security. The opposition to this measure expressed by some BALPA members was, one suspects, partly the result of lack of awareness of the severity of the threat and the general lack of up-to-date knowledge of counter-terrorism developments overseas. There are two practical arguments in favour of the new measures, which should suffice to quash the opposition. First, opponents of intrusion-proof doors and sky marshals should be aware that if boarding gate and in-flight security fail in the face of a suicide hijacking attempt, the crew and their passengers will end up *either* crashing into a building on the ground *or* being shot down by Air Force jets or by surface-to-air missiles to prevent them crashing into a building. Either way they will probably all end up dead. If this practical strategic argument fails, there is a stark com-mercial reality: if they do not employ proper in-flight security measures the US authorities will act to deny them landing rights in US airports. Given the vital importance of transatlantic routes to all the major British carriers, this argument is likely to prevail at the end of the day.

The crisis managers' dilemma: what to do if the suicide hijackers are in control?

If the suicide hijackers gain control of an aircraft it is vital that the information regarding the flight path and possible target(s) is conveyed as rapidly as possible to the crisis decision makers and that air traffic control, civilian aviation authorities and the military authorities coordinate all emergency action as swiftly as possible. The terrorists may be heading for a major target literally only minutes away from the airport where the hijackers boarded. The aircraft is likely to be fully loaded with fuel. The impact of crashing the airliner into a building or over a heavily habited area would be likely to lead to the deaths of hundreds of civilians. Clearly the lesser evil would be to shoot down the hijacked plane, knowing that this will be likely to cause fewer total deaths than allowing the aircraft to proceed to its target. However, the need for speedy response is made all the more vital by the fact that if the hijacked plane is aimed at an urban target the shoot down should be carried out well before it reaches the built-up area. However, we may be talking about minutes in trying to calculate the time available to prevent the possibly huge loss of life that could ensue. For these reasons, some security experts, notably in France, have favoured the deployment of surface-to-air missiles around potential targets to provide a swifter response than is possible with inter-ception by fighter aircraft. In calculating the extremely limited opportunity for preventing the hijacked plane from proceeding to its target, the argument for the use of surface-to-air missiles is certainly attractive. Whichever method is used, however, one needs to ensure that air traffic control is carefully and accurately monitoring the seized aircraft *throughout* the crisis, and that there is a well-prepared plan for dealing with all the likely suicide hijack and suicide sabotage bombing scenarios.

The establishment of strictly policed air exclusion zones over major cities and potential targets limiting access to authorised passenger, cargo and military flights is a valuable measure, because if the air traffic control authorities monitor the zones constantly and report any unauthorised flight immediately to the security authorities there should be more opportunity for a swift response to deal with the threat. The UK system aims to use a combination of air exclusion zones regimes and Air Force fighter aircraft interception to deal with such challenges. However, with a high level of both boarding-gate and in-flight security, one hopes these plans will never have to be put to the test.

The 'Robolander' device

In its constant search for technologies, which enhance aviation security, the aerospace industry has come up with an interesting and novel device, which is currently in the stage of development and could be adopted and built into the next generation of air traffic control systems. The system, called 'Robolander', is designed to allow air traffic controllers to take control of aircraft and land them remotely. The device also includes a 'refuse to crash' computer program designed to steer the airliner away from high buildings if the pilots fail to respond to audible warnings.

A senior US aerospace industries chief executive has indicated that the next logical development should be a computerised system that allows air traffic control to take control of a plane in an emergency. The pilot sending an encrypted signal to air traffic control the moment he became aware of the hijackers breaking through the cockpit door would trigger the system.

One major obstacle to the adoption of this type of remote-control technology is its sheer expense. However, costs could considerably reduce if the system was to be incorporated into the next generation of air traffic control systems and airliners. Hence, this technology does not offer a 'quick fix' to the suicide hijacker threat, but it does offer a potentially valuable tool for future generations of airliners and air traffic control systems which could save the lives of passengers and crews in a wide range of emergency situations, such as intrusion into the cockpit by a mentally disturbed passenger attempting to grab the controls, or a pilot experiencing a heart attack or severe stroke. As one would anticipate, the International Airline Pilots' Association tends to be strongly opposed to remote-control technologies. They are reluctant to accept any system where they would have to surrender command of the aircraft to a computer system. One senior executive of IFALPA has been quoted recently as objecting: 'What would happen if the terrorists took over the air traffic control tower and hacked the codes? They would have a dozen flying bombs.'

It is clear that there is not at present any generally accepted remote-control technology which would be a guaranteed effective counter to the suicide hijacker, though one aerospace company has patented a device that requires a code before the aircraft can be operated. There are, of course, serious problems about all remote-control technologies.

The suicide sabotage bomber threat

The attempt by Richard Reid to blow up an American Airlines plane using a bomb hidden in his shoe, thwarted only by the vigilance and speedy intervention of the cabin crew and other passengers, was a sharp reminder that we now have to face the suicide sabotage bomber threat, a threat that was dismissed as too improbable by those who planned the response to sabotage bombings of airliners in the 1980s.

The emergence of the suicide sabotage bomber greatly strengthens the case for maximising boarding gate and in-flight security. The task at the boarding gate is greatly complicated by the fact that more sophisticated terrorist organisations have now mastered the technique of carrying small components of bombs on board rather than an entire IED, thus making it far more difficult to identify the bomber. Ramzi Yousef, the terrorist master bomb designer, pioneered this method. For example, he used liquid explosive, which was hidden in an apparently innocent contact lenses solution container. The bomber then assembled the bomb in the toilet.

A bomb detonated at any altitude over 30,000 feet is likely to cause the aircraft to crash with the loss of all lives on board. The emergence of Al Qaeda-linked suicide sabotage bombing is therefore a serious challenge. The only effective means of prevention are enhanced intelligence enabling the would-be bomber to be caught before boarding the plane, and greatly improved and extra vigilant boarding gate and in-flight security.

Essential components of an effective aviation security system

The first requirement is the establishment of strong national aviation security systems, particularly in major civil aviation countries: the G8 states. Effective national systems are the essential building blocks of any worthwhile international cooperation. Each national security system should be under the control of a powerful lead agency with the tasks of assisting government in the formulation of aviation security policy, and the overall direction and coordination of all the organisations in both the public and private sectors that have a role in the implementation of the aviation security programme. The lead agency should be backed by strong regulatory powers and the necessary resources, including trained manpower, necessary to monitor, inspect and regulate all aspects of aviation security. It should in addition have the task of evaluating the overall effectiveness of the security policy and recommending any necessary changes to government.

There is much evidence to suggest that the commercial deregulation of airlines has had beneficial consequences for the air traveller. Opening up a far greater choice of services and making vigorous competition for routes and passengers has compelled airlines and airports to strive for a larger market share by offering better quality services and more attractive prices. Experience shows, however, that it would be foolish and irresponsible to leave matters such as air safety and security to the vagaries of the market. Unfortunately the US aviation system has not yet acquired a strong enough regulatory agency, which is absolutely vital if standards of security are to be properly enforced and leadership in research and development and policy direction is to be provided.

There are a number of current and emerging threats to aviation security that call for a concerted response by the UK aviation security authorities working in close cooperation with the US and other allies within the international Coalition Against Terrorism. International cooperation is of the essence here because unless there are reciprocal improvements in aviation security and other related counter-terrorism measures in countries whose airlines fly to and from our countries, we are going to be vulnerable not only to attacks on our homelands, for example, by a foreign-registered aircraft bringing a terrorist bomb or other weaponry and/or terrorists into our airspace but also to our airliners, passengers and crew becoming targets in foreign airspace or airports.

10 The media and terrorism

It is first necessary to define the term used in the title of this chapter. *Media* is a generic term meaning all the methods or channels of information and entertainment. The *mass media* are taken to encompass newspapers, radio and television and other important forms of communications including books, films, music, theatre and the visual arts. The late twentieth century has seen the globalisation of mass media culture, but we should not overlook the fact that throughout history informal methods of communication such as the gossip of the taverns, streets and marketplace have been the standard local media for transmitting information, and these informal channels coexist with all the latest multimedia technology in contemporary societies.

In the process of attempting to spread terror among a wider target group some channel or medium of transmitting information, however informal and localised, will inevitably be involved. The Assassin Sect of Shia Islam,[1] which attempted to sow terror in the Muslim world in the Middle Ages, relied upon word of mouth in the mosques and marketplaces to relay news of their attacks; similar methods of transmitting fear were used by the Russian and Balkan terrorists in the nineteenth century.[2] These and many other historical examples provide abundant evidence to disprove the theory that the development of modern mass media is the prime underlying cause of terrorism. The political weapon of terror, it was believed, would serve their cause, not television producers and journalists. It would be foolish to deny that many modern terrorists and certain sections of the mass media can appear to become locked in a relationship of considerable mutual benefit. The former want to appear on prime-time television to obtain not only massive, possibly worldwide, publicity but also the aura of legitimisation that such media attention gains for them in the eyes of their own followers and sympathisers. For the mass media organisations the coverage of terrorism, especially prolonged incidents such as hijackings and hostage situations, provides an endless source of sensational and visually compelling news stories capable of boosting audience/readership figures.[3]

Common to all acts of terrorism is the threat or use of murder, injury or destruction to coerce the government or other target groups into conceding to the terrorists' demands. It is because terrorists seek to demonstrate the credibility of their threats by spectacular acts of destruction or atrocity that the media reporting of these acts is often held in some sense to have 'caused' the terrorism. In reality it is well beyond the powers even of the modern mass media to create a terrorist movement or a terrorist state. In order to understand how groups espousing terrorism originate one needs to examine their motivations, aims, ideologies or religious beliefs and strategies. However, once terrorist violence is under way the relationship between the terrorists and the mass media tends inevitably to become *symbiotic*. In sociology the term *symbiosis* is taken to mean relations of mutual dependence between different groups within a community when the groups are unlike each other and their relations are complementary. It would be foolish to deny that modern media technology, communications satellites and the rapid spread of television have had a marked effect in increasing the publicity potential of terrorism. A dramatic illustration of this was the seizure and massacre of Israeli athletes by Black September terrorists at the 1972 Munich Olympics. It is estimated that these events were relayed to a world-wide television audience of over 500 million.[4] For as long as the mass media exist, terrorists will hunger for what former British Prime Minister Margaret Thatcher called 'the oxygen of publicity'. And for as long as terrorists commit acts of violence the mass media will continue to scramble for coverage in order to satisfy the desire of their audiences for dramatic stories in which there is inevitably huge public curiosity about both the victimisers and their victims. Even those terrorist incidents where the perpetrators fail to claim responsibility and their identity is unknown or in serious doubt, as in the case of the bombing of the American base at Dhahran in June 1996, the international media coverage given will still be enormous.

The French sociologist Michel Wieviorka, in *The Making of Terrorism* (1993), attempts to dismiss the claim that terrorism and the media are in a symbiotic relationship. He argues that there are four distinct relationships between terrorists and the media. The first of these is described as one of *pure intelligence*, where 'the terrorists neither seek to frighten a given population group neither beyond their intended victims nor to realise a propaganda coup through their acts'.[5] This category is totally unreal because even for the purpose of creating terror in an intended set of victims, the perpetrator relies on some channel or medium of communication to relay the threat. If there is no aim to instil terror, then the violence is not of a terroristic nature.

According to Wieviorka, the 'second relational model is that of *relative indifference* ... In which perpetrators of violence remain indifferent about making the headlines not out of disinterest with regard to the most powerful media, but because there already exists channels of communication through which to discuss and explain their positions.'[6] The kind of channels he lists that 'already exist' are a legal and relatively free press, radio transmitters and centres for free expression such as universities, churches and mosques. But what are these channels that 'already exist' if not alternative media? One might also add the internet, now widely used by terrorist groups. Wieviorka's second category turns out to be a non-category.

Wieviorka's third relational mode, the *media-orientated strategy*, is self-explanatory. He intends this category to cover terrorist efforts to provoke the media into action and a 'calculated manipulation of what they know of media operations'.[7]

Wieviorka appears to think that this is the only case in which the terrorists are 'engaged in an instrumental relationship with the media'.[8] Yet in reality it is intrinsic to the very activity of terrorisation that some form of media, however crude, is utilised as an instrument to disseminate the messages of threat and intimidation.

This applies equally to Wieviorka's fourth relational mode, which he terms as *total break*,[9] and which I think is more accurately described as *coercion* of the media. Wieviorka is referring here to cases where the terrorists come to view the media organisation, editors, journalists and broadcasters as enemies to be punished and destroyed. Those working in the media have often been the targets of terrorist violence in areas of severe conflict such as Italy and Turkey in the 1970s and Lebanon in the 1970s and 1980s. Some journalists and editors have been attacked for in some way offending a terrorist movement. Others have been threatened and attacked in an attempt to prevent them from exposing some detail of terrorist activity which they wish to suppress. But such attacks on sections of the media do not signify that the relationship to the media has suddenly become irrelevant or non-instrumental. The terrorists, however hostile they become towards the major mass media organisations, still depend on mass media's coverage of their attacks to terrorise their particular media enemies into silence and to coerce the rest of the media into submission, or at least into passive neutrality. Moreover, terrorist groups engaged in attacking the established mass media seldom, if ever, regard such activity as an alternative to using their own organs of propaganda, such as communiqués, broadsheets, pamphlets and magazines. However, the more sophisticated terrorist organisations, such as the Al Qaeda network, now rely heavily on the internet as the main channel for spreading their ideas, propaganda and useful information on tactics and methods for their supporters, for example on manufacturing bombs. It is a common mistake to assume that the Al Qaeda network is living in the Middle Ages. Following the toppling of the Taliban regime in the Fall of 2001, and Al Qaeda's loss of training camps in Afghanistan, the movement's leadership swiftly expanded its use of the internet and video and audio tapes to provide an alternative and globally accessible means of communication which is entirely under their own control. Bin Laden and Ayman Zawahiri, the chief ideologue and strategist of the movement, have also made extensive use of new technology to get their message across. However, as Gilles Kepel, one of the world's leading scholars on contemporary Islam, has observed:

> ... the principal ideologues who have spoken in the name of Al Qaeda or about it, have published on the Internet, and abundant literature that mainly, it would seem, targets circles of militants and potential sympathisers ... it provides the rationale for action ... in the absence of any organisational chart for a hypothetical organisation named Al Qaeda, this written body of work remains the most tangible element in the identity of such a phenomenon.[10]

In an uncanny way this intensive use of the internet, a globalised system of communication, mirrors the transnational globalised ideology of Al Qaeda and its complex network of affiliates and cells. Gilles Kepel observes that the ideological battle between the Al Qaeda jihadists and their opponents in the Muslim world are being fought out on the internet, the space:

> ... Overwhelmingly occupied by a movement that has structured itself like the Web and shaped itself according to the same model: the term *al qaeda*, in Arabic, also suggests a database or reservoir, for example, of information (*aqedat al-ma'lumat*).[11]

In dealing with the relationship between terrorism and the media, the most useful approach is to attempt to understand the terrorist view of the problem of communications.[12] It cannot be denied that although terrorism has proved remarkably ineffective as the major weapon for toppling governments and capturing political power, it has been a remarkably successful means of publicising a political cause and relaying the terrorist threat to a wider audience, particularly in the open and pluralistic countries of the West. When one says 'terrorism' in a democratic society, one also says 'media'. For terrorism by its very nature is a psychological weapon which depends upon communicating a threat to the wider society. This, in essence, is why terrorism and the media enjoy a symbiotic relationship. The free media clearly do not represent terrorist values. Generally they tend to reflect the underlying values of the democratic society. But the media in an open society are in a fiercely competitive market for their audiences, are constantly under pressure to be first with the news and to provide more information, excitement and entertainment than their rivals. Hence, they are almost bound to respond to terrorist propaganda of the deed because it is dramatic bad news. Thus, as explained earlier, the media are in a kind of symbiotic relationship with terrorism. This does not, of course, mean that the mass media are controlled by the terrorists. It does mean that they are continually attempting to manipulate and exploit the free media for their own ends. It also means that responsible media professionals and the public need to be constantly on their guard against terrorist attempts to manipulate them.

Terrorists view the mass media in a free society in entirely cynical and opportunistic terms. They have nothing but contempt for the values and attitudes of the democratic mass media. For example, they view the media's expressed concern for protecting human life as mere hypocrisy and sentimentality. However, many terrorist leaders are well aware that their cause can be damaged by unfavourable publicity. Hence the more established and sophisticated terrorist movements and their political 'Front' organisations, such as Herri Batasuna, invest considerable time and effort in waging propaganda warfare both at domestic and international audiences.

For this purpose sophisticated terrorist groups such as the Al Qaeda network make extensive use of audio-visual taped messages from their leaders and videos showing pictures of successful attacks on their designated 'enemies', and images of the death and suffering of Muslim civilians they always portray as the victims of attacks by Americans or their allies. They exploit the enormous scope of the global internet to disseminate their propaganda around the world. They can use their computers to send coded and encrypted messages to provide secret communications systems for the network as well as for reaching their wider audience of supporters and sympathisers. Recently the Al Qaeda network has acquired its own broadcasting network, *Voice of Caliphate*, to help speak their propaganda, and to give a predictably twisted version of international news.

In this propaganda war,[13] the terrorists constantly emphasise the absolute justice or righteousness of their cause. Usually, this claim of justice is founded on a secular ideology. However, today we should note the significance of the resurgence of religious justifications for terrorism. Beliefs like those of the pro-Iranian fundamentalist terrorists – that acts of violence are ordained by God and that martyrdom in the course of the struggle against the infidel leads to Paradise – present a very potent threat to opponents. Whether based on secular ideology or religious faith, however, this belief in the absolute justice of the cause has characterised the propaganda of all terrorist organisations.

These beliefs carry some important corollaries. First, the terrorists can and do claim that because their violence is in a just cause they are freedom fighters or soldiers of liberation fighting a just war,[14] and they passionately deny that their acts can be described as crimes or murders. Second, because of their belief in their own righteousness, the terrorists can portray their opponents not simply as misguided but as totally evil, as corrupt oppressors beyond redemption. Because their enemies are corrupt beyond redemption, the terrorists have the duty to kill them and indeed anyone who resists or obstructs the just war of the terrorists.

Third, because the terrorist organisation believes it is waging a Manichaean struggle with the forces of oppression or reaction, it cannot tolerate neutrals – you must be either with us or against us. If you are with us, join our cause and fight against the enemy. If you are not actively with us, we will assume you are a traitor and therefore we are entitled to kill you.

The other three key propaganda themes vividly illustrate the potency of the terrorists' use of the claim of total righteousness as a psychological weapon. For example, it is used to undermine all claims to legitimacy on the part of the incumbents: 'Our enemies, by denying the justice of our cause and by acting against us, have forfeited all rights to obedience and respect. It is no longer they who are legitimate and whose authority and word you should believe, but we the terrorist organisation.' The righteousness theme is also deployed in order to push the blame for all the violence on to the terrorists' opponents. The government started the violence: 'Our violence was simply a totally justified reaction to the violence imposed on us by our enemies; hence, all the blame for the sufferings caused to the people should be placed on our opponents. The masses should recognise this and throw in their lot with our movement, which will inevitably triumph in the end.' All these themes can be recognised in the propaganda of numerous contemporary terrorist organisations. We should never underestimate their skill in disseminating these illusions among the public and among politicians and other influential groups. At its most subtle and effective, this form of propaganda campaign may more than compensate for the military weaknesses and security failures of a terrorist organisation. If government, faced with these more sophisticated challenges, does not succeed in dealing effectively with the terrorists' political and psychological subversion, they may indeed be on the slide to disaster.

The most frequent terrorist technique for influencing the mass media and reaching a wider public is the creation of terrorist events and armed propaganda with the object of seducing or trapping the mass media into giving the terrorists huge publicity and portraying them as such a powerful force that it would be folly to resist them.[15]

To summarise briefly on the symbiotic nature of the relationship between terrorists and the media, the recent history of terrorism in many democratic countries vividly demonstrates that terrorists do thrive on the oxygen of publicity, and it is foolish to deny this. This does not mean that the established democratic media share the values of the terrorists. It does demonstrate, however, that the free media in an open society are particularly vulnerable to exploitation and manipulation by ruthless terrorist organisations. In using television, radio and the print media the terrorists generally have four main objectives:

to convey the propaganda of the deed and to create extreme fear among their target groups;

to mobilise wider support for their cause among the general population and international opinion by emphasising such themes as the righteousness of their cause and the inevitability of their victory;

to frustrate and disrupt the response of the government and security forces, for example by suggesting that all their practical anti-terrorist measures are inherently tyrannical and counterproductive;

to mobilise, incite and boost their constituency of actual and potential supporters and in doing so to increase recruitment, raise more funds and inspire further attacks.

In a valuable empirical study of the mass media's coverage of the hijacking to Beirut of TWA Flight 847 while *en route* from Cairo to Rome, Alex P. Schmid demonstrates convincingly how the terrorists were able to use the 'pseudo-event' to obtain vast publicity.[16] For example, Schmid observes that NBC devoted no less than two-thirds of their total news time to the crisis over the fate of the American hostages taken to Beirut throughout the 17 days of the hijacking. Significantly the hostages received roughly ten times the attention given to the terrorists in the over-all news coverage. As Schmid wryly observes, 'The exposure increased the price of the 39 US hostages and made their potential sacrifice extremely costly for the American and Israeli governments.'[17] He also points out that opinion polls showed an overwhelming majority of the American public (89 per cent) applauded the media's coverage, reflecting public perceptions of the media's role in the previous terrorist spectaculars.

In their intense competition for audience share all the major US television networks gave huge exposure to the hostages, thus ensuring that huge numbers of Americans would completely identify with the hostages. This, inevitably, greatly increased the pressure on the US government, and indirectly on the Israeli government, to do any deal that would secure the release of the hostages. The Shi'ite Islamic Jihad hijackers had originally demanded the release of the 776 Shi'ites held in Israel. In the event they secured the release of no less than 756 imprisoned Shi'ites in return for the release of the 39 hostages. As Alex Schmid rightly concludes:

> The media's profuse exposure of the hostage families and their grief thereby played into the hands of the terrorists. The outcome – successful for the hostages and the terrorists – undermined the American administration's declaratory policy of 'No bargaining, no concessions' and probably increased the likelihood of imitation by other terrorists.[18]

Moreover, we would be deceiving ourselves if we believed that this dangerous media hype of terrorist 'spectaculars' was simply the result of media organisations' unintended mistakes. The major US networks all compete fiercely for an increased market share of the audience and for the higher advertising revenue they can gain through exploiting the public's insatiable interest in the coverage of major terrorist 'pseudo-events'. For example, in the first three weeks of the Tehran hostage crisis in 1979 all the major television networks achieved an 18 per cent increase in audience rating. According to Hamid Mowlana, the networks were able to secure, in 1979, an annual revenue increase of £30 million for each percentage point of audience rating increase.[19] On the other hand it may well be the case that the owners and chief executives of the media organisations are unaware of the wider *political* implications of their frenetic pursuit of ratings. In the case of the Tehran hostage situation, the networks' constant and disproportionate emphasis on the fate of the hostages and their portrayal of an administration apparently powerless to obtain their release helped to undermine Carter and to pave the way for the election of Ronald Reagan.

The cases of the TWA Flight 847 hijacking and the Tehran hostage crisis certainly bring home the power of the mass media. There is no evidence to suggest that the Western-dominated mass media organisations share the political aims of the terrorist organisations, but sophisticated media-wise terrorists can certainly exploit and manipulate the power of the mass media for their own malevolent purpose.

So far I have been examining the complex relationships between the terrorists and the media without taking proper account of other key players such as the law-enforcement agencies and the government of the day. It is important to emphasise that the objectives and concerns of the law-enforcement agencies in terrorist situations are not only at variance with the aims of the media: they are intrinsically in conflict with them.[20] The mass media aim to 'scoop' their rivals with news stories that will grip and sustain the public's attention and hence increase their ratings and revenue. The police, on the other hand, are first and foremost concerned with the protection of life, the enforcement of the law and apprehending those guilty of committing crimes and bringing them to justice before courts of law. There have been many notorious examples where the efforts of the police have been directly threatened by the behaviour of sections of the media. For example, during the Iranian Embassy siege at Princes Gate, London, in 1980, the Metropolitan Police were particularly concerned to ensure total secrecy and surprise for the hostage rescue by the SAS. However, one ITN film crew defied police instructions and succeeded in filming the rescuers as they were abseiling down the walls of the embassy. If those pictures had been shown on live television they could have jeopardised the entire hostage rescue.

Another striking example of media irresponsibility occurred during the hijacking of a Kuwait airliner by Hezbollah terrorists in 1988. While the airliner was on the ground at Larnaca, Cyprus, there might have been an opportunity to mount a hostage rescue operation by an elite commando group. A major obstacle to such an operation was the unrelenting intrusiveness of the international media surrounding the aircraft with infrared equipment, so that during the hours of darkness it would have been impossible for a rescue operation to have been launched without its presence being given away.

A different kind of media irresponsibility led to a British court abandoning a trial in January 1997 of five IRA terrorists and an armed robber in connection with an escape from a top security prison at Whitemoor. The specific reason given by the trial judge was that the London *Evening Standard* newspaper had published material that prevented the men from having a fair trial. This kind of problem is less likely to occur in Scotland where the *sub judice* rule has traditionally been rigorously enforced by the courts and adhered to by the media.

In an open society with free media it is impossible to guarantee that police anti-terrorist operations will be safeguarded against being compromised or disrupted by irresponsible media activity. However, a great deal can be achieved by ensuring that expert press liaison and news management are an intrinsic part of the police response to any terrorist campaign and the contingency planning and crisis management processes. Indeed, in a democratic society, a sound and effective public information policy, harnessing the great power of the mass media insofar as this is possible, is a vital element in a successful strategy against terrorism.

This power of the media and the political leadership to mobilise democratic public opinion, so contemptuously ignored by the terrorist movements, reveals a crucial flaw in terrorist strategy. The terrorist assumes that the target group he or she seeks to coerce will always fall victim to intimidation if his or her threatened or actual violence is sufficiently severe. The terrorist believes in the ultimate inevitability of a collapse of will on the part of the adversary. Even on the face of it this is a somewhat naïve assumption. Why should people subjected to threats behave with such docility and weakness? Not only do terrorists frequently score an 'own goal', they also often succeed in hardening society's resistance towards them, and in provoking tougher, more effective counter-measures of a kind which may decimate or permanently debilitate their revolutionary movement.

There are a number of other important ways in which responsible media in a democracy serve to frustrate the aims of the terrorists. Terrorists like to present themselves as noble Robin Hoods, champions of the oppressed and downtrodden. By showing the savage cruelty of terrorists' violence and the way in which they violate the rights of the innocent, the media can help to shatter this myth. It is quite easy to show, by plain photographic evidence, how terrorists have failed to observe any laws or rules of war, how they have murdered children and women, the old and the sick, without compunction. For in terrorist practice no one is innocent, no one can be neutral, for all are potentially expendable for the transcendental ends of the terrorist cause.

What else can the media do in a positive way to aid in the struggle against terrorism? There are numerous practical forms of help they can provide. Responsible and accurate reporting of incidents can create a heightened vigilance among the public to observe, for example, unusual packages and suspicious persons or behaviour. At the practical level the media can carry warnings to the public from the police, and instructions as to how they should react in an emergency. Frequently media with international coverage can provide valuable data and leads concerning foreign movements, links between different terrorist personalities and different terrorist organisations, new types of weaponry and possible future threats, such as the planning of an international terrorist 'spectacular' or warning signs of a new threat.

Finally the media also provide an indispensable forum for informed discussion concerning the social and political implications of terrorism and the development of adequate policies and countermeasures. Media which place a high value on democratic freedoms will, rightly and necessarily, continually remind the authorities of their broader responsibilities to ensure that the response to terrorism is consistent with the rule of law, respect for basic rights and demands of social justice.

An excellent example of the media making a truly constructive contribution by triggering a serious domestic and international debate on alleged serious violations of human rights and the rule of law committed in the name of the war on terror occurred in the autumn of 2005, when a report in the *Washington Post* raised very serious allegations that the CIA had allegedly abducted terrorist suspects in Europe, used European airports to transfer them to 'secret prisons' somewhere in Europe where they could be secretly tortured. Unusually for the *Washington Post*, the sources of these allegations were not named in the report. However, the article raised alarm in the US Congress, where Senator John McCain had strong backing for his amendment seeking to extend the prohibition on torture to all US agents acting overseas as well as those operating on US soil. However, Congress and European governments, the Council of Europe (which set up a pan-continental inquiry led by the Swiss Senator, Dick Marty), and the European Commission, were all getting increasingly exasperated by the Bush administration's refusal to confirm or deny the allegations.

During the British presidency of the EU it fell to the then Foreign Secretary Jack Straw to raise the issue of these alleged 'extraordinary renditions' with the US government. The newly appointed German Chancellor, Angela Merkel, raised the issue with the then Secretary of State Condoleezza Rice when she paid an official visit to Berlin, and the European Commission threatened to issue sanctions possibly including suspending the offending state's voting rights or suspending talks with any offending applicant countries if they were found to be allowing 'secret prisons' to operate in their territory. However, it is clear that the mass media played a key part in pressuring political leaders in EU member states to put tough questions to the US government about the alleged use of CIA aircraft to engage in extraordinary rendition of terrorist suspects to 'secret prisons' in Europe and, most serious of all, the allegation that suspects were tortured. These allegations by the media were given much greater force by the cases of Khaled Masri and Abu Omar which allegedly occurred in 2003. Khaled Mari, a Lebanese, is alleged to have been abducted by the CIA in Macedonia in 2003, flown to Afghanistan and imprisoned for five months before being freed. In the case of Abu Omar, an Egyptian cleric, the allegation is that he was kidnapped in Milan, taken to Egypt and tortured while US personnel were present.

The mass media can therefore take some of the credit for the u-turn in US policy on terrorist suspects. On 7 December 2005 Secretary of State Condoleezza Rice announced that no US personnel could use cruel or degrading practices on suspects at home or overseas. It is still not known how much knowledge European governments had, if any, about these covert activities. In late 2005 it was also unclear whether the practice of extraordinary rendition was being shut down, or whether it had been transferred to Africa.

American and European media were generally very enthusiastic about the election of President Obama. He had not voted for the increasingly unpopular war in Iraq and he appeared to be making a welcome departure from President George W. Bush's administration's policies. However, once elected he has found it hard to disentangle himself from the Bush–Cheney legacy. Some of the liberal media, such as the *Washington Post* and the *New York Times*, have been criticised for turning on their hero. What the critics tend to forget is that the media perform a useful service to democracy by raising issues and questions of crucial importance, not least on counter-terrorism, security and human rights.

In sum it can be argued that these contributions by the media to the war against terrorism are so valuable that they outweigh the disadvantages, risks and the undoubted damage caused by a small minority of irresponsible journalists and broadcasters. The positive work of the media has been either gravely under-estimated or ignored. It is always fair game, especially for politicians, to attack the media. A more considered assessment suggests that the media in Western liberal states are a weapon that can be used as a major tool in the defeat of terrorism. The media need not become the instrument of the terrorist.

I have briefly examined the perspective of the law-enforcement authorities on media coverage of terrorism. I have also noted that although the mass media in an open society are highly vulnerable to manipulations and exploitation by terrorists, they can also make an invaluable contribution to the defeat of terrorism. What are the major policy options for a democratic society in regard to the media's response to terrorism?

First, there is the policy of *laissez-faire*. This assumes that no specific steps should be taken as regards media coverage of terrorism, however serious the violence or threat of violence may be. The dangers of this approach are fairly obvious:

sophisticated and media-wise terrorist organisations will exploit the enormous power of the media to enhance their ability to create a climate of fear and disruption, to amplify their propaganda of the deed to publicise their cause or to force concessions of ransoms out of the government or out of companies or wealthy individuals. At best the *laissez-faire* approach is likely to encourage attacks which endanger life and limb and place property at risk. At the most severe end of the spectrum of violence, the tame acquiescence of the mass media as an ally of a terrorist campaign may help to induce a situation of incipient or actual civil war with a concomitant threat to the stability and survival of the democracy in question.

A second policy option on media response to terrorism is some form of *media censorship or statutory regulation*. In view of the great power wielded by the media for good or ill, it is hardly surprising to find that, when faced with severe terrorist campaigns, several domestic countries have sought to deny the terrorist direct access to the important platform of the broadcast media. Thus Prime Minister Margaret Thatcher's demand that the terrorists should be starved of the oxygen of publicity, and the British government's ban, since rescinded, on the broadcasting of the voice of terrorist spokespersons caused controversy.

The closest parallel to the media ban on the use of IRA/Sinn Fein voices in interview with Ulster terrorists is the Irish Republicans' ban, under Section 31 of their 1960 Broadcasting Authority Act, on the carrying of interviews with the IRA, Sinn Fein and other terrorist spokespersons. Sinn Fein protested that it was a legal political party in the Republic of Ireland and therefore had the legal right to broadcasting time. However, the minister who imposed the ban, Conor Cruise O'Brien, said that Sinn Fein was not a legitimate political party, but rather a 'public relations agency for a murder gang'.[21] Predictably, a similar debate surrounded the British ban on Sinn Fein voices.

Students of Irish politics have argued that their media ban (rescinded during the IRA's ceasefire) did actually damage Sinn Fein's efforts to build electoral support and sympathy in the Republic by denying it the aura of legitimacy accorded by television appearances. The angry protests of Sinn Fein in response to the British ban on the voices of their spokespersons suggest that Sinn Fein leaders were also convinced the ban damaged them. However, in due course the television news programmes became so skilled at providing actors' voices to accompany film footage of Sinn Fein leaders that they turned the voice ban into a farce.

In the wake of the Dunblane and Tasmania massacres of 1996 there was a revival of interest in the proposals to curb film and television violence. In July 1996 the Australian government announced new censorship guidelines for films and videos and a requirement that all new television sets be fitted with V-chip, an electronic locking device that allows parents to block reception of programmes coded as violent or offensive. It is noteworthy that Australia is the only country so far to have introduced these measures, the most far-reaching efforts to curb film and television violence, even though its government admits that 'No one pretends that you can demonstrate a linear connection between electronic violence and real-life violence'. It is also interesting to note that measures of this kind have not been proposed or adopted by states experiencing high levels of politically motivated violence. At the more draconian end of the spectrum, of democratic states' efforts to starve terrorists of publicity, the Spanish government introduced a law in 1984 that makes it a criminal offence to support or praise 'the activities typical of a terrorist organisation … Or the deeds or commemorative dates of their members by publishing or broadcasting via the mass media, articles expressing opinion, news reports, graphical illustrations, communiqués, and in general by any other forms of dissemination'. Spanish judges were at one stage even empowered to close down radio stations as an exceptional precautionary measure.

In 1976 the Federal Republic of Germany brought in the Anti Constitutional Advocacy Act, making an offence of publicy advocating and/or encouraging others to commit an offence against the stability of the Federal Republic.

In general, however, even the democratic states most plagued by terrorism have been reluctant to take the route of comprehensive censorship of the media's coverage of terrorism. It is widely recognised that it is important to avoid mass media being hijacked and manipulated by terrorists, but if the freedom of the media is sacrificed in the name of combating terrorism one has allowed small groups of terrorists to destroy one of the key foundations of a democratic society. Censorship, in whatever guise, plays into the hands of enemies of democracy. It is also an insult to the intelligence of the general public, and would totally undermine confidence in the veracity of the media if censorship was to be introduced. We should try to uphold the vital principle of free speech so eloquently championed by Thomas Jefferson two centuries ago: 'that truth is great and will prevail if left to herself; that she is the proper and sufficient antagonist of error, and has nothing to fear from the conflict unless disarmed of her natural weapons, free argument and debate'.

However, in any free and responsible society no freedom of expression is totally unlimited. Most of us believe, for example, that pornography should be banned from television and radio. Most decent citizens would also be horrified if the mass media began to provide a platform for race-hate propaganda, or for drug pushers or rapists to come on the screen to boast of their crimes and to incite others to commit crimes.

The third option on media policy on terrorism coverage, and the approach most favoured by the more responsible mass media organisations, is *voluntary self-restraint* to try to avoid the dangers of manipulation and exploitation by terrorist groups. Many major media organisations have adopted guidelines for their staff with the aim of helping to prevent the more obvious pitfalls. For example, CBS News' guidelines commit the organisation to 'thoughtful, conscientious care and restraint' in its coverage of terrorism, avoiding giving an 'excessive platform for the terrorist/kidnapper', 'no live coverage of the terrorist/kidnapper' (though live on the spot reporting by CBS News reporters is not limited thereby), avoiding interference with the authorities' communications (e.g. telephone lines), using expert advisers in hostage situations to help avoid questions or reports that 'might tend to exacerbate the situation', obeying 'all police instructions' (but reporting to their superiors any instructions that seem to be intended to massage or suppress the news) and attempting to achieve 'such overall balance as to length' that 'the (terrorist) story does not unduly crowd out other important news of the hour/day'.

The above guidelines are for the most part entirely laudable, and, if properly and consistently implemented, they would help to avoid the worst excesses of media coverage of terrorism. However, one needs to bear in mind that many of those who work in mass media organisations appear blissfully unaware of any guidelines on terrorism news coverage. There is very little evidence of necessary briefing and training of editors and journalists in this sensitive area, and no evidence of any serious effort by media organisations to enforce their own guidelines.[22] It is governments' frustration over the apparent inadequacy of media self-restraints that leads some to advocate some form of statutory regulation. If the mass media genuinely wish to exercise due care and responsibility in covering the exceedingly sensitive subject of terrorism, in situations where lives may well be at grave risk, they will need to work harder at devising measures of self-restraint that are both appropriate and effective.[23]

The internet, terrorism and counter-terrorism

Earlier in this chapter we noted how Al Qaeda and its affiliates have made extensive use of the internet for a whole range of purposes including communicating the movement's main doctrines, propaganda, recruitment and for teaching militants how to make IEDs, etc. Another important use of the internet for the Al Qaeda network is to send coded messages to those involved in planning terrorist operations. The great attractions of the internet for the terrorists are (1) it is an almost entirely unregulated medium of communication (countries that have tried to control and censor this medium have found it virtually impossible to totally suppress this means of communication even for brief periods); (2) it is extremely difficult, if not impossible, to identify the source of a message and to authenticate its real authorship. Very often terrorist groups set up websites under apparently innocuous names, disguising the identity of the individuals who authored the online material. In the period 2008–10, terrorists started making increasing use of well-known social networking sites in order to identify potential recruits and to lure them into the virtual world of jihadi extremism. Intelligence agencies and other organisations concerned with preventing and combating terrorism have greatly increased the resources and effort devoted to monitoring the internet to learn more about terrorists' evolving ideas and plans and to seek actionable information to enable them to prevent terrorist attacks. Hence, the counter-terrorism agencies can themselves gain from the unregulated character of the internet. The internet has become an indispensable tool for security organisations in both the public and private sectors. However, some of the many current and emerging trends in computing technology are wide open to exploitation by terrorist groups and by the often highly sophisticated hackers in their support networks. For example, cloud-based data storage, so attractive to those with heavily overloaded storage systems, could become an open door for theft of private and confidential data if rigorous security protections are not put in place. Similarly, failure to maintain secrecy of passwords and to update firewall security could lead to hackers obtaining huge amounts of confidential and private information. Potentially disastrous leaks of data can occur if wireless-routed data has not been installed with full security protection. There is no such thing as total security of computerised data. The best way to reduce the dangers of major leaks of secure information is to ensure that efficient security procedures are made a key part of the IT curriculum, especially for those employed in the police, the military, the criminal justice system and the private security industry in combating organised crime and terrorism.[24]

11 International cooperation against terrorism

The evolution of international cooperation

Terrorism is inherently international. The archetypal international terrorist act involves the citizens and territory of more than one country, as for example in the attack on the World Trade Center on 11 September 2001, which killed nearly 3,000 citizens including British, German, French, Italian and Indians. In view of globalisation and increasing interdependence almost every significant terrorist campaign has an international dimension, even when it is mounting a challenge to a specific government within its own territory. For example, the IRA raised funds in the United States and used the Republic of Ireland as a safe haven, as a logistic, organisational base and as a source of recruits. Similarly the Basque terrorist group ETA has used French territory as a sanctuary and as a base of planning operations. Another manifestation of this international dimension is terrorist groups' and states' constant search for political support from like-minded groups overseas, and many examples exist of bilateral collaboration between extremist groups involved in terrorism and states that sponsor and support them.

Efforts to develop international cooperation against terrorism go back to the 1930s. The assassination of King Alexander of Yugoslavia and French foreign minister Louis Barthou at Marseilles in 1934 led to France proposing the establishment of an international criminal court to try terrorist criminals. The somewhat dilatory response of the League of Nations was to summon a conference on the subject at Geneva in 1937. This resulted in the drafting of two conventions.[1]

The first proscribed acts of terrorism, which included attempts on the life of heads of state or their spouses and other government representatives. It also prohibited acts of international terrorism involving injury to persons or damage to property committed by citizens of one state against citizens of another state. The other convention set up an International Criminal Court and accorded it jurisdiction over terrorist crimes. But these bold and radical measures never came into effect because only 13 states had ratified the conventions before war broke out in 1939. The idea of an International Criminal Court for terrorist offences remains, however, a favourite cause among certain international lawyers, though the 1998 Rome conference decided against including crimes of international terrorism in the remit of the proposed ICC.

It is not sufficiently recognised that the United Nations' measures on human rights are directly applicable to the case of terrorism. The *Universal Declaration of*

Human Rights (1984), in addition to guaranteeing the right to life, liberty and security of the person, also states that 'no one shall be subjected to torture or to cruel, inhuman or degrading treatment or punishment'. The right to enjoy 'freedom from fear' is stressed in the preambles of both the *International Covenant on Economic, Social and Cultural Rights* (1966) and the *International Covenant on Civil and Political Rights* (1966). Under Article 6 of the latter, 'no one shall be arbitrarily deprived of his life'.

The UN *Convention on the Prevention of Punishment of the Crime of Genocide* (1948) forbids the killing, serious bodily harm or severe mental distress to members of a national, racial, ethnic or religious group. This is clearly an explicit prohibition of terror violence, whether committed by states, factions or individuals. In addition the UN *Declaration on Principles of International Law Concerning Friendly Relations and Co-Operation Among States* (1970) enjoins states to refrain from 'organising and assisting or participating in acts of civil strife or terrorist acts in another state'.

In the *Declaration on Principles of International Law* the principle of equal rights and self-determination of people is put on the same level as the principle that states 'shall refrain in their international relations from the threat or use of force against ... any State, or in any manner inconsistent with the purpose of the UN'. Significantly it proceeds to spell out that all states have a 'duty to promote ... realisation of the principle (of self-determination) ... in order to bring a speedy end to colonialism' and that 'every state has the duty to refrain from any forcible action which deprives peoples ... of their right to self-determination'. The *Declaration* continues: 'In their actions against, and resistance to, such forcible action in pursuit of their right to self-determination, such peoples are entitled to seek and receive support.'

Naturally enough these clauses can be read as a legitimisation by the UN of any struggle undertaken in the name of the principle of national liberation and an open invitation for international support for such struggles. Thus the UN is seen to be supporting both sides at once in such conflicts. For example, Israel, as a member state, is accorded full 'sovereign equality' and protection of that sovereignty. Simultaneously other member states of the UN can claim that they are fully entitled to arm and support movements dedicated to the liquidation of Israel, on the grounds that they are merely supporting a legitimate national liberation struggle aimed at self-determination.

This double standard was clearly reflected in the UN's faltering attempts to deal with terrorism in the 1970s and 1980s. Following the Munich Olympics massacre in 1972, Secretary General Kurt Waldheim requested the UN to deal with the menace of international terrorism. A study undertaken by the Secretariat was entitled 'Measures to Prevent International Terrorism which Endangers or Takes Innocent Human Lives or Jeopardises Fundamental Freedoms, and Study of the Underlying Causes of those Forms of Terrorism and Acts of Terrorism which Lie in Misery, Frustration, Grievance and Despair, and which Cause some People to Sacrifice Human Lives Including their own, in an Attempt to Effect Radical Changes'.

The discussion revealed a clear split between those states wishing the UN to condemn and act against factional terrorism and those pro-terrorist states wanting to legalise terrorism by factions as a justifiable means of struggle. The latter group used the opportunity to attack Western states for 'colonial and racist terror', and blamed them for 'compelling' those engaged in 'freedom struggles' to use violence to secure 'justice'. In the ensuing Ad Hoc Committee on International Terrorism, consisting of 35 states, which met in the summer of 1973, the Third World states concentrated all their attention on attacking 'state terrorism'.

The UN General Assembly did however agree, in December 1973, to adopt a *Convention on the Prevention and Punishment of Crimes Against Internationally Protected Persons, Including Diplomatic Agents* (1973),[2] and this Convention has now acquired sufficient ratifications by member states to come into effect. Further progress was made in the special field of international measures against aircraft hijacking. The Tokyo *Convention on Offences and Certain Other Acts Committed on Board Aircraft* (1963)[3] sets out the jurisdiction guiding principles requiring contracting states to make every effort to restore control of the aircraft to its lawful commander and to ensure the prompt onward passage or return of the hijacked aircraft together with its crew, passengers and cargo.

The 1970 Hague Convention[4] requires contracting states either to extradite apprehended hijackers to their country of origin or to prosecute them under the judicial code of the recipient state. The Montreal Convention of 1971[5] extended the scope of international law to encompass sabotage and attacks on airports and grounded aircraft. It also laid down the principle that such offences be subject to severe penalties. Unfortunately, despite the encouraging readiness of the majority of states to ratify these conventions, there is still no international convention providing for effective sanctions to ensure enforcement and the punishment of states that aid or give sanctuary to hijackers.

In December 1976 the UN established an ad hoc committee to draft a *Convention Against the Taking of Hostages* (1979).[6] This was an initiative urged by West Germany and other Western states, but it was so weakened in the process of drafting as to become practically useless. However, the Security Council did use sanctions to help compel Libya to hand over two of its citizens indicted for the Lockerbie bombing for trial.

More recently the UN has taken the initiative to launch two new conventions on terrorism, the first is the *International Convention for the Suppression of Terrorist Bombings* (1998) and the second, to help combat terrorist financial infrastructure, is the *International Convention for the Suppression of the Financing of Terrorism* (1999). The texts employ formulas similar to those adopted in the other UN conventions dealing with aspects of terrorism. It remains to be seen how long it will take to obtain sufficient ratification from states to bring these conventions into effect. The convention dealing with terrorist finances is particularly welcome, as most terrorist groups involved in prolonged campaigns of violence set up networks to obtain funding from supporters and sponsors overseas, to launder money gained from organised crime and to purchase weaponry.

The difficulty with all these conventions and with the declarations of other bodies, such as G8, is that they are statements of good intentions, and not a guarantee of action. If, for example, we examine the recommendations of the

Paris Ministerial Summit on Terrorism we find many states have an extremely patchy record on implementation of anti-terrorism measures.

Pro-terrorist states, such as Iran and Syria, still give substantial aid and succour to terrorist groups. It is important to note that pro-terrorist countries go considerably beyond mere ideological and diplomatic support: they are in fact an important part of the problem. They have provided considerable sums of money and supplies of modern weapons to their protégé terrorist gangs. For example, shipments of weapons including Semtex, from Gaddafi, in the mid 1980s made the IRA the best-equipped terrorist group in Europe. They also made available to selected client groups extensive terrorist training facilities, sanctuary for terrorists on the run, the use of embassies as hideouts – and as sources of weapons and false documents, and of the diplomatic pouch to smuggle weapons and explosives – and, when necessary, their own radio communication links.

After the spate of diplomatic kidnappings in Latin America between 1968 and 1971 the Organisation of American States (OAS) formulated a *Convention to Prevent and Punish Acts of Terrorism Taking the Form of Crimes Against Persons and Related Extortion that are of International Significance.*[7] In terms of the Latin American legal tradition this was a remarkably bold innovation, for Latin American states have always held the principle of political asylum to be sacrosanct. The OAS convention circumvented this by defining attacks against internationally protected persons common crimes, regardless of motive, thus making it possible to apply the *aut dedere aut punire* (extradite or prosecute) formula in all such cases. Unfortunately, however, ratification and effective implementation of this formula were resisted by legal conservatism.

Substantial progress has been made in the field of international cooperation within Europe, but this has not sufficed to prevent this region from experiencing a high proportion of terrorist attacks. EU Ministers of the Interior and police forces and intelligence services of the member states have, since 1976, developed regular machinery for discussion and practical multilateral cooperation, for example through the TREVI group.

But the earliest and most ambitious attempt at European cooperation at the judicial level is the *Convention on the Suppression of Terrorism*,[8] which 17 out of the 19 Council of Europe member states signed in January 1977, when the convention was opened for signature. At the time of writing, all European Union member states are now party to the European Convention on the Suppression of Terrorism 1977.

The convention provides, in effect, that all ratifying states will exclude the whole range of major terrorist offences, such as assassinations, hostage-takings, bomb attacks and hijackings, from the political offence exception clauses that had previously been used to justify refusal of extradition; in other words to ensure that all contracting states would treat such offences as common crimes. In cases where, because of some technical or constitutional difficulty, a contracting state is unable to carry out extradition, the convention obliges the authorities to bring the case before their own prosecuting authority. Mutual assistance in criminal investigation of such offences is also made mandatory.

However, the admirable intentions of this convention were seriously obstructed by two major shortcomings. First, a possible escape clause was inserted into the convention permitting a contracting state to reserve the right to regard a certain offence as political and hence to withhold extradition. In 1996 this loophole was closed by the EU states' strengthening of the Convention on Extradition. Use of the political offence exception as grounds for refusing extradition of a terrorist suspect is now excluded.

It is now generally realised that one of the most effective methods of cooperation against terrorism takes the form of bilateral agreements between neighbouring states. A notable instance of this occurred in the US–Cuba hijack pact[9] of February 1973, in which both governments agreed to return hijacked aircraft, crews and passengers and hijackers. It is true that Cuba insisted on a caveat enabling her to refuse to return terrorists affiliated to a national liberation movement recognised by Cuba. But as most hijackers who sought sanctuary in Cuba from the US were criminals or psychopaths this clause did not undermine the effectiveness of the agreement. Moreover, even though Cuba refused formally to renew the agreement, following the blowing up of a Cuban airliner by anti-Castro exiles in October 1976, the fact is that Cuba has continued to operate in the spirit of the pact, and it has undoubtedly contributed to the defeat of the hijacking plague that afflicted the United States between 1970 and 1972.

An even more unlikely example of partnership was the cooperation between Somalia and West Germany in the GSG-9 (Grenzschutzgruppe 9 – the German anti-terrorist unit) operation to rescue the Lufthansa hostages in Mogadishu. After all, Somalia was a Marxist regime which had previously been used as a base by terrorists organising the Air France hijack to Entebbe. Yet, encouraged by the prospect of economic assistance, the new state rendered valuable service by allowing in the German rescue squad.

If such diverse political systems can cooperate profitably, surely it should not be beyond the power of European states to improve their own bilateral security cooperation? This form of bilateral collaboration made a big contribution to combating two particularly intractable terrorist campaigns in Europe: in Northern Ireland in the period 1980–98 and in regard to the Basque region and ETA's terrorist campaign since 1979. In January 1979 France abolished refugee status for Spanish nationals in France on the sensible grounds that Spain, as a democracy, no longer had political refugees. Almost simultaneously 13 Basques living near the Spanish border were banished to the remote Hautes-Alpes in eastern France. This was France's very positive response to the Spanish government's demands for more vigorous cooperation to stamp out terrorism.

French border country has long been regarded as valuable sanctuary and a launching point of ETA terrorism and the new measures did much to assist the Spanish authorities' counter-terrorism drive. Spanish–French cross-border cooperation against terrorism has been vastly more effective than British–Irish cooperation in recent years. The French authorities began to change their attitude towards cooperation when the terrorism began to spill over to their side of the border, particularly when an extreme right-wing death squad calling itself GAL (the

Anti-Terrorist Liberation Group) began to step up its assassination attacks against Basque targets on French territory. At last they strengthened their controls on the frontier and started to deport and extradite ETA activists in Spain. This cooperation has led, for example, to the dismantling of ETA's itinerant network in France. In 1991, 40 ETA members, Spanish and French, were arrested in France, and the following year the French and Spanish police arrested three terrorist leaders and 199 terrorists and collaborators, thereby totally disrupting ETA's financial and logistical support. In 1993, French–Spanish cooperation led to the arrest of the leader of ETA's Barcelona cell. Despite this disruption, however, ETA's hardcore continued their terrorist campaign. During the summer of 1993, it planted some small bombs in hotels in the Costa del Sol and in Barcelona.

French–Spanish cooperation in 1994 led to the capture of the deputy leader of ETA and the discovery of a bomb factory. The pressure from the police and intelligence cooperation and an increasingly sophisticated use of police informers by the authorities continues and has undoubtedly reduced ETA's capabilities to sustain major terrorist activity.

If the international community is to minimise the rewards of terrorism and maximise the risks and costs, it must be seen to be possible to bring terrorist suspects to justice even when they slip across frontiers. But extradition is a highly complex and unpredictable process. Many states do not have extradition agreements, and where these do exist they frequently exclude political offences – the term *political* is often very liberally construed. Differences in criminal codes, procedures and judicial traditions also have to be taken into account. Often the extradition procedures become highly protracted, owing to difficulties in obtaining evidence and witnesses from abroad. In the British extradition hearings in the case of Astrid Poll in 1978–79 there was further complication – a dispute over nationality.

Extradition proceedings succeed in the cases of only a small minority of terrorist suspects. Many states use deportation as a form of 'disguised extradition' and as this is a civil – as opposed to criminal – proceeding it does not afford the individual the same opportunities to present his or her own case. However, deportation merely shifts the problem to another state, and does not ensure that a suspected terrorist is brought to justice. On all these grounds this method ought not to be encouraged. A far more desirable course is for states to attempt to standardise their criminal codes and procedures to facilitate the application of the 'extradite or prosecute' principle. However, 'extraordinary rendition', i.e. abducting a suspect, with or without the knowledge and approval of the state where it occurs, and secretly transporting the suspect to a third country where torture is known to be used, has been a tactic employed extensively during the 'war on terrorism'; this method is a serious violation of international law.

Far and away the most important advances in international cooperation against terrorism among the democratic countries have taken place at police and intelligence service levels.[10] It is a measure of the sensitivities of the EU member states about their sovereignty over national security matters that all the improvements that have taken place on these operational aspects of combating terrorism fall under the heading of intergovernmental cooperation rather than arising from the community method.[11] It is significant that even under the Maastricht Treaty, despite all the talk of a Common Foreign and Security Policy the 'third pillar' of cooperation in internal security matters is firmly under the direction of the EU governments. Articles K1–9 of the treaty accorded the governments' responsibility for coordinating their approach to a whole range of key issues from combating organised crime and terrorism to matters such as asylum, visa requirements and refugee status. But the mechanism designated for the task of coordinating the EU response is the intergovernmental K4 Committee.

As early as 1976 the EU (formerly the European Economic Community) has established a valuable structure for exchanging intelligence and helping to coordinate the efforts of EU states to combat organised crime and terrorism. This was TREVI (International Terrorism, Radicalism, Extremism and Violence), a structure established in 1976 under the direction of the EU Ministers of Interior. TREVI's working groups of senior officials addressed problems of international organised crime, including drug trafficking and money laundering, as well as terrorism. It provided an ideal mechanism for developing informal collaboration and exchanges of information between national police and intelligence officials. Routine liaison work was carried out by national police coordinating bureaux. However, now that EUROPOL has been authorised to include terrorism within its remit, it is expected that EUROPOL will take on some of the valuable work previously done by TREVI.

Police and intelligence cooperation is generally most effective at the bilateral level, where there is a considerable degree of personal trust between the officials involved.[12] However, there can be serious obstructions and even failures in cooperation where a particular agency is blamed for a major intelligence failure or where it is suspected of compromising vital sources. As a means of fostering a culture of international cooperation, the secondment of police officers and officials to work with friendly countries has proved most effective in building up a network of informal international cooperation.

Among EU member states the need for enhanced cooperation on security issues, including terrorism, was given added urgency by the introduction of the Single European Act, which established a European internal market. In preparation for this the governments of Germany, France, Belgium, the Netherlands and Luxemburg signed the Schengen Agreement, committing them to dismantle controls on their common frontiers. Their plan was to enable free movement of persons, goods and services across borders. However, in practice this radical scheme created complex problems which have taken a long time to resolve, such as the establishment of a satisfactory computer link between the national police forces, arrangements for the hot pursuit of criminals and terrorists, firearms control, visa requirement and work permits for aliens.

When one takes into account that the EU has the most fully developed structures for regional integration in the world, it is evident that international police and intelligence cooperation on terrorism and related matters in other parts of the world is going to remain fairly limited in scope.

Some observers point to Interpol as a possible mechanism for enhancing police cooperation. However, under Article 3 of its constitution, Interpol is explicitly debarred from investigating political matters. Although the organisation's 1984 assembly agreed to allow Interpol to handle cases involving crimes against innocent victims or property outside the area of conflict, the organisation continues to play a relatively modest role in combating terrorism. Among the reasons for this is the fact that the states engaged in sponsoring terrorism belong to Interpol, and hence other states are reluctant to allow highly sensitive information into the Interpol network.

In the 1990s there has been a significant trend towards greater transnational terrorist activity of groups motivated by religious fanaticism, of gangs and cartels involved in transnational organised crime, such as the Cali cartel and the Russian Mafias, and of degenerate guerrilla movements, corrupted by large-scale crime and racketeering.

Last, but by no means least, is the international concern about these developments shared by many governments and international organisations, and the growing realisation that terrorism can only be combated effectively through greater enhanced international cooperation: sound national measures against terrorism are of course essential, but by themselves, they are not going to be adequate to deal with an increasingly transnational phenomenon.

A recurring problem in the evolution of international cooperation against terrorism has been what I have described as 'the politics of the latest outrage'.[13] In the wake of a major atrocity, such as the terrorist bombing of Pan Am 103 over Lockerbie, Scotland, in December 1998 or the US embassy bombings in East Africa in August 1998, public outrage is reflected in numerous promises of major governmental and international action to ensure that 'it never happens again'. However, once the memory of the atrocity begins to fade, the public begins to lose interest in measures against terrorism and governments fail to fully implement the promised preventative measures. Similarly, levels of international cooperation achieved during major crises, such as Operation Desert Shield and Operation Desert Storm in 1990–91, are soon discarded once the coalition partners no longer perceive it as a major priority.

Clear illustrations of the sharp decline in the level of cooperation against terrorism among the former coalition partners since the Gulf conflict were the US government's granting of visas to Gerry Adams, the head of the IRA's political wing; the EU governments' unwillingness to back the US in economic sanctions against Libya and Iran; and the Saudi Arabian authorities' failure to provide adequate assistance and access to US investigators pursuing those responsible for the Dhahran bombing of US servicemen in 1996.

The continuing problems of moving beyond mere rhetoric by governments to the effective implementation of international cooperation against terrorism may at first sight seem surprising. After all, the United States, the sole remaining superpower commanding huge military capabilities and economic leverage, continued to be a major target of international terrorism and remains the leading champion of stronger international action. Perhaps the most striking example of close cooperation between allies is the special relationship between the United Kingdom and the United States. This relationship is founded not only on historical and cultural links and a common language; it has developed out of close alliance relationships in two world wars and the Cold War. It was therefore rather puzzling to learn that a committee of Westminster MPs concluded, before the 2010 general election, that the special relationship was dead. As was publicly acknowledged when Prime Minister David Cameron paid his first visit to President Obama in Washington, political leaders on both sides of the Atlantic recognise the value of the close alliance. It is in the common interests of both countries, especially in the field of counter-terrorism. Naturally there are disagreements between close allies, but this does not mean that the special relationship has suddenly ceased to exist. Nor should we make the mistake of assuming that a healthy special relationship necessarily means that the UK must be subservient to the US. It is valuable for the US government to be able to rely on support from its leading European NATO ally in a crisis and it is invaluable for the UK to be able to benefit from the US superpower capabilities in intelligence and fighting terrorism. It is clear that Prime Minister David Cameron and his coalition colleagues cannot afford to give up their access to US intelligence, the best-resourced and most powerful source of global intelligence in the world. It would be the height of folly to try to abandon the special relationship at a time when the UK and the US face a severe threat of terrorist attack.

Over half of the world's states experience some form of international terrorist attack every year. Other G8 states, such as Britain, France, Russia and Japan, have every reason to favour stronger international measures. India, Israel, Egypt, Spain and Turkey have been among the most active supporters of enhanced international cooperation against terrorism. Above all, the peace process between Israel and the PLO appeared to provide an unprecedented opportunity for reducing one of the major sources of international terrorism.

In June 1995 a flurry of multilateral initiatives appeared to promise significant progress in international cooperation against terrorism. At the meeting of the G7 states plus Russia at Halifax in June 1995 the political leaders called for a special counter-terrorism conference of G8 ministers. This was held at ministerial level in Ottawa in December and pledged to strengthen the sharing of intelligence on terrorism; to pursue measures to prevent terrorists' use of nuclear, chemical and biological weapons (a response to the gas attack by Aum Shinrikyo cult on the Tokyo underground system on 20 March 1995); to inhibit the movement of terrorists; to deprive terrorists of funds; to increase mutual legal assistance; to strengthen protection of aviation, maritime and other forms of transport against terrorism; to enhance measures to prevent the falsification of documents; and to work towards universal adherence to international treaties and conventions on terrorism by the year 2000.

The assassination of Prime Minister Yitzhak Rabin by a Jewish extremist in November 1995, and the Hamas suicide bombings against Israel in 1996, provided the catalyst for a further summit at Sharm el Sheikh on strengthening international cooperation, and this theme was at the top of the agenda of the G8 meeting in 1996 in Lyon where President Clinton presented 40 US initiatives designed to enhance the counter-terrorism effort. The G8 summit agreed to hold an unprecedented three-day ministerial meeting on countering terrorism in Paris in July 1996.

At the Paris meeting 16 foreign and security ministers of the G7 states plus Russia agreed to back 25 measures. Some of the counter-terrorism steps agreed, such as improved sharing of intelligence and easing of extradition of suspected terrorists, have been the subject of many previous declarations and agreements. Some, however, are quite new. For example, ministers agreed to clamp down on the use of charitable organisations as a front for terrorist fund raising, and on the use of the internet by terrorists. Another fresh measure adopted, proposed by the British government, was for the establishment of a directory of counter-terrorist skills and expertise to enable agencies in different states to share expertise on combating different types of terrorism.

The intensive activity on international cooperation against terrorism in 1995–96 needs to be placed into perspective. It reflects the undoubted growing concern at that time among the world's leading industrialised nations about the growing threat of terrorism, as manifested in the 1993 World Trade Center bombing in New York City, the huge car bomb attacks on the Israeli Embassy and a Jewish cultural centre in Buenos Aires in 1992 and 1994 respectively, the intensification of terrorist attacks in the Middle East and the assassination of Prime Minister Yitzhak Rabin, the attack on the Tokyo underground system by Aum Shinrikyo using the deadly chemical nerve agent Sarin, the spate of terrorist bombings in France linked with the GIA, the bomb at the Olympic Games in Atlanta in July 1996, the conviction of Ramzi Yousef and others for conspiring to plant bombs on board eleven US airliners in the East Asia region, and the bombings of US embassies in Nairobi and Dar es Salaam in which 250 were killed. When one bears in mind the great lethality of the East African embassy attacks, the failure of the US and its G8 partners to take more effective concerted actions against the growing threat from Al Qaeda seems extraordinary.

However, although there is ample evidence of growing international concern about international terrorism on the part of the US and other G8 states, many other countries afflicted by severe campaigns of international terrorism, such as India, Pakistan, Turkey, Peru, Algeria, Egypt, Sri Lanka and the Philippines, focus primarily, if not exclusively, on domestic counter-terrorism measures. Their main interest in international cooperation was understandably directed at cross-border security relations with their immediate neighbouring states, especially those sharing a land frontier which really counts. High-sounding multilateral declarations and agreements are not seen as having much practical value. One hopes 9/11 and Al Qaeda attacks in Bali, Casablanca, Madrid, Istanbul, London, Riyadh, Egypt, Iraq, etc., have made countries aware that *no* country can assume they are immune.

The state of Israel, assailed by terrorism almost continually throughout its history, has placed little reliance on international cooperation but has followed a deter- mined and often draconian policy of self-help, including military interventions in neighbouring states and collective punishments of the Palestinian population. Indeed Israel's recent devastating bombardment and invasion of Gaza in response to Hamas rocket attacks on Israel, the killing of nine peace activists on the high seas and the hardening of its position on Israel settlements, are a graphic illustration of the way failure to engage in the diplomacy of international cooperation can lead to greater isolation and jeopardise possibilities of achieving progress towards genuine conflict resolution. Both the Israeli government and Hamas have been obstacles to peace. The prolonged and bitter Arab–Israeli conflict is a powerful reminder that the ethnic and religious struggles that have spawned a high proportion of the terrorist violence experienced in the late twentieth century have deeply divided the international community. It is obvious that it is going to be impossible to achieve a common or collective international security policy against terrorism where there is a fundamental disagreement regarding the *legitimacy* of those who use violence to pursue their aims, and those states which utilise overwhelming military power in an attempt to suppress them.

The huge gulf between the rhetoric and the reality of international cooperation against terrorism is a powerful illustration of the extent to which the realist paradigm actually dominates and shapes the perceptions of the majority of political leaders and their citizens in the contemporary international state system. It is obvious that there is no agreed international sovereign authority and hence there are no clearly defined and universally accepted international binding laws, and no mechanisms for enforcing such laws. In our essentially anarchical international system there is no universal agreement as to what constitutes the illegitimate use of violence, or the legitimate suppression of revolt by the state. Each state jealously guards its own national sovereignty, especially on sensitive issues of national security. Each national government inevitably places the pursuit of its own national interest above all other considerations, including even general international declarations about common responsibilities to combat terrorism.

The UN response to 9/11

The UN Security Council's immediate and unusually concerted response to the 9/11 attacks marked a sea change in the role of the UN in relation to international terrorism, and reflected the genuine shock and outrage voiced by the overwhelming majority of governments around the world, including the major powers. The Council responded to the 9/11 attacks by unanimously passing Resolution 1368 on the following day declaring that 9/11 was 'a threat to international peace and security' and that it was willing to take 'all necessary steps to respond to the attacks'. The resolution also explicitly underlined the inherent right of the US to self-defence and the right of collective self-defence in accordance with the UN Charter.

Moreover, as if to indicate the urgency they attached to the situation, and in contrast to numerous lengthy Council debates on terrorism in the past, the Council passed Resolution 1373 two weeks later reiterating these declarations. It is true that these resolutions did not specifically propose or endorse military intervention in Afghanistan to topple the Taliban regime that had given safe haven to Al Qaeda. The US administration was known to have great scepticism about the multilateral cooperation under the UN umbrella and did not seek explicit authorisation for its military action in Afghanistan. (We can already see the rather unilateralist tenor of US response to 9/11 emerging at the UN debates, even though President Bush clearly welcomed the swift formation of an International Coalition Against Terrorism and offers of sympathy and support from other countries on an unprecedented scale.)

The Bush administration was content to justify its actions in Afghanistan on the basis of the self-defence provision (Article 51) of the UN Charter. This position was – at least implicitly – accepted by both Russia and China in the light of the 9/11 attacks. In normal circumstances it could have been very difficult to carry support from the two permanent members traditionally most opposed to US foreign policy and military interventions in particular.

The great value of UNSC Resolution 1373, drafted by the US, is that it became a chapter VII obligation for member states to apply the terms of the resolution, and with the possibility of sanctions being used against them if they fail to.

Moreover, one of the great strengths of the resolution is that it is geared towards achieving goals which are, at least in principle, within the capacity of the UN to attain. It would be no good demanding that the UN organisation itself should take on the roles of enforcement and the suppression of terrorism. It does not have the power or resources to undertake these tasks: these matters are inevitably left in the hands of member states with the necessary means.

The major advantages the UN has are (1) the use of its moral authority and legitimacy to *influence* the behaviour of member states; (2) the ability to *dissuade* or at least *discourage* certain types of behaviour by member states (e.g. by the threat or use of UN sanctions); and (3) the ability to set standards of behaviour (e.g. in the texts of the various UN conventions dealing with aspects of terrorism, which are so useful as models for national governments to use in shaping their own legislation).

Indeed UNSC Resolution 1373 itself is largely based on the language and objectives of the major UN conventions. For example, the resolution obliges member states to concert action to suppress terrorist finances, to freeze assets of those who finance terrorism, and to amend their criminal codes to ensure that the financing of terrorism is treated as a serious criminal offence. The language used is modelled on that of the UN Convention for the Suppression of Terrorist Finances. UNSC 1373 also obliges states to operate effective border controls and procedures for issuing and checking travel documents, to take steps to prevent the supply of weapons to terrorists, and to refrain from permitting their territory to be used by terrorist organisations including recruitment of members. All member states are obliged to ensure that those found to be involved in the financing, planning, preparing, perpetrating or supporting of terrorist acts should be prosecuted under the national criminal code on the basis that these are all serious offences in domestic and international law. Member states are also *required* to exchange intelligence to prevent attacks, especially information about 'actions or movements of terrorist persons or networks; forged or falsified travel documents; traffic in arms; explosives or sensitive materials; use of communication technologies by terrorist groups; and the threat posed by possession of weapons of mass destruction by terrorist groups'.

However, perhaps the most radical and potentially useful new measure introduced by the UN resolution was the establishment of a Counter Terrorism Committee of the Security Council to monitor its implementation. This breaks new ground by giving the UN a proactive role in identifying states failing, or lagging behind, in their implementation. The CTC made a good start under the Chairmanship of the British representative to the UN, Sir Jeremy Greenstock, creating an initial set of procedures and a plan to carry out its work. It has already served as a valuable clearing house for developing best practice in countering terrorism among member states.

In short there is no doubt that the UN Security Council's response to 9/11 acted as a catalyst to transform the UN's role and influence in this difficult field, and despite the difficulties and disagreements, for example over the US–UK invasion of Iraq, it has continued to make a valuable and very practical contribution.

The EU's response to 9/11

The EU also reacted very swiftly to 9/11 by issuing a very wide-ranging 'action plan' covering six main aspects of counter-terrorism cooperation:

1. police and judicial cooperation;
2. diplomatic activity, including the relaunch of the Middle East peace process;
3. humanitarian aid to Afghanistan;
4. improving airport security through the EU;
5. enhancing cooperation on the suppression of terrorist financing;
6. sharing expertise in emergency planning, including dealing with possible terrorist attacks using CBRN materials.

The flagship of EU counter-terrorism efforts since 9/11 was the introduction of the European Arrest Warrant in 2002. The value of this measure to combat international terrorism is *in theory* all too clear. It would make the lengthy, cumbersome and unpredictable method of extradition between the EU states unnecessary. The EU Arrest Warrant is based on the principle of mutual recognition of criminal judgements of the courts of all member states by fellow member states. It becomes an administrative procedure, and is aimed at being a fast-track means of transferring suspects. However, *in practice*, the European Arrest Warrant, which was supposedly to come into force from January 2004, was initially undermined by the reluctance or unwillingness of some key member states to ratify it, and by the continuing desire of certain member states to maintain total national political control on these matters.

As in the past, however, the pressure of events has conspired to push the EU into great counter-terrorism activity. A major catalyst was the Madrid bombing on 11 March 2004, which killed almost 200 civilians. This led the EU to launch an ambitious Plan of Action to Combat Terrorism (March 2004). The strategic objectives of the plan are as follows:

*   To deepen the international consensus and enhance international efforts to combat terrorism.

- To reduce the access of terrorists to financial and other economic resources.
- To maximise capability within EU bodies and member states to detect, investigate and prosecute terrorists and prevent terrorist attacks.
- To protect the security of international transport and ensure effective systems of border control.
- To enhance the capability of the European Union and of member states to deal with the consequences of terrorist attack.
- To address the factors which contribute to support for, and recruitment into, terrorism.
- To target actions under EU external relations towards priority third countries where counter-terrorism capacity or commitment to combating terrorism needs to be enhanced.

This plan was accompanied by an EU Declaration on Combating Terrorism, a powerful statement of solidarity against terrorism in the wake of the Madrid bombings. The European Council stated it was 'deeply shocked by the terrorist attacks in Madrid and expressed its sympathy and solidarity to the victims, their families, and to the Spanish people. The callous and cowardly attacks served as a terrible reminder of the threat posed by terrorism to our society.'

The most recent catalyst for promoting further action from the EU in the prevention and combating of terrorism was the coordinated bombing attack in London in July 2005 that killed 52 members of the public and injured over 700. Charles Clarke, the UK's Home Secretary, taking the initiative under the British EU Presidency, called an Extraordinary Council meeting of Justice and Home Affairs in the wake of the 7 July London bombings. After condemning the terrorist attacks on London and sending condolences to the victims and their families, the meeting declared that its immediate priority was to build on the existing EU framework 'for pursuing and investigating terrorists across borders'. The Council decided to:[14]

> Agree the Framework Decisions on the Retention of Telecommunications Data (October 2005), on the European Evidence Warrant (December 2005) and on the exchange of information between law enforcement authorities (December 2005); adopt the Decision on the exchange of information concerning terrorist offences (September 2005); combat terrorist financing by: agreeing by December 2005 a Regulation on Wire Transfers; adopting the Third Money Laundering Directive and Regulation on cash control by September 2005; agreeing a Code of Conduct to prevent the misuse of charities by terrorists (December 2005); reviewing the EU's performance overall (December 2005) and urging Member States to ensure that comprehensive financial investigation is a part of all terrorist investigations and to develop robust asset freezing powers.

In addition the Council urged member states to intensify exchange of police and judicial information, including the sharing of information on lost and stolen explosives. Member states were also urged to reduce vulnerability to attack by improved measures to protect citizens and infrastructures. On the issue of managing and minimising the consequences of terrorist attacks the Council invited member states to undertake regular joint counter-terrorism exercises to test resilience, and invited the EU Counter-Terrorism Coordinator and the Commission to report on the development of emergency response capabilities and to arrange sharing of information and coordination to enable collective decision making in an emergency, particularly for terrorist attacks on more than one member state.

In a key part of their press release, the Council stressed that their recommendations were to be seen as part of a worldwide agenda to develop a global counter-terrorism strategy and to help reach an agreed Comprehensive Convention Against Terrorism at the UN Summit in September 2003.[15] The Council and the Commission pledged to work with priority third countries, by increasing technical assistance and capacity-building to support them, including the areas of countering radicalisation and terrorist financing. These matters are clearly to be given high priority in the EU's counter-terrorism activity.

In a valuable and informative interview with Mr Gijs de Vries, the EU's Counter-Terrorism Coordinator, the author was impressed by the Coordinator's total commitment to these tasks. He gave special emphasis to the work of the EU in assisting priority third countries, especially in the field of capacity building for preventing and combating terrorism.[16] This emphasis is, in the author's view, absolutely correct, because the major form of terrorism threat we face is from Al Qaeda's transnational network. Unless we can develop an effective global strategy and coordination, and ensure that it is implemented, we will not succeed in unravelling the Al Qaeda network of networks.

In a potentially important initiative the EU's executive is preparing a paper on the radicalisation of European youth and measures to counter this trend, such as enhanced communication efforts with religious communities and better cooperation with third countries linked to terrorist training.

A further useful initiative was the adoption in mid July 2005 of a European Commission Communication to work on the EU plan for the enhancement of security of explosives and firearms:

> ... on ensuring greater security of explosives, detonators, bomb-making equipment and firearms that constitutes an integral part of the Commission's work in developing a coherent preventive strategy in the fight against terrorism and complements parallel work being done in the fight against terrorism financing and violent radicalisation and recruitment. The communication provides the state of play regarding security of explosives in all the fields in which the EU has competences and also makes a series of concrete proposals in all related fields – from a proposal to make the purchase of fertilisers subject to an authorisation obligation to the creation of a network of EU bomb disposal squads that would share information on new threats particularly those coming from home-made explosives. The communication places emphasis on improving security arrangements all along the production and supply chain but particularly during storage and transport.

The above measures are clearly very practical and should secure broad support. Far more controversial, because of their civil liberties implications, are the EU Ministers' proposals from the 13 July 2005 meeting which would lead to: telecom companies being mandated to retain details of all telephone calls, e-mails and web traffic for a minimum period; a strategy to counter radicalisation and recruitment; and a strengthening of the visa information system and the Schengen information system, which causes concerns to civil liberties groups worried about the concentration of data held and who would have access to it. The role of data exchange and intelligence cooperation is so crucial that we must now consider this in more detail.

The role of intelligence data exchange in EU counter-terrorism activities

The EU Declaration on Combating Terrorism can be seen as a powerful call for solidarity and firm action from member states, but it is clear from the language of the declaration and the Plan of Action that the call for action is primarily directed at the member states' own national authorities, because in reality it is they who have the power and resources to carry out the plan. It is true that under Objective 3, the plan speaks of enhancing the 'capacity of appropriate EU bodies (i.e. Europol, Eurojust and the Police Chiefs' Task Force) in the preparation of intelligence assessments of all aspects of the terrorist threat ... '.

However, the key source for this intelligence is inevitably the secret intelligence services and police forces of the individual member states. The reality is that national governments are unwilling to allow other governments' intelligence services and police anything more than limited access to their secret intelligence on terrorism (or indeed on other key security issues). There are a number of reasons for this:

- They are afraid of disclosing their sources and possibly compromising them.
- They do not trust other countries to keep the secret intelligence secret.
- They fear that other countries might take action on the basis of the information given to them, which would be contrary to the sending state's interest.
- They are afraid of revealing gaps and errors in their intelligence, which an unlimited access would disclose.
- In the extremely competitive world of intelligence, agencies are reluctant to part with intelligence, which they assess as giving them an advantage over their rival agencies within their own nation-state.

For all the above reasons national intelligence agencies working with Europol and other EU collaborative bodies will only provide *sanitised* intelligence data for sharing purposes. Hence it is *national governments* and not the EU that are inevitably and understandably the key recipients and gatekeepers for sensitive counter-terrorism intelligence. When they do engage in serious international cooperation it is almost invariably at the bilateral or trilateral level. When there is a well-established and trusted bilateral cooperation, as between France and Spain in regard to Basque terrorism, there will be a concomitant sharing of high-grade and sensitive intelligence.

This does not mean that intelligence sharing at the EU level is a waste of time. It may have a valuable part to play in developing threat awareness and vigilance in member states. Although access to raw intelligence data will inevitably be restricted by the collecting authorities' national governments, we should bear in mind that the sharing of *analyses* and *assessments* may be highly beneficial in persuading national authorities to provide enhanced or more urgent action in support of a threatened or victim state.

In the light of the above, I support the 8 June 2004 proposal by Javier Solana, EU High Representative for the CFSP, for charging the EU's Joint Situation Centre (SITCEN) with the production of intelligence analyses with a view to supporting EU policymaking.

In his statement at Luxemburg on 8 June 2004,[17] Javier Solana reported that the heads of the security services of the member states have given their support to the proposal and that he hoped to reach 'a final consensus on the proposal in the next European Council'. Mr Solana correctly pointed out in his statement that his proposal would 'build on the existing cooperation within the SITCEN, established between the external intelligence services of the member states since early 2002'.

Mr Solana put forward what he termed 'core ideas' which he hoped the Council would endorse:

1. Moves by the Heads of the EU's 25 Security Services to meet regularly together as a group in the format of the existing Counter-Terrorist Group (CTG).
2. The work of CTG would allow for close cooperation *in the field of analytical exchange* between Security Services, and would provide scope for improved operation cooperation.
3. Moves by the European Police Office (EUROPOL) to reactivate their Counter-Terrorist Task Force and efforts to improve the flow of criminal intelligence to EUROPOL.

Mr Solana argued that these measures would mean that:

1. EU decision makers would be better informed, inter alia, about threats, terrorist methods, organisation of terrorist groups and thus better prepared to devise effective EU counter-terrorism policies.
2. Member states would receive better support from European bodies. They would get assessment material from the EU's SITCEN and their police services in particular would get better support from EUROPOL.
3. Member states would retain the lead in the operational field but would be working more closely together through CTG, EUROPOL, as well as through existing bilateral arrangements to strengthen information exchange and cooperation.

I fully accept the logic of Javier Solana's proposal. It is realistic in recognising that member states will retain the lead in the operational field and that his proposal, if implemented will simply complement 'existing bilateral arrangements'.

However, there is an overwhelming counter-terrorism case which Mr Solana does not deploy but which should persuade all member states to adopt his proposal. The threat from the Al Qaeda network is quintessentially transnational. As we saw in the investigation of the Madrid bombings and many other acts of the Al Qaeda network and its affiliates, the terrorist cells and their support networks operate across national boundaries. We need to greatly improve our transnational networking in order to prevent and combat Al Qaeda, the most lethal network in the modern history of non-state terror.

To sum up: the EU has made small and often faltering steps towards greater counter-terrorism cooperation. The role of national governments and their counter-terrorism agencies and their bilateral cooperation with other states' authorities have made a far more significant and effective contribution. But, 9/11 and the Madrid bombings have had the effect of triggering a more proactive approach by the EU. We should, in my view, warmly encourage this approach, viewing it as a way of adding to our existing methods of cooperation. Because of the changed nature of the threat it could develop into something very useful. I hope that Her Majesty's Government will encourage and contribute to this process.

There are other measures which the EU has already initiated or is proposing to initiate that I believe to be urgent priorities in the fight against international terrorism, which the EU is particularly well placed to push forward:

- The inclusion of biometrics in passports and the strengthening of European border controls.
- Efforts to get member states to adhere to the commitment they made in the EU Action Plan for Combating Terrorism, especially implementation of the European Arrest Warrant and Joint Investigation Teams.
- Facilitating joint training for police and emergency services.
- Enhancing EU capabilities for combating terrorist financing and money laundering.

We must bear in mind, however, that national authorities of member states carry prime responsibility for protecting their citizens. In the next section the author proposes some general principles that should underpin the counter-terrorism policies of EU member states and which are fully compatible with EU legislation and the European Convention on Human Rights.

Conclusion

Even if groupings of states at regional or global levels do agree on the nature and seriousness of terrorist challenges to their security, this does not necessarily mean that they will agree on *what* needs to be done or on which international organisation is the appropriate mechanism for countermeasures. For example, on matters of European security concerning NATO, the EU, WEU and OSCE all have a finger in the pie. Which organisation, if any, should take the leading role in regional matters against terrorism?

What are the policy options open to cooperating states? Which are likely to tackle the terrorist threat without at the same time putting the wider interests of the state or alliance at risk? In situations where diplomatic pressure and economic sanctions are impracticable or inadequate, should the use of military force be considered? If so, what kind of force? How can the use of military force in such circumstances be prevented from acting as a catalyst for a wider conflict? Terrorism is a complex phenomenon presenting the international community with daunting decisions and dilemmas. There are no easy solutions. The response of the liberal democratic state at international level should be firm and courageous, but *always* within the rule of law. Massive military retaliation against states or groups involved in terrorism will only tend to substitute the even greater evil of war, with its attendant massive loss of life and destruction, in place of the lesser evil of terrorism. Yet equally it is essential to avoid cowardly under-reaction and surrender. Terrorism is a fundamental attack on human rights, and the international community has a moral as well as a legal duty to combat this international scourge of the innocent. The traditional realist paradigm is all too clearly and inherently incapable of contending with the new transnational threats to human rights and security posed by international terrorism. Ideally all countries should cooperate fully to ensure that those involved in terrorist crimes are brought to justice. In practice, the anarchic nature of the international system and the fact there are states that use, sponsor, support and sympathise with specific terrorist groups are basic reasons why terrorism is likely to remain the most ubiquitous form of political violence well into the future.

12 The future of terrorism

America's sense of invulnerability to large-scale terrorist attacks within its own borders suffered a huge blow with the 9/11 attacks. There is no doubt that the sheer scale of the loss of life, unprecedented in the history of acts of international terrorism by non-state organisations, was a traumatic awakening for Americans to their vulnerability.

As noted in Chapter 4, one of the Al Qaeda movement's most worrying features is the intense interest it has shown in acquiring the necessary expertise and technology to construct CBRN (chemical, biological, radiological and nuclear) weapons. In a notorious statement issued in 1998 Osama bin Laden said it was the duty of Muslims to prepare the maximum force to terrorise the infidel enemy. The statement was entitled, 'The Nuclear Bomb of Islam'. There have been numerous reports of Al Qaeda seeking to obtain WMD from former Soviet Union countries and trying to buy uranium, presumably to make an atomic bomb. This interest in CBRN weaponry is chilling and entirely credible. A terrorist movement that is explicitly committed to mass killing of civilians and which massacred nearly 3,000 civilians on 9/11 without any compunction is clearly capable of using its suicide attackers in a CBRN attack of some kind. For all these reasons I believe that since 9/11 the threat of CBRN terrorism has increased from low probability to medium probability, high consequence. Al Qaeda appears to have had some difficulty in implementing this type of attack and this may partly be because of the major disruption they suffered after being moved out of their Afghan bases when the Taliban regime was overthrown in autumn 2001. However, though this may have given the world breathing space, it is hard to believe that it will take Al Qaeda more than a few years to produce its own atomic weapon, however crude. It is all the more important for the international community to inflict greater disruption on Al Qaeda to help stop this happening.

The significance of the first known cases of the use of chemical weapons by a terrorist group in Japan should be heavily emphasised.[1] Sarin and other nerve gas agents have been known for decades. Until the gas attack at Matsumoto, Japan in June 1994, however, it had been widely assumed that terrorists would be inhibited in their use of chemical, biological and nuclear weapons because of the political backlash it would provoke, and because of the very real risks to the lives of the perpetrators in manufacturing and deploying such weapons.

Now that a fanatical Japanese group has shown that it can be done, and that even a crude homemade chemical weapon attack can potentially cause massive loss of life, a climate of fear and huge disruption, there is a real danger that either the residue of the Aum Shinrikyo group in Japan or elsewhere, or another group seeking to emulate their mode of attack, will seek to copy this tactic or resort to other forms of weapons of mass destruction terrorism.

Japan has no monopoly on groups with bizarre beliefs capable of attempting mass murder. It should be stressed that the profiles and track records of the overwhelming majority of terrorist groups suggests that there are very few that appear to have the propensity for using weapons of mass destruction, and hence this type of terrorist attack by groups other than those which are part of the Al Qaeda network remains a low probability event. It is encouraging to note that in the 15 years since the Tokyo Sarin attack in 1995, there has been no attack emulating the Aum's choice of weapon.

However, it is worth noting that the Japanese police discovered some evidence suggesting that Aum Shinrikyo, the group suspected of the Tokyo underground attack, was also studying the possibilities of producing biological and nuclear weapons.

It should also be borne in mind that the Aum cult had been setting up branches in other countries, including Russia, and that many activists and loyal adherents in the organisation are still at large. Hence, it would be dangerous to assume that we have heard the last of this cult, despite the capture and trial of its leader Shoko Asahara. Indeed media reports in early 1999 confirmed that Aum was still raising funds and recruiting support in Japan. The group has not been suppressed.

Taking into account these developments in Japan, and the strong evidence of the smuggling of nuclear materials from the former Soviet Union countries, it is vital that democratic governments develop the specialist counter-terrorism intelligence and contingency planning designed to thwart the acquisition and deployment of weapons of mass destruction by terrorists, and the disaster management of capabilities to deal with the consequences of a chemical, biological and nuclear attack.

Even though the probability of such an attack is still relatively low, the consequences could be so catastrophic that it is vital for government authorities to plan for the worst-case scenario. Dealing with nuclear, biological and chemical threats requires highly specialised personnel and equipment of a type not generally available to the civilian police and emergency services. In the Tokyo attack the Japanese anti-chemical warfare units of the Self Defence Force had to be deployed. They and the emergency services performed well in circumstances which were almost unprecedented in peacetime. Other countries should now be studying the Japanese experience and applying the lessons to their own planning. The American and Japanese police would also gain by examining the experience of democratic countries that have suffered prolonged and intensive internal terrorism and have developed particular expertise. However, it cannot be sufficiently emphasised that such studies and the tasks of threat analysis, intelligence gathering, counter-proliferation measures, contingency planning and crisis management exercises for mass-destruction terrorism should be conducted quietly and discreetly, out of the public gaze. Too much strident public comment may have the effect of encouraging weapons of mass-destruction terrorism.

Wider lessons for democratic response

Some general lessons can be drawn from the tragic attacks of 9/11.

First, terrorist attacks have grown far more lethal over the past 25 years, as shown in the shift from hijacking to the sabotage bombings of jumbo jets and suicide hijackings – turning airliners into cruise missiles – and the escalation from small car bombs to huge truck bombs capable of killing hundreds of people. This greater capability for mass murder can be achieved by traditional terrorist weapons. After Tokyo, however, we now have to consider the possibility of other terrorists using chemical weapons or even biological or nuclear materials.

Second, in an open pluralistic society, physical security measures alone will never be enough to combat terrorism. Well-planned and coordinated measures can greatly reduce the threat.

But the key to the success against terrorism in a democracy is winning the intelligence war and mobilising the political will and democratic support for a multipronged strategy, carefully calibrated to the specific threat posed by a particular campaign.

Third, it is important not to lose sight of the international dimension of response. There is a danger that countries like America and Japan may become too preoccupied with their internal threats, forgetting perhaps that international terrorist threats are still very much alive, and hence they must be vigilant in protecting their citizens and facilities abroad. Moreover, many 'domestic' terrorist movements seek weapons, training, funds and other assistance from abroad, from closely allied groups, sponsors or through links with international organised crime and so on.

Fourth, in the final analysis, the inner strength of a liberal democracy against terrorism lies in its citizens' determination not to allow the terrorists to impose by the bomb and the gun what they cannot achieve by the ballot box. The deeper lesson of Tokyo, Oklahoma and 9/11 is that democratic governments must in all circumstances try to avoid, on the one hand, appeasement or weakness in response to terrorism, and on the other, suspending democracy in the name of defending it.

The Japanese authorities have been blamed for under-reacting to the nerve gas attacks. The American government has been criticised for overreaction to 9/11, for hyping the threat of mass destruction weapon terrorism and for devoting so much attention to it that they have paradoxically increased the possibility of such an attack while neglecting necessary measures for combating more probable forms of terrorism.

It is still too early to form a proper evaluation of these responses, but West Europeans should have enough experience of domestic terrorism to put them on their guard against any easy 'solutions' which may be on offer. Every terrorist group and campaign is different and no democratic country has a monopoly of wisdom on this complex challenge.

Likely targets

On the basis of statistical analysis of trends in targeting by international terrorist groups over recent years, it is not difficult to predict the most likely targets in the coming years. Over half of the attacks on property or facilities are likely to involve business or industrial premises, roughly 10 per cent are likely to involve diplomatic premises and about half this number will involve other government premises and military facilities. Owing to the fact that some terrorism is primarily directed at buildings rather than personnel and that military, governmental and diplomatic facilities have been 'target hardened', the vulnerability of personnel in each category does not coincide with the vulnerability of the facilities. The most vulnerable individuals are usually civilian members of the public, such as shoppers or tourists, passengers in public transit systems and worshippers in mosques and churches, who do not have the benefit of any security protection whatsoever.

It is important not to rely too heavily on terrorism incident statistics. These do not bring out the qualitative difference in the effect of specific terrorist attacks. In view of the fact that terrorist groups have shown an increasing tendency to be more lethal over recent years, it is wise to plan for a continuing trend towards massive car and truck bombings in crowded city areas.[2] 'Spectacular' terrorist attacks – for example on civil aviation, governmental, business, transportation or diplomatic targets – are designed to capture maximum attention from the mass media, to cause maximum shock and outrage, and to effect some demands sought by the terrorists.

Nuclear terrorism

Many analysts have endorsed the somewhat sanguine assessment of an American writer that 'the threat of nuclear action by terrorists appears to be exaggerated'. In support of this optimistic view it has been argued that terrorists are not really interested in mass murder, but in gaining publicity and using propaganda to influence people. Of course publicity and propaganda are generally key tactical objectives. But in many cases the terrorists' cardinal aim is to create a climate of fear and collapse, essentially by terrifying and demoralising their targets into capitulation. What more potent weapon of psychological coercion can be conceived in the modern age than the threat to explode a nuclear device?

It would be extraordinarily foolish to assume that all terrorist groups shared the same perceptions of rationality, humanity and prudence that inform the consciences of most of humanity. In the strange transcendental logic of the fanatical political terrorist, as I have earlier observed, the end is held to justify any means. If any individual life is expendable in the case of 'global jihad', 'revolutionary justice' or 'liberation', so many hundreds, even thousands of lives may have to be 'sacrificed'. One has only to turn to the hysterical writing of Johannes Most, Pierre Vallieres of the Weathermen, to find mass slaughter of 'bourgeois vermin' not only commended but proudly and enthusiastically advocated. Justifications for mass killings are not confined to religious and ethnic fanatics. As for international terrorists, who may be operating in the heart of the territory of their hated enemy, there has been a similar readiness on their part to regard the 'enemy' civil population as expendable. Hence although a lower probability than chemical terrorism, nuclear terrorism is potentially so high-consequence that we must have contingency plans to prevent such an attack and to deal with possible consequences should it happen, in order to minimise loss of life.

For a whole variety of technical reasons it would probably be easier to manufacture its own home-made nuclear bomb than to acquire a tactical nuclear weapon by theft. However, even a very crude low-yield atomic blast could have a very destructive and deadly effect, well beyond the destruction and deadliness that a conventional high-explosive weapon of similar size could produce. Let us also bear in mind that beyond the immediate effects of a nuclear explosion (intense heat, shock and blast pulse, electro-magnetic phenomenon and initial radiation) the explosion would cause residual radiation, contaminating a wider area and causing deaths and very serious radiation effects on a large number of civilians.

Practical constraints

There are major practical constraints, which help to explain the absence, to date, of terrorists 'going nuclear'. In the first place nuclear weapons, both strategic and tactical, are closely guarded by governments. Their security is the prime responsibility of security forces and secret services in all the nuclear powers. Furthermore, by their very nature their operational use is controlled by a complex secret code of procedures for unlocking the weapon and preparing it for action-readiness. Unless they have confederates within the nuclear military forces of the state concerned, terrorists are unable to operate such weapons. The most they might hope to achieve would be to gravely damage or destroy them by sabotage. It is also clear that no nuclear power, even one sponsoring proxy terrorism, would willingly allow part of its own nuclear armoury to fall into the hands of a terrorist movement. The danger of the movement recklessly triggering a nuclear conflict or a major limited war, or of the sponsor state being blackmailed by the movement with threats of nuclear use, would discourage any such adventurism. The problem is that Al Qaeda is unlikely to be deterred by such factors.

The future of Al Qaeda

It is likely that many of the current terror wars will continue for many years ahead, for the reasons outlined in the previous sections. It is also clear that there will be some fresh outbreaks of this type of warfare in conflict hotspots where it had been hoped that some political resolution had been achieved. Areas which are particularly vulnerable to this reversion to terror war include Central Africa, West Africa, the Horn of Africa, the Caucasus, Sudan, Iraq, Afghanistan, Kashmir and Indonesia.

As the author concluded in an earlier chapter, the Al Qaeda movement, though seriously damaged by extensive international measures against it, seems likely to continue to pose a threat through its global network of networks for some decades ahead. Even if the current leadership is removed from the scene there are likely to be eager successors in the wings ready to pursue the same overall objectives and using the terrorism weapon. Whoever assumes the leadership, it seems almost certain that they will retain key elements of Al Qaeda's ideology and combat doctrine, and hence will continue to wage their jihad within the frontline countries (Iraq, Afghanistan, Pakistan, Saudi Arabia), and urge their networks within Western countries to launch terrorist attacks on the homelands of the Coalition allies, including, of course, the US and the UK.

Investigations into the 7 July London bombings have confirmed that this was the first case of suicide bombing being used in Western Europe. This will have major implications for Europe's counter-terrorism strategy.

The US is likely to continue its policy of using drone attacks to eliminate senior members of Al Qaeda's leadership, concentrating on targets near the Afghan–Pakistan border where they believe a number of them are based. For example, in May 2010, Musafa Abu al-Yazid was reportedly killed with his wife and three children in an American drone attack in the tribal areas of Pakistan. It is known that Egyptian-born al-Yazid was experienced in operational planning and mana-ging finances for Al Qaeda. It is believed that he managed the finances for the 9/11 attacks on New York and Washington. More recently he has been operational commander for Al Qaeda in Afghanistan with a direct link to bin Laden. According to some reports he had risen to be number three in Al Qaeda's leadership structure. There is no doubt that repeated losses of experienced, har-dened militants such as al-Yazid are severe blows against the terrorist network, but it would be a great mistake to assume that a policy of decapitation of the leadership, even the death of bin Laden himself, would put Al Qaeda out of business. The movement has always been able to replace these losses and the likelihood is that successors would be found to replace bin Laden and Zawahiri if they were killed or captured. It should also be borne in mind that very often drone attacks kill innocent civilians, including women and children, in 'collateral damage', increasing hostility towards the US and its allies and making it more difficult to win 'hearts and minds'.

Vulnerable targets

There are extremely grave dangers involved in the diffusion of civil nuclear facilities and technologies in many states. The Chinese decision in 2010 to sell nuclear reactors to foreign countries will undoubtedly accelerate these develop-ments along with their intrinsic risks of nuclear weapon proliferation, not only to states but also to non-state actors. These processes involve the use of substances that could be employed to make a nuclear explosive device. Plutonium, which is used for incorporation into reactor fuel, has to be shipped and in some cases transported by road. It is clearly vulnerable to theft by terrorists while it is in transit. Still more dangerous is the practice, which has developed in the nuclear power industry, of transporting plutonium nitrate in liquid form by road. This is a hazardous process. Plutonium transported as a pure compound, even in small quantities, is a particularly tempting target for terrorist theft or hijack because of the material's obvious value in constructing a nuclear weapon. Because of its extreme toxicity it could be used by terrorists as a weapon of radiological extortion. Reports by scientific experts have underlined both these dangers, but this does not appear to have influenced the policy of the EU member states' authorities regarding the transportation of nuclear fuels. Plutonium is also present in spent reactor fuel. It then has to be stored because there is to date no commercially viable system for reprocessing it. In the special case of liquid metal fast-breeder reactors, more plutonium is produced than is actually consumed, so that the problem of disposal is especially acute.

Terrorists, therefore, might seek to obtain regular small supplies of nuclear materials by various means, including infiltration of the nuclear industry workforce. The particularly vulnerable points for nuclear theft include storage facilities for spent fuel, fuel-reprocessing plants, and fabrication and uranium enrichment plants. There is little doubt that sufficient quantities of enriched uranium and plutonium could be obtained to make possible the manufacture of a primitive device. Recent firm evidence of the smuggling of nuclear materials from Russian installations underlines the growing seriousness of this threat. Even more worrying is the strong possibility that disaffected scientists and engineers from the former Soviet Union's nuclear weapons programme have been lured into the employ of rogue states or terrorist groups. It is certainly credible that a group of competent and qualified scientists and engineers could be recruited for the special purpose of building an atomic weapon or advising the group on techniques of nuclear sabotage and extortion. A team of five or six could probably accomplish this within the space of five or six weeks without incurring any serious risk to their personal health or safety. Estimates of the financial costs involved vary.

A particularly difficult threat to counter would be the terrorist group organising large-scale theft, sabotage or the manufacture of an explosive device with the skilled assistance of many collaborators within the nuclear-power industry. Also, by infiltrating terrorist activists into relatively unskilled work on nuclear-power plants the terrorist organisation could gain vital information and assistance in planning a raid on the nuclear site. Even a relatively small group with a crude general knowledge of a civil nuclear plant and its points of vulnerability could be tempted into seizing control of an installation and threatening to sabotage it as a means of extorting concessions, especially if they were suicide terrorists. This would appeal to certain groups because of the dramatic publicity they would receive. It would also be an extremely difficult and hazardous situation for the authorities. With the possibility of a major disaster that could result, for example, from reactor-core disassembly and fire in a commercial fast-breeder reactor, it would be a dangerous business to assume that the terrorists were bluffing. Prudent authorities would rapidly have to effect a mass evacuation of the population in the surrounding area.

It is sometimes argued that terrorists would be effectively discouraged from sabotage of nuclear installations because of the risk involved to their own safety, lack of knowledge of safety precautions and ignorance of nuclear technology. We have already noted that these weaknesses could be overcome by certain terrorist groups through the employment of their own 'expert' advisers on nuclear technology, or alternatively by the use of employees in the installation as agents and collaborators, and that some fanatical groups include individuals willing to martyr themselves for their cause.

Governments and security forces would be wise to plan for the 'worst possible' terrorist contingencies. Much as they may like to reassure themselves that those anarchist fringe groups or 'crazy state' terrorists are a tiny minority, they cannot afford to discount the possibility of a small number of fanatics launching into nuclear terrorism. It is the duty of the authorities to do all they can to prevent any such attacks from succeeding. There is no shortage of evidence that individuals and groups have been tempted into attacks and threats against nuclear installations. It is noteworthy that the Japanese police discovered documents showing that the Aum cult was very interested in nuclear technology and they believe that they were seeking to purchase a nuclear weapon and/or obtain a supply of uranium.

Chemical and biological weapons

Most specialists in the study of terrorism have been as sceptical about the possibility of terrorists using chemical or biological weapons as they have about the prospect of nuclear terrorism. The late Dr Richard Clutterbuck in his *Terrorism in an Unstable World* concluded:

> Clearly we should not be complacent about nuclear, biological and chemical weapons, both because of the need to evaluate hoax calls … and because all of them would be feasible for a group which was both desperate and suicidal. But the threat is far less, and would in many ways be easier to handle because of its lack of credibility than the terrorist actions to which we are accustomed.

The tragic attack on the Tokyo underground system with the nerve gas Sarin, which killed 12 and injured many more, has made it vital to reconsider the conventional wisdom. It is unlikely that there are more than a tiny number of groups willing to commit such acts. But it clearly could have caused a large number of deaths if the Sarin had been used in a purer form, and this may tempt another group to emulate the Aum group's action.

The methods for making nerve gases and biological pathogens have been known for decades. The formula for making Sarin is on the internet. The materials and equipment for making crude chemical and biological weapons are cheap and easily obtained and the weapons can be made by a person with only basic scientific training.

In these circumstances it is essential that government and security services place the possibility of attack by terrorists using weapons of mass destruction into their future threat scenarios and contingency plans. In the Tokyo underground attack a significant threshold has been crossed by a substate group for the first time. We may find it very hard to understand the thinking of extreme groups that would use such weapons, but we must allow for the possibility that there may be other groups in other countries, in addition to the embittered remaining followers of the Aum cult in Japan and Al Qaeda with their own internal agenda and reasoning, which may be capable of using weapons of mass destruction in their attacks.[1]

Terrorist tactics and the use of conventional weapons

In a recently published symposium edited by myself, a number of experts rightly stressed that the most likely trend in terrorist weaponry and tactics was further refinement, adaptation and deployment of what is already widely available and affordable. Why go to the trouble of acquiring more hazardous and costly weapons when so much death and destruction can be achieved by traditional means? It is worth bearing in mind that the bomb used in Oklahoma, which killed 169, comprised ammonium nitrate and fuel oil; the same bomb was also one of the most effective conventional weapons used by the IRA. The IRA provided us with the outstanding example of an experienced terrorist group improvising and adapting traditional weaponry, for example in its development of the drogue grenade, homemade mortars and booby-trap devices. There are reports that they also developed a remote-control device to guide a driverless car containing a bomb to its target. When terrorist groups are able to achieve 'successes' using such improvisations, they are less likely to feel the need to experiment with entirely new weapons that carry a high risk of death or injury to their own operatives. We are likely to see more developments of this kind in a constant battle to keep ahead of the technology available to the counter-terrorist agencies.[2]

One important source of innovation or switch in tactics and weaponry is the introduction by the authorities of more effective countermeasures against certain types of attack. For example, as the civil aviation system's measures to improve protection against the sabotage bombings of airliners become more efficient, we are likely to see a greater use of alternative means of terrorist attack against aviation, such as surface-to-air missiles. There are clear signs that this was already happening in the 1990s. There have been at least 25 attacks using man-portable SAMs since November 1990 and in 15 of the incidents an aircraft was shot down causing an estimated 300 deaths. So far most of the aircraft involved have been military. However, in view of the clear evidence that terrorist groups in many parts of the world have managed to obtain SAMs, the security authorities in the European democracies should be urgently concentrating efforts to combat this growing threat.[3]

Can we predict terrorist attacks?

So far we have been looking at the future of terrorism from a long-term perspective: in the light of recent experience and emerging trends what are the probable long-term trajectories of different types of terrorism? This is an extremely difficult problem. However, it is an even more daunting challenge to try to predict specific terrorist attacks. As will be clear to anyone who has studied the *9/11 Commission Report*, intelligence is an art rather than a science, and very often intelligence agencies get things disastrously wrong. Fair-minded and realistic academic analysts will sympathise with the problems of the intelligence analysts trying to obtain advance warning in order to prevent attacks. However, Dr Joseph Sinai, an erudite and practical US specialist in terrorism studies, has made a very useful contribution in a recent journal article by identifying seven major attack indicators (Table 12.1). I believe this is a useful tool for counter-terrorism agencies and specialists and I have tabulated the Sinai attack indicators below:

Table 12.1 Attack Indicators

Attack Indicator
1   Previous terrorist attacks, failed attacks, or plots not yet executed, which serve as blueprints for intentions and future targeting.
2   A terrorist group's modus operandi, especially tactics.
3   Use of particular types of weaponry and devices that a terrorist group perceives will achieve its objectives.
4   The objectives of a state sponsor.
5   The geographic factor.
6   Historical dates of particular significance to terrorist groups.
7   Triggers that propel a group to launch attacks in a revenge mode as quickly as possible.

Ref: Dr Joseph Sinai, 'Red Teaming Catastrophic Terrorism by Al Qaeda Jihadists', *The Journal of Counterterrorism and Homeland Security International*, 11: 4 (winter 2005).

Countering international terrorism: the democratic response

In countering international terrorism, the democratic state confronts an inescapable dilemma. It has to deal effectively with the terrorist threat to citizens and to vulnerable potential targets, such as civil aviation, diplomatic and commercial premises, without at the same time destroying basic civil rights, the democratic process and the rule of law. On the one hand, the democratic government and its agencies of law enforcement must avoid a heavy-handed overreaction, which many terrorist groups deliberately seek to provoke. Such a response would only help to alienate the public from the government and could ultimately destroy democracy more swiftly and completely than any small terrorist group ever could. On the other hand, if government, judiciary and police prove incapable of upholding the law and protecting life and property, then their whole credibility and authority would be undermined.

If this balance is to be maintained, the liberal state should seek at all times to combat terrorism using its criminal justice and law-enforcement mechanisms. However, it is clearly the case that some terrorist groups attain a level of firepower that outstrips even the capabilities of elite squads of armed police. It has been proven time and again that in certain circumstances of high emergency, such as the hijacking at Entebbe in 1976 and the Iranian embassy siege of 1980, it may be essential to deploy a highly trained military rescue commando force to save hostages. Military, naval or air forces may be invaluable in interdicting a major terrorist assault, as has been seen in the case of Israel's measures against terrorist groups attacking its borders from land and sea. In the more normal conditions enjoyed by the democratic states in Western Europe, the occasions when military deployment to tackle international terrorists is required will be very rare.

A number of dangers need to be constantly borne in mind when deploying the army in a major internal terrorist emergency role. First, an unnecessarily high military profile may serve to escalate the level of violence by polarising pro- and anti-government elements in the community. Second, there is a constant risk that a repressive overreaction or a minor error in judgement by the military may trigger further civil violence. Internal security duties inevitably impose considerable strains on the soldiers, who are well aware of the hostility of certain sections of the community towards them. Third, anti-terrorist and internal security duties absorb considerable manpower and involve diverting highly trained military technicians from their primary NATO and external defence roles. Fourth, there is a risk that the civil power may become over-dependent on the army's presence and there may be a consequent lack of urgency in preparing the civil police for gradually reassuming the internal security responsibility. Finally, in the event of an international terrorist attack, a military operation to punish a state sponsor or to strike at alleged terrorist bases may trigger an international conflict worse than the act of terrorism one is seeking to oppose.

High-quality intelligence is at the heart of the proactive counter-terrorism strategy. It has been used with notable success against many terrorist groups. By gaining advanced warning of terrorists' planned operations, their weaponry, personnel, financial assets and fund-raising, tactics, communications systems and so on, it becomes feasible to preempt terrorist attacks, and ultimately to crack open the terrorist cell structure and bring its members to trial. Impressive examples of this proactive intelligence-led counter-terrorism strategy are frequently ignored or forgotten by the public, but this should not deceive us into underestimating their value.

Sadly, such high levels of international cooperation against terrorism are hard to find. Just as the lack of intelligence sharing between uniformed and non-uniformed security agencies often damages national counter-terrorism responses, so international mistrust and reluctance to share information often vitiates an effective international response. The most useful enhancements of policy to combat terrorism at the international level need to be made in intelligence gathering, by every means available, intelligence sharing, intelligence analysis and threat assessment. This is my key recommendation and it is my hope that there will be a fuller debate on refining a better proactive strategy for America, G8 and EU friends and allies, and the democratised states of Eastern Europe.

Terrorist attacks against troops and civilians engaged in UN peacekeeping operations are also likely to increase in frequency and lethality. United Nations personnel experienced a wave of attacks of this kind in northern Iraq, for example, in the wake of Operation Desert Storm and the establishment of Kurdish safe havens. In July 1997 SFOR troops and facilities were targeted in a wave of attacks following on from an SAS snatch operation in which one Serb war crimes' suspect, Milan Kovacevic, was arrested, and a second, Simo Drljaca, was killed while resisting arrest. On 17 July a leaflet was found in Banja Luka announcing the re-launch of the Serbian Black Hand terrorist organisation, notorious for its ruthless attacks in the early twentieth century, threatening revenge attacks against Stabilisation Force members and promising that 'the IRA will be child's play compared with our struggle'. We are likely to see a growing trend of terrorist attacks, especially hostage-takings of peacekeeping personnel and international aid workers involved in humanitarian and UN peacekeeping missions, as ethnic or ethnoreligious conflicts increase around the globe. It would be disastrous if the terrorists involved were to succeed in intimidating the contributing peacekeeping countries into withdrawing their contingents and civilian aid workers so desperately needed in these important tasks.[4]

13 Conclusion

Towards a response to terrorism based
on democratic principles and respect for
human rights

Can the end justify the means?

It would be a serious mistake to exaggerate the importance of the new terrorism
of the Al Qaeda movement. There are far greater long-term threats to the
security of the human race and dangers also created by human activity: threats
to the global environment, for example, should be a far higher priority in the
agenda for international cooperation and action. Nor should we overlook the
dangers posed by the possibility of interstate warfare between states possessing
nuclear weapons. However, the global jihad waged by the Al Qaeda movement is the
most dangerous international non-state terrorist threat the world has ever confronted and we should bear in mind that it has had a huge impact on international
relations, in addition to the large-scale loss of life and economic disruption it has
caused. Nor should we overlook the danger of terrorism triggering a wider conflict.
After all, it was a militant supporter of a Balkan terrorist group who triggered the
outbreak of the First World War by assassinating Archduke Ferdinand.

As I hope to have made clear, the Al Qaeda movement is by far the most
serious terrorist threat now faced by the international community. The movement
is not like traditional highly centralised terrorist organisations. It has been able to
adapt and sustain its campaign of terror through its global network of networks
and affiliates, leaving local/regional groups to plan and carry out attacks and to
recruit new militants and suicide bombers while providing ideological leadership
and general strategic goals and inspirations to its followers around the world. It is
therefore just irresponsible to pretend that the Al Qaeda movement is finished,
or that it poses a threat indistinguishable from traditional groups. Last but not
least research into the Al Qaeda movement's aims, ideology and track record of
terrorist activity shows that it comes into the category of an incorrigible group, i.e.
there is no feasible political or diplomatic route to resolving its conflict with the
civilised world. Therefore the only sensible way forward is through a coordinated,
multi-national and multi-pronged approach to unravel the terrorist network and
bring it to justice. In the discussion above on the key elements of a successful
strategy to counter Al Qaeda I have warned of the dangers of both over-reaction
and under-reaction, and have stressed the cardinal importance of ensuring that
basic civil liberties and the rule of law are upheld even in a severe terrorist

emergency. The key roles of high-quality intelligence, public support and cooperation of the mass media and the private sector have been emphasised.

Much confusion occurs in the debate on the morality of terrorism because of a failure to distinguish ends and means. Terrorism is a *method* which can be used for an infinite variety of goals. The cliché that one man's terrorist is another man's freedom fighter simply reflects the paradox that many groups use terror in pursuit of a cause that most liberal democrats in principle regard as just: the goal of self-determination or national liberation.

Yet even in cases where we have firm grounds for believing that a group has a legitimate grievance or sense of grave injustice, this does not mean that we should refrain from posing the question: 'Does a just cause justify the use of terrorism by its supporters?' Terrorism is inherently and inevitably a means of struggle involving indiscriminate and arbitrary violence against the innocent. It is almost universally agreed among the citizens of liberal democracies that the method of terrorism is morally indefensible in a free society in which, by definition, there are always other ways of campaigning for a cause, and methods that do not involve a fundamental attack on the human rights of fellow citizens.

I take an even more determined moral position against the use of terrorism, whether by states or factions. It is frequently claimed by terrorists that actions such as bombings, hostage-taking and assassinations are the only means they have for removing a tyrannical or oppressive authoritarian regime. This claim does not bear serious examination. There is *always* some other means, including moral resistance, civil disobedience and well-planned, concerted economic and political action, either alone or in combination, which may prove extremely effective in removing an unpleasant regime with the minimum of violence. There is no case of non-state terrorism removing an autocracy, but there are many inspiring examples of the relatively bloodless removal of dictatorships, including Portugal and Spain in the mid 1970s, Haiti and the Philippines in early 1986, and the communist regimes in Eastern Europe in 1989–90.

Thus, I would argue, we should question the received wisdom of the radical left, which constantly asserts that terrorism is permissible, even desirable, as a weapon against non-democratic systems. From the humanitarian point of view there is a stench of double standards about such a policy. Should we be less concerned about the rights of the innocent in non-democratic societies? What rights have we, sitting in the comfort of our free political systems, to condone a method of 'freedom fighting' that robs innocent civilians of life, maims many others and destroys their property? How can we ignore the historical evidence that those who use such methods become corrupted and criminalised by the savagery of the infliction of terrorism. Moreover, the idea that terrorism is a precise, highly controlled, almost surgical strategy is a cruel illusion. Once a society starts on a spiral of terror and counter-terror, there may be no way of stopping the carnage. Terrorism will become interwoven with the criminal sub-culture: for many it will become a way of life. Mass killings by the Al Qaeda network in Iraq and elsewhere are gruesome testimony to the effects of habitual terrorism (Iraq body count, 2005).

An alternative to war or a threat to peace?

There can be no doubt that terrorism, despite its savage inhumanity to civilians, is a lesser evil than modern war. Even in a relatively short-lived civil war in a small country the level of violence will be vastly more lethal and destructive. For example, more people died in the Lebanese civil war (1974–76) than were killed in the entire decade of international terrorism 1975–85. The authoritative Oxford Research Group has estimated that almost 25,000 civilians were killed in Iraq from March 2003 to March 2005.

Terrorism is sometimes described as a form of 'surrogate warfare'. In the sense that it is often adopted as a low-cost/low-risk/potentially high-yield instrument of foreign policy by pro-terrorist states, this is a useful concept. But it would be a dangerous error to assume that it therefore follows that the international community can face the growth of terrorism with equanimity. For just as severe international terrorism often leads to a full-scale bloody civil war, so international terrorism has sometimes triggered international war, with all its accompanying wider dangers to international peace. Let us not forget that the First World War was ignited by the assassination of Archduke Francis Ferdinand and his wife at Sarajevo on 28 June 1914 by Gavrilo Princip, a member of Mlada Bosnia, 'Young Bosnia'. More recently, the attempt on the life of Ambassador Argov in 1982 helped to spark the Israeli invasion of Lebanon, with all its inevitable dangers of escalation to a general war in the Middle East. There is a real danger that terrorist attacks across the Line of Control could trigger a full-scale conflict between India and Pakistan, both of which are nuclear-armed states.

Democracies are clearly vulnerable to terrorist attacks because of the openness of their societies and the ease of movement across and within frontiers. It is always easy for extremists to exploit democratic freedoms with the aim of destroying democracy. But a well-established democratic political system also has enormous inner strengths. By definition the majority of the population sees the government as legitimate and accountable. They willingly cooperate in the upholding of the law, and they rally to defend democracy against the petty tyrants who try to substitute the gun and the bomb for the ballot box. There is no case in the modern history of terrorism in which a European democracy has been destroyed by a terrorist group and replaced by a pro-terrorist regime.

Even so, it is clear that prolonged and intensive terrorism can be very damaging to the democratic governments and societies that experience it. For example, in Northern Ireland and Spain, terrorism has not only attacked innocent life and fundamental rights: it has also been used to undermine the democratic values, institutions, processes and rule of law. By scaring away investment and disrupting industry and commerce, terrorism can gravely weaken the economy. At its most intensive, terrorist violence serves to incite hatred, promote and provoke inter-communal conflict and violence and destroy the middle ground of normal politics. If unchecked, terrorism can easily escalate to a civil war situation, which the terrorist may seek to exploit in order to establish a terrorist-style dictatorship.

In the long run, the threat to human freedom from the spread of terrorism in Asia and Africa is far more serious. For terrorism in these often highly unstable areas is much more likely to lead to the undermining of fragile democratic governments and is widely used as part of the repertoire of revolutionary movements, separatists and extreme fundamentalist groups. These wider conflicts clearly alter the regional balance of power in Third World areas. They also threaten general economic interests, such as access to oil and raw materials and lines of maritime communication as strategic choke points.

Internationally terrorism is more than a challenge to the rule of law and a clear threat to individual life and safety. It has the potential to become far more than a minor problem of law and order. For the United States, the major target of international terrorism all over the world, terrorism can be a major national security problem. For example, the handling of the seizure of the entire United States diplomatic mission in Tehran in 1979 became a colossal burden to the Carter administration, crippling other activities and weakening US morale and prestige internationally, particularly in the Middle East. In the early 1980s the tragic bombings of US marines in Lebanon not only took large numbers of lives, but also severely curtailed President Reagan's military options in the Middle East and made it impossible for him to maintain a US presence in Lebanon, either through the multinational force or independently. The suicide bombers' atrocity reached US opinion, Congress and the media, as it was clearly designed to do.

Why has the collective response of democracies been so ineffective?

In a world of sovereign states, it is inherently difficult to secure effective international cooperation. Despite the fact that Western states have cooperated with such organisations as the Organisation for Economic Cooperation and Development (OECD), the North Atlantic Treaty Organisation (NATO) and the European Union (EU), it is extremely hard for them to cooperate in the sensitive area of internal security and law and order. On such matters, they have traditionally taken the view that the national government has total sovereign control. Western politicians and judiciaries are as chauvinistic in this respect as other states, despite the many moral and legal values they have in common with fellow Western organisations.

A major political difficulty in cooperation against terrorism is the lack of a clear single forum for Western democratic cooperation. The European Union does not include all the major Western states, and in any case it is primarily concerned with economic matters. NATO, though it has a larger membership, is by no means comprehensive and essentially remains an intergovernmental organisation in which member states jealously guard their national sovereignty.

Some Western democracies have little or no direct experience of terrorism and thus cannot see the importance of the problem. Enthusiasm for action often dissipates rapidly once shock at a specific outrage has died away. Some Western governments are unwilling to sacrifice or endanger commercial outlets, possible markets, trade links or sources of oil or raw materials by taking really tough action against pro-terrorist states like Iran. Some states are also afraid of attracting revenge attacks from terrorist states; they hope to buy security by appeasement. Some have a double standard; they insist on regarding some terrorists as 'freedom fighters' that need not be condemned (e.g. Irish-American attitudes to the IRA, the French attitude to Armenian terrorists and the Greek attitude to the Palestinian Liberation Organisation).

Worst of all is the widespread defeatist illusion, assiduously cultivated by the propaganda of the terrorist movements, that democracies can do nothing to defeat terrorism. This is a dangerous myth; look at the success of countries like Canada against the FLQ and Italy against the Red Brigades. We do have experience and knowledge showing us how to defeat even severe campaigns and terrorism. It is basically up to each democratic government to learn and apply these lessons, and to improve its cooperation with fellow democracies.

Pathways out of terrorism

The experience of modern terrorism in democratic societies has shown that there are no simple solutions. There are many pathways out of terrorism; some lead in opposite directions, while others provide alternative routes to strengthen democracy and reduce violence. Let us briefly identify six main possible pathways out of terrorism.

1. The terrorists solve the problem on *their* terms: they achieve their goals and abandon the violence as it is no longer seen as necessary. This has only happened very rarely. In a number of colonial independence struggles in the 1950s and 1960s (Palestine, Algeria, Cyprus, Aden) something very close to this did occur. But the conditions of decaying colonialism provided exceptional opportunities for terrorists who no longer exist: for example, the colonial regimes lacked the will to maintain their control and were gravely economically and militarily weakened by the exertions of the Second World War. The terrorists in most cases had vast popular support from their own populations.

2. The terrorists perceive the inevitable failure of their campaign, or in any case grow weary of it, and give up their violent struggle without having achieved their goals. An example of this was the abandonment of the struggle by the IRA in Northern Ireland in 1962.

3. The terrorist campaign may be eradicated within the border of the state by determined and efficient military action. For example a draconian military campaign virtually wiped out the Tupamaros' campaign in Uruguay. But this was at a heavy cost of the virtual suspension of democratic government in Uruguay and its replacement by military rule. A frequent effect of this strategy is to drive the terrorist residue into exile. The campaign may thus be continued abroad, including attacks on diplomats of the target state, with the terrorist hopes of carrying their fight back to their homeland.

4. A fourth scenario is a political solution on the state's terms that nevertheless makes sufficient concessions to genuine and deeply felt grievances of a particular group: in effect it dries up the water in which the terrorist 'fish' swim. There are a few examples of the remarkably successful use of this strategy. It was extremely effective in the case of South Tyrol (Alto Adie), where the autonomy measure passed by the Italian Senate in 1971 defused a violent campaign. But in most cases this method has had only limited success because there are always 'maximalists' or 'irreconcilables' among the terrorists who refuse to abandon the struggle unless or until their absolute demands are met. Hence, despite the bold and imaginative measures taken by the French and Spanish government respectively to introduce a real regional autonomy in Corsica and the Basque region, hardline terrorist groups in each case have continued to wage violence.

5. Many democratic states attempt to deal with internal terrorism as essentially a problem of law-enforcement and judicial control, viewing terrorist actions as serious crimes and dealing with them firmly under the criminal code. There have been some remarkably successful applications of this approach, for example against the early generation of the Red Army Faction in West Germany and against the Red Brigades and other terrorist groups in Italy. In both these cases it is true that the laws and the judicial process had to be strengthened in order to cope with the ruthlessness and cunning of the terrorists. But it is manifestly the case that in both countries essential democratic values and institutions and the rule of law remain intact, despite these long and bitter campaigns of terrorists to undermine the state and provoke it into overreaction. There are often serious residual problems with this approach, however. Some terrorists will inevitably succeed in escaping justice by fleeing abroad, as has been the case with many Red Brigades and Red Army Faction members, who have fled to France, 'Terre d'Asile'. From their new bases abroad they may then continue to wage violence and attempt to rebuild their networks within their home countries. Nor does the problem end when terrorists are successfully apprehended, tried and convicted. As our penal systems are ill-adapted and under-equipped to handle large numbers of imprisoned terrorists, it is all too easy for militant and determined terrorists with considerable expertise of covert activity outside gaol to begin to re-establish their terrorist organisations within the prison system. In addition, using the aid of pro-terrorist lawyers and friends, they can even hope to establish a network outside the prison which they can direct, or at least strongly influence, from inside. Hence the law-enforcement solution by itself is inevitably incomplete. Without additional measures there is the strong likelihood of new terrorist movements recreating themselves from the ashes of the old.

6. Finally there is the educative solution, in which the combination of education effort by democratic political parties, the mass media, trade unions, churches, schools, colleges and other major social institutions succeeds in persuading the terrorists or a sufficient proportion of their supporters that

terrorism is both undesirable and counterproductive to the realisation of their political ideals. This approach is, of course, fraught with enormous difficulties and requires many years of patient work before it yields results. It has rarely been tried on a major scale. However, small-scale experiments in the re-education and rehabilitation of former members of ETA-militar and the Red Brigades indicate that it can be extraordinarily successful in certain cases.

Democratic pathways out of terrorism (models 4, 5 and 6) are obviously not mutually exclusive. Undoubtedly the most effective policy will be multipronged, involving skilful coordinated elements of each. However, with the exception of models 1 and 2 in which the terrorist group itself takes the decision to abandon its violence, there is no sound basis for assuming that the *total* eradication of terrorist violence from democratic society is feasible. It is part of the price we must pay for our democratic freedoms that some may choose to abuse these freedoms for the purpose of destroying democracy, or some other goal.

It follows that an essential part of the democratic effort must be to provide effective pathways out of terrorism for the individual. By so doing we will constantly be aiming to minimise the threat of residual or irreconcilable terrorism, which may otherwise slowly regroup and regain sufficient support and strength to launch fresh campaigns of violence. In this constant moral and psychological battle of attrition, democratic authorities must continually seek more imaginative and effective ways of enabling individual members of terrorist organisations to make a complete break with their comrades and leaders who, for their part, strive to keep their members under an iron grip.

Individual pathways out of terrorism

The first thing to understand about the problem is the colossal pressure that keeps the individual terrorist bonded to the terrorist group. He or she will have been intensively indoctrinated, literally brainwashed, into seeing the world through terrorist spectacles. They will have been taught to hate everyone associated with the government and legal system, especially the police, with a blind loathing. They will be schooled into suspecting the authorities' every move, basically disbelieving their every statement, constantly vigilant for new traps or ruses set by the 'enemy'. Moreover, they will have it instilled into them that the only important thing in life is the furtherance of their cause. Every involvement in a terrorist action will further reinforce this and will be rationalised as the dedicated pursuit of justice. They are taught to see each bombing, shooting or fresh act of violence against the 'enemy' state as a heroic act, as the living of the true revolutionary existence. Terrorist violence is thus transvalued in their minds to provide meaning and purpose to their hitherto 'wasted' lives. Once this process of indoctrination and mental bonding to the ideology of the group has reached a certain point, it is extremely difficult to bring the terrorists to *question* their fundamental ideological assumptions and beliefs, let alone to abandon them.

A second major constraint is the individual terrorist fear of his/her own group. Terror has always been the method used to ruthlessly control discipline within the conspiratorial world of the terrorist organisation. Knee-capping, shooting in the hand or foot and torture are punishments frequently meted out for relatively minor violations of the rules laid down by the leadership. Major infractions or repeated disobedience of the leaders' orders usually mean death. If an individual terrorist 'disappears' or is suspected of having gone over to the side of the authorities, the group will try to mete out vengeance on their closest family member. Faced with such deadly threats from within their own group, it is little wonder that few terrorists find the courage to try to break with the past.

Third, even if a terrorist can break these bonds, some individuals will be deterred from breaking with their group because of the apparently insuperable difficulties of rehabilitating themselves into normal society. They live in constant fear of being handed over to the authorities. In order to get a job, buy a car or obtain a home, they will need false identity papers, and will be constantly fearful of their true identity being discovered by their employers and by the police. If they wish to get married, register a birth or death, obtain a passport, open a bank account or acquire social security benefits, then these difficulties will be compounded. If a terrorist knows the normal sentence for the crime(s) of which they have been guilty is severe, say at least ten years' imprisonment, they may calculate that the dangers of leaving the group's protective 'underground' cover and the added risk of arrest outweigh the disadvantages of continued terrorist membership.

Countries such as Italy and the United Kingdom already have some considerable experience of the ways in which these conflicting pressures tug at the emotions and divide the loyalties of those who are hesitating on the brink of turning state's evidence. The 'repentant terrorist' legislation in Italy (which is not being used to combat the Mafia) and the 'Supergrass' system in Northern Ireland have both provided invaluable intelligence about the operations, membership and plans for their respective terrorist groups. It is notoriously difficult for the police to infiltrate the cell structures of modern terrorist organisations. Hence this type of 'inside information' from the informers is often the sole means of securing the information to bring terrorists to trial and to convict them. This experience has also led to an intensification of the terrorist leaderships' attempts to punish and deter those who may seek to betray them, for they know that once such a process gets under way it can rapidly demoralise and destroy a whole campaign. This underlines the absolute necessity of providing 'supergrasses' with new identities and securing new lives to protect them from assassination by their former comrades.

In spite of this important and fascinating experience, which incidentally has hardly begun to be subjected to any serious research by social scientists, it must be said that our democratic legal and penal systems remain extraordinarily ill-suited to the specialised tasks of winning over individual members of the terror organisations and setting about their long-term rehabilitation in normal society.

There are many who would deny the need to bother with such efforts. It is easy to pour cold water on theories and policies of rehabilitation which have proved of very limited value in application to conventional crime. Yet there is reason to believe that the terrorist who has been subjected to intensive political indoctrination and conditioned by the terrorist training and way of life, especially when under the direct influence of fanatical terrorist mentors, is potentially susceptible to determined skilful and well-planned and re-education and rehabilitation techniques, if only we could make these available within our penal systems. Moreover, within the prison system it should be possible to ensure that those showing a potential for re-education and rehabilitation are insulated from terrorist bosses, militant activists and propagandists.

It is of course a very important consideration in any rule of law system that there should be no special privileges or discrimination in favour of those who plead political motives for their crimes of violence. According terrorists special status only serves to legitimise and perpetuate their own self-perception as 'freedom fighters' and 'heroes', and simultaneously undermines the general public's confidence in the impartiality and consistency of the judicial system. But why should we not be more innovative and sophisticated in our *application* of penal policy? The prisons already have the broad tasks of education and rehabilitation, though few have the resources to do the jobs well. There is already considerable flexibility in reviewing sentences and in the parole system. There is no reason whatsoever, in principle, why we should not make a more serious effort within prisons to re-educate and rehabilitate, and to inject the expertise and relatively modest resources necessary to cope with the special problems of terrorist offenders, in just the same way we make special provision for weaning drug addicts away from their addictions. In the long term such measures would make a substantial contribution by significantly reducing the danger of terrorist cells reconstituting within the prison systems and of terrorists returning to their careers of violence when released. Currently in most penal systems little or nothing is being done to open up these individual pathways out of terrorism. Intense efforts in this field will be required if they are to have any effect, but experience shows that it will not be easy to win back committed terrorists. However, recent evidence suggests that recruiters for Al Qaeda have managed to penetrate penal systems and it is important to combat this.

Prophylaxis, prevention diplomacy and efforts towards conflict resolution

So far this study has concentrated on the security policies that have a proven track record in reducing, or in some cases eradicating, terrorist campaigns against liberal states. An effective proactive counter-terrorism policy based on a high-quality intelligence system and effective coordination and professionalism, determination and courage among the policy and judiciary may be enough to eradicate ideological groupuscules such as the CCC in Belgium, the AD in France and the BR in Italy. But they are unlikely to be sufficient to quell a terrorist movement with a genuine base of mass support among an ethnic or ethnoreligious constituency. No truly liberal democratic government can afford to ignore the demands and aspirations of a genuinely popular movement, even if that movement only has the full support of a sizeable minority of the population. The democratic authorities need to defeat the terrorist leadership at the *political* level by showing that the government is capable of responding imaginatively to the legitimate demands and aspirations of the very social groups terrorists seek to mobilise.

An efficient democratic government will attempt to remain sensitive to the needs of all sectors of society and take effective action to remedy widely perceived injustices before they fester into full-blown rebellion. It is a common mistake to assume that such injustices are always perceived in purely materialistic terms, such as access to jobs, housing and so forth. Social scientific research suggests that perceived deprivation of civil and political rights, such as downgrading the status of a religious or ethnic group or a language, is far more of a danger to stability than purely material deprivation.

Timely and effective political, social and economic reform measures should be introduced because of their inherent worth and the degree of popular support they enjoy. At the same time, such measures can have the inestimable advantage of serving as prophylaxis against violence, insurrection and terrorism.

In cases of long-standing and potentially bitter and violent ethnic conflicts within liberal democratic states, imaginative policies designed to give fuller recognition and rights to a minority population can be the most effective way of preventing or greatly diminishing polarisation and armed conflict. An outstanding example of this method of heading off a potentially bitter and prolonged civil war was the Italian government's 1972 statute granting a considerable degree of autonomy to the German-speaking province of South Tyrol, where terrorist violence was an increasing danger at that time. There is wide agreement that Italy's handling of the South Tyrol issue was pretty effective.

Similarly, the 1978 Statute of Autonomy granted to the Basque region by the Madrid government appears to have been very successful and has led to the increasing isolation of ETA. The Statute of Autonomy has not been sufficient to eradicate ETA violence, but it has helped to marginalise it and has captured the allegiance of the overwhelming majority of Basques.

However, attempts to resolve bitter international conflicts which have spawned international terrorism are fraught with even more difficulties and dangers. The current efforts by the Israeli government and the moderates in the Palestinian movement to counteract rejectionist terrorism deserve the widest possible support from the liberal democratic countries throughout the world. There is no doubt that the terrorist bomb attacks by Hamas and Islamic Jihad were aimed at derailing the peace process. All states supporting the peace process must constantly reaffirm their determination not to allow the terrorists to get their way and to press on with the patient and determined peace efforts that are so vital to the long-term security of Israel and its Arab neighbours.

Realistically, in the light of the ideologies and track records of the terrorist groups involved, and the authoritarian elements in the Iranian Islamic fundamentalist regime that sponsor and succour them, we must expect more desperate attempts to block the peace process. Indeed, the closer we come to negotiated diplomatic settlement of major outstanding issues, the more likely it is that we shall see bloody terrorist attacks by the maximalist groups who view any such agreements as a betrayal of their commitment to the total eradication of the state of Israel. Similarly, fanatical right-wing Israeli groups are likely to use violence to derail the peace process if they see it moving forward by trading more land in the occupied territories in return for peace. Hence, an important part of the strategy for countering international terrorism is to adopt and implement the principle that 'one democracy's terrorist is another democracy's terrorist', and to give the fullest possible political and moral support, and wholehearted international intelligence, police and judicial cooperation, towards efforts to defeat terrorism and keep the peace process on track. Solidarity between all the democracies, the other EU states and the United States is a vital part of this strategy.

A principled response

There is no universally applicable counter-terrorism policy for democracies. Every conflict involving terrorism has its own unique characteristics. In order to design an appropriate and effective response each national government and its security advisers will need to take into account the nature and severity of the threat and the political, social, economic and strategic context and the capabilities and pre-paredness of their intelligence, police and judicial systems, their anti-terrorism legislation (if any) and, when necessary, the availability and potential value of their military forces in aid to the civil power in combating terrorism. The level of response against terrorism in Northern Ireland and the Basque region, for example, would have been totally inappropriate in, for instance, the Benelux countries, where experience of indigenous terrorist groups is negligible. The tightrope between under-reaction, or toleration of terrorism, on the one hand, and draconian over-reaction, leading to serious infringement of civil liberties, on the other, is pitched at a different height and angle in each case. It is, of course, not only the scale and intensity of the democratic states' responses that will vary: the key *components* if the counter-terrorism strategy must be geared to the type of terrorist threat confronted.

In combating challenges from terrorist movements with some degree of mass support and significant resources, the democratic authorities need to win the battle for popular legitimacy and support by showing that they can respond to the basic needs and demands of the population. Popular consent and support are the foundations of an effective democratic government. Terrorist groups such as ETA have invested huge efforts in political and propaganda warfare, but they have failed to win the electoral support of the ethnic populations they claim to represent. Nevertheless, very often these propaganda efforts can help to damage democratic processes and institutions even in well-established democracies, and even limited political successes for terrorist groups and their front organisations may help to compensate for setbacks in their battle against security forces. Against groups which enjoy at least some degree of mass support, democratic governments need to wage simultaneously both a security campaign to contain and reduce terrorist violence and a political and information campaign to secure popular consent and support to sustain it.

However, it is fallacious to assume that terrorists need mass support before they can perpetrate murder and destruction; as I have already observed, many contemporary terrorist groups are numerically tiny. Examples of this are the group that carried out the first World Trade Center bombing in 1993 and the extreme right-wing cell in Israel to which the assassin of Prime Minister Yitzhak Rabin belonged. Other groups, such as the Aum Shinrikyo in Japan, extreme right-wing terrorist groups in the United States and the Al Qaeda network, may have larger numbers of members but are following a religious or ideological agenda that so totally rejects the existing political and social order that there is no basis for negotiation with democratic governments on political, social and economic demands. No democratic government worthy of the name could enter into political negotiations with the Al Qaeda network responsible for the 9/11 attacks or those who carried out the nerve gas attack on the Tokyo underground system.

The appropriate democratic response to murderous terrorist sects of this kind is to deploy the counter-terrorism resources of the intelligence and police services and the judicial and prison system to deter and suppress this threat to the innocent. To be successful this strategy demands a unified control of all counter-terrorism operations, an intelligence service of the highest quality, adequate security forces possessing the full range of counter-terrorism skills and complete loyalty to the government, and last but not least enormous reserves of patience and determination.

There are rarely any easy victories over terrorism. The characteristic features of political terrorism, its undeclared and clandestine nature, and its employment by desperate fanatics, often already on the run from the authorities, imply a struggle of attrition constantly erupting into murder and destruction. Moreover, the terrorists know that the security forces in a liberal democracy are forced to operate at mid levels of coerciveness. Judicial restraints and civil control and accountability, all of which are essential safeguards in a democracy, prevent the security forces from deploying their full strength and fire power. These constraints are inevitable and desirable, but they do mean that the task of countering terrorism in a democracy, under the constant scrutiny of the free media, becomes an enormously complex and demanding task. It also means that a serious error of judgement, negligence or hasty over-reaction can have very serious long-term consequences. They can provide a powerful propaganda weapon and a recruiting sergeant for the terrorist group, and can severely damage the government and the security forces in their efforts to maintain popular legitimacy and support.

High-quality intelligence is at the heart of the proactive counter-terrorism strategy. It has been used with notable success against many terrorist groups. By gaining advanced warning of terrorist-planned operations, terrorist weaponry, personnel, financial assets and fundraising tactics, communications systems and so on, it becomes feasible to pre-empt terrorist attacks, and ultimately to crack open the terrorist cell structure and bring its members to trial. Impressive examples of proactive intelligence-led counter-terrorism are frequently ignored or forgotten by the public, but this should not deceive us into underestimating their value. At the international level, the most impressive example was the brilliant intelligence cooperation among the Allies to thwart Saddam Hussein's much-vaunted campaign of 'holy terror' during Operations Desert Shield and Desert Storm.

Sadly, such high levels of international cooperation against terrorism are hard to find. Just as the lack of intelligence sharing between uniformed and non-uniformed security agencies often damages national counter-terrorism responses, so international mistrust and reluctance to share information often vitiates an effective international response. The most useful enhancements of policy to combat terrorism at the international level need to be made in intelligence gathering, by every means available, intelligence sharing, intelligence analysis and threat assessments.

International judicial cooperation against terrorism remains pathetically weak at global level. In some cases this is due to the absence of extradition between the states concerned: in others it results from differences in legal codes and procedures. In many cases fugitive terrorists can rely on the protection of a sponsoring or supporting state to provide them with safe haven; pro-terrorist states would of course refuse to participate in a convention establishing an international criminal court. Nevertheless, if the United States and other states with a common interest in suppressing terrorism were to collaborate in establishing the new court, many other law-abiding states could be encouraged to join, and strong sanctions could be placed on those states which adamantly refused to cooperate. After all, there is a precedent. The International War Crimes Tribunal that sits at The Hague has tried individuals accused of war crimes in the former Yugoslavia. Despite the fact that this lacks universal support from the international community, it is clearly able to hear cases involving allegations of gross violations of human rights, and observers have been impressed by the great care and rigour displayed by the tribunal in its extremely difficult and harrowing task. The international community has now agreed (at the 1998 Rome diplomatic conference) to set up an international criminal court, but regrettably its mandate does not include international terrorism crimes. In principle there is no reason why an international tribunal to try those alleged to have committed terrorist crimes against human rights should not be successfully established: the prime obstacle is the absence of political will. However, if an international criminal law statute is one day accepted by a majority of member states of the UN, it will have enormous practical benefits. The confusion, political abuse and unreliability of the present extradition process could, in effect, be bypassed so far as serious international crimes are concerned. Small countries would not be so vulnerable to intimidation by fear of terrorist retaliation in prosecuting members of a terrorist group and terrorists would have to come to terms with the fact there would be far fewer places to hide from justice. The pro-terrorist states remaining could then be subject to sanctions based on the encouraging precedent of UNSC sanctions between 1991 and 1999 against Libya for refusing to render the two Lockerbie suspects for trial. A major advantage would be the concentration of judicial expertise in the handling of international terrorism cases. At present there is enormous variation in the levels of specialist knowledge of terrorism available to national judicial systems. In France, Judge Jean-Louis Bruguière and his fellow specialist judges handling terrorism cases are able to draw upon a wealth of knowledge and experience of investigating such cases. In countries with little or no experience of terrorism there may be no knowledge of terrorism among members of the judiciary. And in Britain and the US, where you would expect such expertise to be available, the court procedures and the structure of the legal profession often lead to judges hearing major terrorist cases when they have absolutely no previous knowledge or experience of this field. Another problem that is in urgent need of solution in the UK is the recurrent conflict between the executive and the judiciary. Judges repeatedly rule that counter-terrorism measures adopted by the government, such as detention without trial and control orders imposed on terrorist suspects, are illegal on the grounds that they violate the Human Rights Act. Surely a round table of senior members of the judiciary, parliament and ministers of the Department of Justice and the Home Office should be able to find sensible solutions to these problems. Other European countries signatory to the European Convention on Human Rights have found ways of making their counter-terrorism measures fully compatible with the ECHR. It is high time that the UK followed their example.

Conclusion

Faced with the scenario of terrorism continuing well into the next century, what are the prospects of the international community achieving radical improvements in their policies and measures to combat terrorism? It would be foolish to be sanguine. So much depends on the quality of the political leaders and their advisers and the moral strength and determination of the democratic societies. The true litmus tests will be the major democracies' consistency and courage in maintaining a firm line against terrorism in all its forms. They must abhor the idea that terrorism can be tolerated as long as it is only affecting someone else's democratic rule of law. They must adopt the clear principle that 'one democracy's terrorist is another democracy's terrorist'. The general principles of the firm hardline strategy for liberal democracies in combating terrorism have the best track record in reducing terrorism. I have noted that the threat of terrorism is changing in a number of ways, but we still confront a very wide range of terrorist groups and states. Some of the major principles and measures to combat terrorism which I examined in *Terrorism and the Liberal State* (1977 and 1986) are still as relevant to the world's problems today. The major principles are:

- No surrender to the terrorists, and an absolute determination to defeat terrorism within the framework of the rule of law and the democratic process.
- No deals and no concessions, even in the face of the most severe intimidation and blackmail.
- An intensified effort to bring terrorists to justice by prosecution and conviction before courts of law.

- Tough measures to penalise the state sponsors who give terrorist movements safe haven, explosives, cash, and moral and diplomatic support.
- A determination never to allow terrorist intimidation to block or derail international diplomatic efforts to resolve major conflicts in strife-torn regions, such as the Middle East; in many such cases terrorism has become a major threat to peace and stability and its suppression or termination therefore is in the common interests of international society.

Where do we stand now in the 'war against terrorism'?

In attempting to construct an overall balance sheet of the failures and successes of the 'war against terrorism' as we approached 2011 a number of health warnings are required. The Al Qaeda network fanatically believes that Allah is on their side and that their self-proclaimed global jihad will ultimately obtain victory over its designated enemies. Their leaders have a very different historical calendar from that of secularised Western societies. They refer to historical events such as the collapse of the last Caliphate in the nineteenth century as if it was only yesterday. Hence they are psychologically prepared to wage a long-term struggle. Their concept of war is therefore very different from Western ideas of war.

Second, we need to bear in mind that Al Qaeda's leaders believe that they must wage a *global* jihad, and for this purpose their development of a global network of affiliated groups, operational cells and support networks has been an ideal structure: it gives them a truly global reach and it means that even when they have suffered a major setback, as in the overthrow of the Taliban regime in Afghanistan in the autumn of 2001, or after the blows suffered by Al Qaeda in Iraq as a result of the US troop surge and the Awakening movement, or when Sunnis turned on the Al Qaeda gangs that had been intimidating them, they can gain comfort and encouragement from successful jihadi attacks elsewhere. Moreover, as they want to exploit every conflict in which Muslims confront non-Muslims from Iraq and Afghanistan to Kashmir, Chechnya, Bosnia and Palestine, they have a wide range of major theatres of conflict in which to exploit and manipulate events to serve their cause.

As is made clear by Ayman Zawahiri, bin Laden's deputy and the Al Qaeda movement's major strategist, a central objective of their campaign is to seize control over a piece of territory in the heart of the Muslim world which they can use as a base for expanding their operations, training more jihadis, weapons development and other activities to support their global terrorist network. Needless to say they have set their sights on setting up such a base in Iraq. Once the coalition forces have been withdrawn they will attempt to undermine, penetrate or topple the new extremely fragile Iraq government and use the continuing conflict and tensions between Sunnis and Shiites to bring about what would undoubtedly be a huge strategic success for them. (This is one of the major reasons why it would be both irresponsible and dangerous for the coalition to withdraw its troops before the Iraqi army and police force are strong enough to preserve national security and law and order.)

However, there are other key so-called 'frontline' Muslim countries where, despite undoubted local successes by government security forces against Al Qaeda, the threat from the Al Qaeda network is still very real. Pakistan and Afghanistan are the most obvious examples. At the time of writing (spring 2010) it was impossible to make a confident prediction about the outcome of the 'war on terror'. The severe threats to Afghanistan and Pakistan posed by insurgents using hypermobile warfare and the growing pressure on the US and UK governments and other contributors to the NATO force to withdraw their troops at the earliest opportunity, are key factors. President Karzai was increasingly outspoken in his criticisms of the NATO forces and appeared anxious to strike a deal with the Taliban. There have been more allegations of Pakistan's ISI being complicit in the Afghan insurgency resurfacing.[1] There was also growing evidence of abundant financial support reaching the Taliban via Pakistan, some coming from wealthy donors in Saudi Arabia.[2]

Another central strategic objective of Al Qaeda is to use terrorist attacks to carry their global jihad into the heart of the Western countries' homelands. They have not abandoned this part of their strategy in the wake of 9/11. On the contrary, what they have done is focus more closely on Europe. As we noted in earlier chapters they have been able to rely on locally recruited, in some cases almost entirely 'home-grown', cells to carry out deadly attacks.

The March 2004 Madrid train bombings and the July 2005 London Underground and bus bombings are evidence that these networks are capable of mass-killing attacks against Western homeland targets. Moreover, the 7 July attacks in London are the first cases of suicide bombing in Western Europe, a type of attack which is particularly difficult to prevent in open societies.

Against this complex global background it would be foolish to predict the precise outcome of the Al Qaeda network's global jihad, or even the approximate length of time it might take to defeat it. However, what I shall attempt is a kind of interim balance sheet, identifying, on the one hand, reasons why one might be pessimistic about the long term, and, on the other, reasons why one might, at least in the long term, be much more optimistic.

The author does not share the rather apocalyptic view of some authors that the Coalition against Terrorism is losing the battle against Al Qaeda, yet he has to admit that there are a number of very worrying adverse developments. Partly as a result of its horizontal network of networks it has succeeded in adapting and surviving following the loss of its Afghan base in the autumn of 2001. The invasion and occupation of Iraq, whatever the arguments for and against these policies, did create an enormous opportunity for Al Qaeda to boost its support. It was able to portray the invasions as an act of imperialism, and has used the conflict to increase recruitment, intensify anti-US and anti-Western propaganda, and to increase donations from wealthy supporters and sympathisers. It has also provided them with a wealth of civilian and military targets to attack, easily accessible across the borders of Iraq. It has tied down huge numbers of US and UK troops and financial resources which might otherwise have gone to help President Karzai to consolidate security in Afghanistan, where the Taliban and Al Qaeda, in alliance with warlords, are already reasserting themselves.

The other major reason for being pessimistic is the apparent success of the Al Qaeda Network in inspiring and mobilising new networks and cells within Western and other countries, with both the intent and capability to mount deadly terrorist attacks, including suicide attacks. Although there have been arrests and convictions of some cell members and others involved in support activities, there is a well-founded concern among police and intelligence services that the networks are managing to replace captured operatives and to recruit additional potential suicide bombers, more than outstripping the authorities' ability to identify and apprehend them. This is the most serious worry of all, for, if this trend continues, it is going to take many more years, perhaps decades, to unravel the networks.

As the author has argued repeatedly in earlier chapters a major reason for the failure to stem the flow of fresh recruits into jihadi networks is the failure of the democracies to make a serious effort to wage the battle of ideas against the perverted ideology of Al Qaeda.

Moreover, as I have argued in detail in earlier chapters, it is very hard, if not impossible, to have real success in this battle of ideas if leading Western democracies are seen to violate their own proclaimed norms of protection of human rights and the rule of law. It is vital to understand that human rights protection is not an optional extra in the fight against terrorism; it is an *essential weapon or asset* in the protection of democracy.

Despite these very serious mistakes and weaknesses I remain an optimist and believe that there are a number of good reasons for being optimistic about the long-term outcome of the struggle against Al Qaeda. Like so many terrorist groups in history the Al Qaeda leaders hopelessly overestimate the effectiveness of terrorism, even mass-killing attacks, to coerce governments and societies to bend to the terrorists' will. Second, Al Qaeda underestimates the extent to which its mass-killing attacks have alienated opinion within the Muslim world. Although the Al Qaeda network is still recruiting and indoctrinating new generations of suicide bombers, Al Qaeda is facing more angry condemnation from mainstream Muslim leaders and from influential radical Islamists. They denounce Al Qaeda for its mass murder of fellow Muslims. Also, countries such as Indonesia and Turkey have had some successes in their de-radicalisation programmes. At the end of the day in the struggle against Al Qaeda, its affiliates and cells will be won or lost by the political will of leaders and the general public, and the crucial but extremely challenging battle of ideas. It is reasonable to hope that democracies and emerging democracies seeking to uphold the rule of law and respect human rights will prevail against international terrorism. Democracies are far from perfect political systems but they are infinitely preferable to the deadly anarchy of terror. If democracies live up to their basic values and keep the public behind them, they will prevail. Even if the Al Qaeda network is simply replaced by one of its fanatical affiliate groups such as Lashkar-e-Tayyiba, expect that it will eventually fade away and become overshadowed by other forms of terrorists with different ideologies and causes.

It is unrealistic to aim to rid the world completely of all terrorisms, but recent experience shows that it is perfectly possible for wise democratic governments and their citizens to greatly reduce the capability of terrorists to murder, maim and destroy. Experience also shows that this can be achieved without abandoning the rule of law and the protection of fundamental human rights and civil liberties.

Similar trends in public opinion following Al Qaeda-linked attacks have been identified in Indonesia, Morocco and Turkey. Admittedly terrorist groups do not need large numbers to carry out attacks, but if they are trying to shape opinion and win wider political support this is bad news for the terrorists.

Last, but not least, one can be encouraged by the fact that nine years after the 9/11 attacks, Al Qaeda has not been able to take power in any Muslim country.

If the Coalition against Terrorism remains solid and determined and unites behind a balanced multi-pronged strategy, I am optimistic enough to believe the Al Qaeda network can be unravalled.

Notes

Introduction to the third edition

1 These figures are drawn from the National Council on Terrorism Center website at http://www.nctc.gov/.
2 For a discussion of the implications of terrorism for the theory and practice of liberal democracy see the author: *Terrorism and the Liberal State* (2nd ed.), Basingstoke: Macmillan, 1986.
3 Paul Wilkinson, 'Transnational Terrorism Threat to Europe: An Interim Assessment', in Franz Eder and Martin Senn (eds.), *Europe and Transnational Terrorism: Assessing Threats and Countermeasures*, Baden-Baden: Nomos, 2009, pp. 21–34.

1 Terrorism, insurgency and asymmetrical conflict

1 For an excellent historical survey, see Walter Laqueur, *Guerrilla* (London: Weidenfeld & Nicolson, 1977).
2 The International Institute for Strategic Studies, *The Military Balance 1995/96* (London: Oxford University Press, 1995), p. 234.
3 Ibid., p. 258.
4 Robert Taber, *The War of the Flea* (New York: Citadel, 1965).
5 See A. J. Jongman and A. P. Schmid, 'Mapping Dimensions of Contemporary Conflict', *The Military Balance 1995/96*, The International Institute for Strategic Studies (London: Oxford University Press, 1995), p. 234.
6 For a penetrating analysis of this phenomenon see Richard Clutterbuck, *Terrorism and Guerrilla Warfare* (London: Routledge, 1992).
7 On this phase in Hezbollah's campaign, see Magnus Ranstorp, *Hizb'allah in Lebanon: The Politics of the Western Hostage Crisis* (New York: St Martin's Press, 1997).

2 The emergence of modern terrorism

1 On the implication of liberal democratic theory for the regulation of internal conflict and civil violence, see Paul Wilkinson, *Terrorism and the Liberal State* (Basingstoke: Macmillan, 1986).
2 On Mussolini's rise to power, see Adrian Lyttelton, *The Seizure of Power: Fascism in Italy – 1919–29* (London: Weidenfeld & Nicolson, 1973).
3 For example: the bibliography included in William Gutteridge and J. E. Spence (eds), *Violence in Southern Africa* (London: Frank Cass, 1997); Edward F. Mickolus with Peter A. Fleming, *Terrorism, 1980–1987: A Selectively Annotated Bibliography* (New York: Greenwood, 1988); and Amos Lakos, *International Terrorism: A Bibliography* (Boulder, CO: Westview Press, 1986).

4 For useful surveys of these conflicts, see, for example, Patrick Brogan, *World Conflict: Why and Where They are Happening* (London: Bloomsbury, 1992); Gerald Chaliand, *Minority Peoples in the Age of Nation-States* (London: Pluto Press, 1989); and Ted Robert Gurr and Barbara Harff, *Ethnic Conflict in World Politics* (Boulder, CO: Westview Press, 1994).

5 For a discussion on these ideas and their influence on extreme left-wing terrorist groups see: Paul Wilkinson, *Terrorism and the Liberal State* (Basingstoke: Macmillan, 1986), Ch 3, pp. 71–80.

6 See John Amos, *Palestinian Resistance: Organisation of a National Movement* (New York: Pergamon Press, 1980), for a useful account of the origins of this group and its role in the wider Palestinian Movement.

7 Ibid.

8 On the origins and political backgrounds of this group see Peter Savigear, 'Separatism and Centralism in Corsica', *World Today*, September 1980, pp. 351–55.

9 Amos, op. cit.

10 Ibid.

11 Jillian Becker, *Hitler's Children: The Story of the Baader-Meinhof Gang* (St Albans: Granada, 1978).

12 See Galia Golan, *The Soviet Union and the Palestine Liberation Organisation* (London: International Institute for Strategic Studies, 1976).

13 Carlos Marighela, trans. John Butt and Rosemary Sheed, *For the Liberation of Brazil* (Harmondsworth: Penguin, 1971).

14 See A. Labrousse, *The Tupamaros: Urban Guerrillas in Uruguay* (Harmondsworth: Penguin, 1973) and J. A. Miller. 'The Tupamaros Insurgents of Uruguay', in B. E. O'Neill, D. J Albers and S. J Rossetti (eds), *Political Violence and Insurgency: A Comparative Approach* (Arvada, CO: Phoenix, 1974), pp. 199–283.

15 For the historical and political background to this conflict see Conor Cruise O'Brien, *States of Ireland* (London: Panther, 1972); Richard Rose, *Governing Without Consensus* (London: Faber, 1971); Charles Townshend, *Political Violence in Ireland: Government and Resistance Since 1848* (Oxford: Oxford University Press, 1984); Patrick Buckland, *A History of Northern Ireland* (Dublin: Gill & MacMillan, 1981); and Robert McKee, *Ireland: A History* (London: Weidenfeld & Nicolson, 1987).

16 Conor Cruise O'Brien, *States of Ireland* (London: Hutchinson, 1972).

17 On the emergence of the Provisionals see Patrick Bishop and Eamonn Mallie, *The Provisional IRA* (London: Heinemann, 1987).

18 The best analysis of the Loyalist terror groups is Steve Bruce, *The Red Hand: Protestant Paramilitaries in Northern Ireland* (Oxford: Oxford University Press, 1992).

19 Ibid.

20 For a collection of hitherto unpublished eye-witness accounts of Bloody Sunday, which threw into doubt the findings of Lord Widgery's official inquiry, see Don Mullan (ed.), *Eyewitness Bloody Sunday: The Truth* (Dublin: Wolfhound Press, 1997).

21 For accounts of the bitter disputes and tensions between Goulding and MacStiofain, see Patrick Bishop and Eamonn Mallie, *The Provisional IRA* (London: Heinemann, 1987); Ed Maloney, *A Secret History of the IRA* (London: Penguin Books, 2002); and Richard English, *Armed Struggle: The History of the IRA* (London: Macmillan, 2003).

22 See Steve Bruce: *The Red Hand*, op. cit., for example.

23 For basic data on al-Gama'al al-Islamiyya, see the glossary in this book.

24 See Magnus Ranstorp, 'Hezbollah's Command Leadership – Its Structure, Decision Making and Relationship with Iranian Clergy and Institutions', *Terrorism and Political Violence*, 6:3 (autumn 1994), pp. 303–39.

25 Indeed, in the early 1970s the Shi'ites of southern Lebanon and the poorest districts of Beirut had already cast aside Sunni and Maronite attempts to lead them. Large numbers of them became won over to Musa Sadr, founder of the Amal Militia, and hence became involved in the Lebanese civil war, often in alliance with the Palestinians and

in opposition to the Lebanese Government. Musa Sadr disappeared in 1978 and is widely presumed to have been murdered on the order of Colonel Gaddafi. See also Robert Fisk, *Pity the Nation: Lebanon at War*, 2nd ed. (Oxford: Oxford University Press, 1992).

26 For a detailed analysis of the Iranian-Contra Arms for hostages affair and its impact on US domestic politics see Theodore Draper, *A Very Thin Line: The Iran Contra Affair* (New York: Simon & Schuster, 1991).

27 See Harvey W. Kushner, 'Suicide Bombers: Business As Usual', *Studies in Conflict and Terrorism*, 19:4 (October–December 1996), and for a fuller scholarly debate, see *Terrorism and Political Violence*, 15:3 (autumn 2003) (articles by Ivan Strenski, Richard D. Hecht and Richard C. Martin).

28 See Bruce Hoffman, *Inside Terrorism* (London: Victor Gollancz, 1998).

29 For terrorist fundraising generally see James Adams, *The Financing of Terror* (New York: Simon & Schuster, 1986) and Loretta Napoleoni, *Terror Inc: Tracing the Money Behind Global Terrorism* (London: Penguin Books, 2004).

30 See the report by Tunku Varadarajan, 'ETA kills Businessman Who Resisted Extortion', in *The Times*, 27 July 1996.

31 See comments by the head of Italy's parliamentary anti-Mafia commission after the Iffizi Gallery bomb, *Daily Telegraph*, 29 May 1993 and report 'Bombers Paid £111.00 for Bombay Attacks', *The Scotsman*, 19 May 1992.

32 See *Guardian*, 25 May 1992 and commentary by Ed Eulliamy, 'The Man Who Got Too Close', *Guardian*, 26 May 1992.

33 See report, 'Mafia Blows up Judge', *Guardian*, 20 July 1992.

34 See report, 'Mafia Arsenal Seized by Police in Sicily Raid', *The Times*, 23 July 1997.

35 This worrying trend is emphasised by Richard Owen, 'Fugitive Godfather Leading Mafia Revival', *The Times*, 20 October 1997.

36 *The Economist*, 16–22 August 1997, p. 13.

3 Origins and key characteristics of Al Qaeda

1 For accounts of the origins of Al Qaeda see: Rohan Gunaratna, *Inside Al Qaeda* (London: Hurst, 2002); Jane Corbin, *The Base: In Search of Al Qaeda* (London and New York: Simon & Schuster, 2002); and Fawaz A. Gerges, *The Far Enemy: Why Jihad Went Global* (Cambridge: Cambridge University Press, 2005).

2 See Mariam Abou Zahab and Olivier Roy, *Islamist Network: The Afghan–Pakistan Connection* (London: Hurst & Co., 2004).

3 Lawrence Wright, 'The Man Behind Bin Laden: How an Egyptian Doctor Became a Master of Terror', *The New Yorker*, 24 September 2002, gives a useful account.

4 On Al Qaeda ideology see Rohan Gunaratna, *Inside Al Qaeda*, op. cit.

5 See Ayman Zawahiri, 'Knights Under the Prophet's Banner', 3 December 2001, English translation in Walter Laqueur (ed.), *Voices of Terror* (New York: Reed Publishers, 2004).

6 On Al Qaeda and global networks, see Mariam Abou Zahab and Olivier Roy, *Islamist Network*, op. cit., and Rohan Gunaratna, *Inside Al Qaeda*, op. cit.

7 For a translation of this notorious 'Fatwa', see Walter Laqueur, *Voices of Terror*, op. cit.

4 Terrorist-backed insurgencies

1 See http://english.aljazeera.net/English/archive/archive?ArchiveID=7403 (accessed on 30 June 2010) for unedited transcript.

2 For valuable estimates of casualty figures in Iraq, see Iraq Body Count Website: http:// www.iraqbodycount.org (accessed on 7 September 2010).

3 Nigel Aylwin-Foster, *The Military Review*, http://usacac.leavenworth.army.mil/CAC/milreview/English/NovDec05/index.asp (accessed on 30 June 2010).

4 Hala Jaber, 'Terror Reborn in Fallujah Ruins', *Sunday Times*, 18 December 2005, p. 24.

5, 6, 7 Figures derived from the independent (www.icasualties.org) website (accessed on 30 June 2010).
8 Allan Mallinson, 'The MOD cannot run a war or a budget', *The Times*, 4 June 2010, p. 28.
9 Report, *Daily Telegraph*, 7 June 2010.
10 Ibid.
11 It is estimated that the Haqqani group of militants totals approximately 10,000. It is believed that the Pakistan government secretly uses the Haqqani army as a cat's paw to oppose Indian influence in Afghanistan.
12 See report by Tim Reid, 'Analysis', *The Times*, 7 June 2010, p. 25.
13 See James Dobbins *et al.*, *The UN's Role in Nation Building: from the Congo to Iraq* (Santa Monica, CA: RAND, 2005).
14 For an interesting and detailed discussion of the challenges of counterinsurgency, see Robert M. Cassidy, *Counterinsurgency and the Global War on Terror* (Westport, CT: Praeger Security International, 2006). For an influential military analysis of counterinsurgency, see David Kilcullen, *The Accidental Guerrilla* (London: Hurst Publishers, 2009) and *Counterinsurgency* (London: Hurst Publishers, 2010). Kilcullen has been Senior Counter-insurgency Advisor to General David Petraeus.

5 Politics, diplomacy and peace processes

1 For useful annual surveys of major tension and conflicts see *Strategic Survey*, produced by the International Institute for Strategic Studies and published by Oxford University Press. The post-Cold War issues of *Strategic Survey* are now available on CD-ROM: *The Military Balance and Strategic Survey. 1992/96* http://www.ism.etliz.eh/iiss (accessed on 30 June 2010). On the linkage between recent and current patterns of conflict and terrorism see Richard Clutterbuck, *Terrorism in an Unstable World* (London: Routledge, 1994) and Paul Wilkinson, 'International Terrorism: New Risks to World Order', in John Baylis and N. J. Rengger (eds), *Dilemmas of World Politics* (Oxford: Clarendon Press, 1992), pp. 228–60.
2 Among the many instances, some of the most dramatic failures of terrorism came in the 1970s. For example in Uruguay, the Tupamaros campaign led to the establishment of an emergency government and the suppression of the insurgent movement within Uruguay; in West Germany the success of the government of Chancellor Schmidt in facing down the Red Army Faction demands and defeating the gang that hijacked a Lufthansa jet to Mogadishu triggered the suicide of the RAF's leaders and the beginning of their demise as an effective force; and in Italy the Red Brigade's kidnap and brutal murder of Aldo Moro signalled the beginning of the end for Red Brigades' terrorism.
3 A notable dissenter from this hardline policy has been Japan, which was prepared to make major concessions to terrorist demands by the Japanese Red Army in the 1970s and 1980s. However, the policy of the Japanese government appears to have undergone something of a sea change in the light of the Aum nerve gas attack on the Tokyo subway system and the MRTA's hostage seizure of the Japanese ambassador's residence in Lima in 1996.
4 This is an underlying assumption of the contributors to a number of major academic symposia on democratic responses to terrorism, for example: Juliet Lodge (ed.), *The Threat of Terrorism* (Brighton: Wheatsheaf, 1988); David A. Charters (ed.), *Democratic Responses to International Terrorism* (New York: Transnational Publishers, 1990); and Alex P. Schmid and Ronald D. Crelinsten (eds), *Western Responses to Terrorism* (London: Frank Cass, 1993). However, there is a real need for an up-to-date and in-depth social scientific study focused exclusively on the relationship between public opinion and terrorism in democratic societies.
5 Feliks Gross, 'Political violence and terror in nineteenth and twentieth century Russia and Eastern Europe', in vol. 8 of *A Report to the National Commission on Causes and*

Prevention of Violence, James F. Kirkham, Sheldon G. Levy and William J. Crotty (eds) (Washington, DC: US Government Printing Office, 1969), pp. 421–76.

6 See, for example, Langston Hughes, *Fight for Freedom: The Story of the NAACP* (New York: Berkeley Medallion Books, 1962).

7 For valuable analyses of these factors, see Michael E. Brown, 'The Causes and Regional Dimensions of Internal Conflict', in *The International Dimensions of Internal Conflict*, Michael E. Brown (ed.) (Cambridge, MA: MIT Press, 1996); Pauline H. Baker and John A. Ausink, 'State Collapse and Ethnic Violence: Toward a Predictive C Model', *Parameters*, 26:1 (spring 1996), pp. 19–31; and Carnegie Commission on Preventing Deadly Conflict Final Report, *Preventing Deadly Conflict* (New York: Carnegie Corporation, December 1997), Ch. 2.

8 See Alan Bullock, *Hitler: A Study in Tyranny* (London: Odhams, 1952); W. S. Allen, *The Nazi Seizure of Power* (London: Quadrangle, 1965); and J. P. Stern, *Hitler: The Führer and the People* (London: Collins/Fontana, 1975).

9 For a thoughtful and balanced English language account, see D. W. Brackett, *Holy Terror: Armageddon in Tokyo* (New York: Weatherhill, 1996).

10 For an overview of current trends, see Jeffrey Kaplan, 'Right-Wing Violence in North America', in Tore Bjorgo (ed.), *Terror from the Extreme Right* (London: Frank Cass, 1995), pp. 44–95.

11 See 'Massacre by the Nile', *Daily Telegraph*, 19 November 1997.

12 This point is made powerfully in the Carnegie Commission Report, *Preventing Deadly Conflict*.

13 On the possibilities of a strengthened UN in the wake of the Cold War, see Boutros Boutros-Ghali, *An Agenda for Peace Preventative Diplomacy: Peacemaking and Peacekeeping* (New York: United Nations, 1992) and Erskine Childers and Brian Urquhart, *Towards a More Effective United Nations* (New York: Dag Hammarskjöld Foundation, 1991) and on peacekeeping potentialities specifically, see Paul F. Diehl, *International Peacekeeping* (Baltimore, MD: Johns Hopkins University Press, 1993) and Thomas C. Weiss, 'New Challenges for UN Military Operations: Implementing an Agenda for Peace', *Washington Quarterly*, winter 1993.

14 See, for example, Trevor Findlay, *Cambodia: The Legacy and Lessons of UNTAC*, SIPRI Research Report No. 9 (New York: Oxford University Press, 1995) and United Nations, *The Blue Helmets: a Review of UN Peacekeeping* (New York: UN Department of Public Information, 1996).

15 Allister Sparks, *Tomorrow is Another Country: The Inside Story of South Africa's Road to Change* (New York: Hill & Wang, 1995).

16 See Supplement to *An Agenda for Peace*, General Assembly/Security Council AI5/60S/I 995/1, 3 (January 1995).

17 But for analyses of some of the huge problems involved in implementing the peace process, see Anthony H. Cordesman, *Perilous Prospect: the Peace Process and the Arab–Israeli Balance* (Boulder, CO: Westview Press, 1996) and Joseph Alpher, *The Netanyahu Government and the Israeli Peace Process*, JPR policy paper No. 4 (London: Institute for Jewish Policy Research, January 1997).

18 For the key role of Palestinian terrorism, see Walter Laqueur, *The Age of Terrorism* (Boston, MA: Little, Brown, 1987); Barry Rubin, *Revolution until Victory? The Politics and History of the PLO* (Cambridge, MA: Harvard University Press, 1994); and Bruce Hoffman, *Inside Terrorism* (London: Gollancz, 1998), Ch 3, 'The Internationalisation of Terrorism'.

19 See Barton Gellman and Laura Blumenfeld, 'The Religious Obsessions that Drove Rabin's Killer', *International Herald Tribune*, 13 November 1995.

20 This position was later implicitly retracted. However, Mr Netanyahu continued, from summer 1997 to May 1998, taking a hard line on the issue of further Israeli withdrawals from the West Bank and the continuation of settlement building at Har Homa.

21 On the origins of the ceasefires, see Brian Rowan, *Behind the Lines: The Story of the IRA and Loyalist Ceasefires* (Belfast: Blackstaff Press, 1995).

22 The IRA retracted its refusal to accept decommissioning of weapons in a statement published in the *Republican News*, 30 April 1998.
23 On Sunningdale, see Patrick Buckland, *A History of Northern Ireland* (Dublin: Gill & Macmillan, 1981) and Paul Arthur, *Government and Politics of Northern Ireland* (Harlow: Longman, 1984).
24 It is worth noting that the June 1999 agreement between the Kosovo Liberation Army (KLA) and NATO committed the KLA to disarming as part of a general process of demilitarisation. Under the agreement, the KLA undertook to place its weapons in storage depots. The total time allocated for the disarmament process was 90 days. It was immediately apparent that some KLA units resented these terms and that there were some factions determined to defy the KLA's political leadership.

6 Law-enforcement, criminal justice and the liberal state

1 For a useful symposium on Western responses to terrorism, including successful cases, see Alex P. Schmid and Ronald D. Crelinsten (eds), *Western Responses to Terrorism* (London: Frank Cass, 1993).
2 See Richard Drake, *The Aldo Moro Murder Case* (Cambridge, MA: Harvard University Press, 1995) and Alison Jamieson, *The Heart Attacked: Terrorism and Conflict in the Italian State* (London: Marion Bayars, 1989).
3 See Jamieson, *The Heart Attacked*, op. cit.
4 The most perceptive survey of the West German experience in English recently is Peter Merkl, 'West German Left-wing Terrorism', in Martha Crenshaw (ed.), *Terrorism in Context* (Pennsylvania, PA: Pennsylvania State University Press, 1995), pp. 160–210.
5 The statistics are derived from the RUC Chief Constables annual reports.
6 The main Republican splinter groups, both of which appear to have access to expertise from defectors from the IRA and considerable supplies of explosives and weapons, are Continuity IRA and the 32 Counties' Sovereignty Committee formed by Bernadette Sands-McKevitt, the sister of IRA hunger-striker Bobby Sands.
7 On Aum Shinrikyo, see D. W. Brackett, *Holy Terror: Armageddon in Tokyo* (New York: Weatherhill, 1996), and a useful assessment in James Campbell, *Weapons of Mass Destruction Terrorism* (Seminole, FL: Interpact Press, 1997).
8 A notable example of this approach is the collection of articles edited by Binyamin Netanyahu, *Terrorism: How the West can Win* (New York: Avon, 1986).
9 See Benjamin S. Lambeth, 'Russia's Air War in Chechnya', *Studies in Conflict and Terrorism*, 19:4 (October–December 1996), pp. 365–84.
10 Assuming that the indictments issued against two Libyans for their alleged involvement in the Lockerbie bombing are backed up with solid proof, the destruction of Pan Am Flight 103 could have been motivated by the desire to avenge the 1986 US raid on Libya. It has also been widely assumed that Libya's decision to send major consignments of weapons to the IRA was also an act of revenge for British assistance to the US raid on Libya.
11 See Robert Fisk, *Pity the Nation: Lebanon at War*, 2nd ed. (Oxford: Oxford University Press, 1992).
12 Moreover, in the light of nuclear tests by both India and Pakistan in June 1998 and the border war along the Line of Control in summer 1999, we must recognise the real danger that an escalation of conflict between India and Pakistan could well lead to the unleashing of missiles with nuclear warheads. In the sub-continent terrorism could potentially trigger a nuclear war.
13 Christopher Andrew, *For the President's Eyes Only: Secret Intelligence and the American Revolutionary Violence* (London: HarperCollins, 1995).
14 There is a useful collection of these international legal measures and agreements in Robert Friedlander (ed.), *Terrorism: Documents of International and Local Control*, Vols I–IV (Dobbs Ferry, NY: Oceana Publications, 1979–84).

15 Under the Maastricht Treaty (1992) setting out the terms for the European Union, it was agreed that matters of law and order should be the subject of intergovernmental cooperation (The Third Pillar). K4 is the intergovernmental committee dealing with this aspect of cooperation.

16 See the valuable testimony of my colleague Professor Didier Bigo of the Institute of Political Science, Paris at the hearing of the European Parliament Committee on Civil Liberties and International Affairs on 21 February 1996. See Doc EN/CM.305/ 3005696, where we both addressed the members of the European Community's response to terrorism.

17 See Friedlander, *Terrorism*, Vol. II, op. cit., pp. 565–70.

18 Ibid.

19 Ibid.

7 The role of the military in combating terrorism

1 For an authoritative account see Michael Dewar, *The British Army in Northern Ireland* (London: Guild, 1985).

2 Caroline Kennedy-Pipe and Colin McInnes, 'The British Army in Northern Ireland, 1969–72: From Policing to Counter-Terror', *Journal of Strategic Studies*, 20:2 (June 1997), pp. 1–24.

3 See David McKittrick, Seamus Kelters, Brian Feeney and Chris Thornton, *Lost Lives* (Edinburgh: Mainstream Publishing, 1999), p. 1482.

4 See Derrick Patrick, *Fetch Felix: The Fight Against the Ulster Bombers, 1976–77* (London: Hamish Hamilton, 1981).

8 Hostage-taking, sieges and problems of response

1 On hostage-taking generally see Richard Clutterbuck, *Kidnap and Ransom: The Response* (London: Faber, 1978); C. C. Aston, 'Political Hostage-taking in Western Europe: A Statistical Analysis', in L. Z. Freedman and Y Alexander (eds), *Perspectives on Terrorism* (Wilmington, DE: Scholarly Resources, 1983); M. S. Miron and A. P. Goldstein, *Hostage* (New York: Pergamon Press, 1979); C. C. Aston, *Governments to Ransom: The Emergency of Political Hostage-taking as a Form of Crisis* (Westport, CT: Greenwood Press, 1982); R. D. Crelinsten and D. Szabo, *Hostage Taking* (Lexington, MA: Lexington Books, 1979); B. M. Jenkins, J. Johnson and D. Ronfeldt, 'Numbered Lives: Some Statistical Observations from Seventy-seven International Hostage Episodes', *Conflict*, 1:1 (1978); and C. Moorehead, *Fortune's Hostages: Kidnapping in the World Today* (London: Hamish Hamilton, 1980).

2 See Richard Clutterbuck, *Terrorism in an Unstable World* (London: Routledge, 1994), pp. 172–76.

3 Roberta Wohlstetter, 'Kidnapping to Win Friends and Influence People', *Survey*, 20:4 (1993), p. 2.

4 Ibid.

5 The most authoritative analysis of the earlier phase of diplomatic kidnappings is provided in Edler Baumann, *The Diplomatic Kidnappings* (The Hague: Martinus Nijhoff, 1973). For the later phase see Andrew Selth, *Against Every Human Law: The Terrorist Threat to Diplomacy* (Rushcutters Bay, NSW: Australian National University Press, 1988).

6 See Alfred P. Rubin, 'The Hostage Incident: the United States and Iran', in G. W. Keeton and G. Schwarzenberger (eds), *The Yearbook of World Affairs* (London: Stevens, 1982), pp. 213–40; Francis A. Boyle, 'The United Nation Charter and the Iranian Hostage Crisis', in H. H Han (ed.), *Terrorism, Political Violence and World Order* (Lanham, MD: University Press of America, 1983), pp. 537–58; and Gary Sick, *All Fell Down: America's Tragic Encounter with Iran* (New York: Random House, 1985).

7 See Selth, *Against Every Human Law*, op. cit.

8 See Aston, *Governments to Ransom*, op. cit.

9 See Tim Lewis and Josie Brookes, *The Human Shield* (Litchfield: Leomansley Press, 1991).
10 See 'Hope for Hostages: Reaction Force Plans', *Independent*, 31 May 1995, p.2, on the problems facing UN peacekeeping troops held hostage by the Bosnian Serbs.
11 For a vivid personal memoir of the failed rescue mission by its leader, see Charlie A. Beckwith and Donald Knox, *Delta Force* (London: Collins/Fontana, 1984).
12 Much of the pressure stemmed from the mass media coverage: see Alex P. Schmid, 'Terrorism and the Media', *Terrorism and Political Violence*, 1:4 1989, pp. 539–65.
13 See Terry Waite, *Taken on Trust* (Sevenoaks: Hodder & Stoughton, 1993); Brian Keenan, *An Evil Cradling* (London: Hutchinson, 1992); and Terry Anderson, *Den of Lions: Memoirs of Seven Years in Captivity* (Sevenoaks: Hodder & Stoughton, 1994).
14 On the Western governments' handling of the crisis and the key role of Mr Picco, see Magnus Ranstorp, *Hizb'allah in Lebanon: The Politics of the Western Hostage Crisis* (Basingstoke: Macmillan, 1997).
15 For analysis of the Stockholm Syndrome see F. M. Ochberg, 'What is Happening to the Hostages in Tehran?', *Psychiatric Annals*, 10 1980; and T. Strentz, 'The Stockholm Syndrome', in D. A. Soskis and F. M. Ochberg (eds), *Victims of Terrorism* (Boulder, CO: Westview Press, 1982).
16 See reports on the ending of the siege in the *New York Times, Washington Post* and *International Herald Tribune*, 23–25 April 1997.
17 For an account of the lessons learned from the Balcombe Street siege, see Clutterbuck, *Kidnap and Ransom*, op. cit., Ch 11.
18 See Valentine Herman and Rob van der Laan Bouma, 'Nationalists Without a Nation: South Moluccan Terrorism in the Netherlands', in J. Lodge (ed.), *Terrorism: A Challenge to the State* (Oxford: Martin Robertson, 1981), pp. 119–46; and Robert Hauben, 'Hostage-Taking: The Dutch Experience', in L. Z. Freedman and Y. Alexander (eds), *Perspectives on Terrorism* (Wilmington, DE: Scholarly Resources, 1982).
19 See Chris Kramer and Sim Harris, *Hostage* (London: John Care Books, 1982) and *Sunday Times* Insight Team, *Siege* (London: Hamlyn, 1980).
20 See George Henderson, 'Murder in the Square', *Middle East International*, 4 May 1984, pp. 4–5.
21 For analysis of this episode see William F. Slater, 'Terrorist Kidnappings in Colombia', in Brian M. Jenkins (ed.), *Terrorism and Personal Protection* (Boston, MA: Butterworth Publishers, 1985), pp. 116–19.
22 See James D. Tabor, *Why Waco? Cults and the Battle for Religious Freedom in America* (Berkeley, CA: University of California Press, 1995).
23 See 'Oklahoma Bomb was Revenge for Waco Cult Deaths', *The Times*, 8 February 1997.
24 See Diane Curran, Fiona Hill and Elena Kostrit-Syna, *The Search for Peace in Chechnya: A Sourcebook* (Cambridge, MA: Harvard University, Department of Government, 1997), pp. 10–11; also report by Carlotta Gali and Carey Scott, 'Carnage in Hostage Hospital', *Sunday Times*, 18 June 1995, p. 15.
25 See 'Russia Offers Halt to Chechen War if Hostages are Freed', *The Times*, 19 June 1995.
26 On the criticisms of President Yeltsin's Chechen policy at the G7 summit in Halifax, Nova Scotia, see Martin Fletcher, 'Yeltsin Defends Attack on World Terrorism Centre', *The Times*, 1995.
27 See Alan Philips and Robert Fox, 'Chechens Seize 2000 Hostages', *Daily Telegraph*, 10 January 1996, and James Meel and David Hearst, 'Nobody Gets out Alive', *Guardian*, 10 January 1996.
28 Quoted in Alan Philips and Robert Fox, 'Chechen Seize 200 Hostages', op. cit.
29 See Thomas de Waal and Carlotta Call, 'Villagers See Tanks Blast Their Homes into Rubble', *The Times*, 10 January 1996.
30 The seizure of the ferry lasted four days. The armed Chechen sympathisers, who had been holding 170 hostages, surrendered peacefully to Turkish security forces on 19 January 1996.

31 See Aledsandr Lebed, 'How I made Peace with the Chechens', *The Times*, 10 October 1996 and Richard Beeston, 'Chechen Success Boosts Lebed's Poll Popularity', *The Times*, 30 December 1996.

32 See Richard Beeston, 'Troop Withdrawal Seals Moscow's Chechnya Debacle', *The Times*, 30 December 1996.

33 BBC's *Horizon* television programme carried out a detailed investigation of the Moscow theatre siege and gathered valuable expert opinions from scientists in a number of countries on the mystery of the gas used by the Russians.

34 For commentary on the MRTA, see Mary Powers, 'Latin American Diehard Rebels Press on Despite Cold War Thaw', *Reuters*, 1 January 1992, and 'Death of Americans Underscores Risks of Drug War', *Reuters*, 22 January 1992.

35 See *Patterns of Global Terrorism 1993* (Washington, DC: Department of State, 1994).

36 See, for example, UN Convention Against the Taking of Hostages (1978), and the UN Convention on the Prevention of Punishment of Crimes against Internationally Protected Persons, Including Diplomatic Agents (1973).

37 See Taiji Miyaoke, 'Terrorist Crisis Management in Japan: Historical Development and Changing Response', *Terrorism and Political Violence*, 10:2 (summer 1998), pp. 23–52.

38 On the strategic options during the Lima hostage crisis, see Paul Wilkinson, 'Beleaguered in Lima', *Times Higher Educational Supplement*, 21 February 1997.

39 See reports on the ending of the siege in the *New York Times*, *Washington Post* and *International Herald Tribune*, 23–25 April 1997.

40 The position of employees of corporations is somewhat different, however. For a clear analysis of the pros and cons of allowing corporations to pay ransom for the release of hostages, see Brian Jenkins, *Should Corporations Be Prevented From Paying Ransom?* (Santa Monica, CA: Rand Corporation, 1974).

9 Aviation security

1 See, for example, the view of the Airline Pilots' Association in their representations to national governments, commissions of inquiry and parliamentary committees, and the international aviation bodies. For clear evidence of the views of the industry on security measures against terrorism, see the report of the House of Commons Select Committee on Transport, 1989: Transport Committee, third report, Aviation Security, HC 509, 1989, in the case of the UK, and the *Report of the President's Commission on Aviation Security and Terrorism* (Washington, DC: Government Printing Office, 1990), in the case of the United States.

2 In 1970 there were 46 successful and 26 unsuccessful hijackings – a total of 72 (Source: International Federation of Airline Pilots' Association).

3 For a valuable analysis of the lessons of the 16-day Kuwait Airways B747 hijacking, which began on 5 April 1988, see Rodney Wallis, *Combating Air Terrorism* (Washington, DC: Brassey's, 1993).

4 Two survivors of the Ethiopian Airways hijacking have written a dramatic account of their ordeal, see Lizzie Anders and Katie Hayes, *Hijack – Our Story of Survival* (London: André Deutsch, 1998).

5 For the figures for each decade and a list of the sabotage bombings of aircraft and recorded attempts, see Paul Wilkinson, *The Lessons of Lockerbie* (Conflict Studies 226), London: RISCT, 1989.

6 Ibid., pp. 2–4.

7 See report by Christopher Walker, 'Plot to Blow Up El Al Jet Triggers Airport Alert', *The Times*, 17 May 1996.

8 For hijacking statistics for that period see Paul Wilkinson, *Terrorism and the Liberal State* (Basingstoke: Macmillan, 1986), pp. 227–45.

9 Ibid., p. 228.

10 A thought-provoking essay on this problem is Marvin B. Schaffer, 'The Missile Threat to Civil Aviation', in Paul Wilkinson and Brian Jenkins (eds), *Aviation, Terrorism and Security* (London: Frank Cass, 1998).
11 Ibid.

10 The media and terrorism

1 This sect is the subject of a classic study: Bernard Lewis, *The Assassins: A Radical Sect in Islam* (London: Weidenfeld & Nicolson, 1967).
2 Russian and Balkan terrorist movements of the nineteenth and early twentieth centuries are described in Walter Laqueur, *Terrorism* (London: Weidenfeld & Nicolson, 1977).
3 The relationship between mass media and coverage of terrorism is analysed in Alex P. Schmid and Janny de Graaf, *Violence as Communication: Insurgent Terrorism and the Western News Media* (Beverly Hills, CA: Sage, 1982); Richard Clutterbuck, *The Media and Political Violence* (London: Macmillan, 1981); and Abraham Miller (ed.), *Terror, the Media and the Law* (Dobbs Ferry, NY: Transaction, 1982).
4 On the Munich Olympics massacre, see Schmid and de Graaf, *Violence as Communication*, op. cit., pp. 30ff.
5 Michel Wieviorka, *The Making of Terrorism* (Chicago, IL: University of Chicago Press, 1993), p. 43.
6 Ibid.
7 Ibid., p. 44.
8 Ibid.
9 Ibid., pp. 44–45.
10 *Al Qaeda in its Own Words*, Gilles Kepel and Jean-Pierre Milelli (eds) (Cambridge, MA: The Belknap Press of Harvard University, 2008), p. 3.
11 Ibid., p. 7.
12 This is a point made very powerfully in Alex P. Schmid, 'Terrorism and the Media: The Ethics of Publicity', *Terrorism and Political Violence*, 1:4 (October 1989), pp. 539–65.
13 On the terrorists' use of the propaganda war, see Maurice Tugwell, 'Politics and Propaganda of the Provisional IRA', in Paul Wilkinson (ed.), *British Perspectives on Terrorism* (London: George Allen & Unwin, 1981), pp. 13–40, and Maurice Tugwell, 'Revolutionary Propaganda and Possible Counter-measures', unpublished PhD thesis (London: King's College, University of London, 1978).
14 In this connection the author has observed in a recent article in Martin Warner and Roger Crisp (eds), *Terrorism Protest and Power* (London: Elgar, 1990), p. 52: 'Terrorists are fond of using romantic euphemisms; they claim to be revolutionary heroes yet they commit cowardly acts, and lack the heroic qualities of humanity and magnanimity. They profess to be revolutionary soldiers yet they attack only by stealth, murder and maim the innocent and disdain all conventions of war. They claim to bring liberation when in reality they generally seek power for themselves.'
15 On terrorists' manufacture of media events see the useful discussion in Schmid and de Graaf, *Violence as Communication*, op. cit., pp. 9–56.
16 See Schmid, 'Terrorism and the Media', op. cit., pp. 539–65.
17 Ibid., p. 549.
18 Ibid., p. 555.
19 Hamid Mowlana, 'The Role of the Media in the US–Iranian Conflict', in Andrew Arno and Wimal Dissanake (eds), *The News Media in National International Conflict* (Boulder, CO: Westview Press, 1984).
20 On this point, see the particularly useful discussion in Clutterbuck, *Media and Political Violence*.
21 Statement by Dr O'Brien reported in *The Times*, 20 October 1976.

22 Evidence for this assessment can be found in Tim Gallimore's valuable paper, 'Media Compliance with Voluntary Press Guidelines for Covering Terrorism', presented at the Terrorism and News Media Research Project conference, 'Communication in Terrorist Events: Functions, Themes and Consequences', 1988. For a thoughtful discussion of some of the problems involved see Ronald D. Crenlinsten, 'Terrorism and the Media: Problems, Solutions and Counter-problems', in David Charters (ed.), *Democratic Responses to International Terrorism* (New York: Transnational Publisher, 1991), pp. 267–308.

23 Baroness Thatcher, the former British Prime Minister, made a powerful point in an interview published in *The Times*, 30 March 1988: 'The news media should consider whether those who, like terrorists, use freedom to destroy freedom, should have so much publicity for their work.'

24 For recent IT security stories which underline the importance of consistently applying rigorous security measures see: http://www.computerweekly.com/Articles/2010/01/12/235782/Top-five-cloud-computing-security-issues.htm; http://arstechnica.com/apple/news/2009/11/dutch-hacker-holds-jailbroken-iphones-hostage-for-5.ars (accessed on 30 June 2010); http://online.wsj.com/article/SB10001424052748704575304575297210 807737710.html; http://news.bbc.co.uk/1/hi/technology/10116606.stm (accessed on 30 June 2010); http://www.infoworld.com/d/security-central/gartner-seven-cloud-computing-security-risks-853 (accessed on 30 June 2010).

11 International cooperation against terrorism

1 For the record of the League of Nations Council Debate on International Terrorism, November–December 1934, and the ensuing draft Convention, opened for signature on November 1937, see Robert A. Friedlander (ed.), *Terrorism: Documents of International and Local Control*, 4 vols (Dobbs Ferry, NY: Oceana Publications Inc., 1979–84), vol. 1, pp. 253–58.

2 For the text of this Convention see ibid., vol. 1, pp. 501–6.

3 Ibid., vol. 1, pp. 1–8.

4 Ibid., vol. 1, pp. 102–6.

5 Ibid., vol. 1, pp. 107–12.

6 For the definitive analysis see Joseph J. Lambert, *Terrorism and Hostages in International Law* (Cambridge: Grotius Publications, 1990) and see Appendix 1 for the text of the International Convention Against the Taking of Hostages, 1979.

7 Friedlander, *Terrorism*, op. cit., vol. 2, pp. 599–646 for the resolution of the OAS and the Draft Convention.

8 Ibid., vol. 2, pp. 565–70.

9 Ibid., vol. 2, pp. 137–50.

10 For a fuller discussion of the role of this form of cooperation see G. Davidson Smith, *Combating Terrorism* (London: Routledge, 1990). See also Richard Clutterbuck, *Terrorism, Drugs and Crime in Europe After 1992* (London: Routledge, 1990).

11 See Paul Wilkinson, 'Can the European Community Develop a Concerted Policy on Terrorism?', in L. Howard (ed.), *Terrorism: Roots, Impacts and Responses* (New York: Praeger, 1992), Ch. 10.

12 See Clutterbuck, *Terrorism*, op. cit.

13 See my *The Lessons of Lockerbie* (Conflict Studies 226), London: RISCT, 1989, p. 7.

14 See http://ue.eu.int/ueDocs/cms_Data/docs.pressData/en/jha/85703.pdf (accessed on 30 June 2010).

15 See http://www.europa.eu.int/rapid.pressReleaseAction.do?reference+IP/05/969&fo (accessed on 30 June 2010); http://euobserver.com/?sid=9&aid=19610 (accessed on 30 June 2010).

16 Interview with Mr de Vries conducted by the author in January 2005.

17 The full text of Mr Solana's remarks can be accessed at http://ue.eu.int/ueDocs/cms-Data/docs/pressdata/EN/declarations/80852.pdf (accessed on 30 June 2010).

12 The future of terrorism

1 See David E. Kaplan and Andrew Marshall, *The Cult at the End of the World* (New York: Crown Publishers, 1996) and James K. Campbell, 'Weapons of Mass Destruction and Terrorism: Proliferation by Non-State Actors', unpublished Master's thesis (Monterey, CA: Naval Postgraduate School, 1996).
2 This is a recurrent theme in the contributions to Paul Wilkinson (ed.), *Technology and Terrorism* (London: Frank Cass, 1993).
3 See Thomas B. Hunter, 'The Proliferation of Man Portable SAM's, Counter Terrorism and Security Report', 6:2 (July/August 1997), pp. 2–5.
4 See BBC Summary of World Broadcasts, 17 July 1997, Section: Part 2 Central Europe: the Balkans' Former Yugoslavia: Bosnia Herzegovina; Tom Walker, 'British Base is Attacked as Bosnia Serbs Vow Revenge', *The Times*, 18 July 1997 and Julius Strauss, 'Serb Attack on British Base: Explosives Lobbed into Vehicle Park', *Daily Telegraph*, 18 July 1997.

13 Conclusion

1 Matt Waldman, special report on the influence of Pakistan's Inter Services Intelligence on the Taliban, published by London School of Economics, June 2010.
2 Anthony Lloyd, 'Saudi Dollars Flood into Afghan War Zone', *The Times*, May 2010.

Bibliography and further reading

Bibliographies and guides to the literature

Lakos, Amos, *International Terrorism: A Bibliography*, Boulder, CO: Westview Press, 1986.
Mickolus, Edward F., *The Literature of Terrorism: A Selectively Annotated Bibliography*, Westport, CT: Greenwood Press, 1980.
——, *Terrorism 1989–91: A Chronology and Selectively Annotated Bibliography*, Westport, CT: Greenwood Press, 1993.
Mickolus, Edward F., with Fleming, Peter A., *Terrorism, 1980–1987: A Selectively Annotated Bibliography*, Westport, CT: Greenwood Press, 1988.
Norton, Augustus R. and Greenberg, Martin H., *International Terrorism: An Annotated Bibliography and Research Guide*, Boulder, CO: Westview Press, 1979.
Schmid, Alex P., Jongman, Albert J., *et al.*, *Political Terrorism: A New Guide to Actors, Authors, Concepts, Data Bases, Theories and Literature*, Amsterdam: North Holland Publishing Co., 1988.
Schmid, Alex P., Jongman, Albert J., *et al.*, *Handbook of Terrorism Research*, London: Routledge, 2010.

General and conceptual

Apter, David E. (ed.), *The Legitimization of Violence*, Basingstoke: Macmillan, 1997.
Arendt, Hannah, *The Origins of Totalitarianism*, London: Allen & Unwin, 1973.
——, 'On Violence', in *Crises of the Republic*, Harmondsworth: Penguin, 1973.
Aron, Raymond, *Peace and War*, London: Weidenfeld & Nicolson, 1966.
Benjamin, Daniel and Simon, Steven, *The Age of Sacred Terror*, New York: Random House, 2002.
Buckley, Mary and Fawn, Rick (eds), *Global Responses to Terrorism*, London: Routledge, 2003.
Chaliand, Gerard, *Terrorismes et Guerillas*, Paris: Flammarion, 1985.
——, *Minority Peoples in the Age of Nation-States*, London: Pluto Press, 1989.
Clarke, Richard A., *Against All Enemies*, London: Free Press, 2004.
Clutterbuck, Richard, *Terrorism and Guerrilla Warfare*, London: Routledge, 1990.
Conquest, Robert, *The Great Terror*, London: Macmillan, 1968.
Fanon, Frantz, *The Wretched of the Earth*, Harmondsworth: Penguin, 1990.
Foreign Affairs, *Understanding the War on Terror*, New York: Foreign Affairs/Council on Foreign Relations, Distributed by W. W. Norton & Co., 2005.
Fromm, Erich, *The Anatomy of Human Destructiveness*, London: Cape, 1974.
Gaddis, John Lewis, *We Now Know: Rethinking Cold War History*, Oxford: Clarendon Press, 1997.

Gilbert, Martin, *The Holocaust: The Jewish Tragedy*, London: Collins, 1996.

Gilbert, Paul, *New Terror, New Wars*, Edinburgh: Edinburgh University Press Ltd., 2002.

Gross, Feliks, *The Seizure of Political Power*, New York: Philosophical Library, 1958.

Gurr, Ted R., *Why Men Rebel*, Princeton, NJ: Princeton University Press, 1970.

Harmon, Christopher C., *Terrorism Today*, 2nd ed., London and New York: Routledge, 2007.

Hoffman, Bruce, *Inside Terrorism*, London: Victor Gollancz, 1983.

Horgan, John, *The Psychology of Terrorism*, London: Routledge, 2005.

Johnson, Chalmers, *Revolutionary Change*, Harlow: Longman, 1983.

Johnson, James Turner, *Can Modern War be Just?*, New Haven, CT: Yale University Press, 1984.

Kegley Jr, Charles (ed.), *International Terrorism, Characteristics, Causes, Controls*, New York: St Martin's Press, 1990.

Kuper, Leo, *Genocide*, New Haven, CT: Yale University Press, 1981.

Laqueur, Walter, *The Age of Terrorism*, Boston: Little, Brown, 1987.

Laqueur, Walter and Alexander, Yonah (eds), *The Terrorism Reader*, New York: Meridian, 1987.

Lesser, Ian O. *et al.*, *Countering the New Terrorism*, Santa Monica, CA: RAND Corporation, 1999.

Lutz, James and Lutz, Brenda J., *Global Terrorism*, 2nd ed., London and New York: Routledge, 2008.

O'Kane, Rosemary (ed.), *Terrorism* (2 vols), Cheltenham: Edward Elgar, 2005.

Pillar, Paul R., *Terrorism and US Foreign Policy*, Washington, DC: Brookings Institution Press, 2001.

Ranstorp, Magnus (ed.), *Mapping Terrorism Research*, London and New York: Routledge, 2006.

Rashid, Ahmed, *Jihad, the Rise of Militant Islam in Central Asia*, New Haven, CT: Yale University Press, 2002.

Richardson, Louise, *What Terrorists Want: Understanding the Terrorist Threat*, London: John Murray, 2006.

Russell, Howard D. and Sawyer, Reid L. (eds), *Terrorism and Counterterrorism: Understanding the New Security Environment*, Guilford, CT: McGraw-Hill/Dushkin, 2002.

Sartre, Jean-Paul, *Critique de la raison dialectique*, Paris: Gallimard, 1960.

Solzhenitsyn, Alexander, *The Gulag Archipelago*, New York: Harper & Row, 1973.

Taylor, Max, *The Fanatics*, London: Brassey's, 1991.

Taylor, Max and Quayle, Ethel, *Terrorist Lives*, London: Brassey's, 1994.

Taylor, Peter, *States of Terror: Democracy and Political Violence*, London: BBC Books, 1993.

The 9/11 Commission Report, New York: W. Norton, 2004.

Van den Haag, Ernest, *Political Violence and Civil Disobedience*, New York: Harper & Row, 1972.

Walter, Eugene, *Terror and Resistance*, London: Oxford University Press, 1969.

Walzer, Michael, *Just and Unjust Wars*, London: Allen Lane, 1978.

Wieviorka, Michel, *The Making of Terrorism*, Chicago: Chicago University Press, 1993.

Wilkinson, Paul, *Political Terrorism*, London: Macmillan, 1974.

——, *Terrorism and the Liberal State*, Basingstoke: Macmillan, 1986.

Wilkinson, Paul and Stewart, Alastair (eds), *Contemporary Research on Terrorism*, Aberdeen: Aberdeen University Press, 1987.

The emergence of modern terrorism

Alexander, Yonah and Pluchinsky, Dennis A., *Europe's Red Terrorists: The Fighting Communist Organisations*, London: Frank Cass, 1992.

Asprey, Robert B., *War in the Shadows: The Guerrilla in History*, London: Macdonald & Jane's, 1976.

Becker, Jillian, *Hitler's Children: The Story of the Baader-Meinhof Gang*, St Albans: Granada, 1978.

Begin, Menachem, *The Revolt: The Story of Irgun*, Jerusalem: Steimatzky, 1977.

Bishop, Patrick and Mallie, Eamonn, *The Provisional IRA*, London: Heinemann, 1987.

Bowyer, Bell J., *The Secret Army: The IRA 1916–79*, Dublin: The Academy Press, 1979.

Bruce, Steve, *The Red Hand: Protestant Paramilitaries in Northern Ireland*, Oxford: Oxford University Press, 1992.

Butterworth, Alex, *The World that Never Was*, London: The Bodley Head, 2010.

Chaliand, Gerard and Blin, Arnaud (eds), *Histoire Du Terrorisme De l'Antiquité à Al Qaida*, Paris: Bayard, 2004.

Cobban, Helen, *The Palestinian Liberation Organisation*, Cambridge: Cambridge University Press, 1984.

Cubert, Harold, *The PFLP's Changing Role in the Middle East*, London: Frank Cass, 1997.

della Porta, Donatella, *Social Movements, Political Violence and the State: A Comparative Analysis of Italy and Germany*, Cambridge: Cambridge University Press, 1995.

Dillon, Martin, *The Dirty War*, London: Arrow Books, 1990.

Drake, Richard, *The Aldo Moro Murder Case*, Cambridge, MA: Harvard University Press, 1995.

English, Richard, *Armed Struggle: The History of the IRA*, 2nd ed., New York: Oxford University Press, 2005.

Fisk, Robert, *Pity the Nation: Lebanon at War*, 2nd ed., Oxford: Oxford University Press, 1992.

Goren, Roberta, *The Soviet Union and Terrorism*, London: Allen & Unwin, 1984.

Gross, Feliks, 'Political Violence in Nineteenth- and Twentieth-Century Russia and Eastern Europe', in James Kirkham *et al.*, *A Report to the National Commission on the Causes and Prevention of Violence*, Vol. 8, Washington, DC: Government Printing Office, 1969.

Horne, Alistair, *A Savage War of Peace: Algeria 1954–62*, Harmondsworh: Penguin, 1977.

Jamieson, Alison, *The Heart Attacked: Terrorism and Conflict in the Italian State*, London: Marion Boyars, 1989.

Jenkins, Brian M., *Embassies Under Siege: A Review of 48 Embassy Takeovers, 1971–1980*, Santa Monica, CA: RAND R-2651-RC, 1981.

Kassimeris, George, *Europe's Last Red Terrorists: The Revolutionary Organisation, 17 November*, London: C. Hurst & Co., 2001.

Kirkham, James F. *et al.*, *A Report to the National Commission on the Causes and Prevention of Violence*, Washington, DC: Government Printing Office, 1969.

Merkl, Peter H., 'West German Left-Wing Terrorism', in Martha Crenshaw (ed.), *Terrorism in Context*, University Park, PA: Pennsylvania State University Press, 1995, pp. 160–210.

Mickolus, Edward F., *Transnational Terrorism: A Chronology of Events, 1968–1979*, Westport, CT: Greenwood Press, 1980.

Mickolus, Edward F., Sandler, Todd and Murdock, Jean M., *International Terrorism in the 1980s: A Chronology of Events, Vol 1: 1980–83*, Ames, IA: Iowa State University Press, 1989.

O'Sullivan, Noel (ed.), *Terrorism, Ideology and Revolution: The Origins of Modern Political Violence*, Brighton: Harvester/Wheatsheaf, 1986.

Parry, Albert, *Terrorism: From Robespierre to Arafat*, New York: Vanguard, 1976.

Rapoport, David C., 'Fear and Trembling: Terrorism in Three Religious Traditions', *American Political Science Review*, 78:3 (September 1984).

Reinares, Fernando, 'The Political Conditioning of Collective Violence: Regime Change and Insurgent Terrorism in Spain', *Research on Democracy and Society*, 3 (1996) (JAI Press), pp. 297–326.

Rubin, Barry, *Revolution Until Victory? The Politics and History of the PLO*, Cambridge, MA: Harvard University Press, 1994.

Saikal, Amin, *Islam and the West*, Basingstoke: Palgrave Macmillan, 2003.

Strong, Simon, *Shining Path: The World's Deadliest Revolutionary Force*, London: HarperCollins, 1992.

Taheri, Amir, *Holy Terror: The Inside Story of Islamic Terrorism*, London: Hutchinson, 1987.

Townshend, Charles, *Britain's Civil Wars: Counterinsurgency in the Twentieth Century*, London: Faber, 1986.

——, 'The Culture of Paramilitarism in Ireland', in Martha Crenshaw (ed.), *Terrorism in Context*, University Park, PA: Pennsylvania State University Press, 1995, pp. 311–51.

Wallace, Paul, 'Political Violence and Terrorism in India: The Crisis of Identity', in Martha Crenshaw (ed.), *Terrorism in Context*, University Park, PA: Pennsylvania State University Press, 1995.

Key trends in contemporary terrorism

Barkun, Michael (ed.), *Millennialism and Violence*, London: Frank Cass, 1996.

Bjorgo, Tore, *Terror from the Extreme Right*, London: Frank Cass, 1995.

Blix, Hans *et al.*, *Weapons of Terror: Freeing the World of Nuclear, Biological and Chemical Weapons*, Stockholm: Weapons of Mass Destruction Commission, 2006.

Campbell, James, *Weapons of Mass Destruction Terrorism*, Seminole, FL: Interpact Press, 1997.

Carnegie Commission on Preventing Deadly Conflict, *Preventing Deadly Conflict*, New York: Carnegie Corporation, December 1997.

Clutterbuck, Richard, *International Crises and Conflict*, London: Macmillan, 1993.

Devost, Matthew and Houghton, Brian K., 'Information Terrorism: The Debate', *Terrorism and Political Violence*, 9:1 (spring 1997).

Dewitt, David, Hagland, David and Kirton, John (eds), *Building a New Global Order: Emerging Trends in International Security*, Toronto: Oxford University Press, 1991.

Israeli, Raphael, 'Islamikaze and their Significance', *Terrorism and Political Violence*, 9:3 (autumn 1997).

Kaplan, Jeffrey, 'Leaderless Resistance', *Terrorism and Political Violence*, 9:3 (autumn 1997).

Kushner, Harvey W., 'Suicide Bombers: Business as Usual', *Studies in Conflict and Terrorism*, 19:4 (October–December 1996).

Maddy-Weitzman, Bruce and Inbar, Efraim (eds), 'Religious Radicalism in the Greater Middle East', *Terrorism and Political Violence*, 8:2 (special issue) (summer 1996).

Schmid, Alex P. and Jongman, Albert J., 'Violent Conflicts and Human Rights Violations in the mid 1990s', *Terrorism and Political Violence*, 9:4 (winter 1997).

US Department of State, *Patterns of Global Terrorism* (annual publication), http://www.state.gov/www/global/terrorism/index.html (accessed on 15 September 2010).

Wilkinson, Paul (ed.), *Technology and Terrorism*, London: Frank Cass, 1993.

Wilkinson, Paul and Jenkins, Brian (eds), *Aviation Terrorism and Security*, London: Frank Cass, 1998.

Politics, diplomacy and peace processes

Bowyer Bell, John, 'Ireland: The Long End Game', *Studies in Conflict and Terrorism*, 21:1 (January–March 1998).

Bregman, Ahron, *Elusive Peace: How the Holy Land Defeated America*, London: Penguin Books, 2005.

Byman, Daniel, *Deadly Connections*, Cambridge: Cambridge University Press, 2005.

Carnegie Commission on Preventing Deadly Conflict, *Preventing Deadly Conflict*, New York: Carnegie Commission, December 1997.

Chalk, Peter, 'The Davao Consensus: A Panacea for the Muslim Insurgency in Mindanao?', *Terrorism and Political Violence*, 9:2 (summer 1997).

Crocker, Chester, *High Noon in Southern Africa: Making Peace in a Rough Neighbourhood*, New York: Norton, 1992.

Curran, Diane, Hill, Fiona and Kostritsyna, Elena, *The Search for Peace in Chechnya*, Cambridge, MA: Harvard University Press, 1997.

Evans, Ernest H., 'The El Salvadoran Peace Process Five Years On: An Assessment', *Studies in Conflict and Terrorism*, 21:2 (April–June 1998), pp. 171–80.

Harari, Haim, *A View from the Edge of the Storm: Terror and Reason in the Middle East*, New York: Regan Books, 2005.

Hinsley, F. H., *Power and the Pursuit of Peace*, Cambridge: Cambridge University Press, 1963.

King, Charles, *Ending Civil Wars*, London: IISS (Adelphi Paper 308), 1997.

Leiden, Carl and Schmitt, Karl, *The Politics of Violence and Revolution in the Modern World*, Englewood Cliffs, NJ: Prentice-Hall, 1968.

Luard, Evan, *Conflict and Peace in Modern International Systems*, Basingstoke: Macmillan, 1988.

Monaghan, Rachel and Shirlow, Peter (eds), 'Special Issue on Northern Ireland 10 Years After the Cease-Fires', *Terrorism and Political Violence*, 16:3 (autumn 2004).

Peres, Shimon, *Battling for Peace*, London: Weidenfeld & Nicolson, 1995.

Rowan, Brian, *Behind the Lines: The Story of the IRA and Loyalist Ceasefires*, Belfast: Blackstaff Press, 1995.

Rummel, Reinhardt, *Report: Common Foreign and Security Policy and Conflict Prevention*, London: Saferworld, 1996.

Selth, Andrew, *Against Every Human Law: The Terrorist Threat to Diplomacy*, Rushcutters Bay, NSW: Australian National University Press, 1998.

Sharp, Gene, *The Politics of Non-Violent Action*, Boston, MA: Porter-Sargent, 1973.

Turner, Stansfield, *Secrecy and Democracy*, London: Sidgwick & Jackson, 1986.

——, *Terrorism and Democracy*, Boston, MA: Houghton Mifflin, 1991.

Waldmeir, Patti, *Anatomy of a Miracle: The End of Apartheid and the Birth of the New South Africa*, Harmondsworth: Penguin, 1997.

The Al Qaeda network

Arquilla, John and Ronfeldt, David, *Networks and Netwars*, Santa Monica, CA: Rand, 2001.

Corbin, Jane, *The Base: Al Qaeda and the Changing Face of Global Terror* (revised ed.), New York: Simon & Schuster, 2003.

Gerges, Fawaz A., *The Far Enemy: Why Jihad Went Global*, New York: Cambridge University Press, 2005.

Gunaratna, Rohan, *Inside Al Qaeda: Global Network of Terror*, London: Hurst & Co., [1999] 2002.

Kepel, Gilles and Milelli, Jean-Pierre (eds), *Al Qaeda in its Own Words*, Cambridge, MA and London: The Belknap Press of Harvard University, 2008.

Randal, Jonathan, *Osama: The Making of a Terrorist*, New York: Knopf, 2004.

Rashid, Ahmed, *Jihad: The Rise of the Militant Islam in Central Asia*, New Haven, CT: Yale University Press, 2002.

Roy, Olivier, *Globalised Islam: Deterritorialisation and the Search for the New Ummah*, London: Hurst & Co., 2004.

Stern, Jessica, 'The Protean Enemy', *Foreign Affairs* (July–August), 2003.

Zahab, Mariam Abou and Roy, Olivier, *Islamist Networks: The Afghan–Pakistan Connection*, London: Hurst & Co., 2004.

Law-enforcement and criminal justice responses to terrorism

Andrew, Christopher, *For the President's Eyes Only: Secret Intelligence and the American Presidency from Washington to Bush*, London: HarperCollins, 1995.

Barkun, Michael, 'Millenarian Groups and Law-Enforcement Agencies: The Lessons of Waco', *Terrorism and Political Violence*, 6:1 (spring 1994), pp. 75–95.

Bianchi, Andrea and Keller, Alexis (eds), *Counterterrorism: Democracy's Challenge*, Oxford and Portland, OR: Hart Publishing, 2008.

Cassese, Antonio, *Violence and the Law in the Modern Age*, Cambridge: Polity Press, 1988.

Charters, David (ed.), *Democratic Responses to International Terrorism*, New York: Transnational Publishers, 1990.

Clutterbuck, Richard, *Terrorism, Drugs and Crime in Europe After 1992*, London: Routledge, 1990.

Davidson Smith, G., *Combating Terrorism*, London: Routledge, 1990.

Dominguez, Jorge I., *et al.*, *Enhancing Global Rights*, New York: McGraw-Hill, 1979.

Fenwick, W. J., 'Investigating Atrocities in the Territory of Former Yugoslavia', *Revue de Droit de la Guerre*, 33 (1995), pp. 1–2, 3–4, 33–71.

Friedlander, Robert A., *Terrorism: Documents of International and Local Control*, New York: Oceana Publications, Vol I–IV, 1979–84.

Godson, Roy, *Dirty Tricks and Trump Cards? US Covert Action and Counter-intelligence*, Washington, DC: Brassey's, 1995.

Gurr, Ted R., *Rogues, Rebels and Reformers: A Political History of Urban Crime and Conflict*, Beverly Hills, CA: Sage, 1976.

Higgins, Rosalyn, *Problems and Process: International Law and How We Use It*, Oxford: Clarendon Press, 1994.

Human Rights Watch, *War Crimes in Bosnia-Herzegovina*, Vol I (1992) and Vol II (1993), New York: Human Rights Watch.

International Committee of the Red Cross, *Protocols Additional to the Geneva Conventions of 12 August 1949*, Geneva: ICRC, 1977.

Lambert, Joseph J., *Terrorism and Hostages in International Law*, Cambridge: Grotius, 1990.

Lord Lloyd of Berwick, *Inquiry into Legislation Against Terrorism*, 2 vols, London: HMSO (CM 3420), 1996.

Mark, Sir Robert, *Policing a Perplexed Society*, London: George Allen & Unwin, 1977.

Moran, Sue Ellen (ed.), *Court Depositions of Three Red Brigadists*, Santa Monica, CA: RAND, N-2391-RC, February 1986.

Murphy, John F., *Punishing International Terrorists*, Totowa, NJ: Rowman & Allanheld, 1985.

Napoleoni, Loretta, *Terror Inc: Tracing the Money Behind Terrorism*, London: Penguin Books, 2004.

Ranstorp, Magnus and Wilkinson, Paul (eds), 'Special Issue on Terrorism and Human Rights', *Terrorism and Political Violence*, 17:1–2 (winter 2005).

Rohan Perera, Amrith, *International Terrorism*, New Delhi: Vikas Publishing, 1997.

Schmid, Alex P. and Crelinsten, Ronald D. (eds), *Western Responses to Terrorism*, London: Frank Cass, 1993.

Sofaer, Abraham D., 'Terrorism and the Law', *Foreign Affairs*, 65: 5 (summer 1986).

Stalker, John, *Stalker*, London: Harrap, 1988.

Walker, Clive, *The Blackstone Guide to Anti-Terrorism Legislation*, 2nd ed., Oxford: Oxford University Press, 2009.

Wilkinson, Paul, 'The Laws of War and Terrorism', in David C. Rapoport and Yonah Alexander (eds), *The Morality of Terrorism*, New York: Pergamon Press, 1982, pp. 308–24.

The role of the military in combating terrorism and insurgency

Brodie, Bernard, *War and Politics*, London: Cassell, 1974.

Brusstar, James H. and Jones, Ellen, *The Russian Military's Role in Politics*, Washington, DC: Institute for National Strategic Studies, 1995.

Dewar, Michael, *Brush Fire Wars: Minor Campaigns of the British Army Since 1945*, New York: St Martin's Press, 1984.

——, *The British Army in Northern Ireland*, London: Guild, 1985.

——, *Weapons and Equipment of Counter-Terrorism*, London: Arms & Armour Press, 1987.

Gunaratna, Rohan, *Indian Intervention in Sri Lanka*, 2nd ed., Colombo: South Asian Network on Conflict Research, 1994.

Harmon, Christopher C., Pratt, Andrew N. and Gorka, Sebastian, *Toward a Grand Strategy Against Terrorism*, New York: McGraw-Hill, 2010.

Horne, Alistair, *A Savage War of Peace: Algeria 1954–1962*, Harmondsworth: Penguin, 1977.

Howard, Michael (ed.), *Restraints on War: Studies in the Limitations of Armed Conflict*, Oxford: Oxford University Press, 1979.

Human Rights Watch, *Bloodshed in the Caucasus: Indiscriminate Bombing and Shelling by Azerbaijani Forces in Nagorno-Karabakh*, New York: Human Rights Watch, 1993.

——, *Genocide in Iraq: The Anfal Campaign Against the Kurds*, New York: Human Rights Watch, 1993.

Kitson, Frank, *Low-Intensity Operations*, London: Faber, 1971.

Lambeth, Benjamin S., 'Russia's Air War in Chechnya', *Studies in Conflict and Terrorism*, 19:4 (1996).

Mullan, Don (ed.), *Eyewitness Bloody Sunday: The Truth*, Dublin: Wolfhound Press, 1987.

O'Neill, Bard E., *Insurgency and Terrorism: From Revolution to Apocalypse*, Dulles, VA: Potomac Books Inc., 2005.

Patrick, Derrick, *Fetch Felix: The Fight Against the Ulster Bombers 1976–1977*, London: Hamish Hamilton, 1981.

Pfaltzgraff, Robert Jr and Schultz, Richard H. Jr (eds), *Ethnic Conflict and Instability: Implications for US Policy and Army Roles and Missions*, Washington, DC: SSI, 1994.

Prunckun, Henry W. Jr and Mohr, Philip B., 'Military Deterrence: An Evaluation of Operation El Dorado Canyon', *Studies in Conflict and Terrorism*, 20:3, 1997.

Ramsbotham, David, *The Changing Nature of Intervention*, London: RISCT (Conflict Studies 282), 1995.

Schiff, Ze'ev, Eitan, Haber and Yeshayahu, Ben-Porat, *Entebbe Rescue*, New York: Dell, 1977.

Townshend, Charles, *Britain's Civil Wars: Counterinsurgency in the Twentieth Century*, London: Faber, 1986.

Hostage-taking, sieges and problems of response

Assersohn, Roy, *The Biggest Deal*, London: Methuen, 1982.

Aston, Clive, 'Political Hostage-taking in Western Europe: A Statistical Analysis', in L. Z. Freedman and Y. Alexander (eds), *Perspectives on Terrorism*, Wilminton, DE: Scholarly Resources, 1983.

Baumann, Edler, *The Diplomatic Kidnappings*, The Hague: Martinus Nijhoff, 1973.

Clutterbuck, Richard, *The Aldo Moro Murder Case*, Cambridge, MA: Harvard University Press, 1995.

Evans, Ernest, *Calling a Truce to Terror: The American Response to International Terrorism*, Westport, CT: Greenwood Press, 1979.

Friedlander, N., 'Hostage Negotiations: Dilemmas about Policy', in L. Z. Freedman and Y. Alexander (eds), *Perspective on Terrorism*, Wilminton, DE: Scholarly Resources, 1983.

Jackson, Geoffrey, *People's Prison*, London: Faber, 1973.

Jenkins, Brian M., *Embassies Under Siege: A Review of 48 Embassy Takeovers, 1971–1980*, Santa Monica, CA: RAND, R-2651-RC, January 1981.

——, (ed.), *Terrorism and Personal Protection*, Boston, MA: Butterworth, 1985.

Keenan, Brian, *An Evil Cradling*, London: Hutchinson, 1992.

Lambert, Joseph, *Terrorism and Hostages in International Law*, Cambridge: Grotius, 1998.

Lewis, Tim and Brookes, Josie, *The Human Shield*, Lichfield: Leomansley Press, 1991.

Miron, M. S. and Goldstein, A. P., *Hostage*, New York: Pergamon Press, 1979.

Moorehead, Caroline, *Fortune's Hostages: Kidnapping in the World Today*, London: Hamish Hamilton, 1980.

Selth, Andrew, *Against Every Human Law: The Terrorist Threat to Diplomacy*, Rushcutters Bay, NSW: Australian National University Press, 1988.

Snow, Peter and Philips, David, *Leila's Hijack War*, London: Pan, 1970.

Soskis, D. A. and Ochberg, F. M., 'Concepts of Terrorist Victimisation', in F. M. Ochberg and D. A. Soskis (eds), *Victims of Terrorism*, Boulder, CO: Westview Press, 1982.

Sunday Times Insight Team, *Siege! Princes Gate, London, 30 April–5 May 1980*, London: Hamlyn, 1980.

Waite, Terry, *Taken on Trust*, Sevenoaks: Hodder & Stoughton, 1993.

Aviation security

Clyne, Peter, *An Anatomy of Skyjacking*, London: Abelard-Schuman, 1973.

Evans, Alona, 'Aerial Hijacking', in Cherif Bassiouni, M. (ed.), *International Terrorism and Political Crimes*, Springfield, IL: Charles C. Thomas, 1974.

Harrison, John, *International Aviation and Terrorism: Evolving Threats, Evolving Security*, London and New York: Routledge, 2009.

Hunter, Thomas B., 'The Proliferation of Man-Portable SAMs', *Counter Terrorism Security Report*, 6:2 (July/August 1997), p. 205.

Jiwa, Salim, *The Death of Air India Flight 182*, London: W. H. Allen, 1986.

Philips, David, *Skyjack*, London: Harrap, 1973.

St John, Peter, *Air Piracy, Airport Security and International Terrorism: Winning the War Against Hijackers*, New York: Quorum Books, 1991.

The 9/11 Commission Report, New York: W. Norton, 2004.

Wallis, Rodney, *Combating Air Terrorism*, Washington, DC: Brassey's, 1993.

White House Commission on Aviation Security, Final Report to President Clinton, Washington, DC: 12 February 1997, esp. Ch 3.

Wilkinson, Paul, *The Lessons of Lockerbie* (Conflict Studies 226), London: RISCT, 1989.

——, 'Aviation Security: The Fight Against Terrorism', *Interdisciplinary Science Review*, 18:2 (June 1993).

International cooperation against terrorism

Doxey, Margaret P., *International Sanctions in Contemporary Perspective*, Basingstoke: Macmillan, 1987.

Evans, Alona E. and Murphy, John F. (eds), *Legal Aspects of International Terrorism*, Lexington, KY: Heath, 1978.

Greene, Owen, *Report: Tackling Light Weapons Proliferation: Issues and Priorities for the EU*, London: Saferworld, 1997.

International Committee of the Red Cross, *Protocols Additional to the Geneva Conventions of 12 August 1949*, Geneva: ICRC, 1977.

Joyner, C. C., 'The United Nations and Terrorism. Rethinking Legal Tensions between National Security, Human Rights and Civil Liberties', *International Studies Perspectives*, 5:2 (2004), pp. 240–57.

Kegley, Charles Jr (ed.), *International Terrorism: Characteristics, Causes, Controls*, New York: St Martin's Press, 1990.

Levitt, Geoffrey M., *Democracies Against Terror: The Western Democracies' Response to State-Supported Terrorism*, New York: Praeger, 1988.

Murphy, John F., *Punishing International Terrorists*, Totowa, NJ: Rowman & Allanheld, 1985.

——, *State Support of International Terrorism*, Boulder, CO: Westview Press, 1989.

Nye, Joseph S. Jr, Satoh, Yukio and Wilkinson, Paul, *Addressing the New International Terrorism: A Report to the Trilateral Commission*, Washington, DC: The Trilateral Commission, 2003.

Prunckun, Henry W. Jr and Mohr, Philip B., 'Military Deterrence of Intestinal Terrorism: An Evaluation of Operation El Dorado Canyon', *Studies in Conflict and Terrorism*, 20: 3, 1997.

Richardson, Louise, 'Terrorists as Transnational Actors', in M. Taylor and J. Horgan (eds), *The Future of Terrorism*, London: Frank Cass, 2000, pp. 209–19.

Schmid, Alex P. and Crelinsten, Ronald D (eds), *Western Responses to Terrorism*, London: Frank Cass, 1993.

Wilkinson, Paul, *International Terrorism: The Changing Threat and the EU's Response*, Paris: Institute for Security Studies, Chaillot Paper, No. 84 (October 2005).

The media and terrorism

Alexander, Yonah and Latter, Richard (eds), *Terrorism and the Media*, McLean, VA: Brassey's, 1990.

Arno, Andrew and Dissanake, Wimal (eds), *The News Media in National and International Conflict*, Boulder, CO: Westview Press, 1984.

Clutterbuck, Richard, *The Media and Political Violence*, London: Macmillan, 1981.

Crelinsten, Ronald D., 'Television and Terrorism', *Terrorism and Political Violence*, 9:4 (autumn 1997), pp. 8–32.

Miller, Abraham H., *Terrorism: The Media and the Law*, Dobbs Ferry, NY: Transnational Publishers, 1982.

Schmid, Alex P., 'Terrorism and the Media: The Ethics of Publicity', *Terrorism and Political Violence*, 1:4 (autumn 1989).

Schmid, Alex P. and de Graaf, Janny, *Violence as Communication, Insurgent Terrorism and the Western News Media*, London: Sage, 1992.

The future of terrorism

Albert, David S., *Defensive Information Warfare*, Washington, DC: Institute for National Strategic Studies, 1996.

Allison, Graham T. *et al.*, *Avoiding Nuclear Anarchy: Containing the Threat of Loose Russian Nuclear Weapons and Fissile Material*, Cambridge, MA: MIT Press, 1996.

——, *Nuclear Terrorism: The Ultimate Preventable Catastrophe*, New York: Times Books, Henry Holt & Co., 2004.

Barkun, Michael (ed.), *Millennialism and Violence*, London: Frank Cass, 1996.

Blix, Hans *et al.*, *Weapons of Terror: Freeing the World of Nuclear, Biological and Chemical Weapons*, Stockholm: Weapons of Mass Destruction Commission, 2006.

Campbell, James K., *Weapons of Mass Destruction in Terrorism*, Seminole, FL: Interpact Press, 1997.

Clutterbuck, Richard, *Terrorism and Guerrilla Warfare: Forecasts and Remedies*, London: Routledge, 1990.

——, *Terrorism in an Unstable World*, London: Routledge, 1994.

Jenkins, Brian M., *Will Terrorists Go Nuclear?* Santa Monica, CA: RAND Corporation, P-5541, 1975.

Leventhal, Raul and Alexander, Yonah (eds), *Nuclear Terrorism: Defining the Threat*, Washington, DC: Pergamon-Brassey's, 1986.

Pillsbury, Michael (ed.), *Chinese Views of Future Warfare*, Washington, DC: National Defense University Press, 1997.

Racket, D. W., *Holy Terror: Armageddon in Tokyo*, New York: Weatherhill, 1996.

Rene Beres, Louis, *Terrorism and Global Security: The Nuclear Threat*, Boulder, CO: Westview Press, 1979.

——, *Apocalypse: Nuclear Catastrophe in World Politics*, Chicago: University of Chicago Press, 1980.

Ross, Ken, *Prospects for Crisis Prediction*, Canberra: Strategic and Defence Studies Centre, Australian National University, 1990.

Spiers, Edward M., *A History of Chemical and Biological Weapons*, London: Reaktion Books, 2010.

Williams, Phil and Woessner, Paul N., 'Nuclear Material Trafficking: An Interim Assessment', *Transnational Organised Crime*, 1:2 (summer 1995).

Wilrich, Mason and Taylor, Theodore B., *Nuclear Theft: Risks and Safeguards*, Cambridge, MA: Ballinger, 1974.

Woessner, Paul N., 'Recent Developments: Chronology of Nuclear Smuggling Incidents July 1991–May 1995', *Transnational Organised Crime*, 1:2 (summer 1995).

Index